GEGE AKUTAMI

As if nothing happened...

GEGE AKUTAMI published a few short works before starting *Jujutsu Kaisen*, which began serialization in *Weekly Shonen Jump* in 2018.

JUJUTSU KAISEN

VOLUME 17
SHONEN JUMP EDITION

BY GEGE AKUTAMI

TRANSLATION John Werry
TOUCH-UP ART & LETTERING Snir Aharon
DESIGN Shawn Carrico
EDITOR John Bae
CONSULTING EDITOR Erika Onabe

JUJUTSU KAISEN © 2018 by Gege Akutami
All rights reserved.
First published in Japan in 2018 by SHUEISHA Inc., Tokyo.
English translation rights arranged by SHUEISHA Inc.

The stories, characters, and incidents mentioned
in this publication are entirely fictional.

Printed in the U.S.A.

Published by VIZ Media, LLC
P.O. Box 77010
San Francisco, CA 94107

10 9 8 7 6 5 4 3 2 1
First printing, August 2022

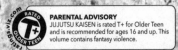

viz.com

JUJUTSU KAISEN

17
PERFECT PREPARATION

STORY AND ART BY GEGE AKUTAMI

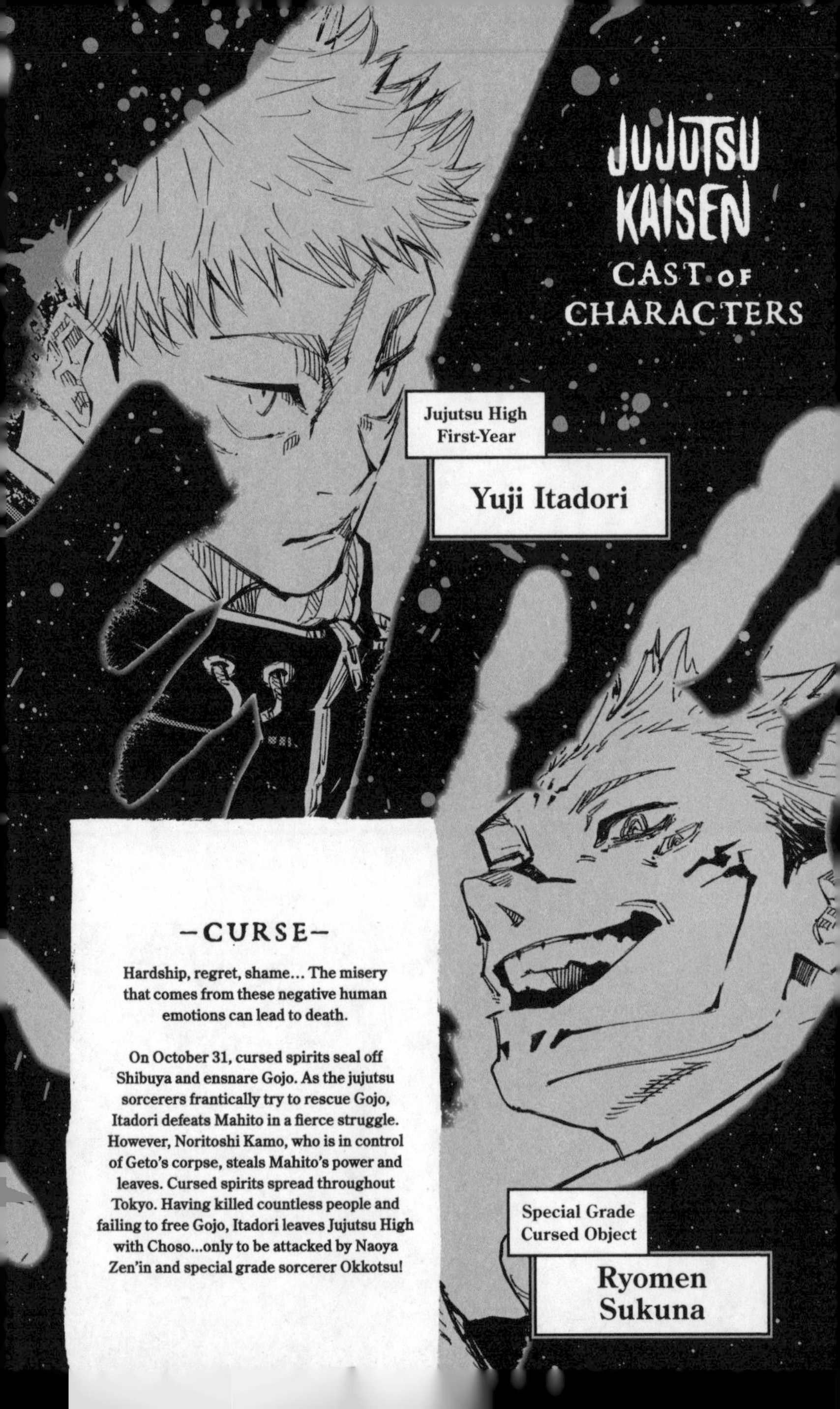
JUJUTSU KAISEN
CAST OF CHARACTERS
Jujutsu High First-Year
Yuji Itadori
Special Grade Cursed Object
Ryomen Sukuna

—CURSE—

Hardship, regret, shame... The misery that comes from these negative human emotions can lead to death.

On October 31, cursed spirits seal off Shibuya and ensnare Gojo. As the jujutsu sorcerers frantically try to rescue Gojo, Itadori defeats Mahito in a fierce struggle. However, Noritoshi Kamo, who is in control of Geto's corpse, steals Mahito's power and leaves. Cursed spirits spread throughout Tokyo. Having killed countless people and failing to free Gojo, Itadori leaves Jujutsu High with Choso...only to be attacked by Naoya Zen'in and special grade sorcerer Okkotsu!

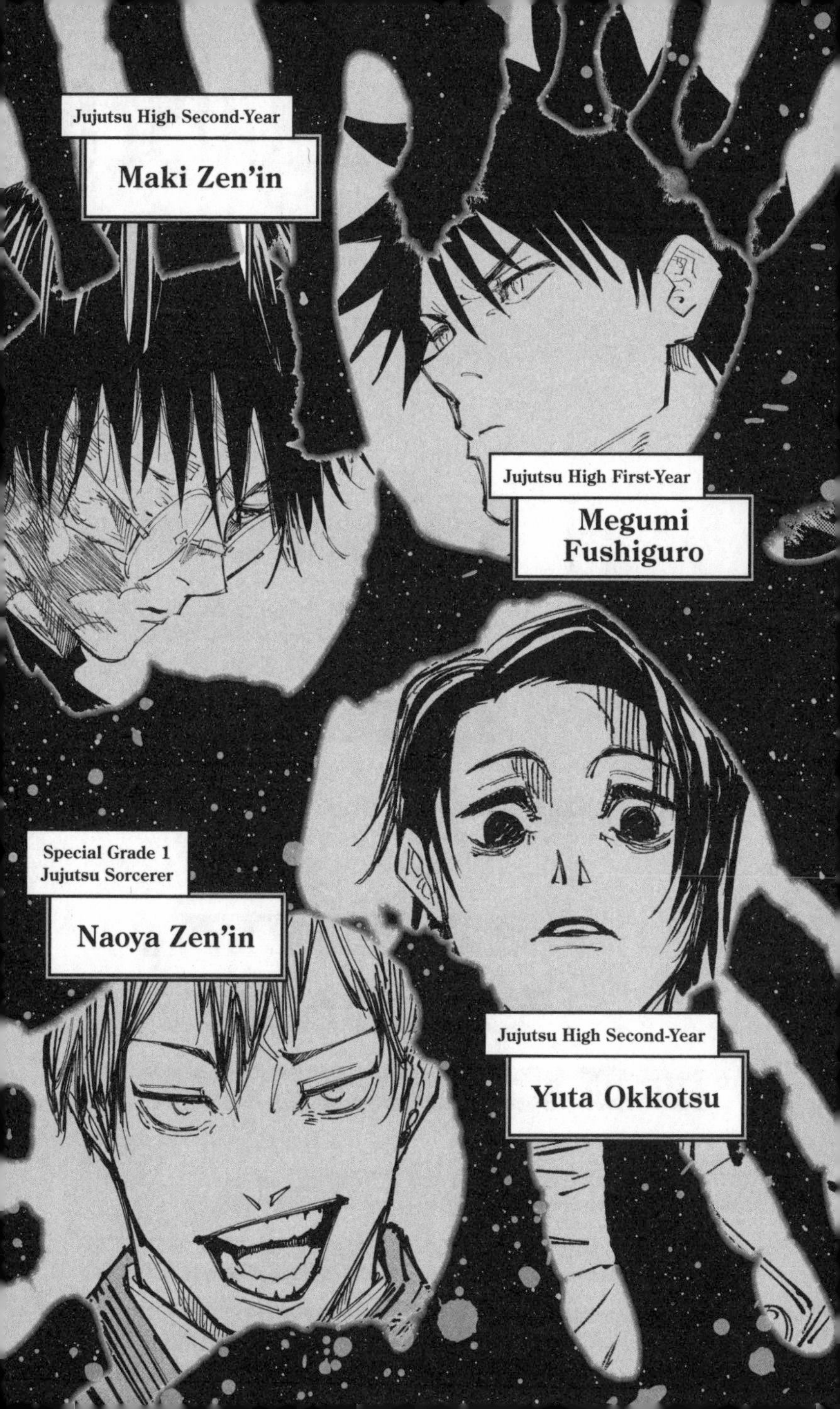
Jujutsu High First-Year
Megumi Fushiguro
Jujutsu High Second-Year
Maki Zen'in
Jujutsu High Second-Year
Yuta Okkotsu
Special Grade 1 Jujutsu Sorcerer
Naoya Zen'in

JUJUTSU KAISEN

17

PERFECT PREPARATION

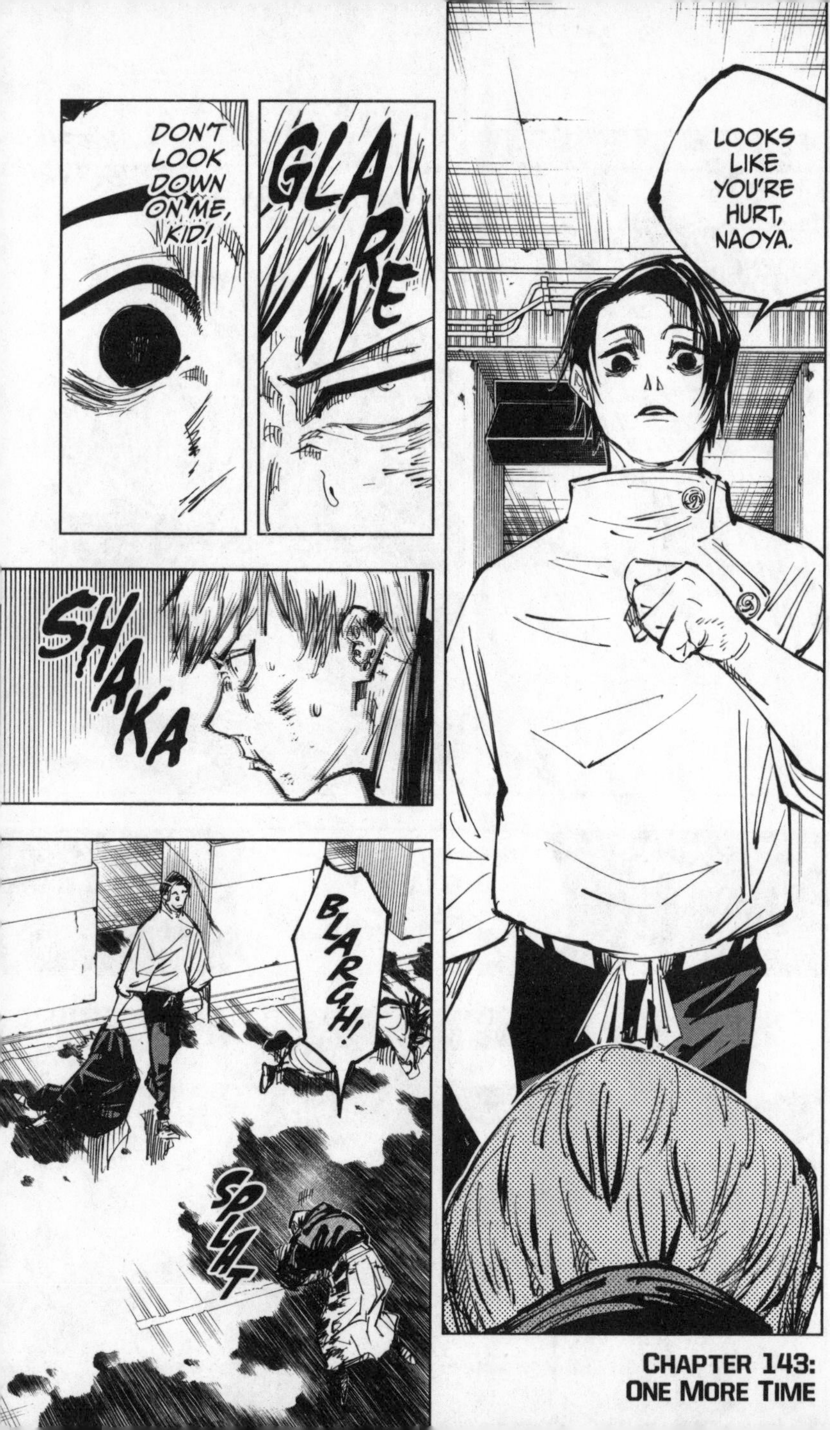
LOOKS LIKE YOU'RE HURT, NAOYA.
GLARE
DON'T LOOK DOWN ON ME, KID!
SHAKA
BLARGH!
SPLAT

CHAPTER 143: ONE MORE TIME

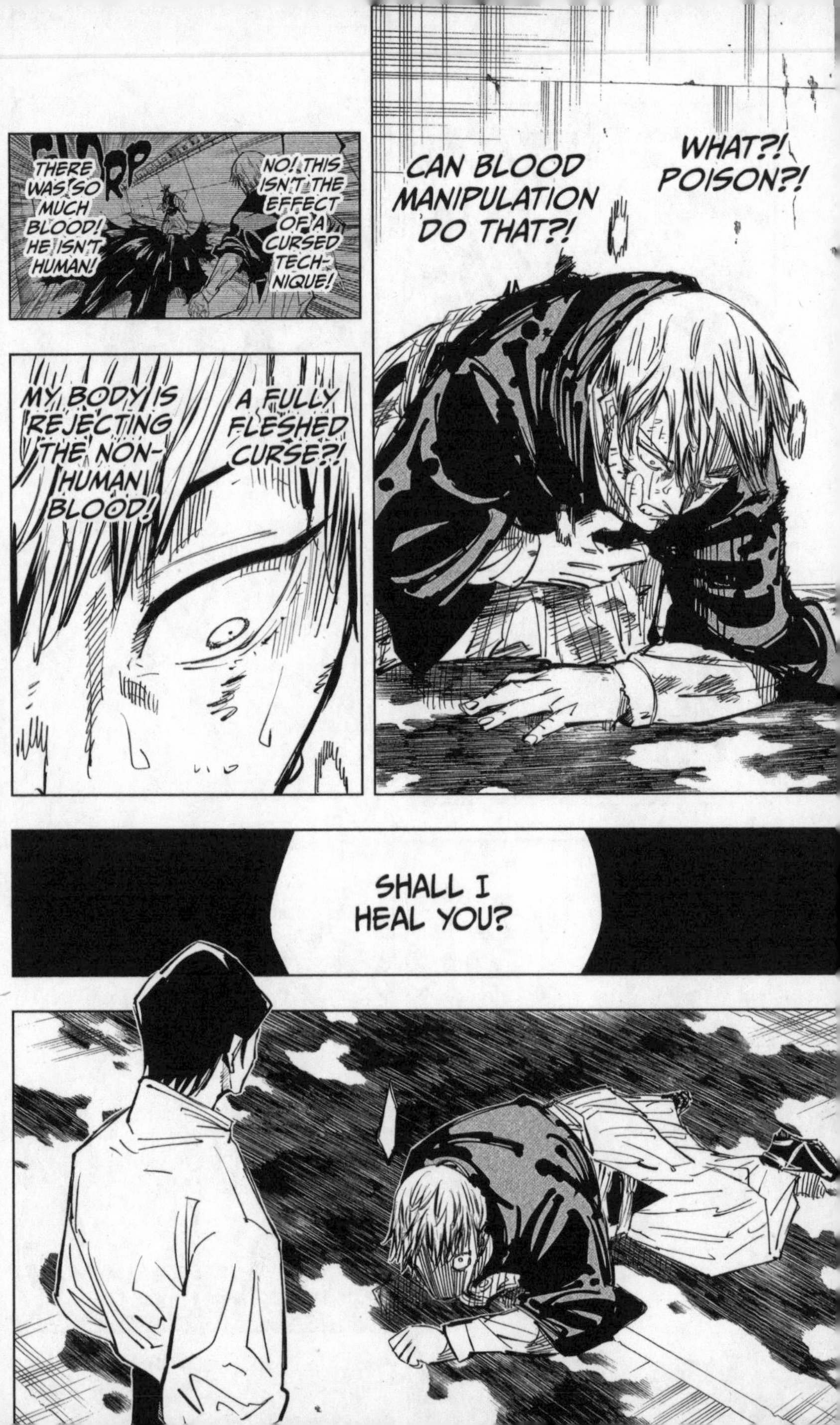
WHAT?! POISON?!
CAN BLOOD MANIPULATION DO THAT?!
NO! THIS ISN'T THE EFFECT OF A CURSED TECH-NIQUE!
THERE WAS SO MUCH BLOOD! HE ISN'T HUMAN!
A FULLY FLESHED CURSE?!
MY BODY IS REJECTING THE NON-HUMAN BLOOD!
SHALL I HEAL YOU?

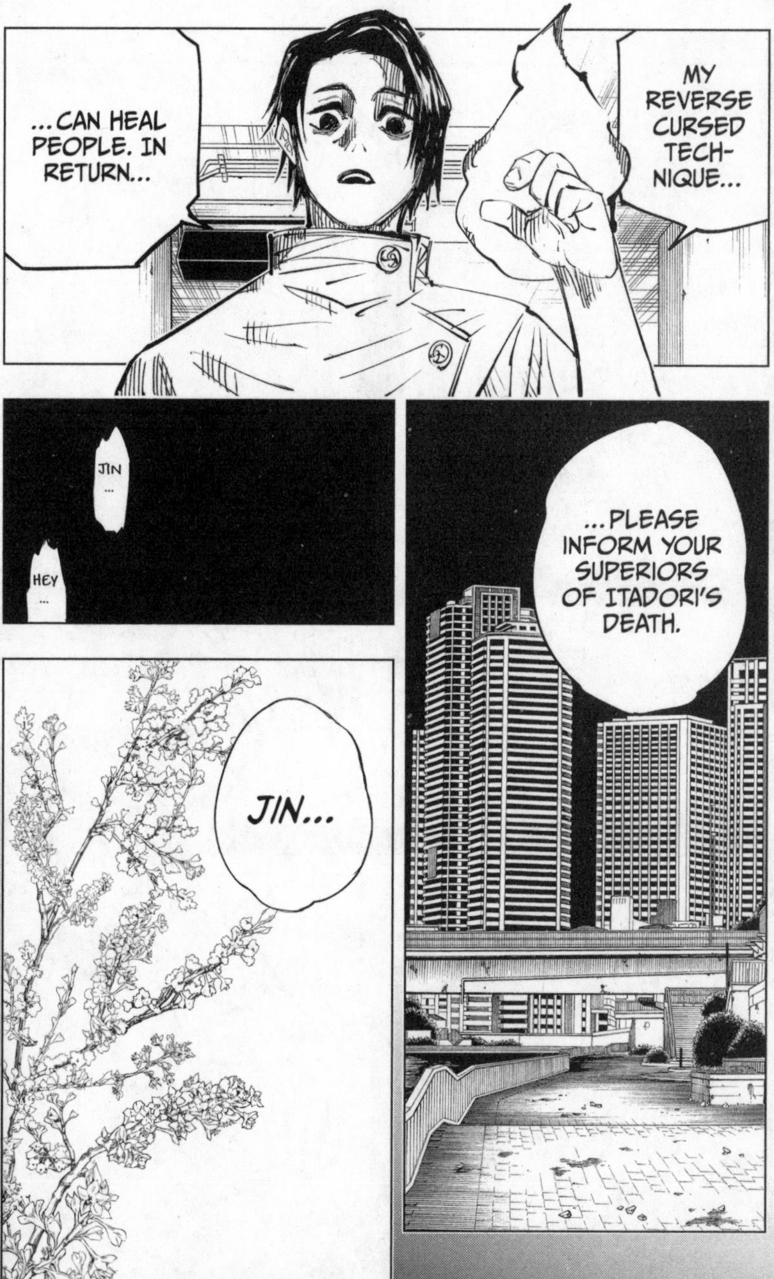
MY REVERSE CURSED TECH-NIQUE...
...CAN HEAL PEOPLE. IN RETURN...
...PLEASE INFORM YOUR SUPERIORS OF ITADORI'S DEATH.
JIN...
HEY...
JIN...

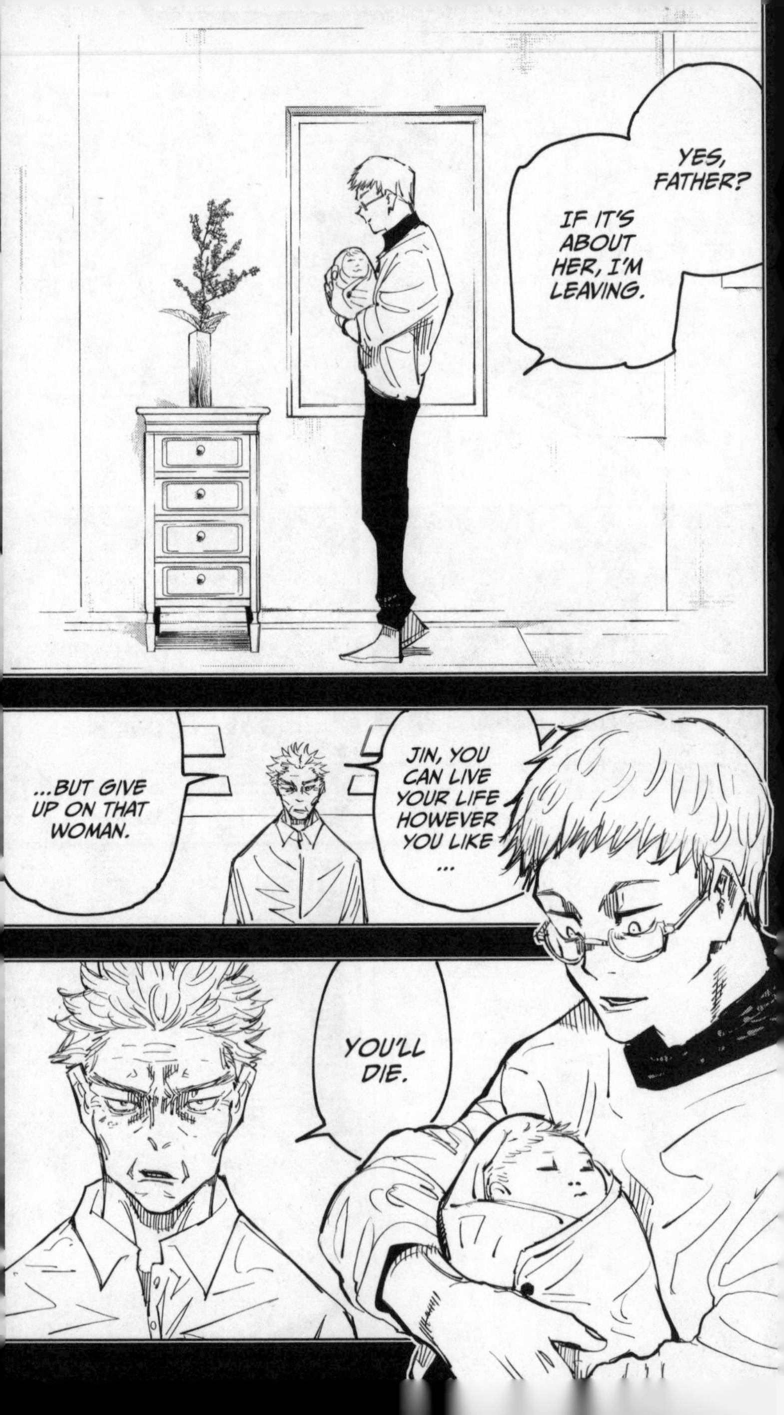
YES, FATHER?
IF IT'S ABOUT HER, I'M LEAVING.
JIN, YOU CAN LIVE YOUR LIFE HOWEVER YOU LIKE ...
...BUT GIVE UP ON THAT WOMAN.
YOU'LL DIE.

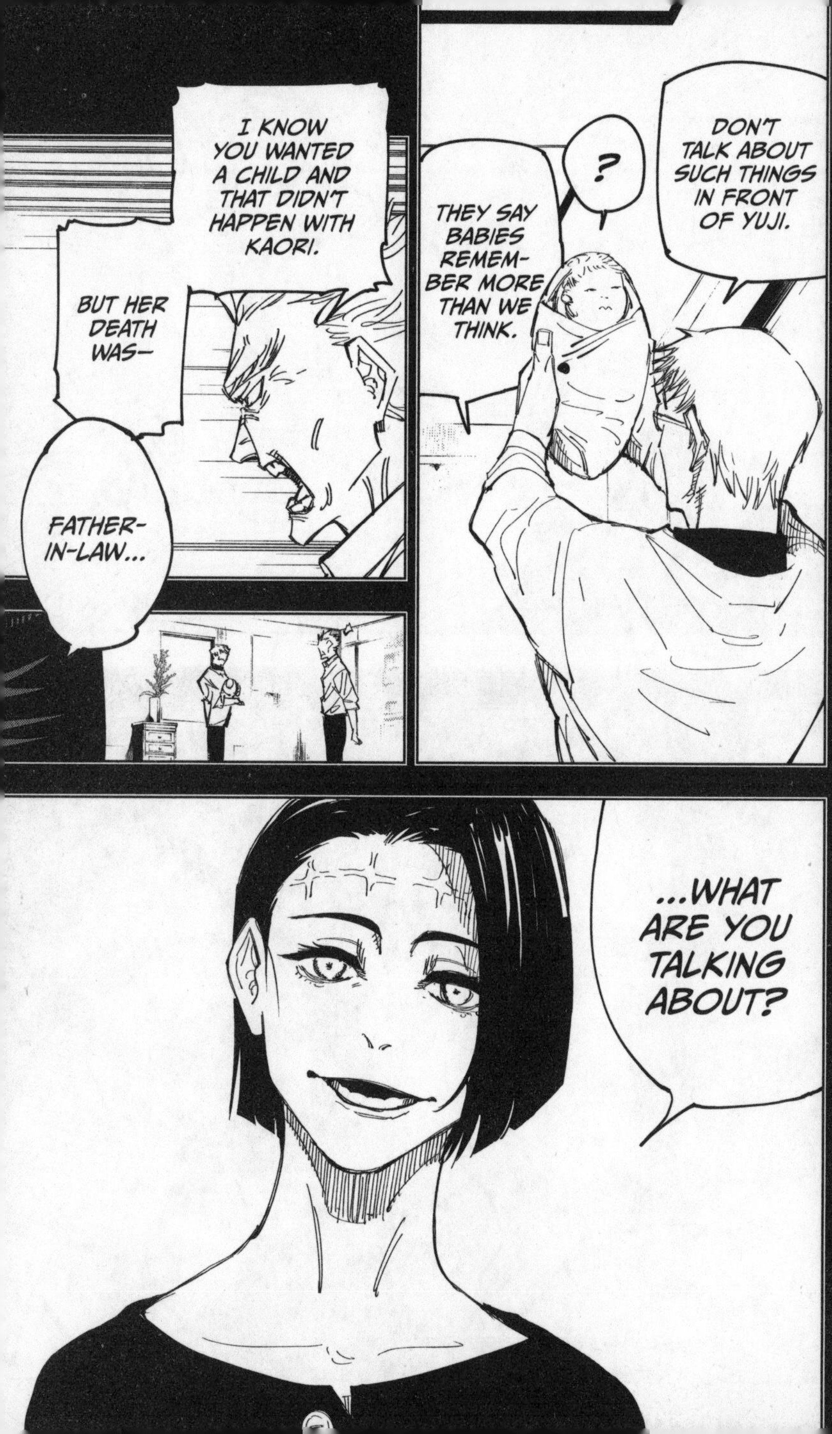
DON'T TALK ABOUT SUCH THINGS IN FRONT OF YUJI.
?
THEY SAY BABIES REMEM-BER MORE THAN WE THINK.
I KNOW YOU WANTED A CHILD AND THAT DIDN'T HAPPEN WITH KAORI.
BUT HER DEATH WAS-
FATHER-IN-LAW...
...WHAT ARE YOU TALKING ABOUT?

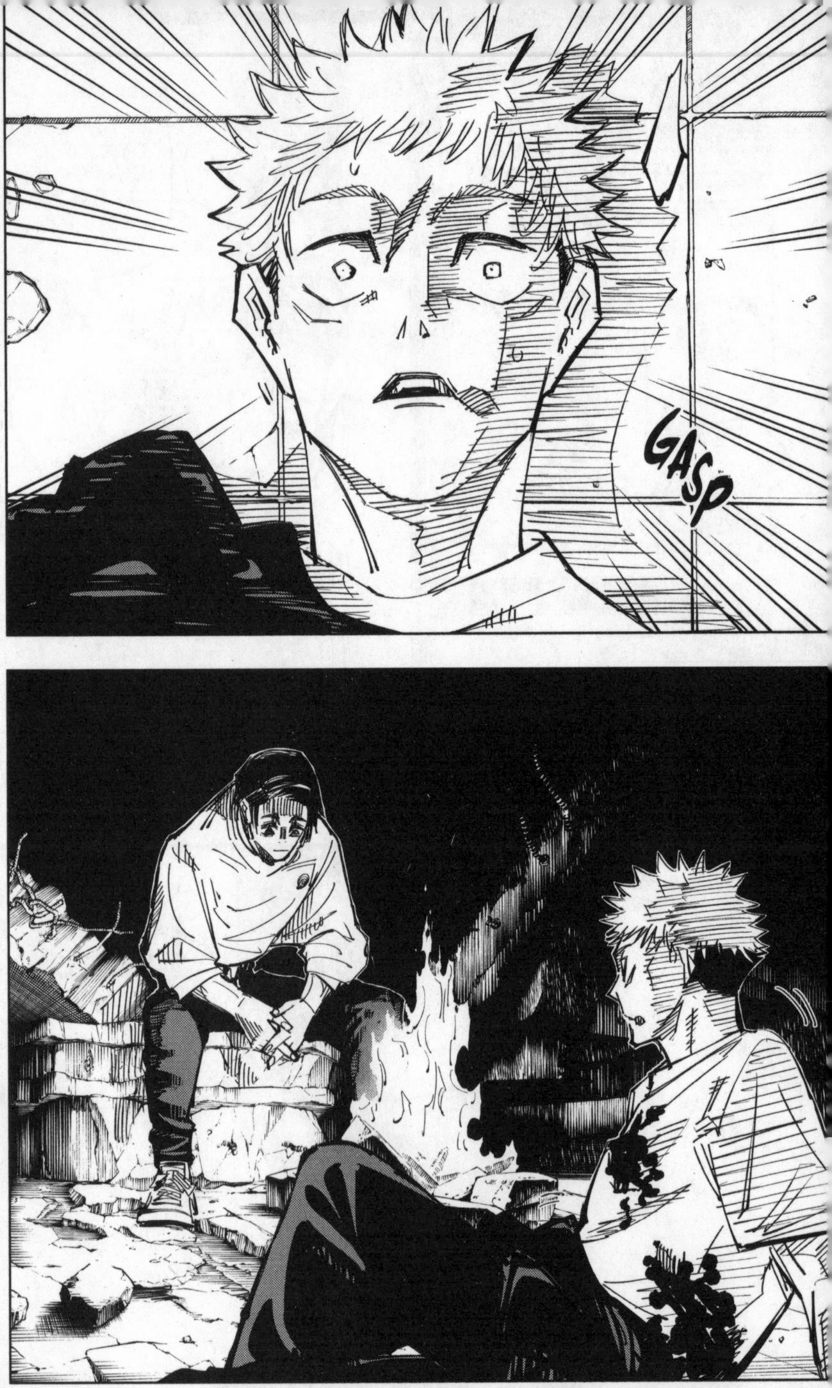
GASP

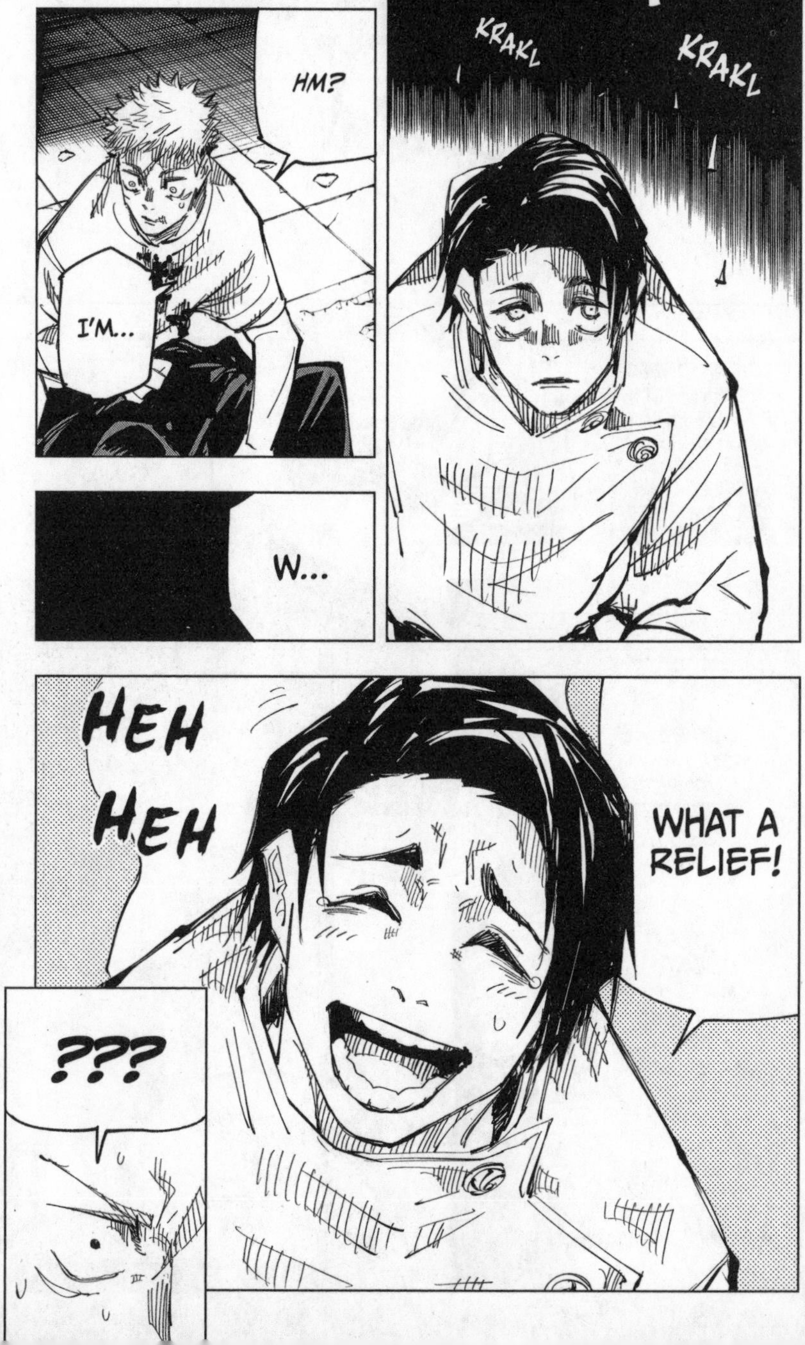
KRAKL
KRAKL
HM?
I'M...
W...
WHAT A RELIEF!
HEH HEH
???

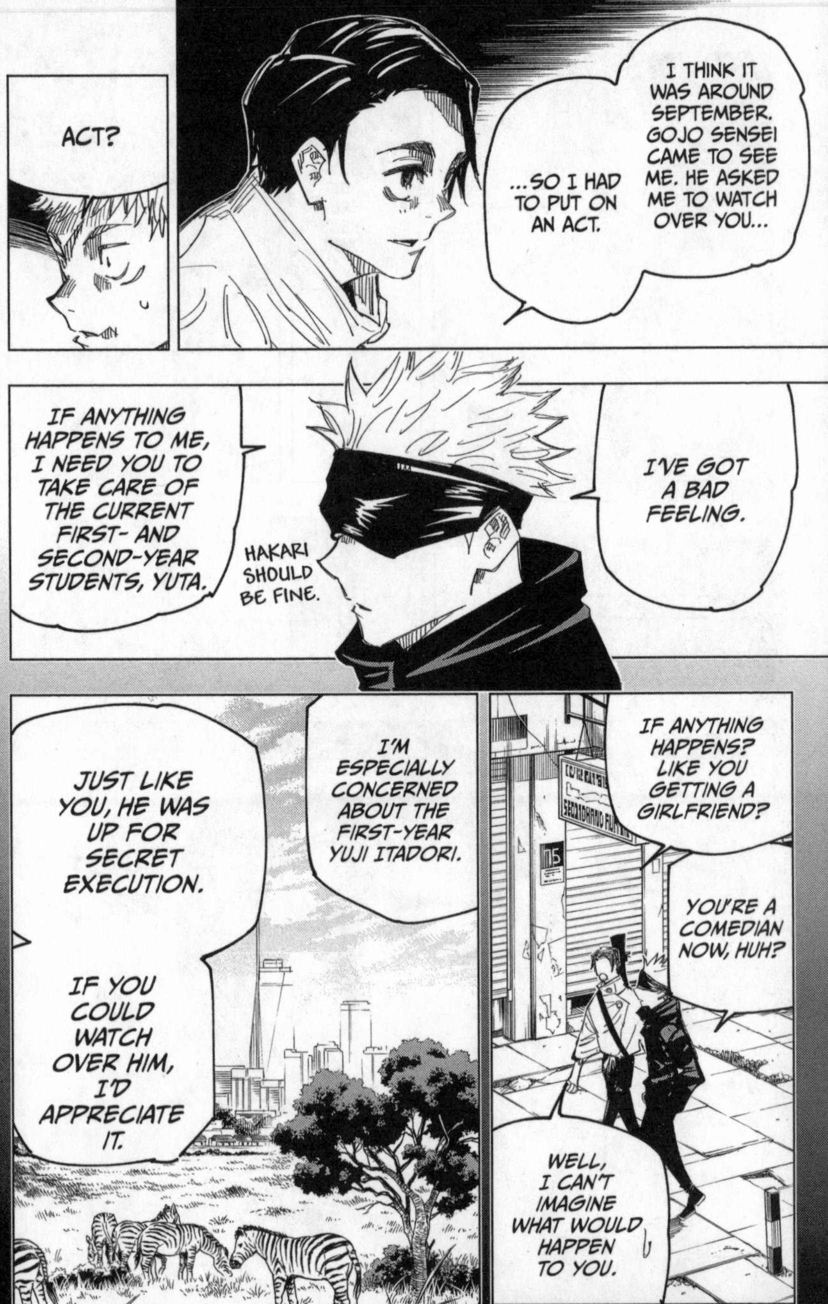
I THINK IT WAS AROUND SEPTEMBER. GOJO SENSEI CAME TO SEE ME. HE ASKED ME TO WATCH OVER YOU...
...SO I HAD TO PUT ON AN ACT.
ACT?
I'VE GOT A BAD FEELING.
IF ANYTHING HAPPENS TO ME, I NEED YOU TO TAKE CARE OF THE CURRENT FIRST- AND SECOND-YEAR STUDENTS, YUTA.
HAKARI SHOULD BE FINE.
IF ANYTHING HAPPENS? LIKE YOU GETTING A GIRLFRIEND?
YOU'RE A COMEDIAN NOW, HUH?
WELL, I CAN'T IMAGINE WHAT WOULD HAPPEN TO YOU.
I'M ESPECIALLY CONCERNED ABOUT THE FIRST-YEAR YUJI ITADORI.
JUST LIKE YOU, HE WAS UP FOR SECRET EXECUTION.
IF YOU COULD WATCH OVER HIM, I'D APPRECIATE IT.

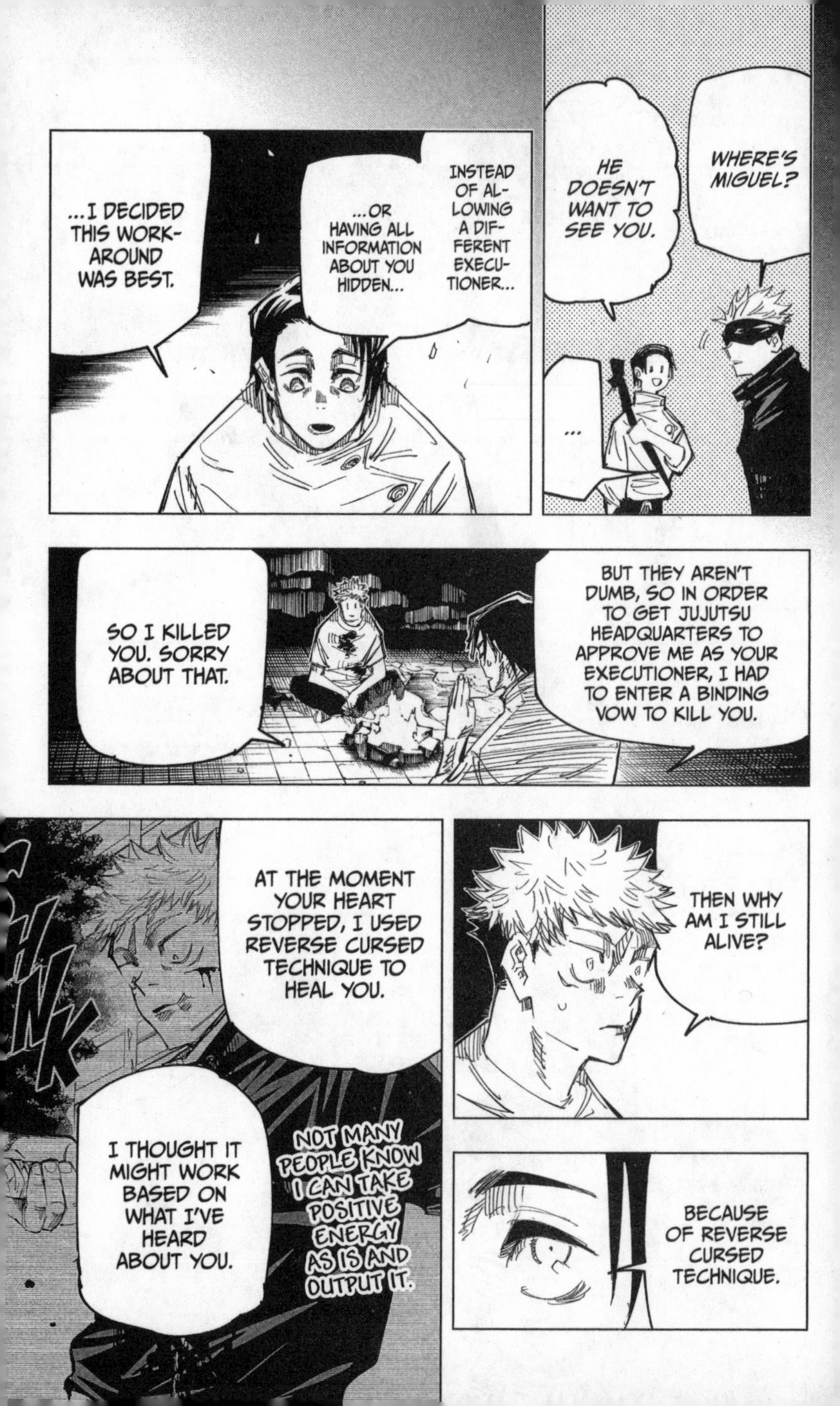
WHERE'S MIGUEL?
HE DOESN'T WANT TO SEE YOU.
...
INSTEAD OF ALLOWING A DIFFERENT EXECUTIONER...
...OR HAVING ALL INFORMATION ABOUT YOU HIDDEN...
...I DECIDED THIS WORK-AROUND WAS BEST.
BUT THEY AREN'T DUMB, SO IN ORDER TO GET JUJUTSU HEADQUARTERS TO APPROVE ME AS YOUR EXECUTIONER, I HAD TO ENTER A BINDING VOW TO KILL YOU.
SO I KILLED YOU. SORRY ABOUT THAT.
THEN WHY AM I STILL ALIVE?
BECAUSE OF REVERSE CURSED TECHNIQUE.
AT THE MOMENT YOUR HEART STOPPED, I USED REVERSE CURSED TECHNIQUE TO HEAL YOU.
NOT MANY PEOPLE KNOW I CAN TAKE POSITIVE ENERGY AS IS AND OUTPUT IT.
I THOUGHT IT MIGHT WORK BASED ON WHAT I'VE HEARD ABOUT YOU.

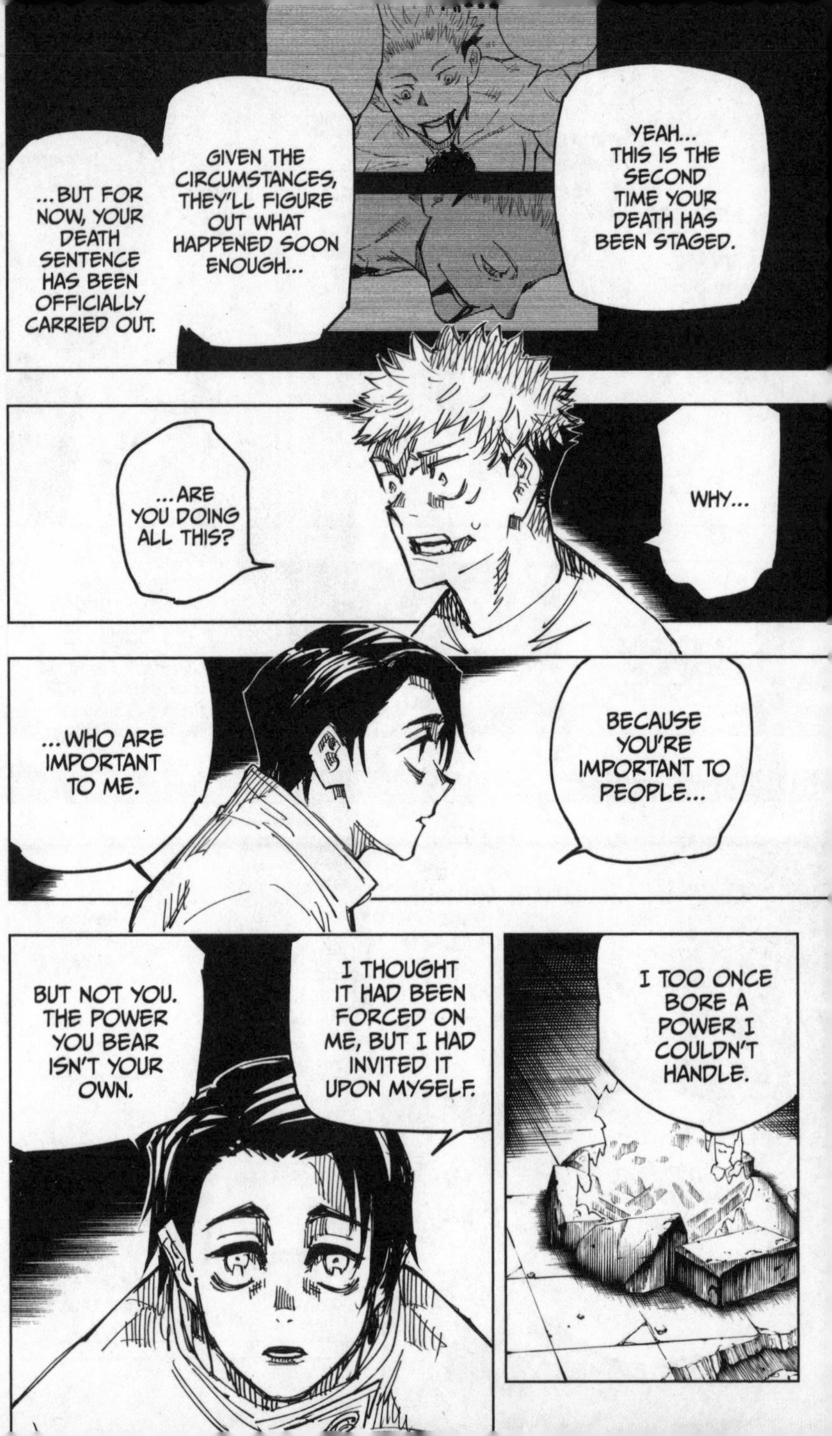
YEAH... THIS IS THE SECOND TIME YOUR DEATH HAS BEEN STAGED.
GIVEN THE CIRCUMSTANCES, THEY'LL FIGURE OUT WHAT HAPPENED SOON ENOUGH...
...BUT FOR NOW, YOUR DEATH SENTENCE HAS BEEN OFFICIALLY CARRIED OUT.
WHY...
...ARE YOU DOING ALL THIS?
BECAUSE YOU'RE IMPORTANT TO PEOPLE...
...WHO ARE IMPORTANT TO ME.
I TOO ONCE BORE A POWER I COULDN'T HANDLE.
I THOUGHT IT HAD BEEN FORCED ON ME, BUT I HAD INVITED IT UPON MYSELF.
BUT NOT YOU. THE POWER YOU BEAR ISN'T YOUR OWN.

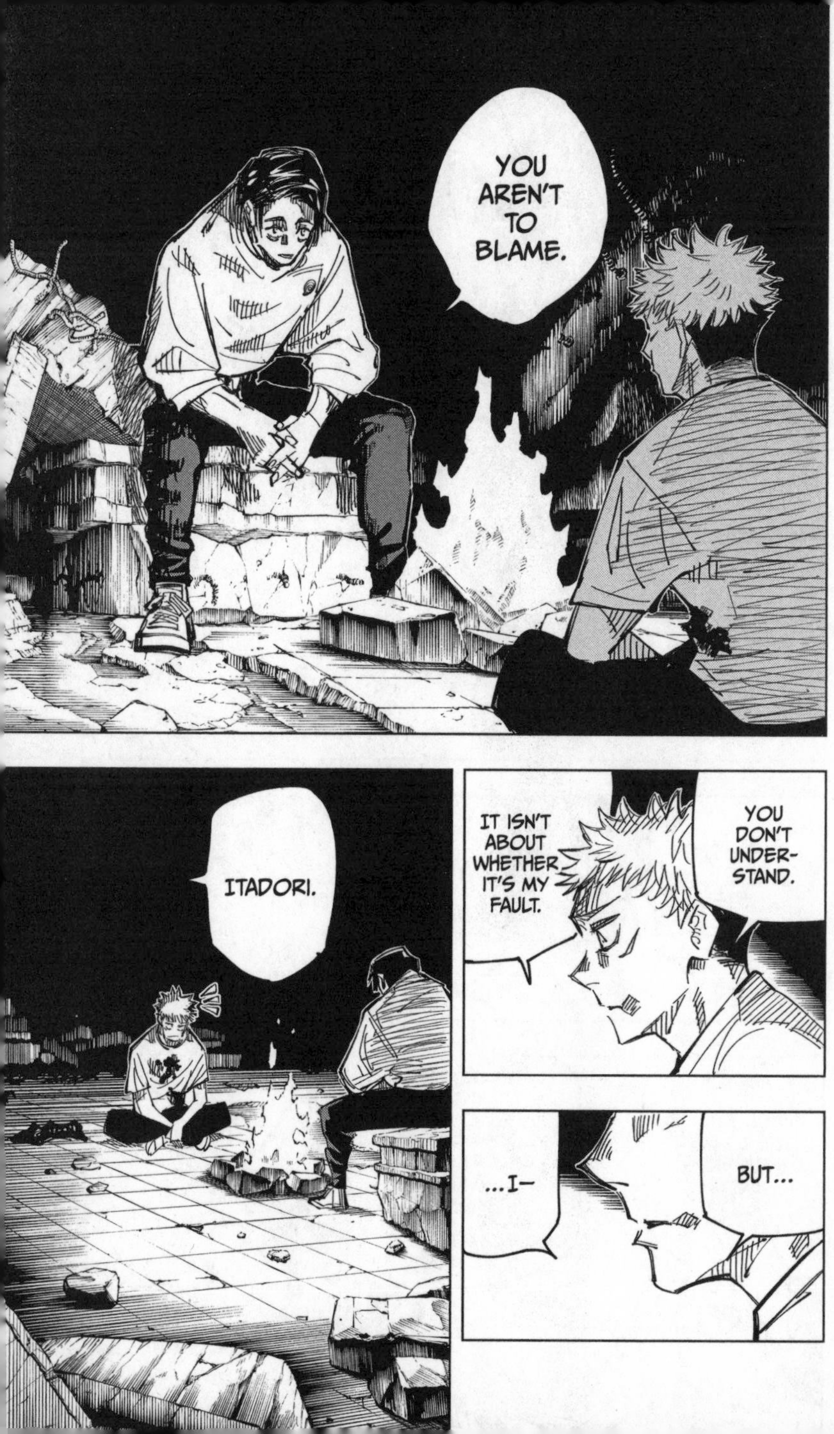
YOU AREN'T TO BLAME.
YOU DON'T UNDERSTAND.
IT ISN'T ABOUT WHETHER IT'S MY FAULT.
BUT...
...I—
ITADORI.

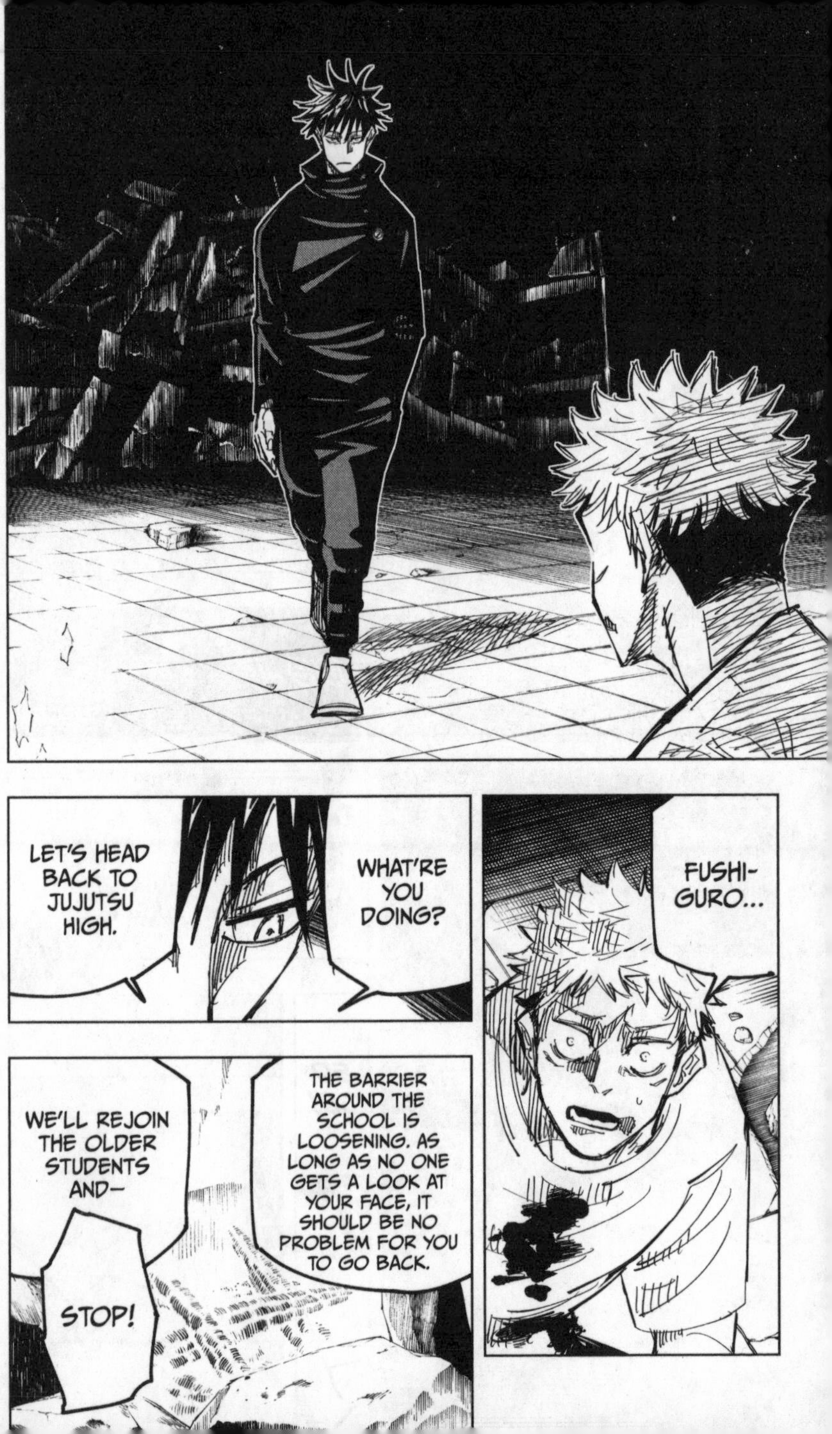
FUSHI-GURO...
WHAT'RE YOU DOING?
LET'S HEAD BACK TO JUJUTSU HIGH.
THE BARRIER AROUND THE SCHOOL IS LOOSENING. AS LONG AS NO ONE GETS A LOOK AT YOUR FACE, IT SHOULD BE NO PROBLEM FOR YOU TO GO BACK.
WE'LL REJOIN THE OLDER STUDENTS AND—
STOP!

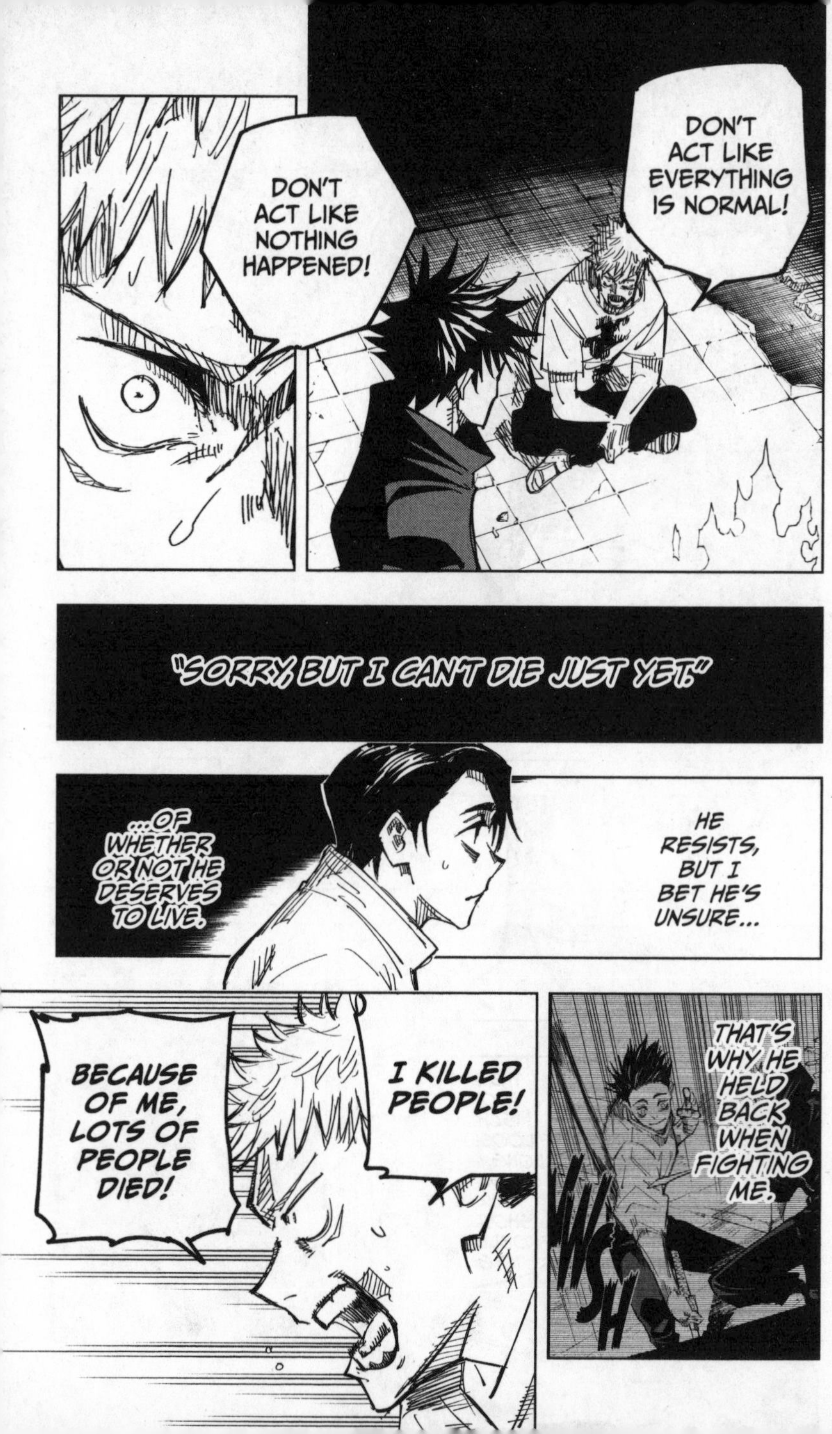
DON'T ACT LIKE EVERYTHING IS NORMAL!
DON'T ACT LIKE NOTHING HAPPENED!
"SORRY, BUT I CAN'T DIE JUST YET."
HE RESISTS, BUT I BET HE'S UNSURE...
...OF WHETHER OR NOT HE DESERVES TO LIVE.
THAT'S WHY HE HELD BACK WHEN FIGHTING ME.
I KILLED PEOPLE!
BECAUSE OF ME, LOTS OF PEOPLE DIED!

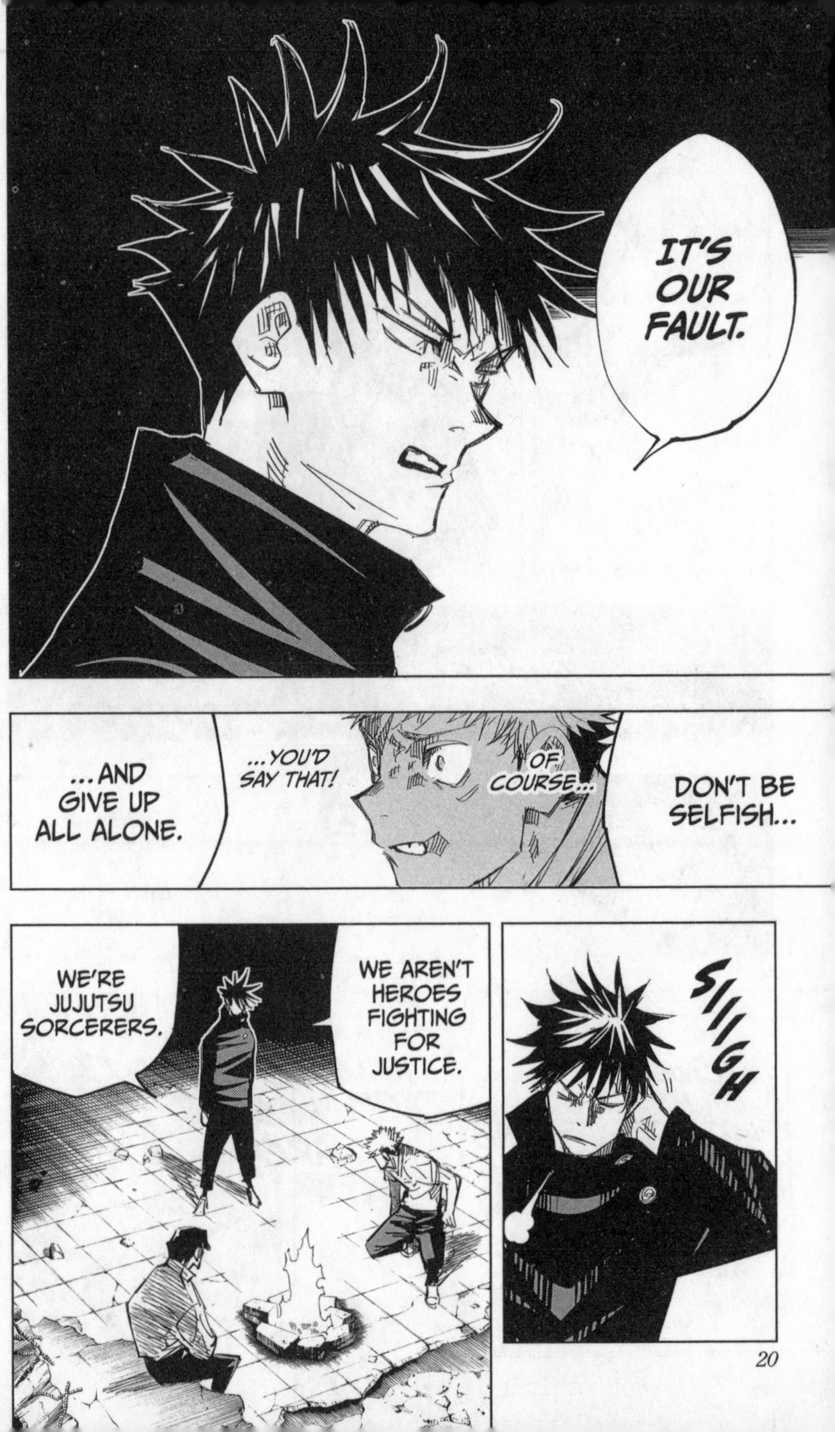
IT'S OUR FAULT.
DON'T BE SELFISH...
OF COURSE...
...YOU'D SAY THAT!
...AND GIVE UP ALL ALONE.
SIIIGH
WE AREN'T HEROES FIGHTING FOR JUSTICE.
WE'RE JUJUTSU SORCERERS.

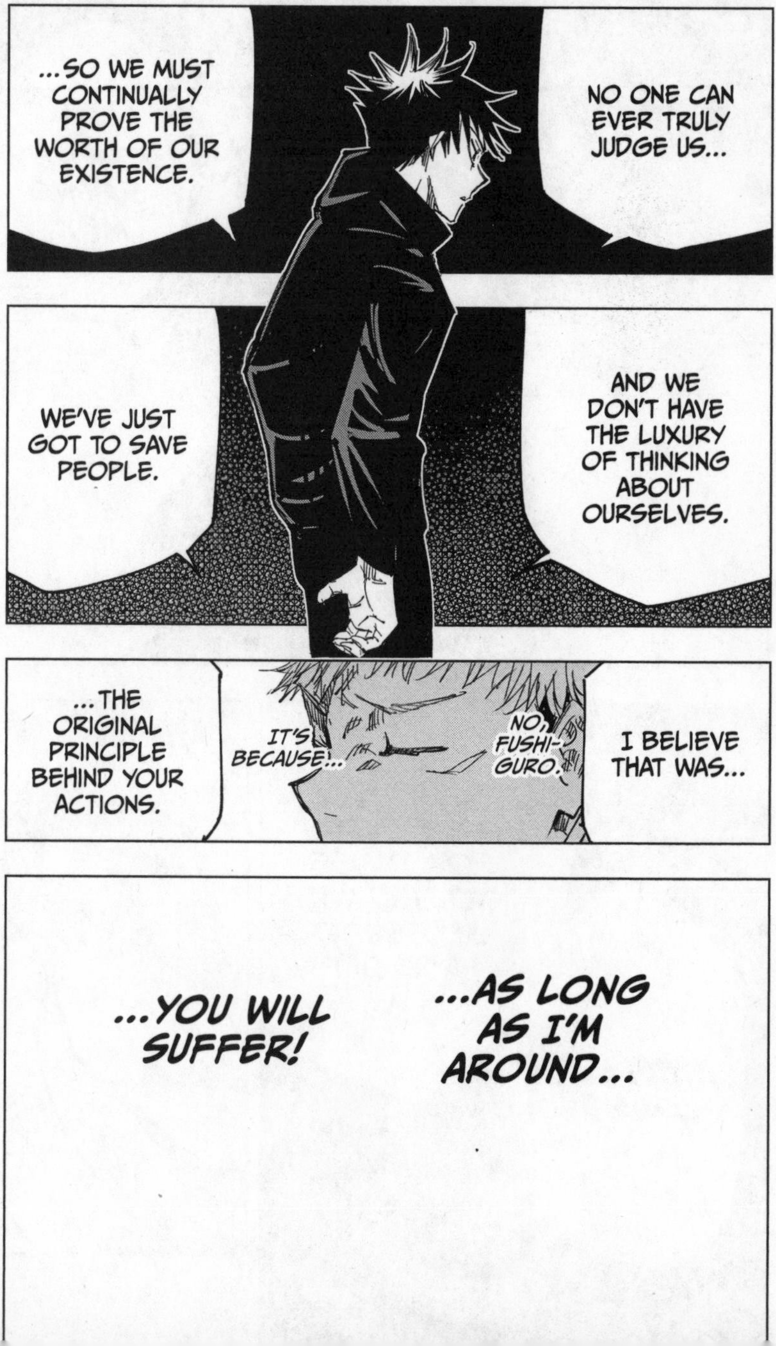
NO ONE CAN EVER TRULY JUDGE US...
...SO WE MUST CONTINUALLY PROVE THE WORTH OF OUR EXISTENCE.
AND WE DON'T HAVE THE LUXURY OF THINKING ABOUT OURSELVES.
WE'VE JUST GOT TO SAVE PEOPLE.
I BELIEVE THAT WAS...
NO, FUSHI-GURO.
IT'S BECAUSE...
...THE ORIGINAL PRINCIPLE BEHIND YOUR ACTIONS.
...AS LONG AS I'M AROUND...
...YOU WILL SUFFER!

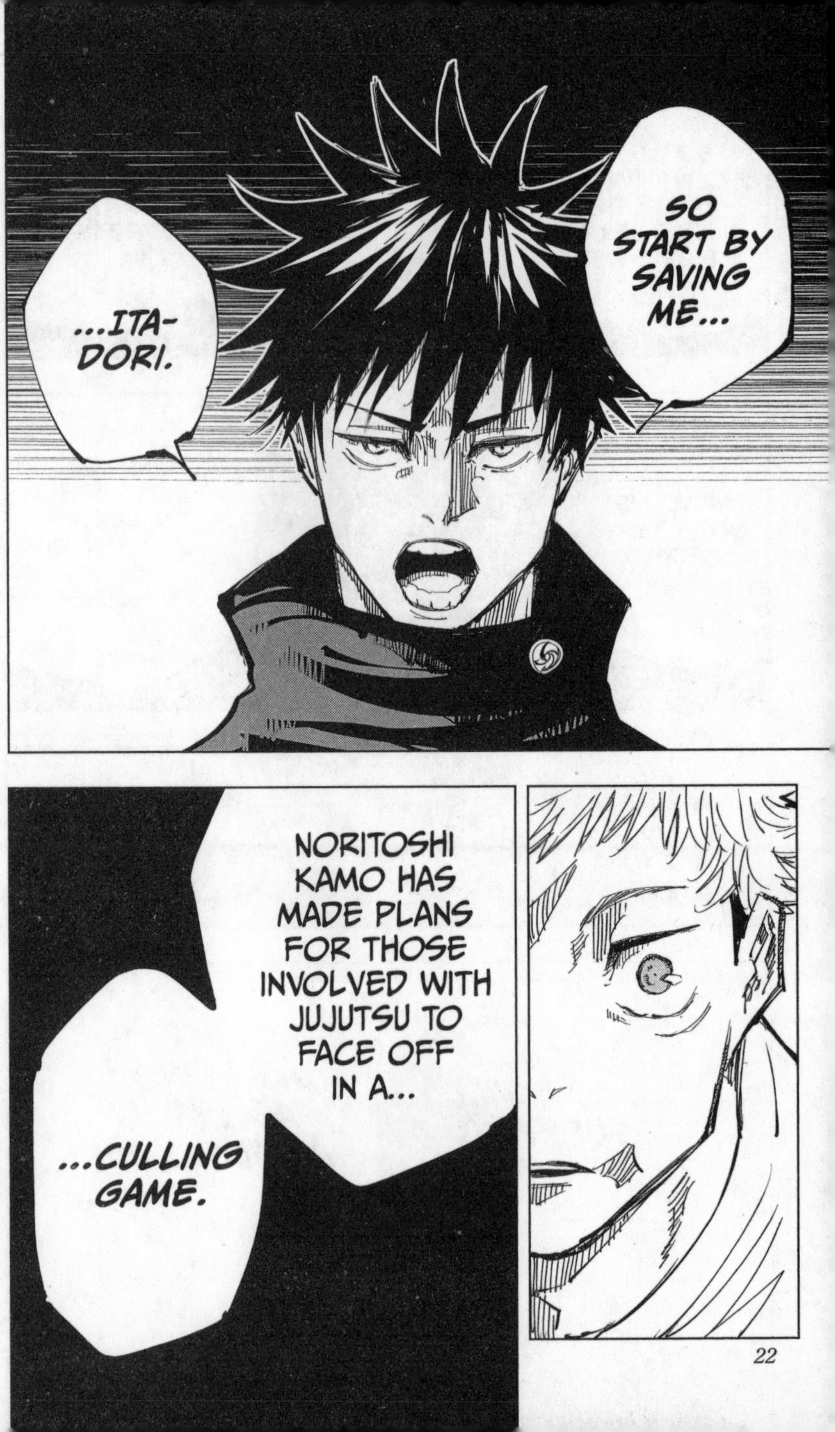
SO START BY SAVING ME...
...ITA-DORI.
NORITOSHI KAMO HAS MADE PLANS FOR THOSE INVOLVED WITH JUJUTSU TO FACE OFF IN A...
...CULLING GAME.

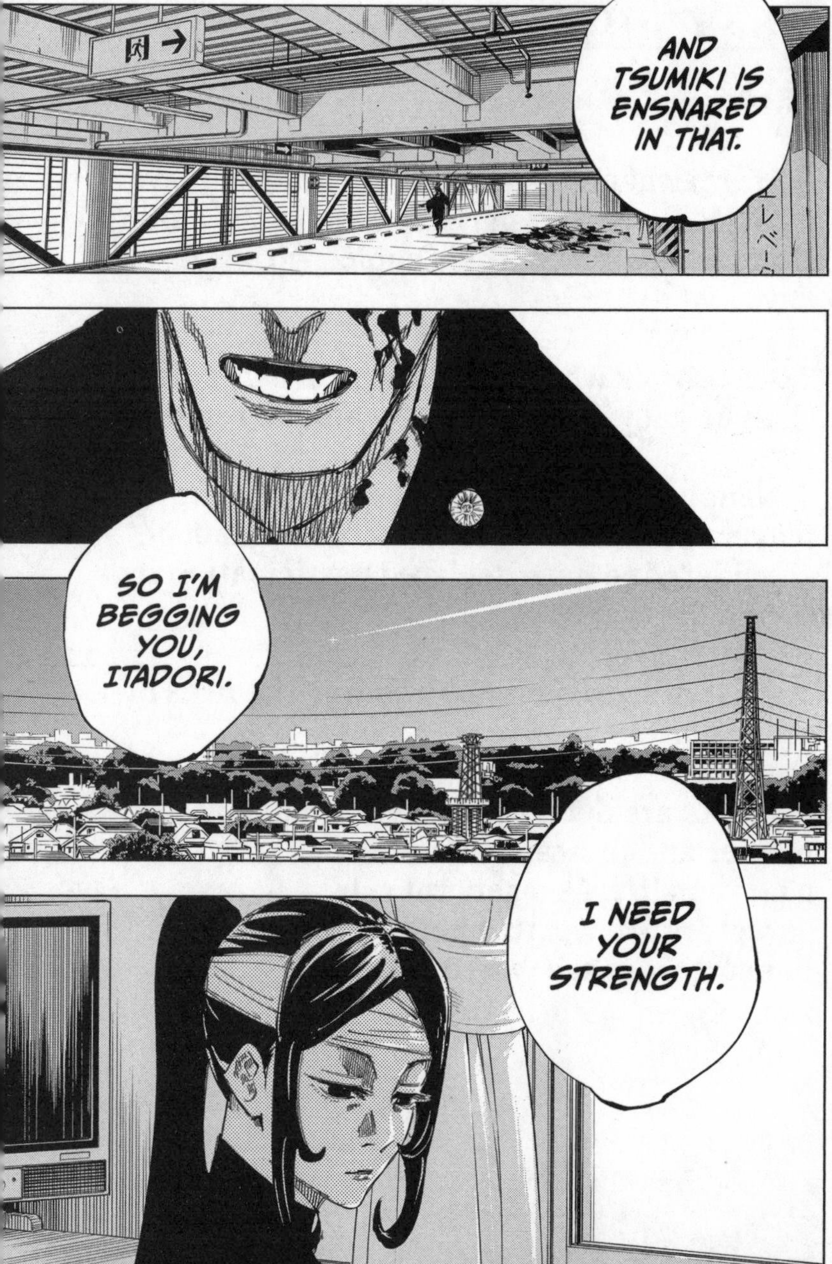
AND TSUMIKI IS ENSNARED IN THAT.
SO I'M BEGGING YOU, ITADORI.
I NEED YOUR STRENGTH.

The Culling Game

<Rules>

1. After awakening a cursed technique, players must declare their participation in the culling game at a colony of their choice within 19 days.

2. Any player who breaks the previous rule shall be subject to cursed technique removal.

3. Nonplayers who enter a colony become players at the moment of entry and shall be considered to have declared participation in the culling game.

4. Players score points by ending the lives of other players.

5. Points are determined by the game master and indicate the value of a player's life. As a general rule, sorcerers are worth 5 points and nonsorcerers are worth 1 point.

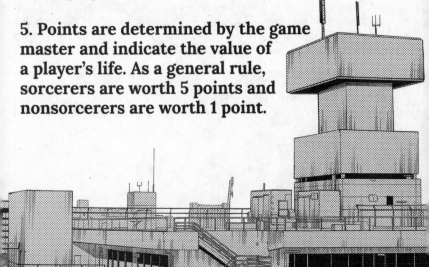

6. Players may expend 100 points to negotiate with the game master to add one new rule to the culling game. However, players cannot add their own life's value to the amount that can be spent.

7. In accordance with the previous rule, the game master must accept any proposed new rule unless it will have a marked and long-lasting effect on the culling game.

8. If a player's score remains the same for 19 days, that player shall be subject to cursed technique removal.

FUSHIGURO

Chapter 144: That Place

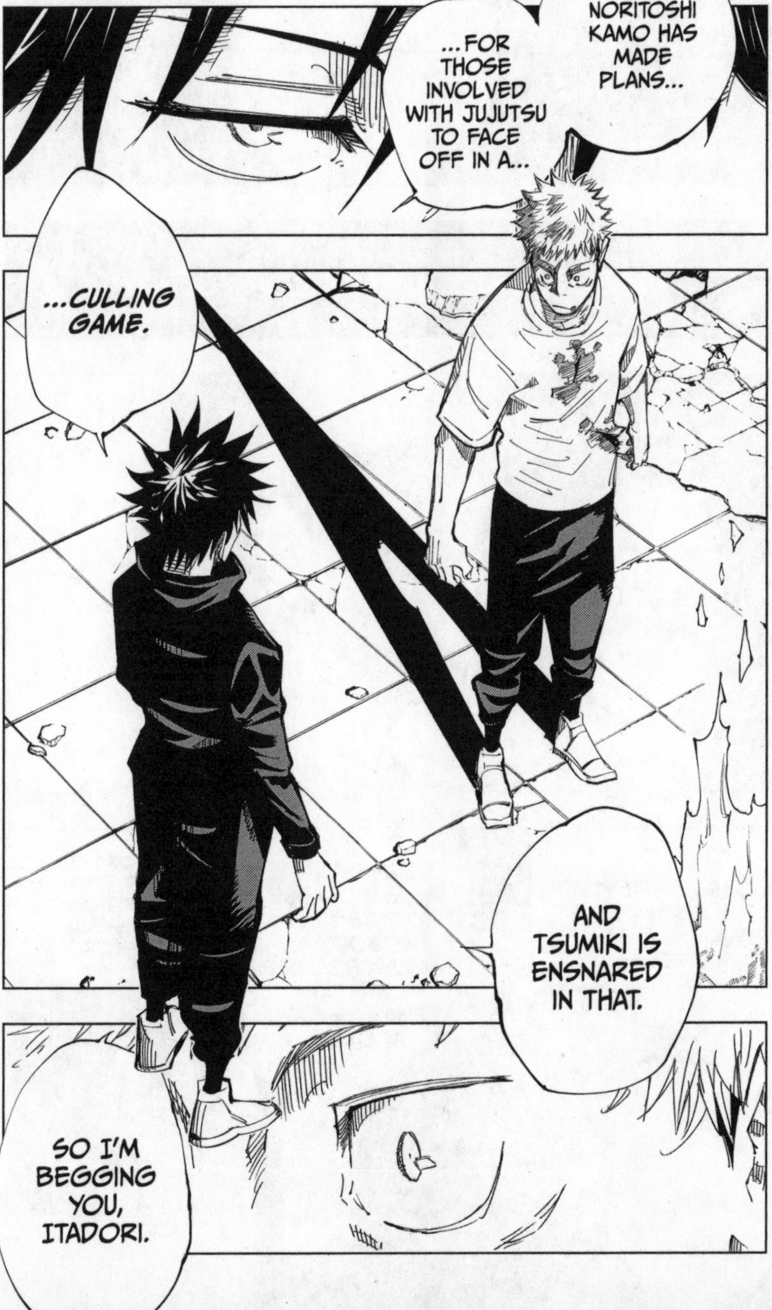
NORITOSHI KAMO HAS MADE PLANS...
...FOR THOSE INVOLVED WITH JUJUTSU TO FACE OFF IN A...
...CULLING GAME.
AND TSUMIKI IS ENSNARED IN THAT.
SO I'M BEGGING YOU, ITADORI.

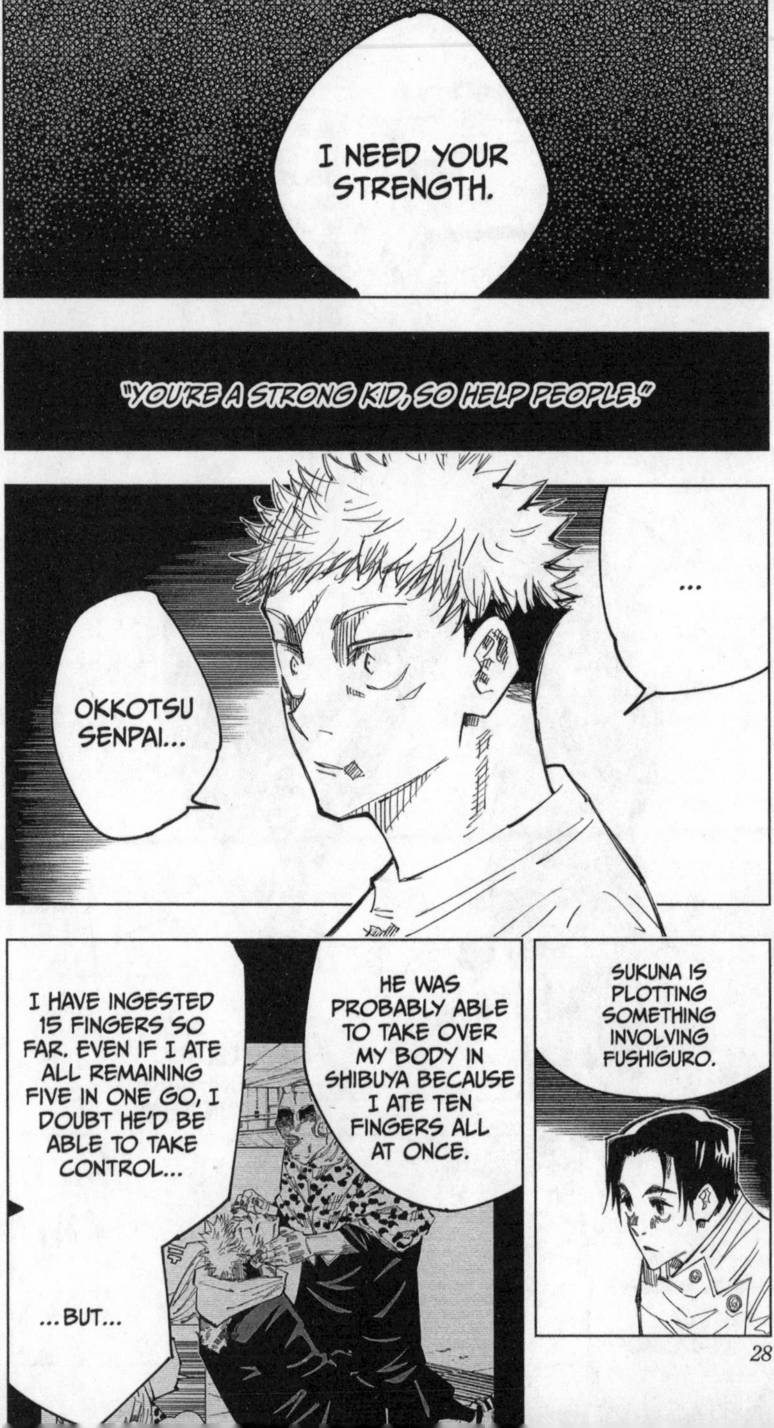

I NEED YOUR STRENGTH.
"YOU'RE A STRONG KID, SO HELP PEOPLE."
...
OKKOTSU SENPAI...
SUKUNA IS PLOTTING SOMETHING INVOLVING FUSHIGURO.
HE WAS PROBABLY ABLE TO TAKE OVER MY BODY IN SHIBUYA BECAUSE I ATE TEN FINGERS ALL AT ONCE.
I HAVE INGESTED 15 FINGERS SO FAR. EVEN IF I ATE ALL REMAINING FIVE IN ONE GO, I DOUBT HE'D BE ABLE TO TAKE CONTROL...
...BUT...

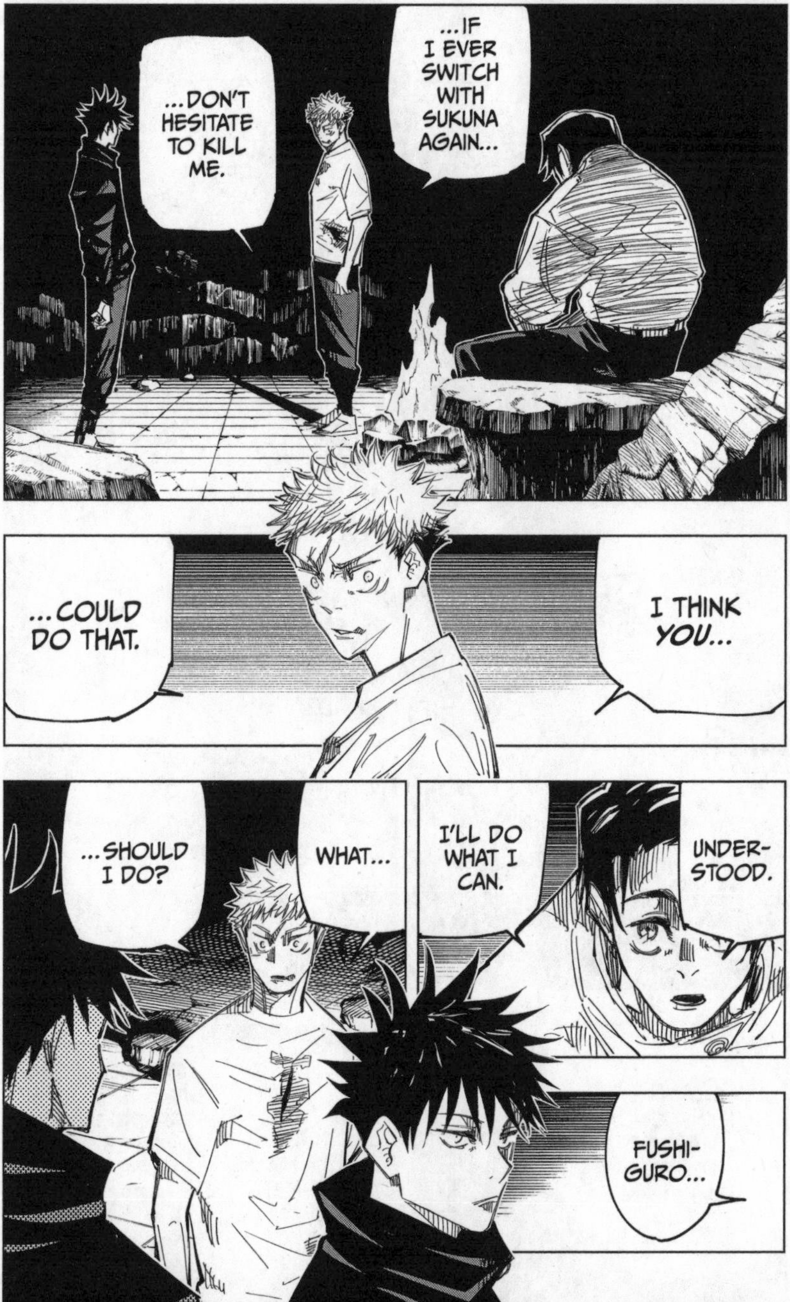
...IF I EVER SWITCH WITH SUKUNA AGAIN...
...DON'T HESITATE TO KILL ME.
I THINK *YOU*...
...COULD DO THAT.
UNDER-STOOD.
I'LL DO WHAT I CAN.
FUSHI-GURO...
WHAT...
...SHOULD I DO?

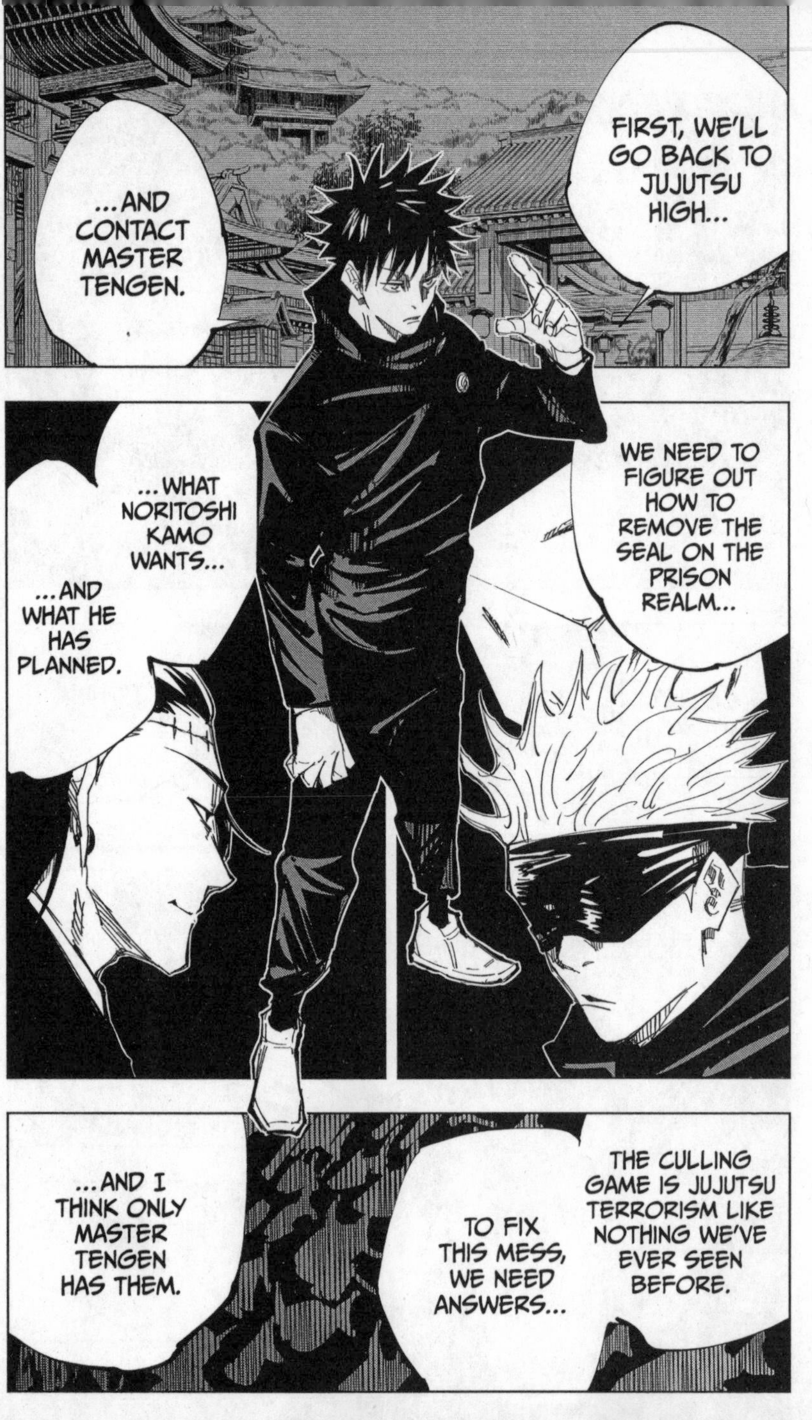
FIRST, WE'LL GO BACK TO JUJUTSU HIGH...
...AND CONTACT MASTER TENGEN.
WE NEED TO FIGURE OUT HOW TO REMOVE THE SEAL ON THE PRISON REALM...
...WHAT NORITOSHI KAMO WANTS...
...AND WHAT HE HAS PLANNED.
THE CULLING GAME IS JUJUTSU TERRORISM LIKE NOTHING WE'VE EVER SEEN BEFORE.
TO FIX THIS MESS, WE NEED ANSWERS...
...AND I THINK ONLY MASTER TENGEN HAS THEM.

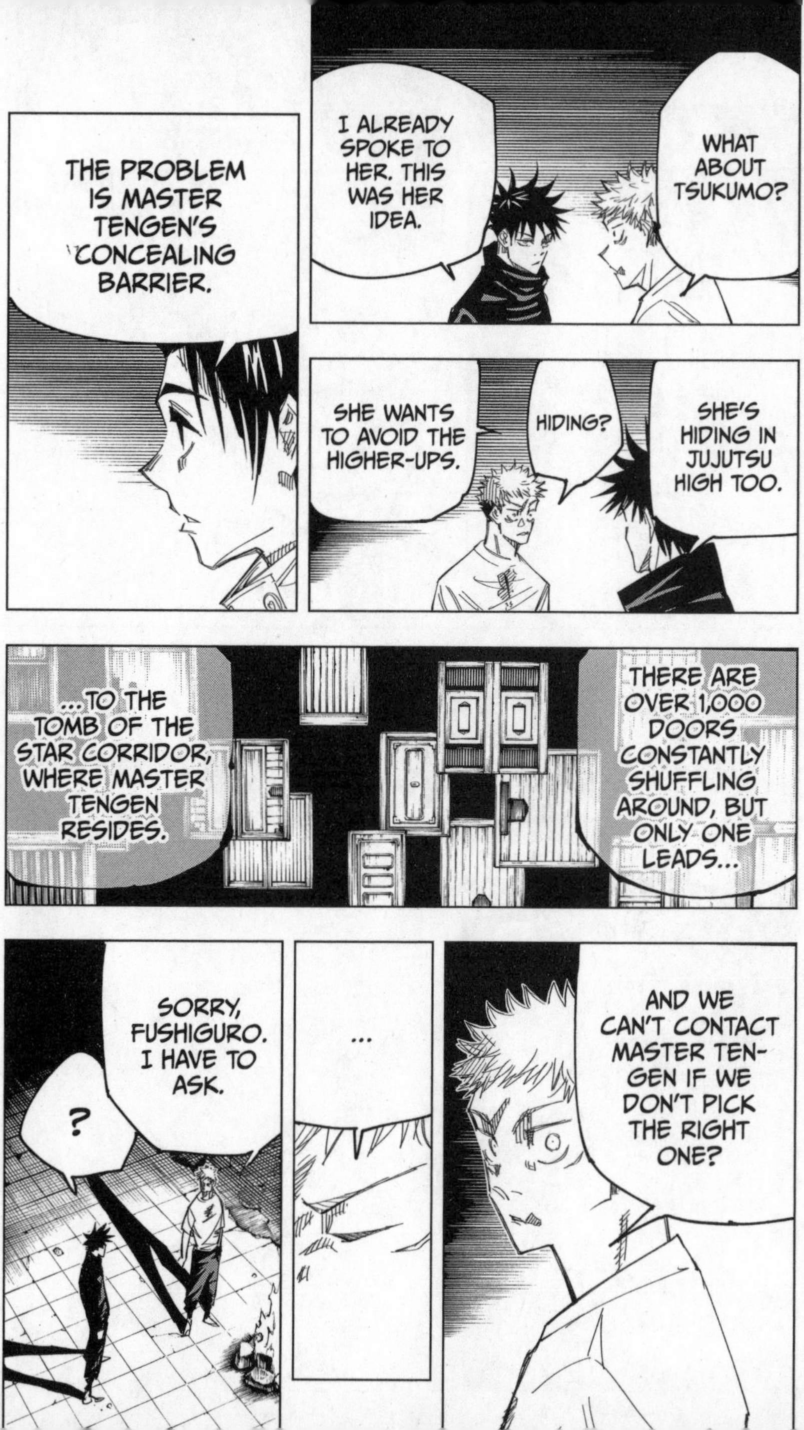
WHAT ABOUT TSUKUMO?
I ALREADY SPOKE TO HER. THIS WAS HER IDEA.
SHE'S HIDING IN JUJUTSU HIGH TOO.
HIDING?
SHE WANTS TO AVOID THE HIGHER-UPS.
THE PROBLEM IS MASTER TENGEN'S CONCEALING BARRIER.
THERE ARE OVER 1,000 DOORS CONSTANTLY SHUFFLING AROUND, BUT ONLY ONE LEADS...
...TO THE TOMB OF THE STAR CORRIDOR, WHERE MASTER TENGEN RESIDES.
AND WE CAN'T CONTACT MASTER TEN-GEN IF WE DON'T PICK THE RIGHT ONE?
...
SORRY, FUSHIGURO. I HAVE TO ASK.
?

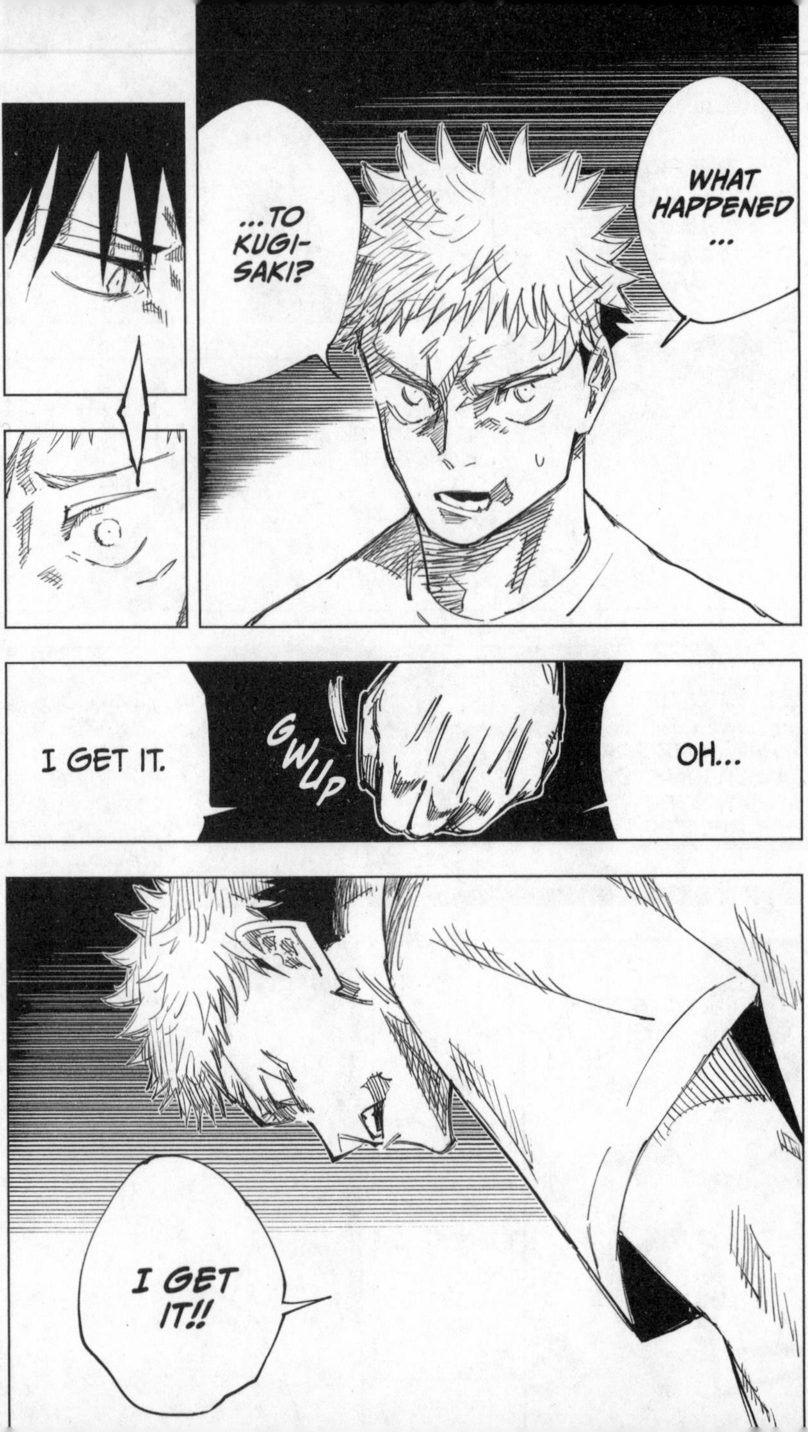
WHAT HAPPENED ...
...TO KUGI-SAKI?
OH...
GWUP
I GET IT.
I GET IT!!

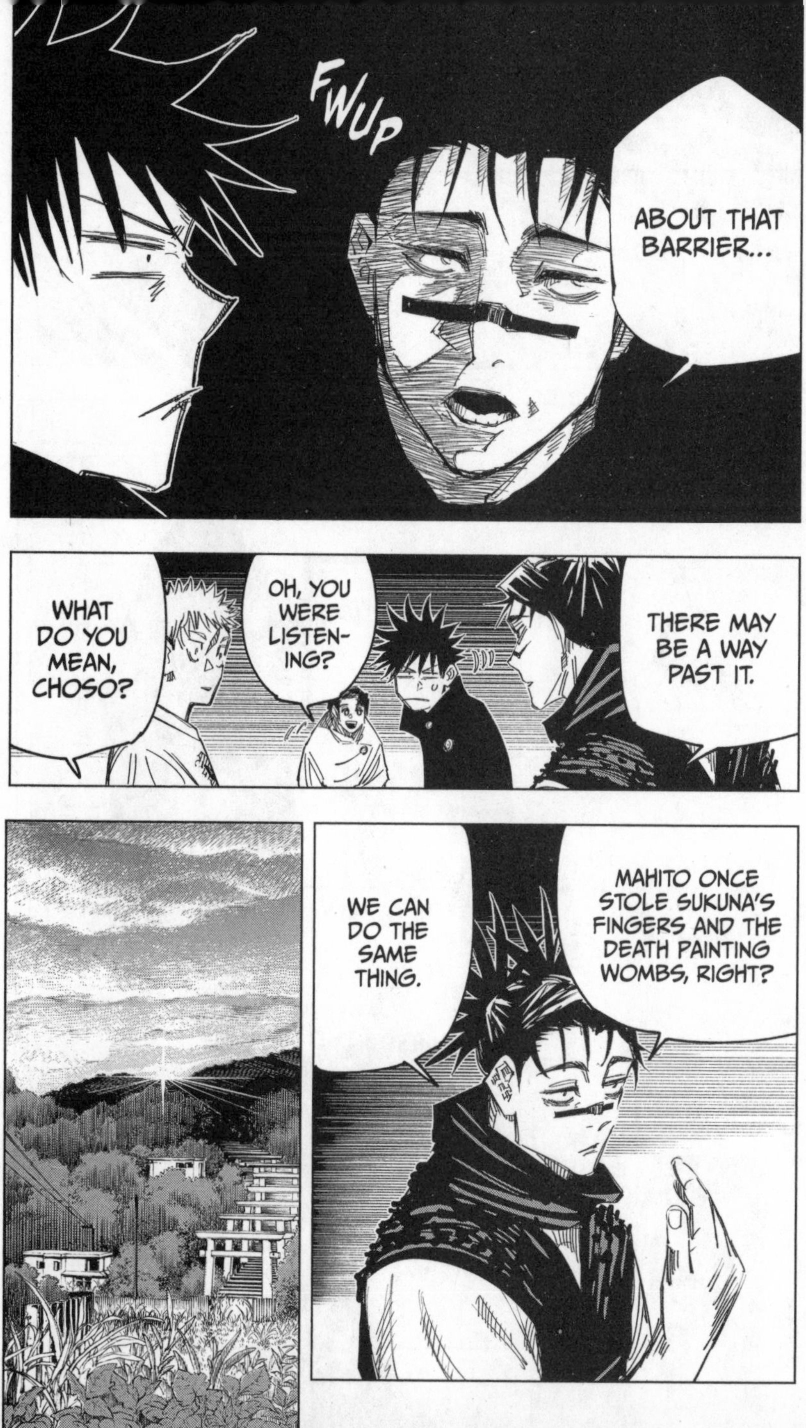
FWUP
ABOUT THAT BARRIER...
THERE MAY BE A WAY PAST IT.
OH, YOU WERE LISTENING?
WHAT DO YOU MEAN, CHOSO?
MAHITO ONCE STOLE SUKUNA'S FINGERS AND THE DEATH PAINTING WOMBS, RIGHT?
WE CAN DO THE SAME THING.

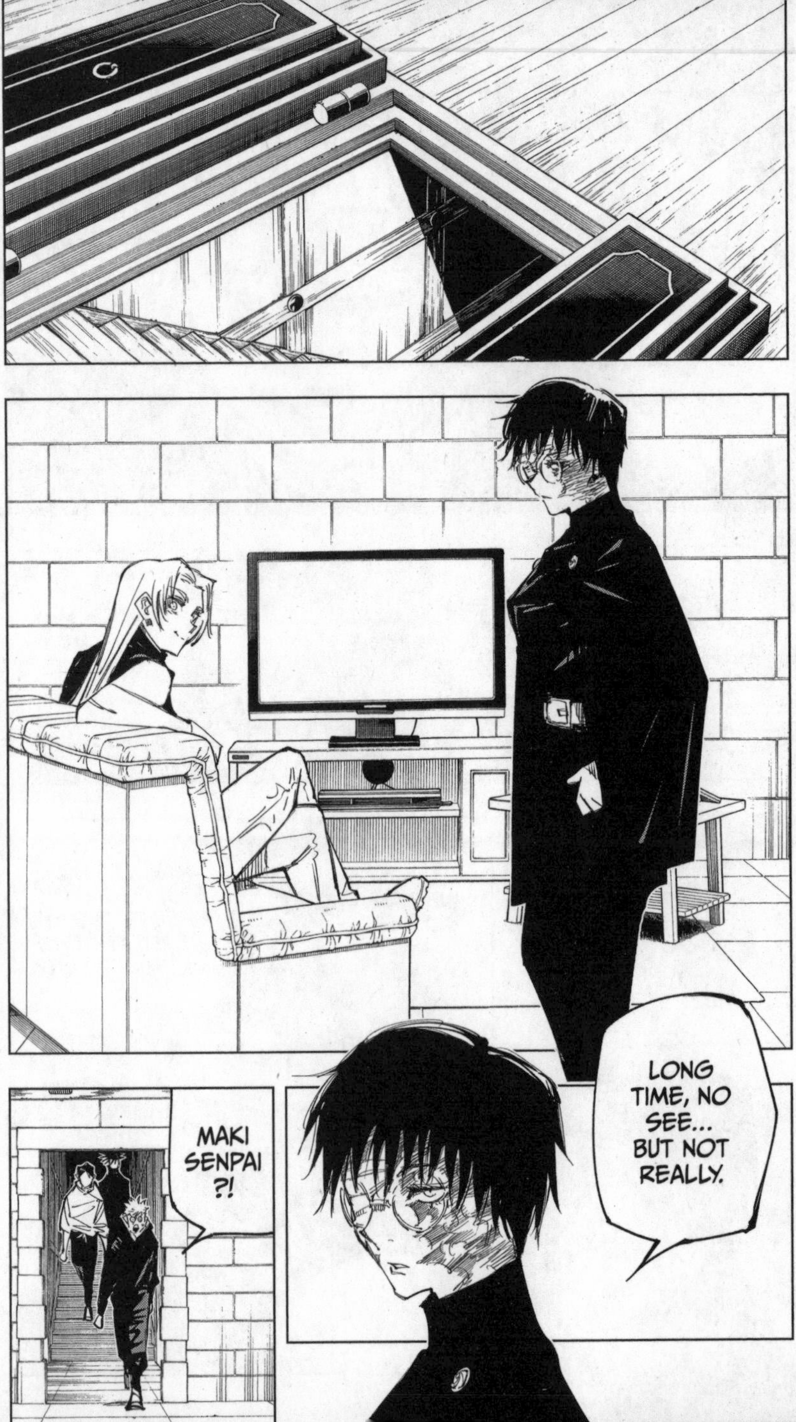
LONG TIME, NO SEE... BUT NOT REALLY.
MAKI SENPAI ?!

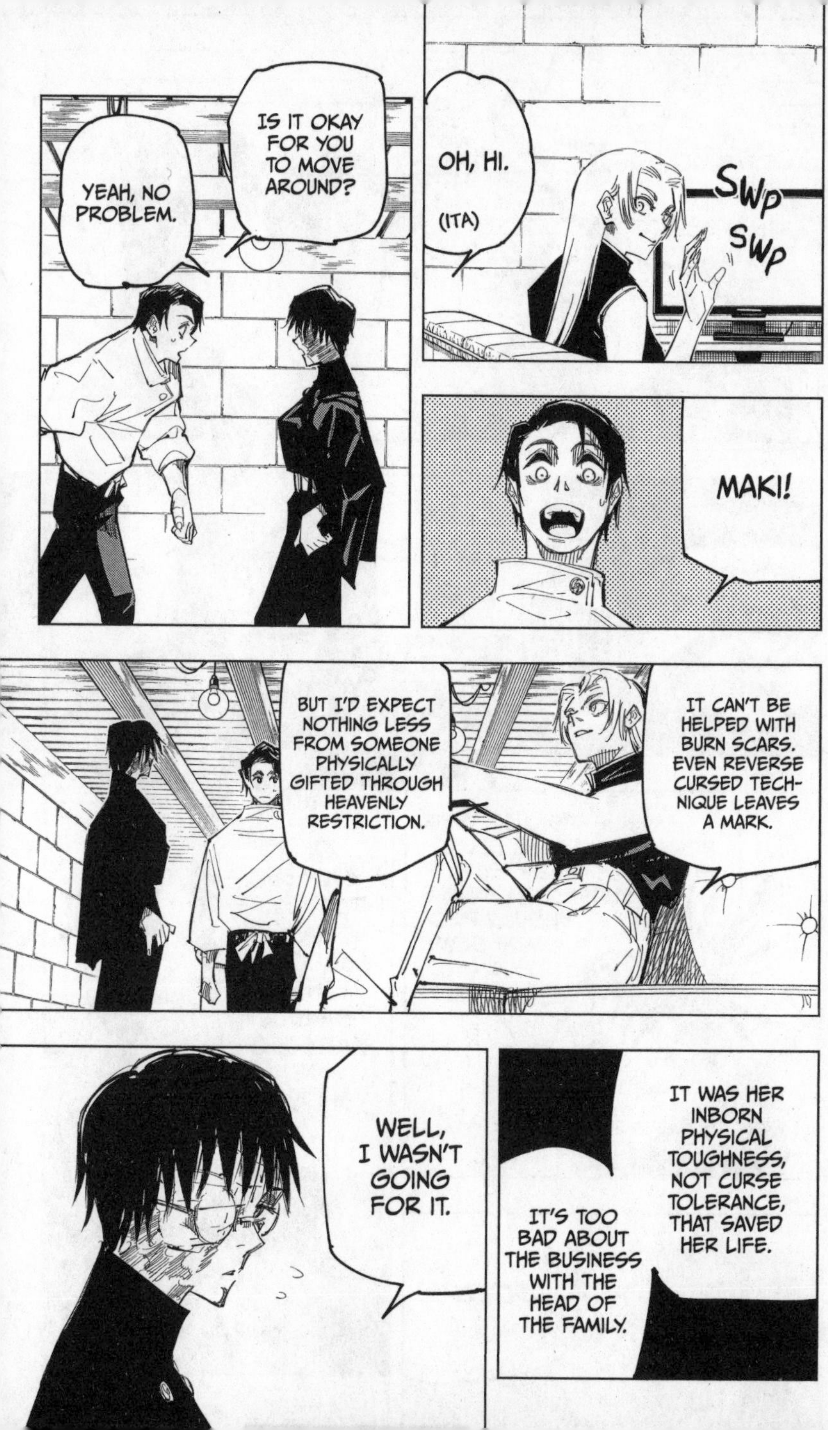
OH, HI.
(ITA)
SWP
SWP
MAKI!
IS IT OKAY FOR YOU TO MOVE AROUND?
YEAH, NO PROBLEM.
IT CAN'T BE HELPED WITH BURN SCARS. EVEN REVERSE CURSED TECH-NIQUE LEAVES A MARK.
BUT I'D EXPECT NOTHING LESS FROM SOMEONE PHYSICALLY GIFTED THROUGH HEAVENLY RESTRICTION.
IT WAS HER INBORN PHYSICAL TOUGHNESS, NOT CURSE TOLERANCE, THAT SAVED HER LIFE.
IT'S TOO BAD ABOUT THE BUSINESS WITH THE HEAD OF THE FAMILY.
WELL, I WASN'T GOING FOR IT.

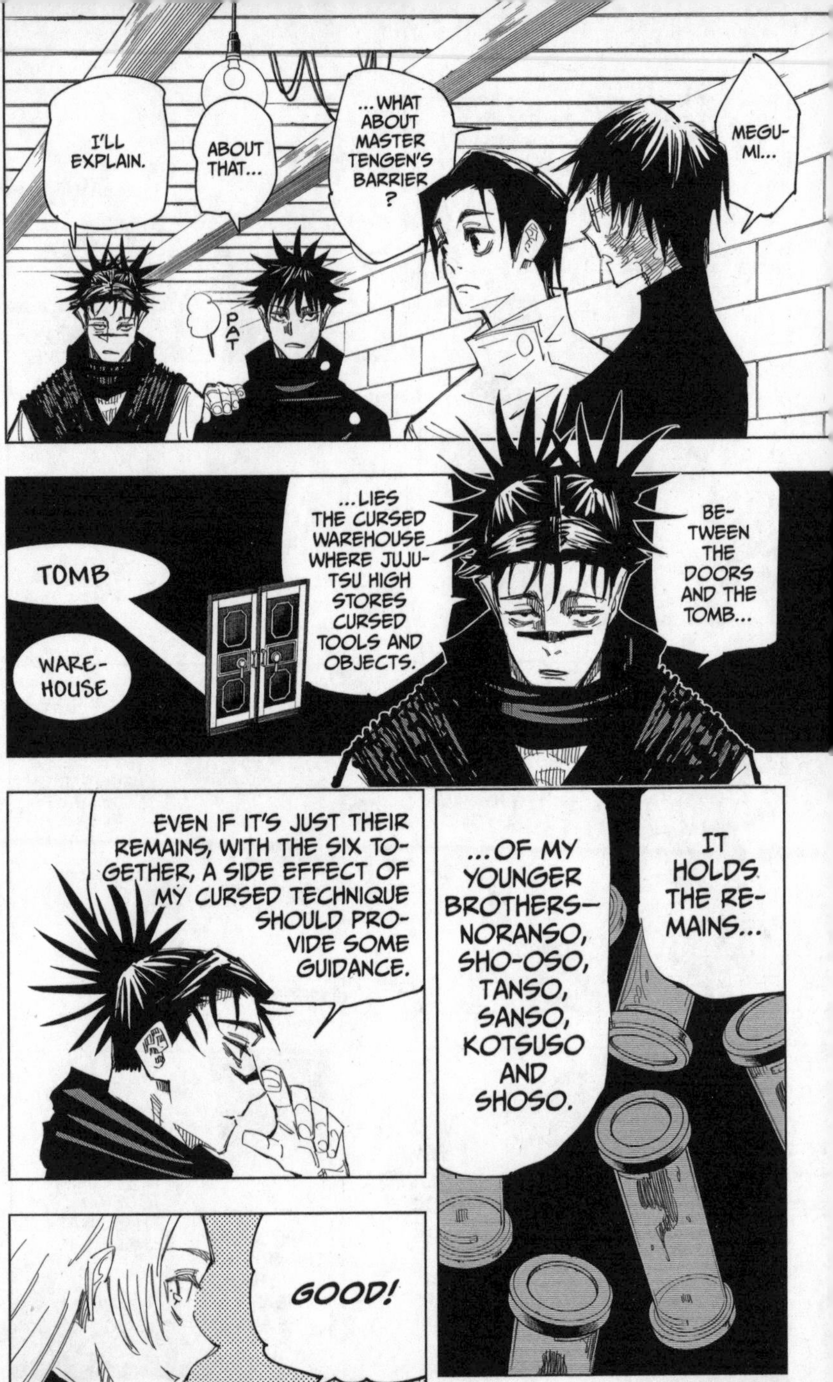
MEGUMI...
...WHAT ABOUT MASTER TENGEN'S BARRIER?
ABOUT THAT...
I'LL EXPLAIN.
PAT
BETWEEN THE DOORS AND THE TOMB...
...LIES THE CURSED WAREHOUSE WHERE JUJUTSU HIGH STORES CURSED TOOLS AND OBJECTS.
TOMB
WAREHOUSE
IT HOLDS THE REMAINS...
...OF MY YOUNGER BROTHERS—NORANSO, SHO-OSO, TANSO, SANSO, KOTSUSO AND SHOSO.
EVEN IF IT'S JUST THEIR REMAINS, WITH THE SIX TOGETHER, A SIDE EFFECT OF MY CURSED TECHNIQUE SHOULD PROVIDE SOME GUIDANCE.
GOOD!

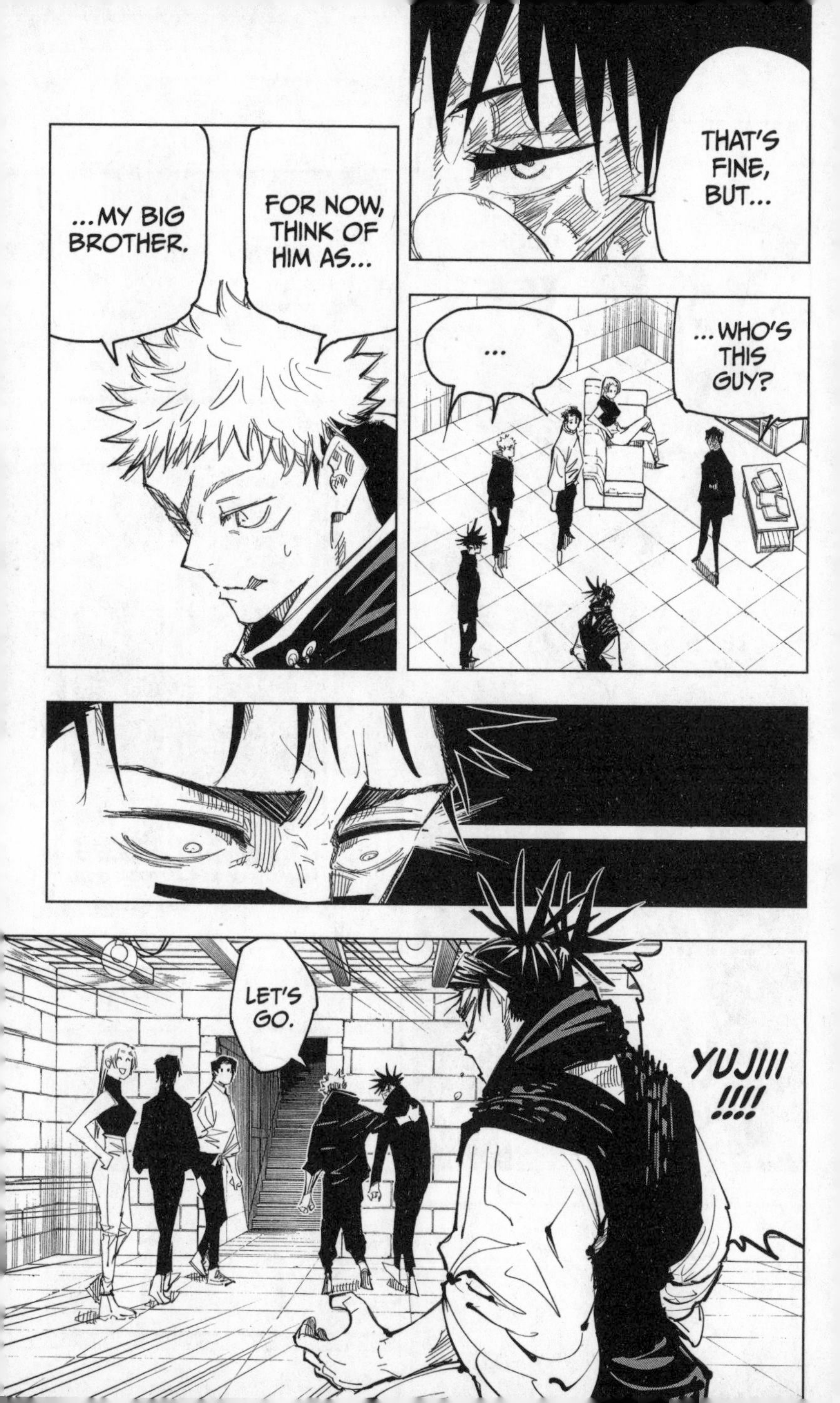
THAT'S FINE, BUT...
...WHO'S THIS GUY?
...
FOR NOW, THINK OF HIM AS...
...MY BIG BROTHER.
LET'S GO.
YUJIII!!!!

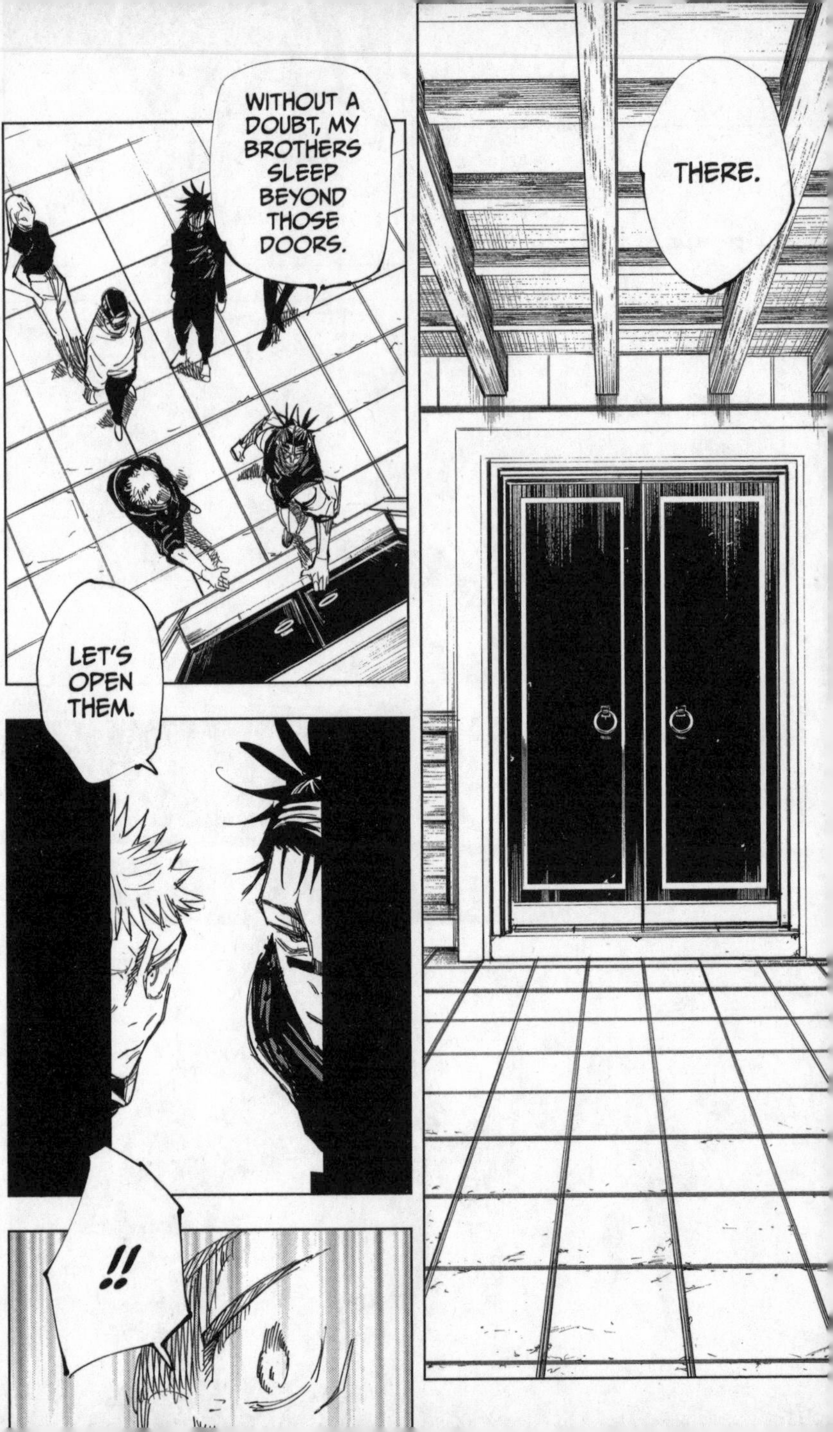
THERE.
WITHOUT A DOUBT, MY BROTHERS SLEEP BEYOND THOSE DOORS.
LET'S OPEN THEM.
!!

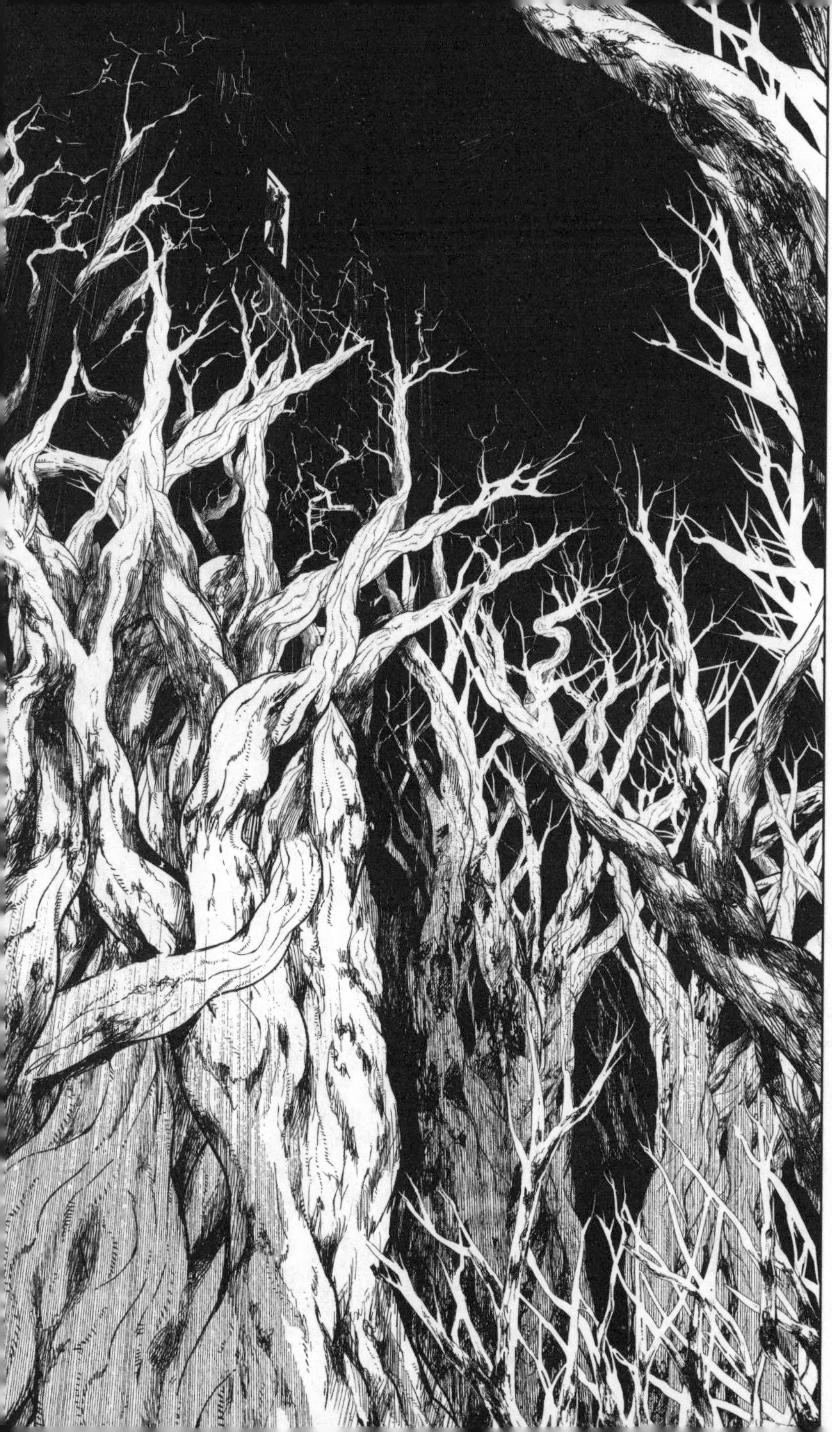

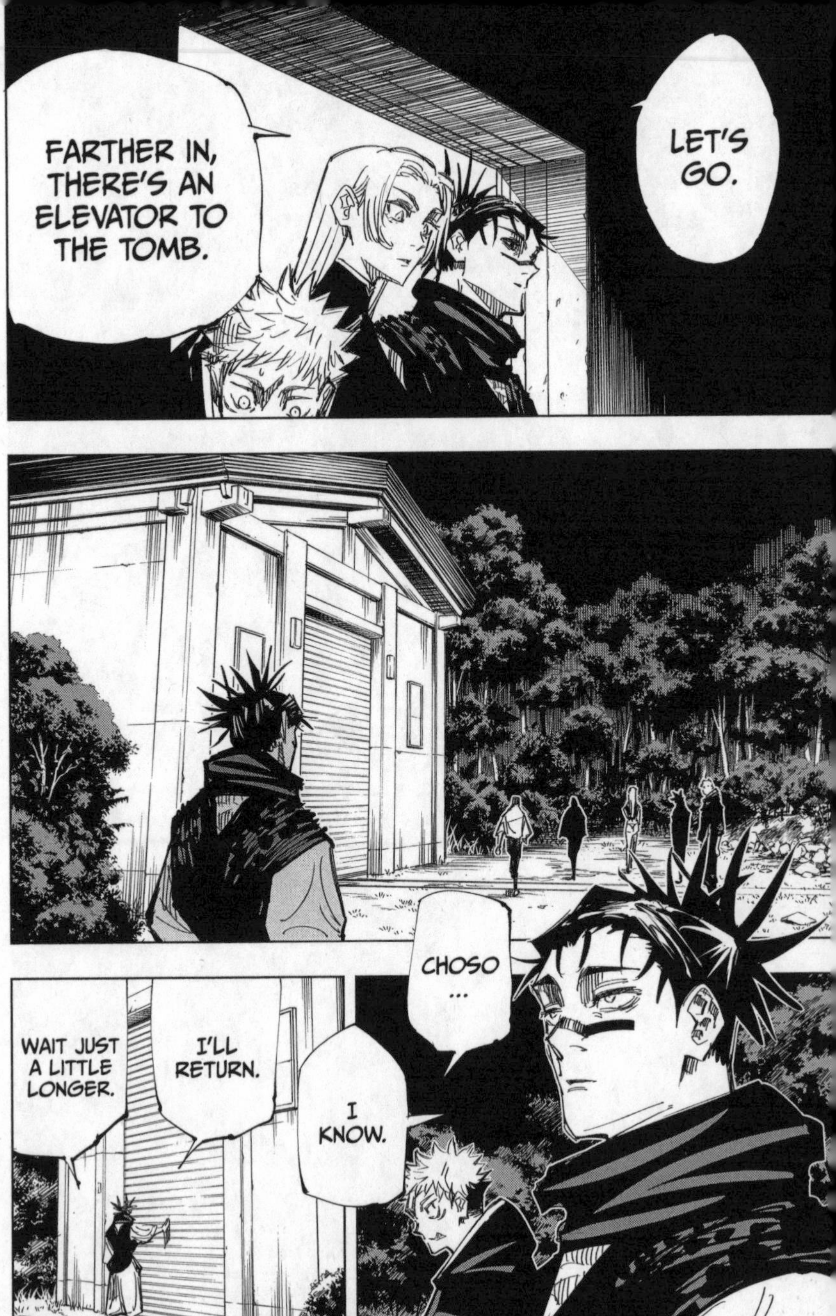
LET'S GO.
FARTHER IN, THERE'S AN ELEVATOR TO THE TOMB.
CHOSO ...
I KNOW.
I'LL RETURN.
WAIT JUST A LITTLE LONGER.

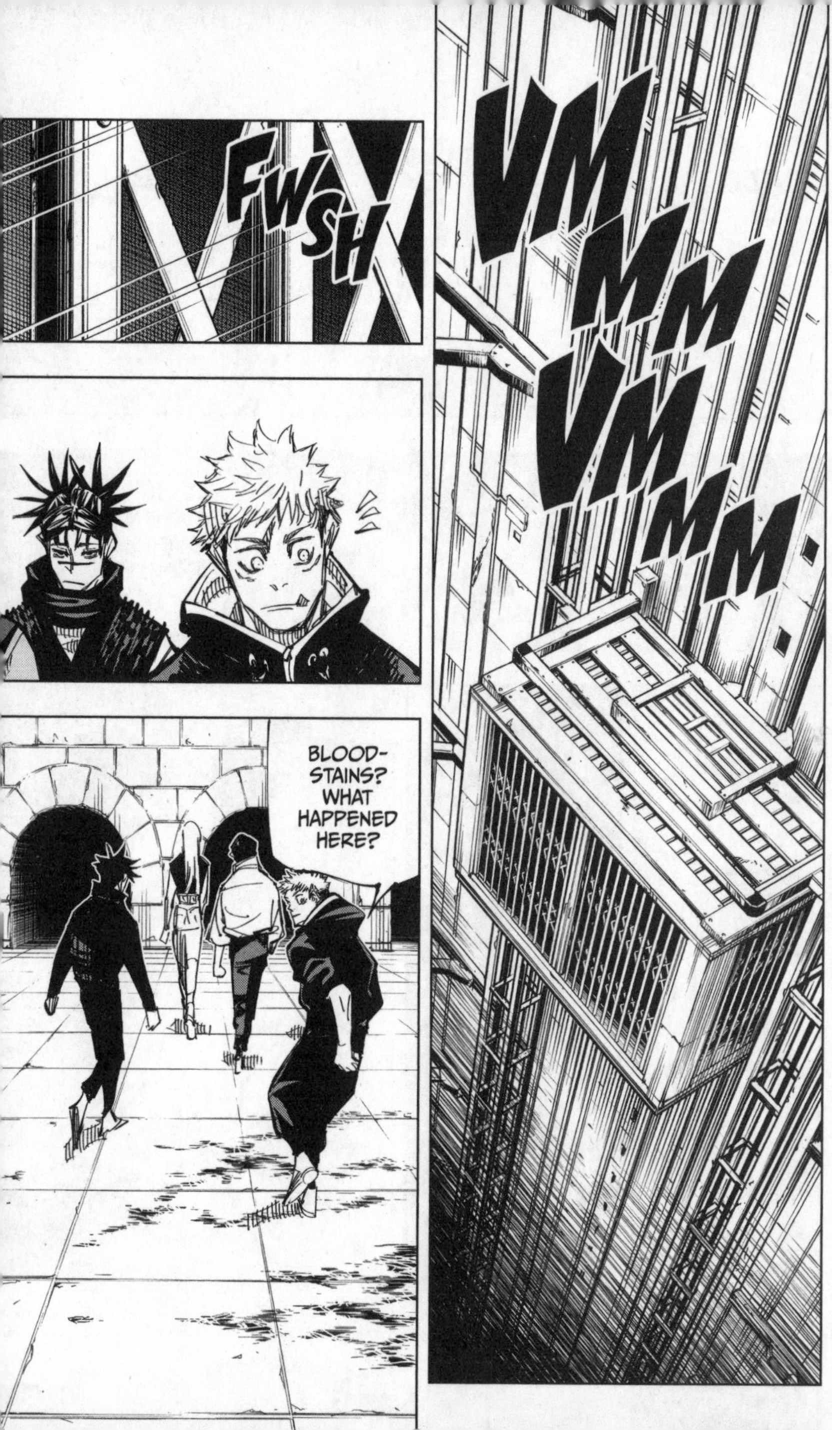
VMMM VMMM
FWSH
BLOOD-STAINS? WHAT HAPPENED HERE?

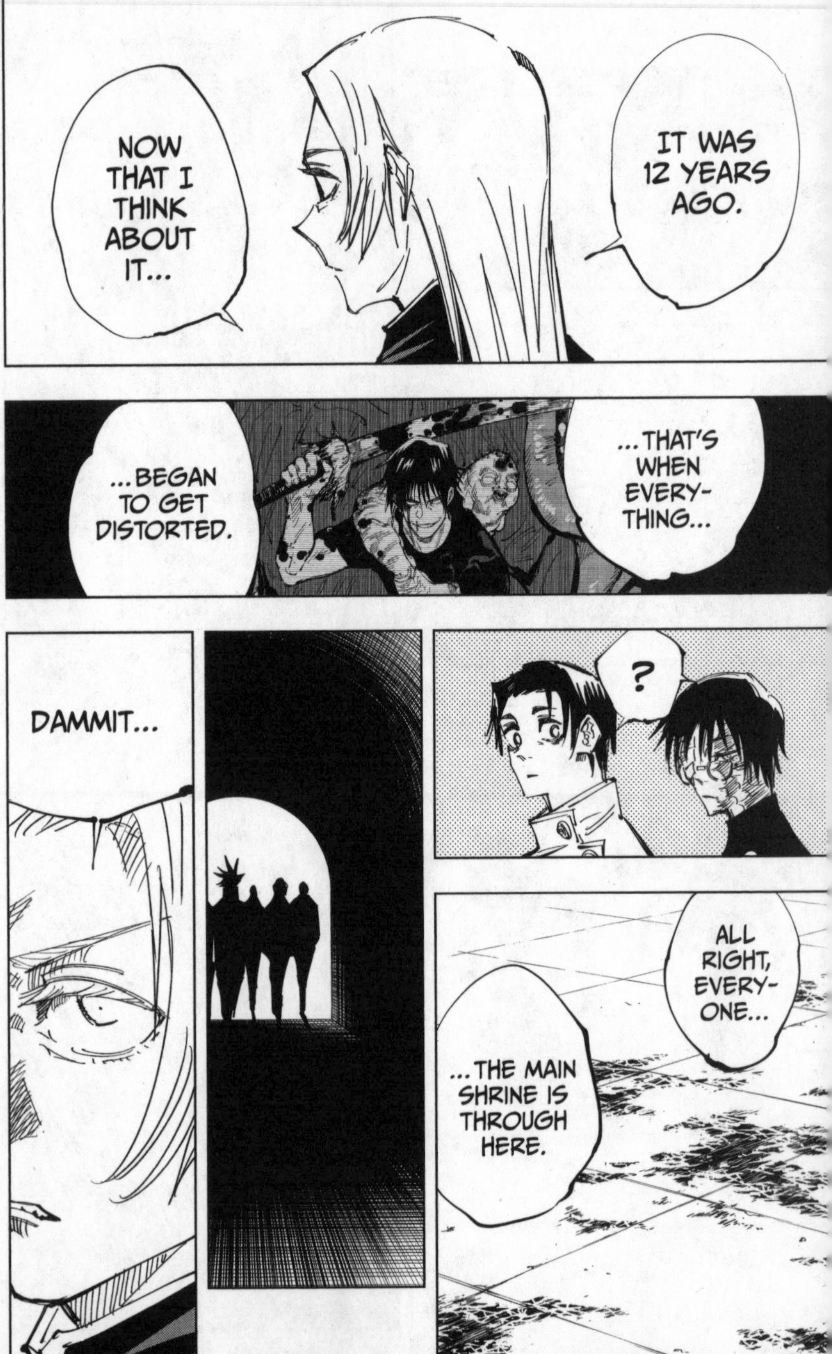
IT WAS 12 YEARS AGO.
NOW THAT I THINK ABOUT IT...
...THAT'S WHEN EVERY-THING...
...BEGAN TO GET DISTORTED.
?
ALL RIGHT, EVERY-ONE...
...THE MAIN SHRINE IS THROUGH HERE.
DAMMIT...

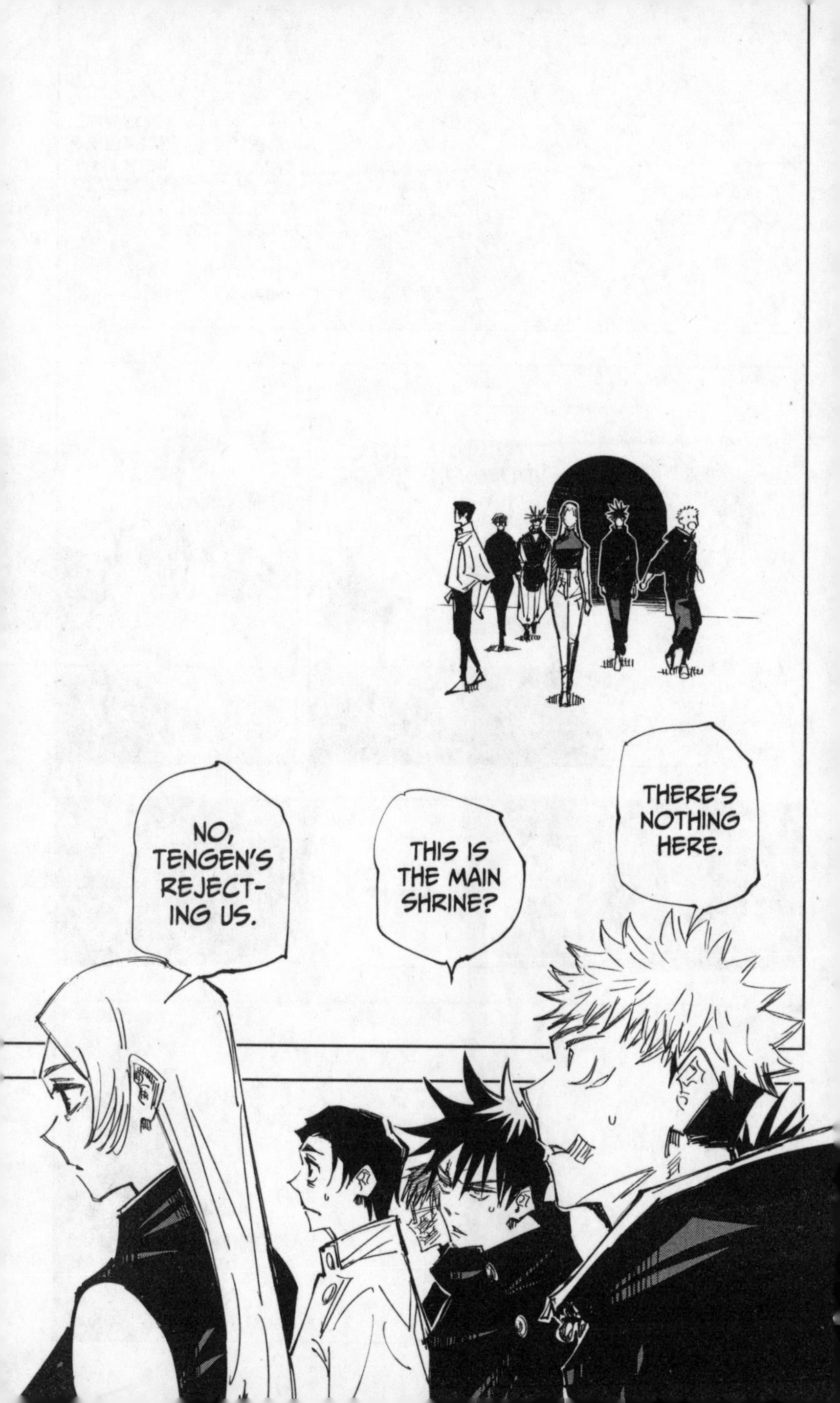
THERE'S NOTHING HERE.
THIS IS THE MAIN SHRINE?
NO, TENGEN'S REJECTING US.

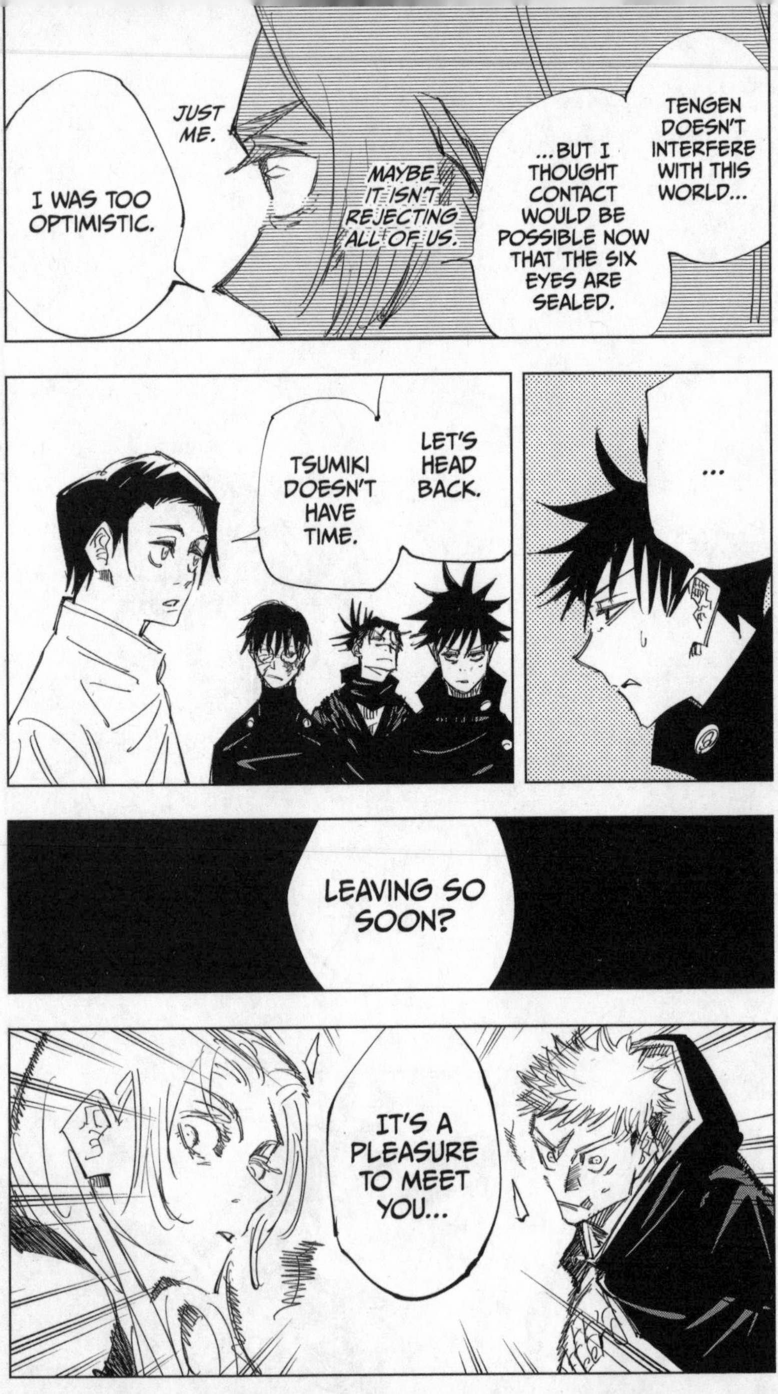
TENGEN DOESN'T INTERFERE WITH THIS WORLD...
...BUT I THOUGHT CONTACT WOULD BE POSSIBLE NOW THAT THE SIX EYES ARE SEALED.
MAYBE IT ISN'T REJECTING ALL OF US.
JUST ME.
I WAS TOO OPTIMISTIC.
...
LET'S HEAD BACK.
TSUMIKI DOESN'T HAVE TIME.
LEAVING SO SOON?
IT'S A PLEASURE TO MEET YOU...

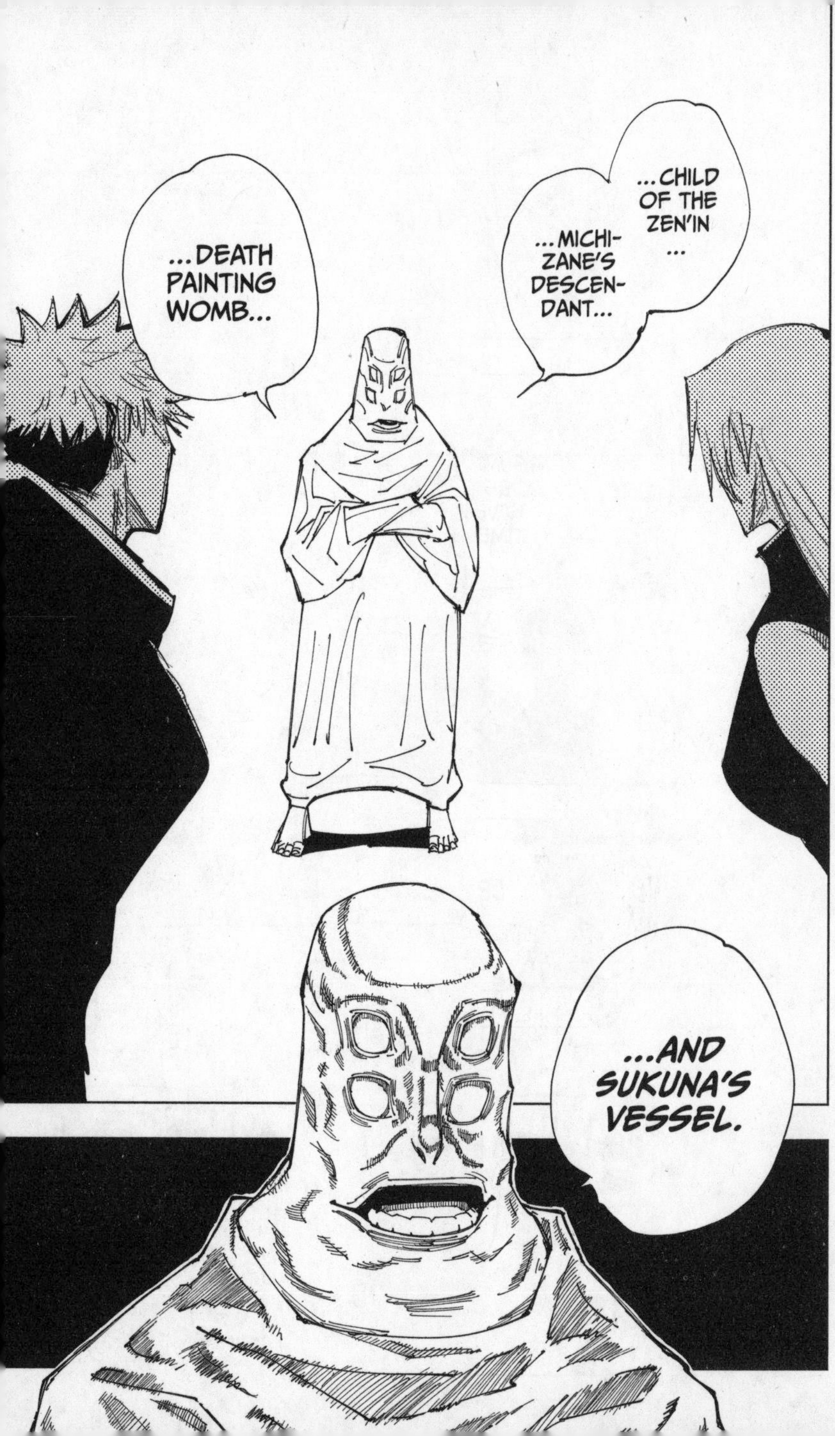
...CHILD OF THE ZEN'IN ...
...MICHIZANE'S DESCENDANT...
...DEATH PAINTING WOMB...
...AND SUKUNA'S VESSEL.

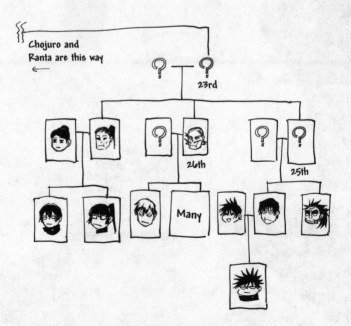

Chojuro and
Ranta are this way
←

23rd

26th

25th

Many

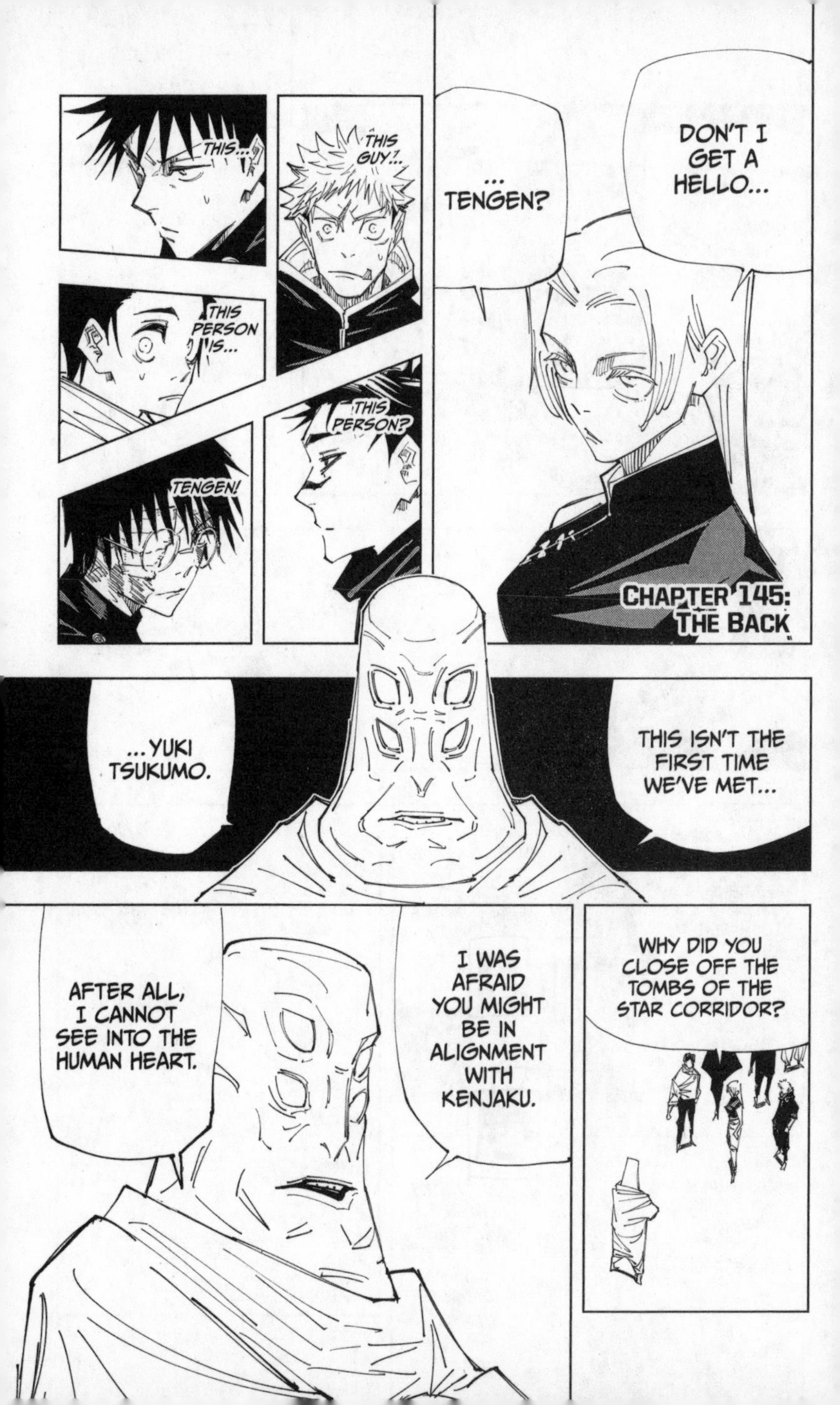
DON'T I GET A HELLO...
... TENGEN?
CHAPTER 145: THE BACK
THIS GUY?...
THIS...
THIS PERSON IS...
THIS PERSON?
TENGEN!
THIS ISN'T THE FIRST TIME WE'VE MET...
...YUKI TSUKUMO.
WHY DID YOU CLOSE OFF THE TOMBS OF THE STAR CORRIDOR?
I WAS AFRAID YOU MIGHT BE IN ALIGNMENT WITH KENJAKU.
AFTER ALL, I CANNOT SEE INTO THE HUMAN HEART.

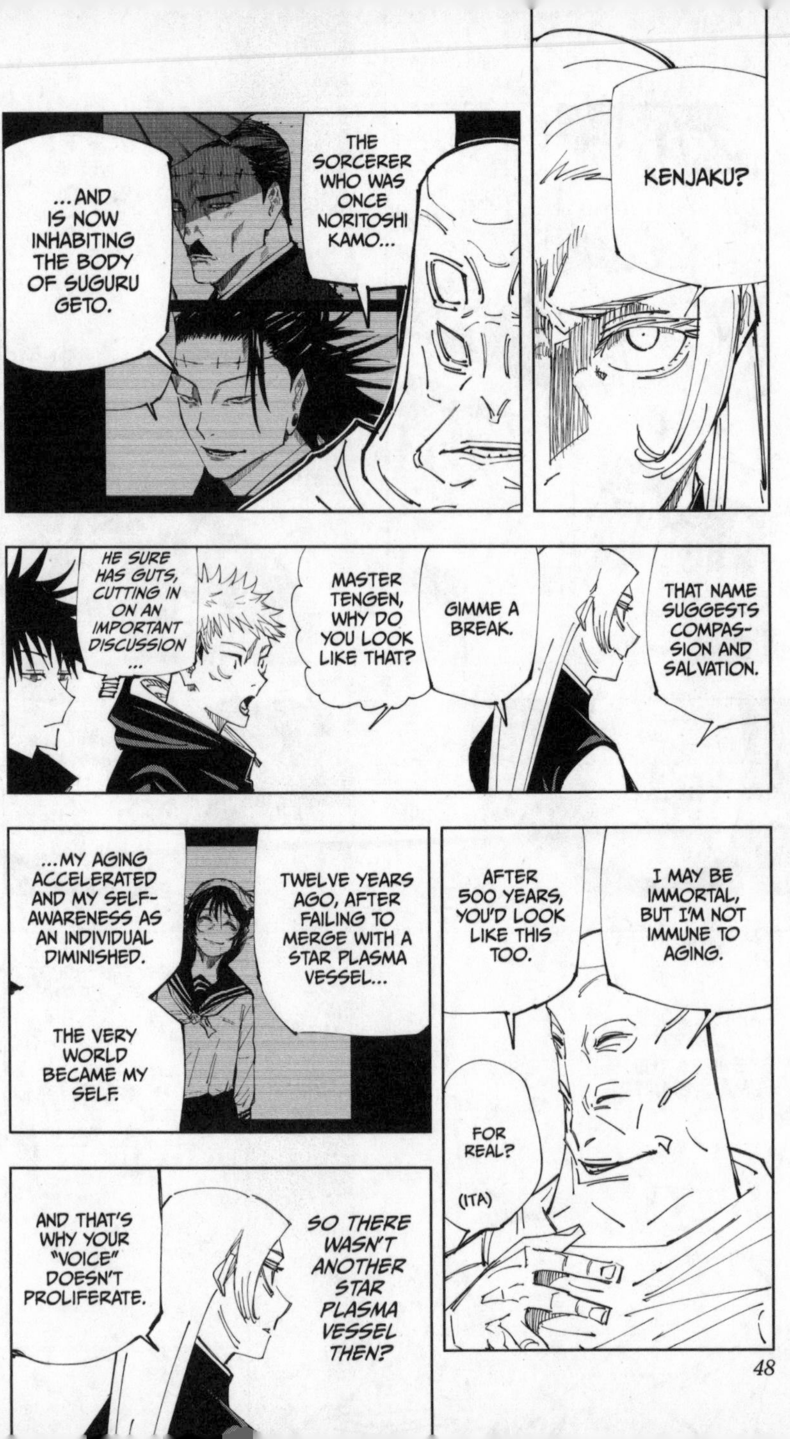
KENJAKU?
THE SORCERER WHO WAS ONCE NORITOSHI KAMO...
...AND IS NOW INHABITING THE BODY OF SUGURU GETO.
THAT NAME SUGGESTS COMPAS-SION AND SALVATION.
GIMME A BREAK.
MASTER TENGEN, WHY DO YOU LOOK LIKE THAT?
HE SURE HAS GUTS, CUTTING IN ON AN IMPORTANT DISCUSSION...
I MAY BE IMMORTAL, BUT I'M NOT IMMUNE TO AGING.
AFTER 500 YEARS, YOU'D LOOK LIKE THIS TOO.
FOR REAL?
(ITA)
TWELVE YEARS AGO, AFTER FAILING TO MERGE WITH A STAR PLASMA VESSEL...
...MY AGING ACCELERATED AND MY SELF-AWARENESS AS AN INDIVIDUAL DIMINISHED.
THE VERY WORLD BECAME MY SELF.
SO THERE WASN'T ANOTHER STAR PLASMA VESSEL THEN?
AND THAT'S WHY YOUR "VOICE" DOESN'T PROLIFERATE.

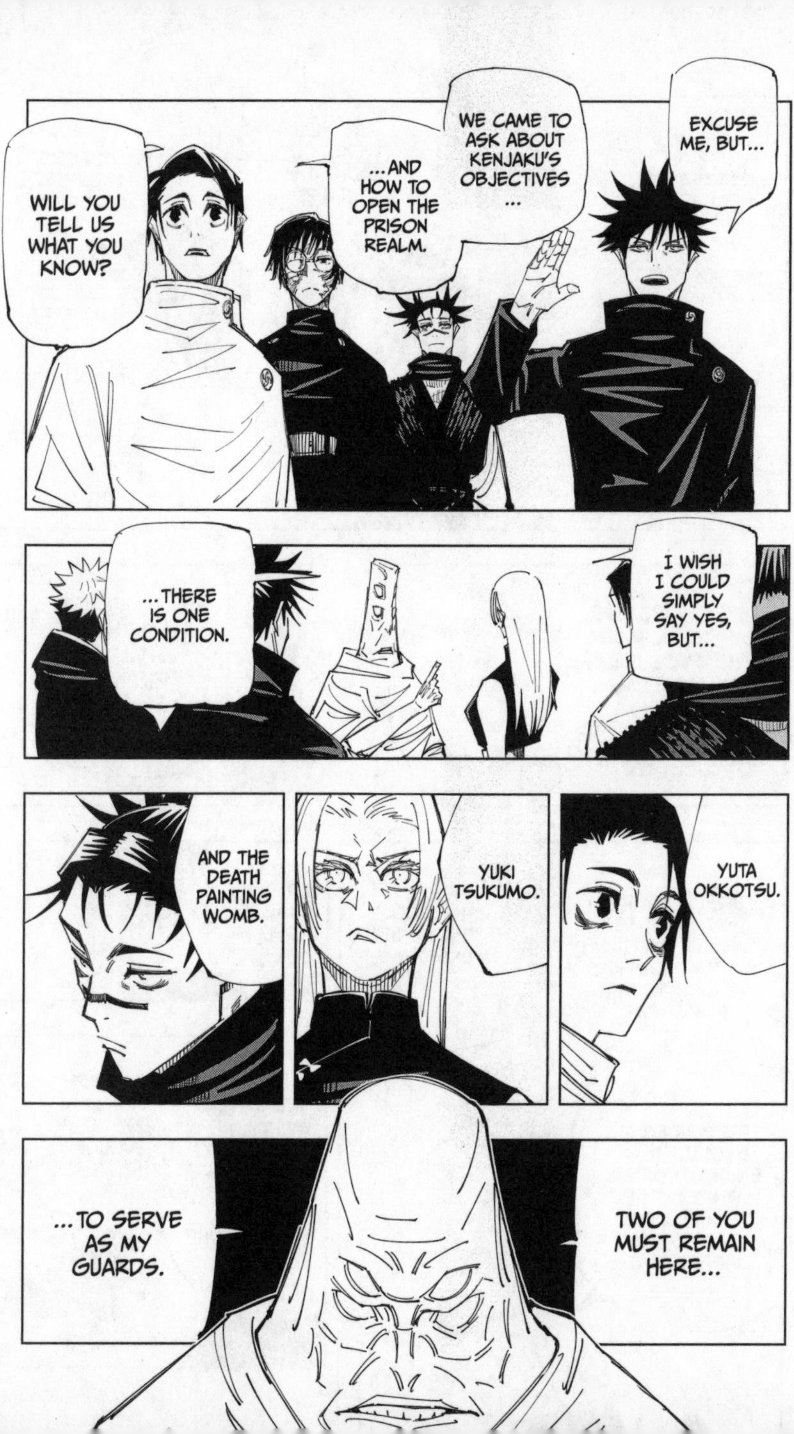
EXCUSE ME, BUT...
WE CAME TO ASK ABOUT KENJAKU'S OBJECTIVES ...
...AND HOW TO OPEN THE PRISON REALM.
WILL YOU TELL US WHAT YOU KNOW?
I WISH I COULD SIMPLY SAY YES, BUT...
...THERE IS ONE CONDITION.
YUTA OKKOTSU.
YUKI TSUKUMO.
AND THE DEATH PAINTING WOMB.
TWO OF YOU MUST REMAIN HERE...
...TO SERVE AS MY GUARDS.

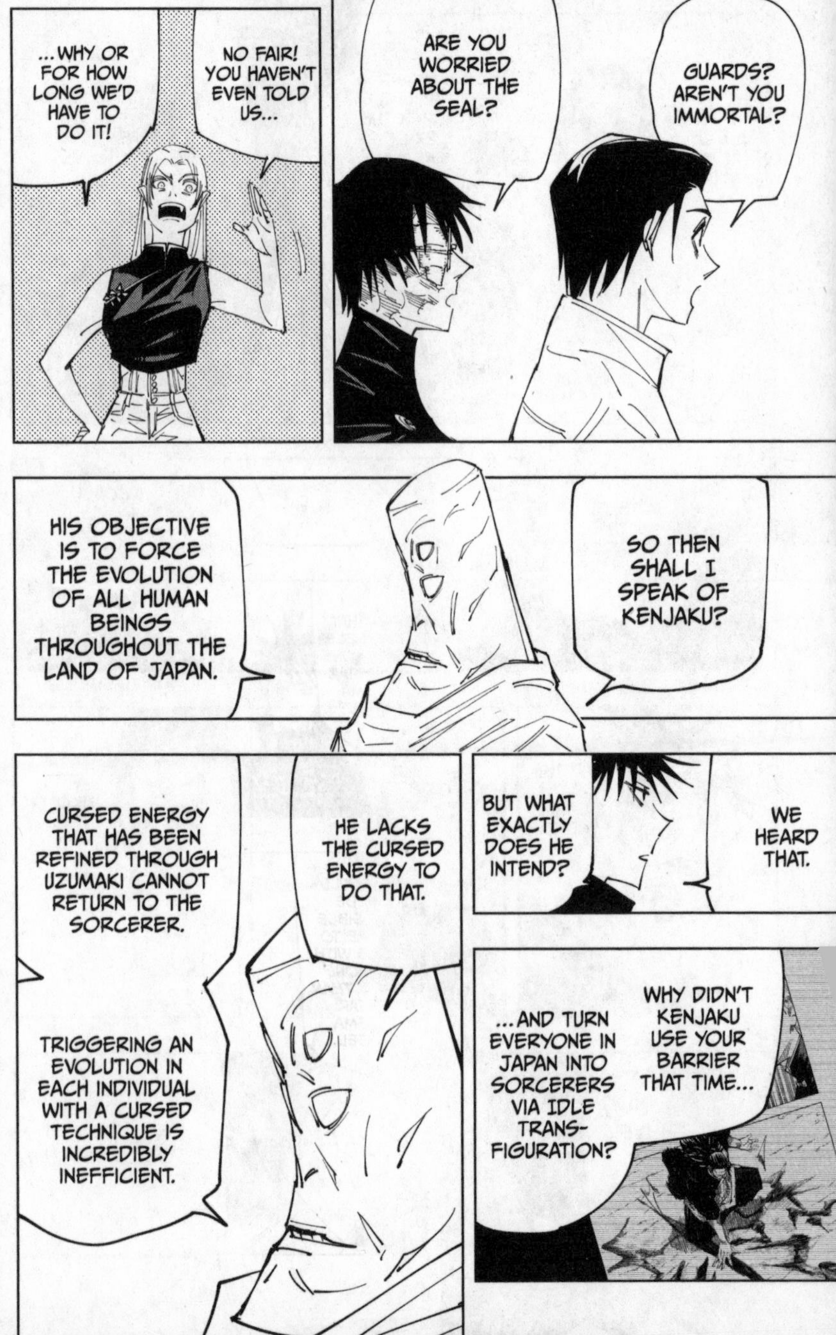
GUARDS? AREN'T YOU IMMORTAL?
ARE YOU WORRIED ABOUT THE SEAL?
NO FAIR! YOU HAVEN'T EVEN TOLD US...
...WHY OR FOR HOW LONG WE'D HAVE TO DO IT!
SO THEN SHALL I SPEAK OF KENJAKU?
HIS OBJECTIVE IS TO FORCE THE EVOLUTION OF ALL HUMAN BEINGS THROUGHOUT THE LAND OF JAPAN.
WE HEARD THAT.
BUT WHAT EXACTLY DOES HE INTEND?
WHY DIDN'T KENJAKU USE YOUR BARRIER THAT TIME...
...AND TURN EVERYONE IN JAPAN INTO SORCERERS VIA IDLE TRANS-FIGURATION?
HE LACKS THE CURSED ENERGY TO DO THAT.
CURSED ENERGY THAT HAS BEEN REFINED THROUGH UZUMAKI CANNOT RETURN TO THE SORCERER.
TRIGGERING AN EVOLUTION IN EACH INDIVIDUAL WITH A CURSED TECHNIQUE IS INCREDIBLY INEFFICIENT.

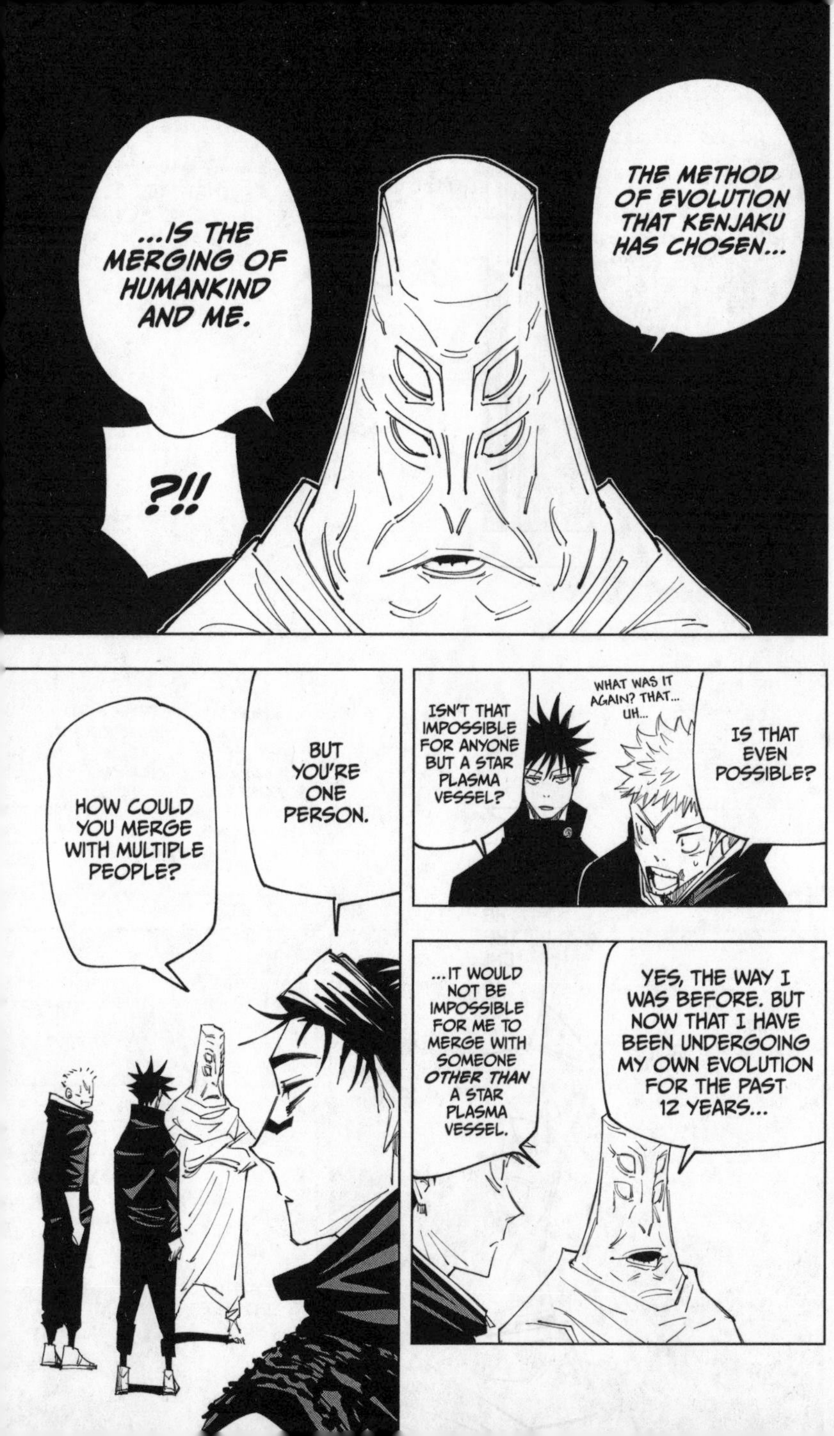
THE METHOD OF EVOLUTION THAT KENJAKU HAS CHOSEN...
...IS THE MERGING OF HUMANKIND AND ME.
?!!
IS THAT EVEN POSSIBLE?
WHAT WAS IT AGAIN? THAT... UH...
ISN'T THAT IMPOSSIBLE FOR ANYONE BUT A STAR PLASMA VESSEL?
YES, THE WAY I WAS BEFORE. BUT NOW THAT I HAVE BEEN UNDERGOING MY OWN EVOLUTION FOR THE PAST 12 YEARS...
...IT WOULD NOT BE IMPOSSIBLE FOR ME TO MERGE WITH SOMEONE *OTHER THAN* A STAR PLASMA VESSEL.
BUT YOU'RE ONE PERSON.
HOW COULD YOU MERGE WITH MULTIPLE PEOPLE?

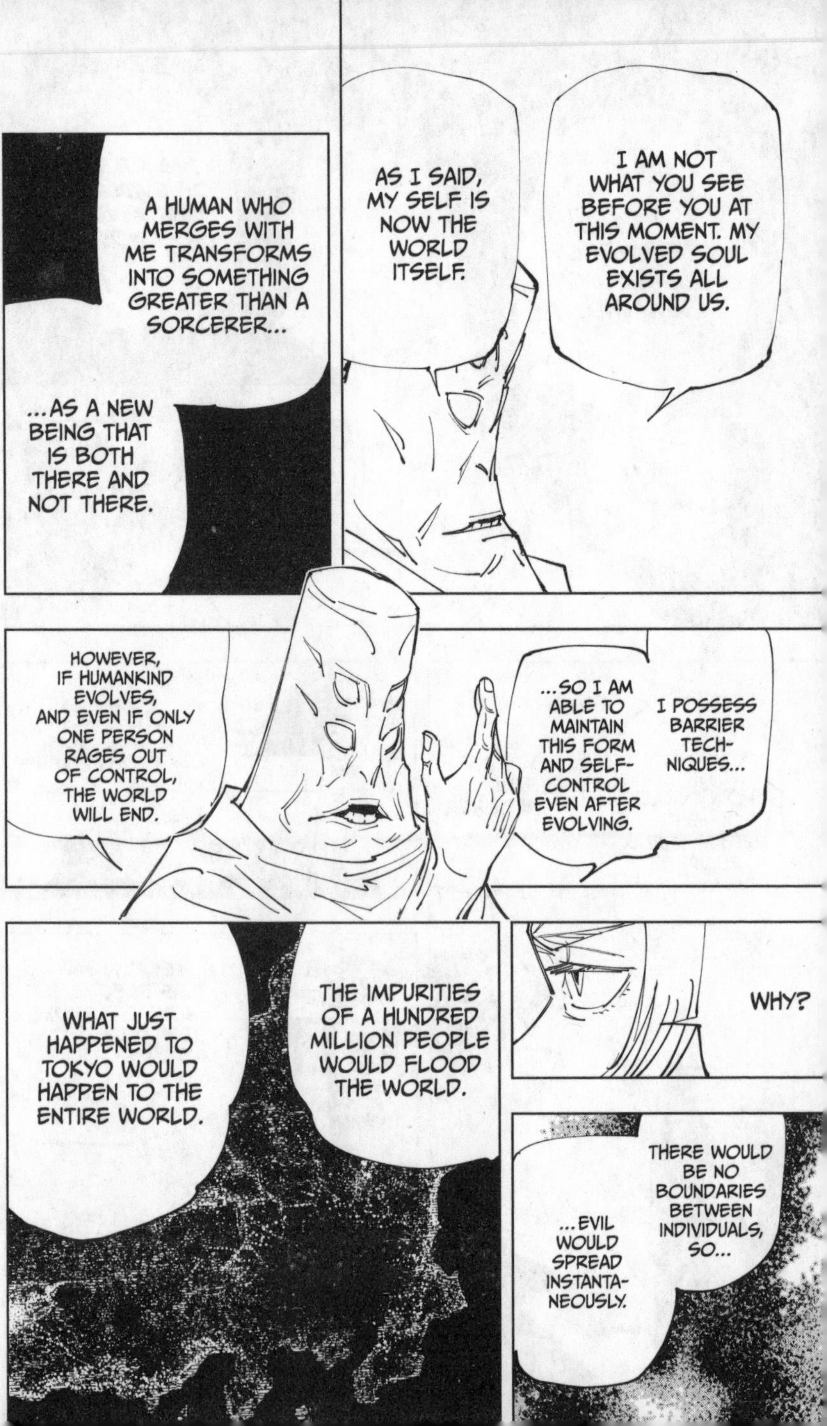
I AM NOT WHAT YOU SEE BEFORE YOU AT THIS MOMENT. MY EVOLVED SOUL EXISTS ALL AROUND US.
AS I SAID, MY SELF IS NOW THE WORLD ITSELF.
A HUMAN WHO MERGES WITH ME TRANSFORMS INTO SOMETHING GREATER THAN A SORCERER...
...AS A NEW BEING THAT IS BOTH THERE AND NOT THERE.
I POSSESS BARRIER TECH-NIQUES...
...SO I AM ABLE TO MAINTAIN THIS FORM AND SELF-CONTROL EVEN AFTER EVOLVING.
HOWEVER, IF HUMANKIND EVOLVES, AND EVEN IF ONLY ONE PERSON RAGES OUT OF CONTROL, THE WORLD WILL END.
WHY?
THERE WOULD BE NO BOUNDARIES BETWEEN INDIVIDUALS, SO...
...EVIL WOULD SPREAD INSTANTA-NEOUSLY.
THE IMPURITIES OF A HUNDRED MILLION PEOPLE WOULD FLOOD THE WORLD.
WHAT JUST HAPPENED TO TOKYO WOULD HAPPEN TO THE ENTIRE WORLD.

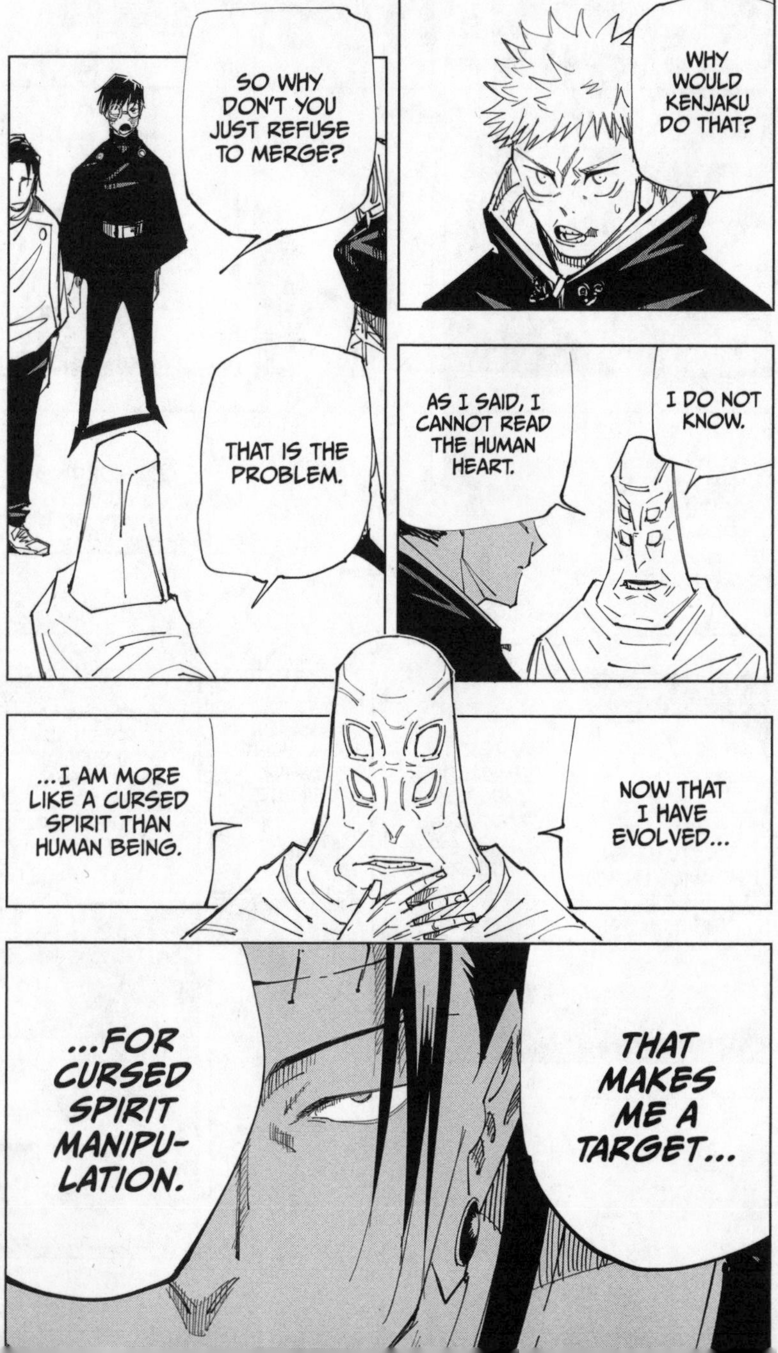
WHY WOULD KENJAKU DO THAT?
I DO NOT KNOW.
AS I SAID, I CANNOT READ THE HUMAN HEART.
SO WHY DON'T YOU JUST REFUSE TO MERGE?
THAT IS THE PROBLEM.
NOW THAT I HAVE EVOLVED...
...I AM MORE LIKE A CURSED SPIRIT THAN HUMAN BEING.
THAT MAKES ME A TARGET...
...FOR CURSED SPIRIT MANIPU-LATION.

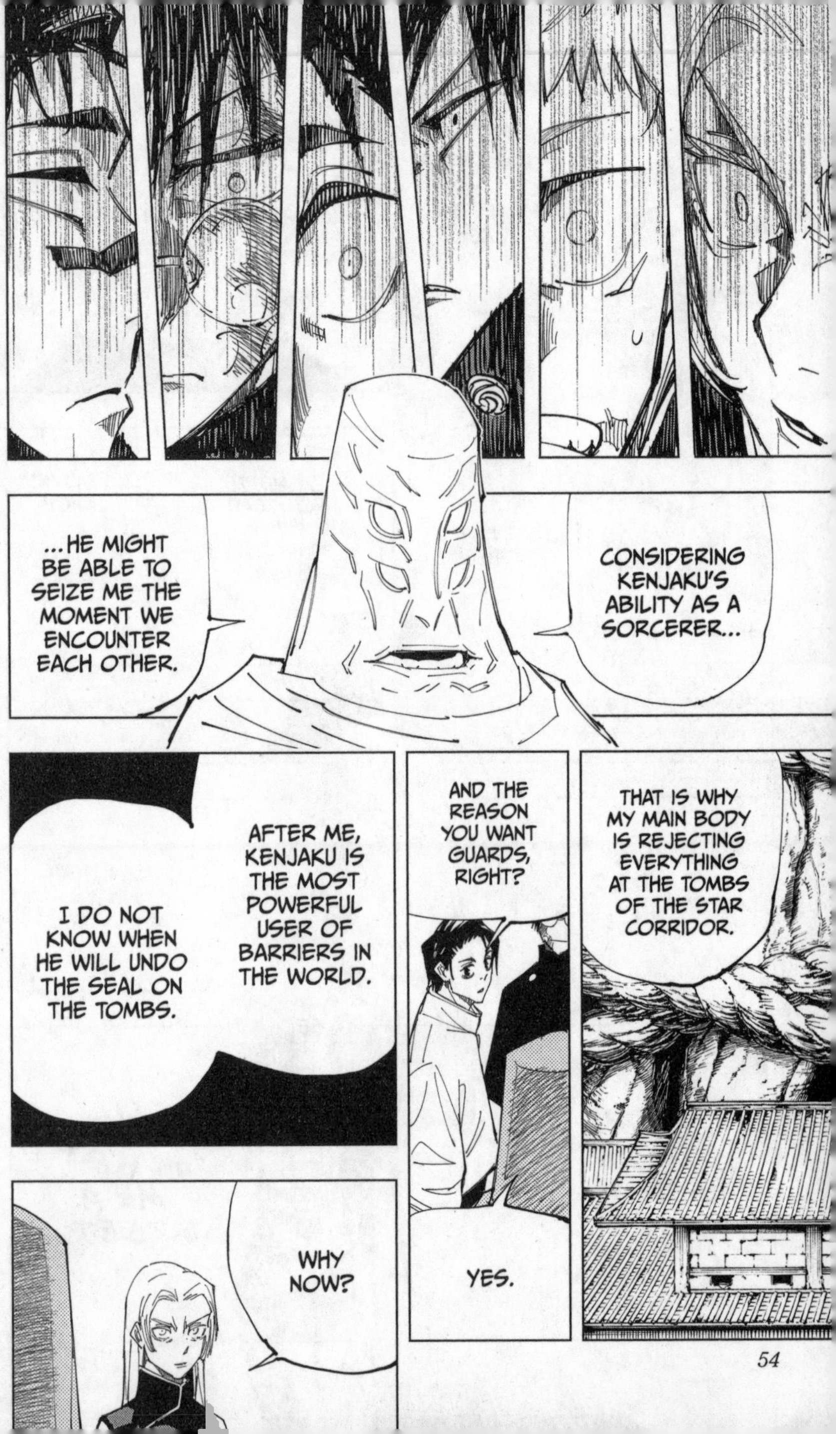
CONSIDERING KENJAKU'S ABILITY AS A SORCERER...
...HE MIGHT BE ABLE TO SEIZE ME THE MOMENT WE ENCOUNTER EACH OTHER.
THAT IS WHY MY MAIN BODY IS REJECTING EVERYTHING AT THE TOMBS OF THE STAR CORRIDOR.
AND THE REASON YOU WANT GUARDS, RIGHT?
YES.
AFTER ME, KENJAKU IS THE MOST POWERFUL USER OF BARRIERS IN THE WORLD.
I DO NOT KNOW WHEN HE WILL UNDO THE SEAL ON THE TOMBS.
WHY NOW?

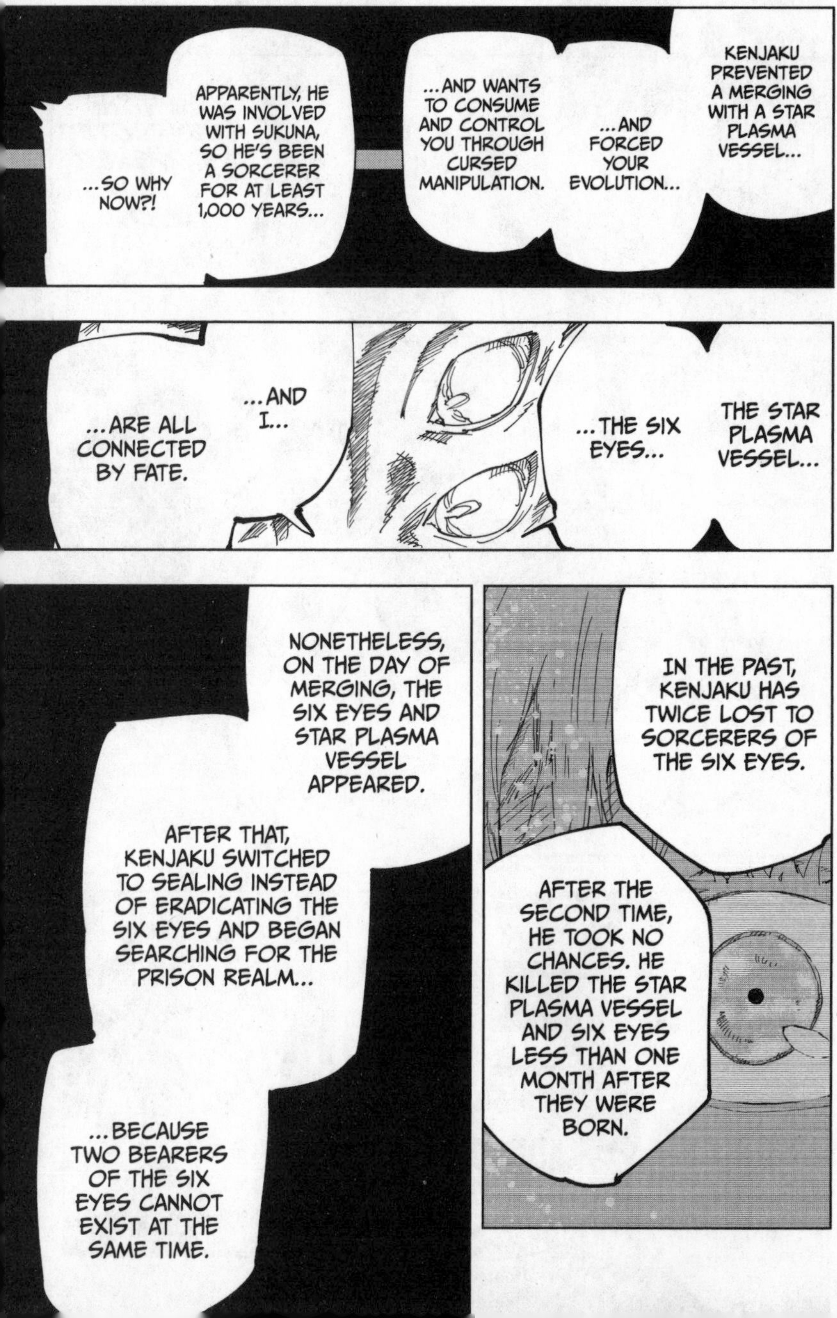
KENJAKU PREVENTED A MERGING WITH A STAR PLASMA VESSEL...
...AND FORCED YOUR EVOLUTION...
...AND WANTS TO CONSUME AND CONTROL YOU THROUGH CURSED MANIPULATION.
APPARENTLY, HE WAS INVOLVED WITH SUKUNA, SO HE'S BEEN A SORCERER FOR AT LEAST 1,000 YEARS...
...SO WHY NOW?!
THE STAR PLASMA VESSEL...
...THE SIX EYES...
...AND I...
...ARE ALL CONNECTED BY FATE.
IN THE PAST, KENJAKU HAS TWICE LOST TO SORCERERS OF THE SIX EYES.
AFTER THE SECOND TIME, HE TOOK NO CHANCES. HE KILLED THE STAR PLASMA VESSEL AND SIX EYES LESS THAN ONE MONTH AFTER THEY WERE BORN.
NONETHELESS, ON THE DAY OF MERGING, THE SIX EYES AND STAR PLASMA VESSEL APPEARED.
AFTER THAT, KENJAKU SWITCHED TO SEALING INSTEAD OF ERADICATING THE SIX EYES AND BEGAN SEARCHING FOR THE PRISON REALM...
...BECAUSE TWO BEARERS OF THE SIX EYES CANNOT EXIST AT THE SAME TIME.

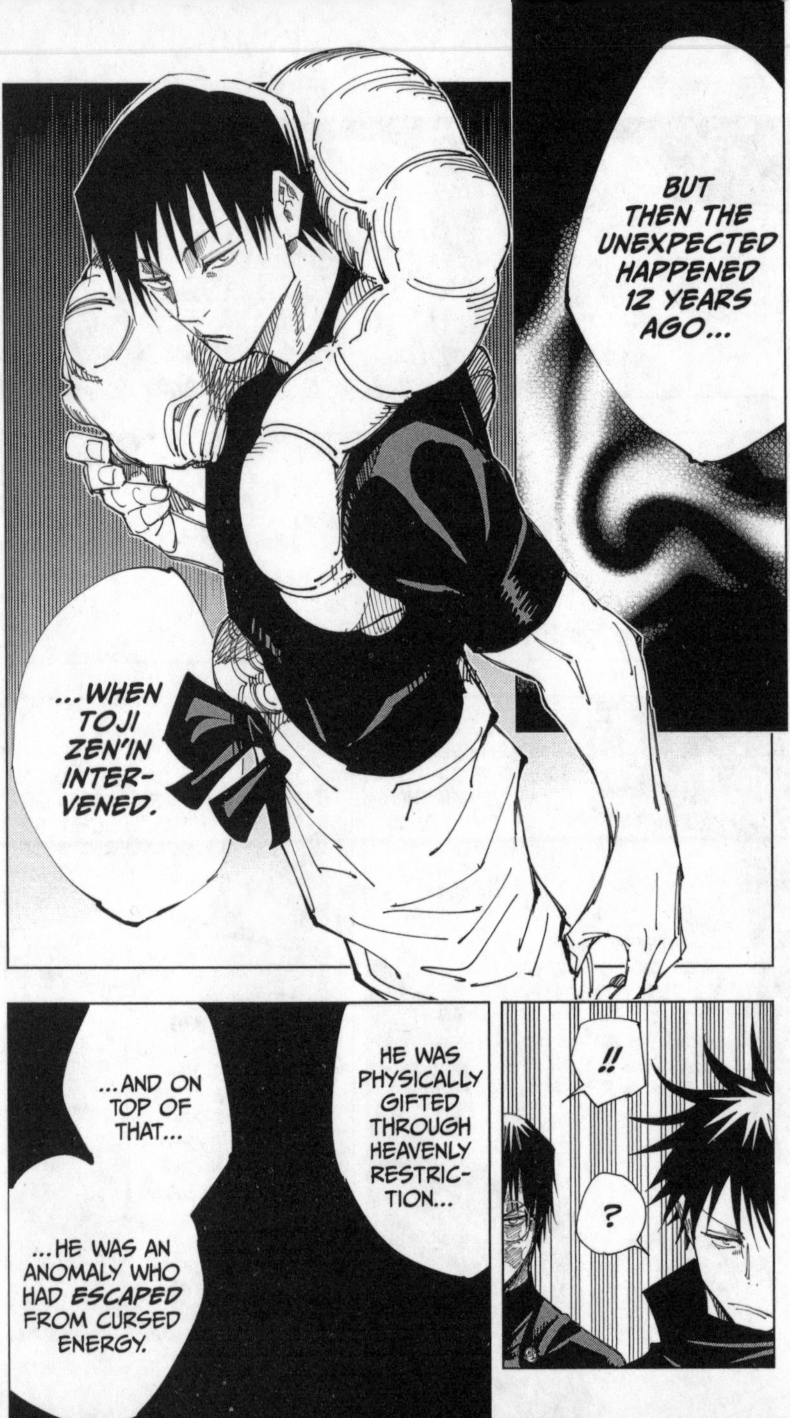
BUT THEN THE UNEXPECTED HAPPENED 12 YEARS AGO...
...WHEN TOJI ZEN'IN INTER-VENED.
!!
?
HE WAS PHYSICALLY GIFTED THROUGH HEAVENLY RESTRIC-TION...
...AND ON TOP OF THAT...
...HE WAS AN ANOMALY WHO HAD *ESCAPED* FROM CURSED ENERGY.

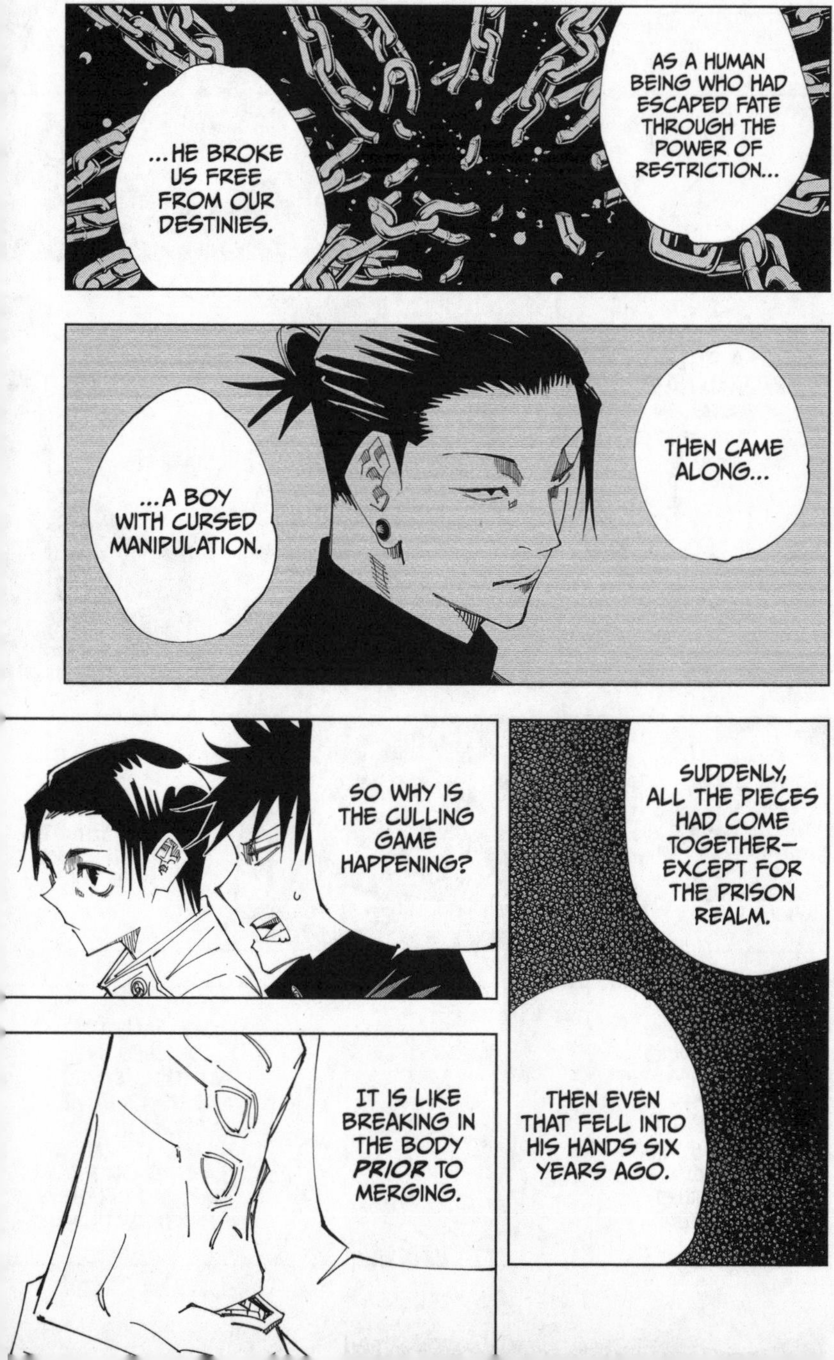
AS A HUMAN BEING WHO HAD ESCAPED FATE THROUGH THE POWER OF RESTRICTION...
...HE BROKE US FREE FROM OUR DESTINIES.
THEN CAME ALONG...
...A BOY WITH CURSED MANIPULATION.
SUDDENLY, ALL THE PIECES HAD COME TOGETHER— EXCEPT FOR THE PRISON REALM.
THEN EVEN THAT FELL INTO HIS HANDS SIX YEARS AGO.
SO WHY IS THE CULLING GAME HAPPENING?
IT IS LIKE BREAKING IN THE BODY *PRIOR* TO MERGING.

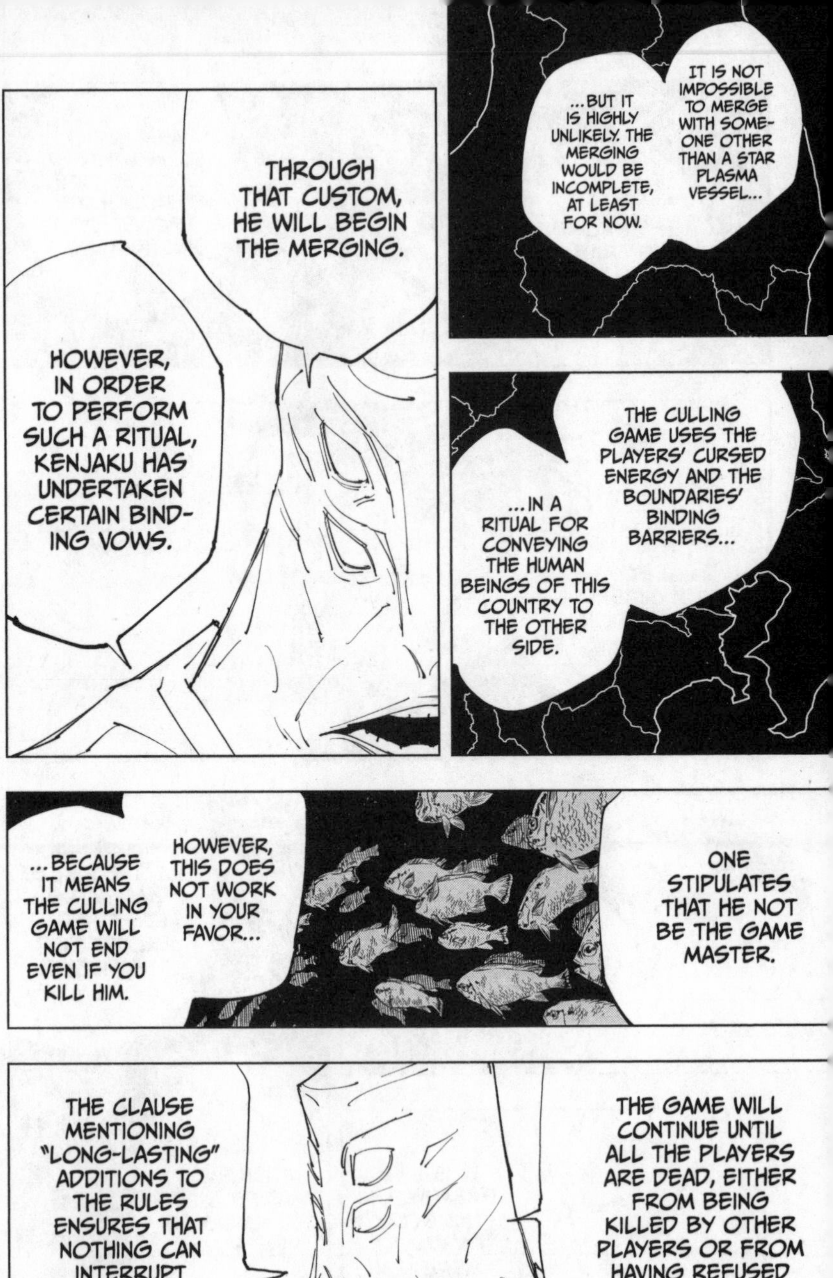
IT IS NOT IMPOSSIBLE TO MERGE WITH SOME-ONE OTHER THAN A STAR PLASMA VESSEL...
...BUT IT IS HIGHLY UNLIKELY. THE MERGING WOULD BE INCOMPLETE, AT LEAST FOR NOW.
THE CULLING GAME USES THE PLAYERS' CURSED ENERGY AND THE BOUNDARIES' BINDING BARRIERS...
...IN A RITUAL FOR CONVEYING THE HUMAN BEINGS OF THIS COUNTRY TO THE OTHER SIDE.
THROUGH THAT CUSTOM, HE WILL BEGIN THE MERGING.
HOWEVER, IN ORDER TO PERFORM SUCH A RITUAL, KENJAKU HAS UNDERTAKEN CERTAIN BIND-ING VOWS.
ONE STIPULATES THAT HE NOT BE THE GAME MASTER.
HOWEVER, THIS DOES NOT WORK IN YOUR FAVOR...
...BECAUSE IT MEANS THE CULLING GAME WILL NOT END EVEN IF YOU KILL HIM.
THE GAME WILL CONTINUE UNTIL ALL THE PLAYERS ARE DEAD, EITHER FROM BEING KILLED BY OTHER PLAYERS OR FROM HAVING REFUSED PARTICIPATION.
THE CLAUSE MENTIONING "LONG-LASTING" ADDITIONS TO THE RULES ENSURES THAT NOTHING CAN INTERRUPT THE RITUAL.

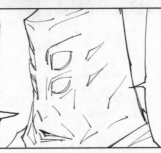

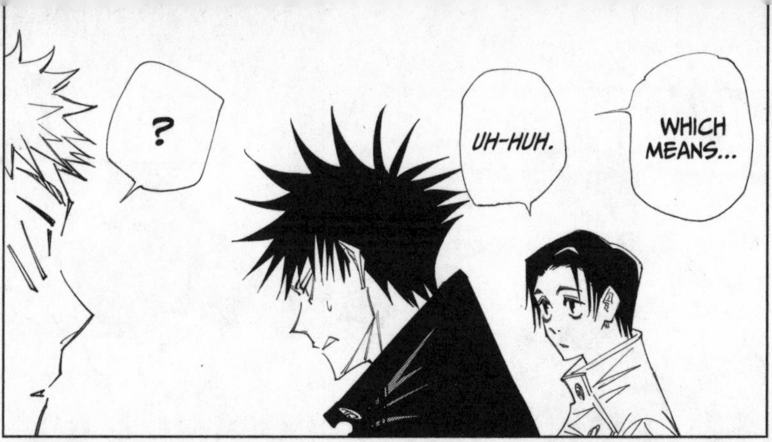
WHICH MEANS...
UH-HUH.
?

6. Players may expend 100 points to negotiate with the game master to add one new rule to the culling game. However, players cannot add their own life's value to the amount that can be spent.

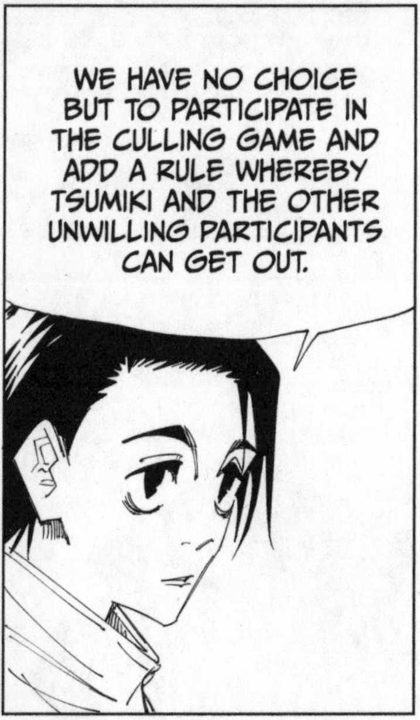
WE HAVE NO CHOICE BUT TO PARTICIPATE IN THE CULLING GAME AND ADD A RULE WHEREBY TSUMIKI AND THE OTHER UNWILLING PARTICIPANTS CAN GET OUT.

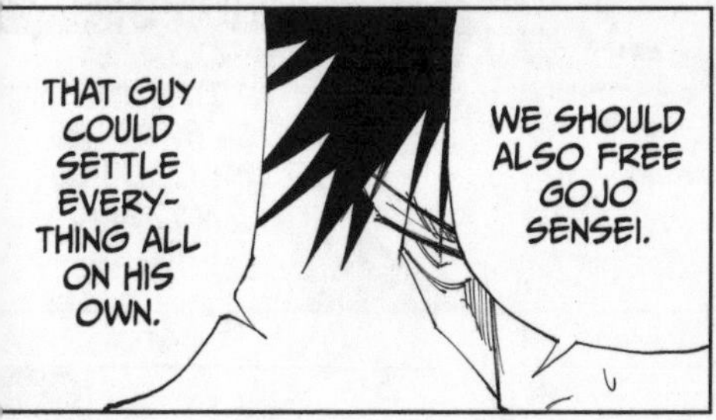
WE SHOULD ALSO FREE GOJO SENSEI.
THAT GUY COULD SETTLE EVERYTHING ALL ON HIS OWN.

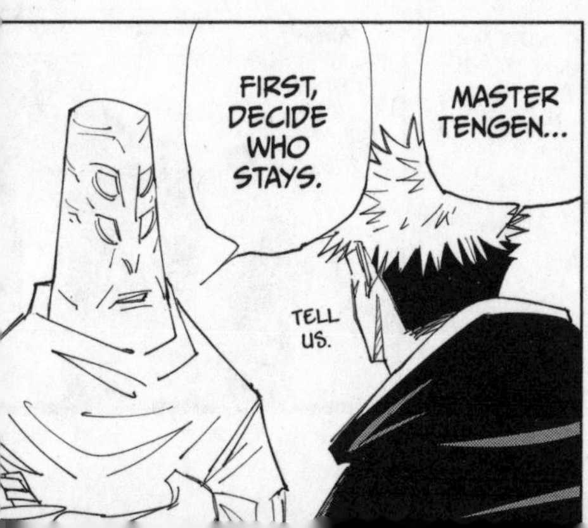
MASTER TENGEN...
FIRST, DECIDE WHO STAYS.
TELL US.

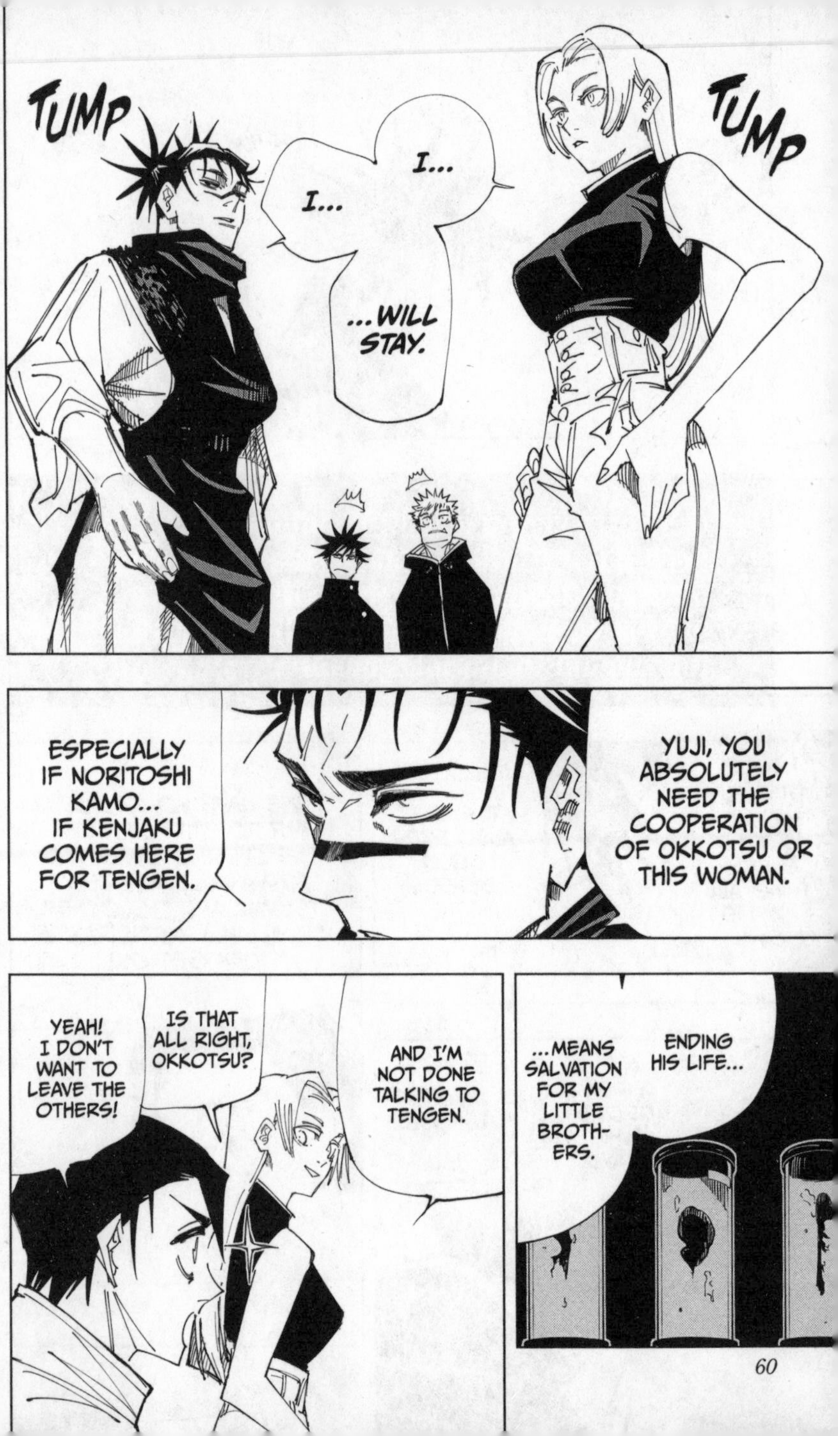
TUMP
TUMP
I...
I...
...WILL STAY.
YUJI, YOU ABSOLUTELY NEED THE COOPERATION OF OKKOTSU OR THIS WOMAN.
ESPECIALLY IF NORITOSHI KAMO... IF KENJAKU COMES HERE FOR TENGEN.
ENDING HIS LIFE...
...MEANS SALVATION FOR MY LITTLE BROTH-ERS.
AND I'M NOT DONE TALKING TO TENGEN.
IS THAT ALL RIGHT, OKKOTSU?
YEAH! I DON'T WANT TO LEAVE THE OTHERS!

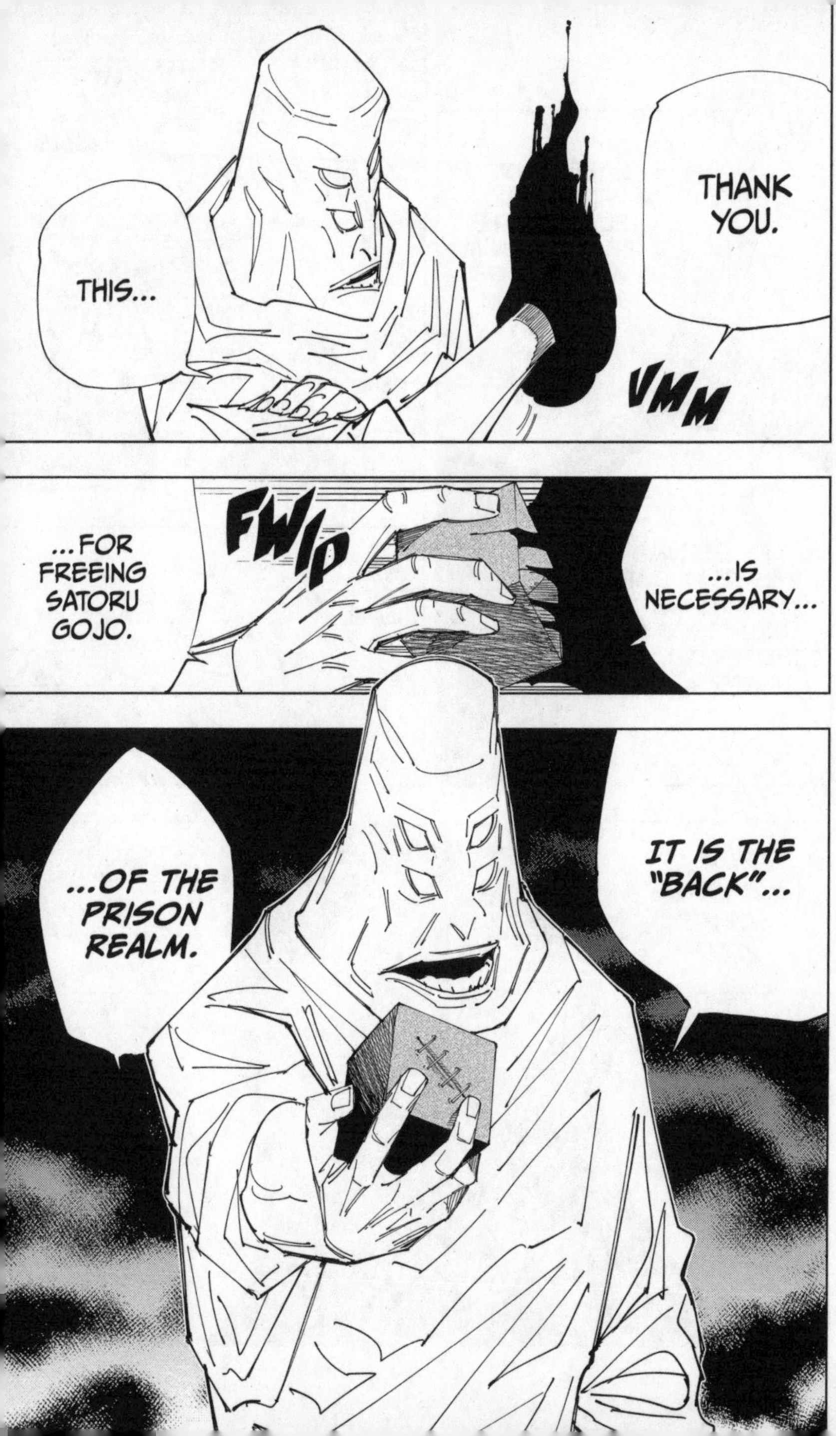
THANK YOU.
VMM
THIS...
...IS NECESSARY...
FWIP
...FOR FREEING SATORU GOJO.
IT IS THE "BACK"...
...OF THE PRISON REALM.

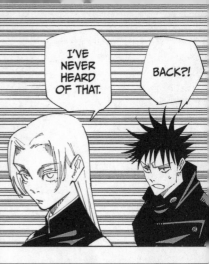

BACK?!
I'VE NEVER HEARD OF THAT.
YOU MEAN LIKE A BACK GATE?
YES, THAT IS RIGHT.
BEFORE KENJAKU FOUND IT, THE PRISON REALM WAS OUTSIDE MY BARRIER. I BELIEVE IT WAS OVERSEAS.
BY SEALING THIS REAR GATE, I WAS HIDING THE EXISTENCE OF THE "FRONT," BUT IT WAS NO USE.
SATORU GOJO IS ALSO SEALED INSIDE THIS REAR GATE.
THEN IF WE OPEN IT, WE CAN—
NO, THE AUTHORITY TO OPEN THE GATE RESTS WITH KENJAKU AS THE BEARER OF THE "FRONT."
BREAKING IT OPEN...

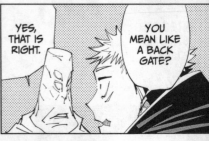

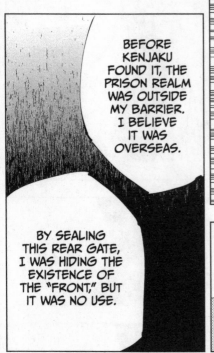

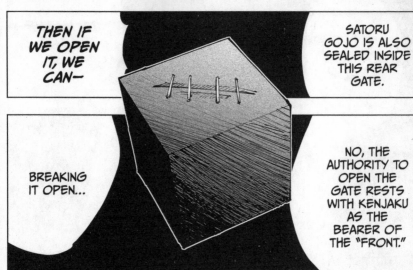

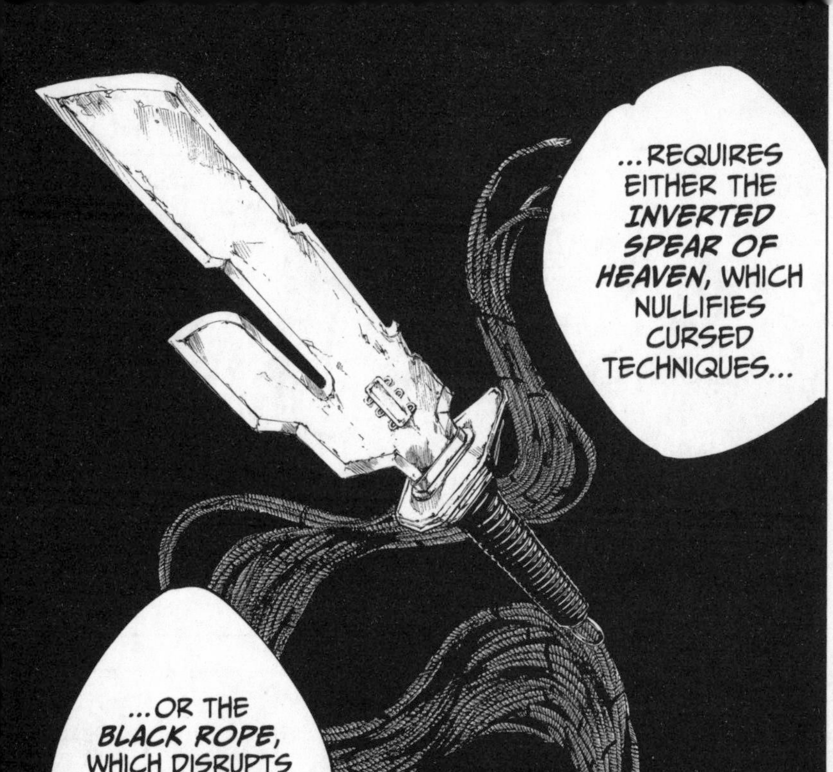
...REQUIRES EITHER THE *INVERTED SPEAR OF HEAVEN*, WHICH NULLIFIES CURSED TECHNIQUES...
...OR THE *BLACK ROPE*, WHICH DISRUPTS AND CANCELS CURSED TECHNIQUE EFFECTS.

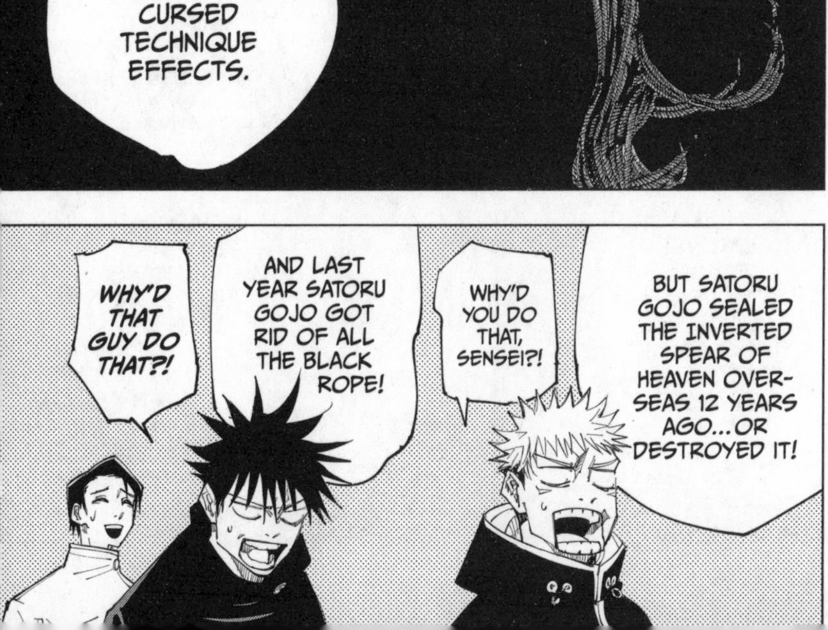
BUT SATORU GOJO SEALED THE INVERTED SPEAR OF HEAVEN OVER-SEAS 12 YEARS AGO...OR DESTROYED IT!
WHY'D YOU DO THAT, SENSEI?!
AND LAST YEAR SATORU GOJO GOT RID OF ALL THE BLACK ROPE!
WHY'D THAT GUY DO THAT?!

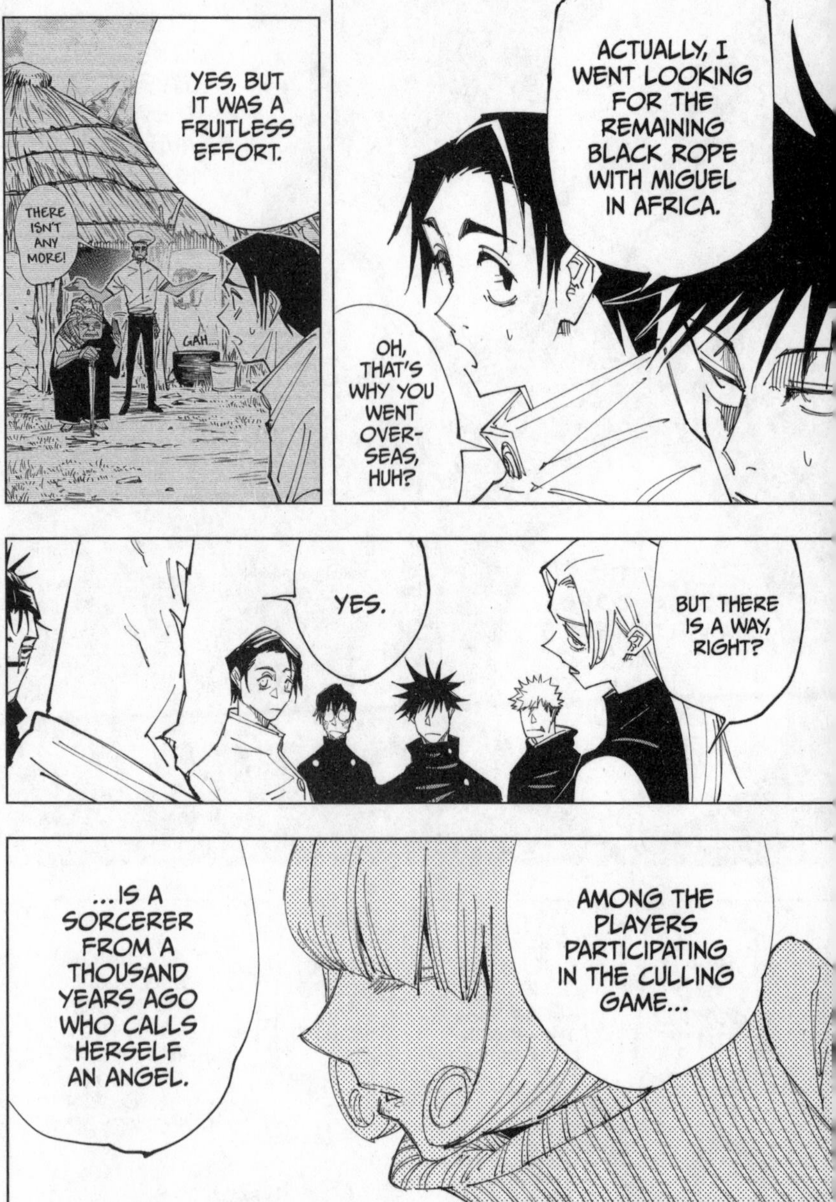
ACTUALLY, I WENT LOOKING FOR THE REMAINING BLACK ROPE WITH MIGUEL IN AFRICA.
OH, THAT'S WHY YOU WENT OVER-SEAS, HUH?
YES, BUT IT WAS A FRUITLESS EFFORT.
THERE ISN'T ANY MORE!
GAH...
BUT THERE IS A WAY, RIGHT?
YES.
AMONG THE PLAYERS PARTICIPATING IN THE CULLING GAME...
...IS A SORCERER FROM A THOUSAND YEARS AGO WHO CALLS HERSELF AN ANGEL.

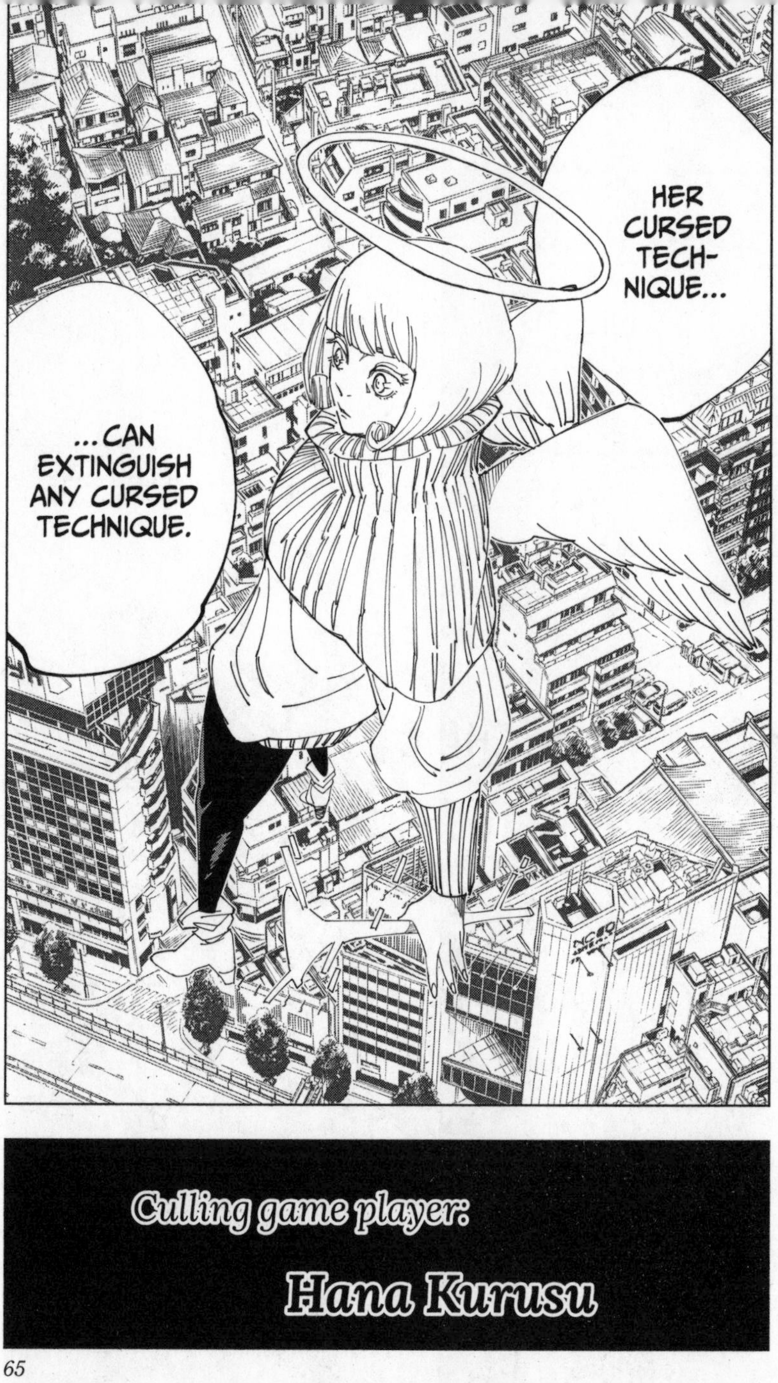
HER CURSED TECH-NIQUE...
...CAN EXTINGUISH ANY CURSED TECHNIQUE.

Culling game player:

Hana Kurusu

JINICHI

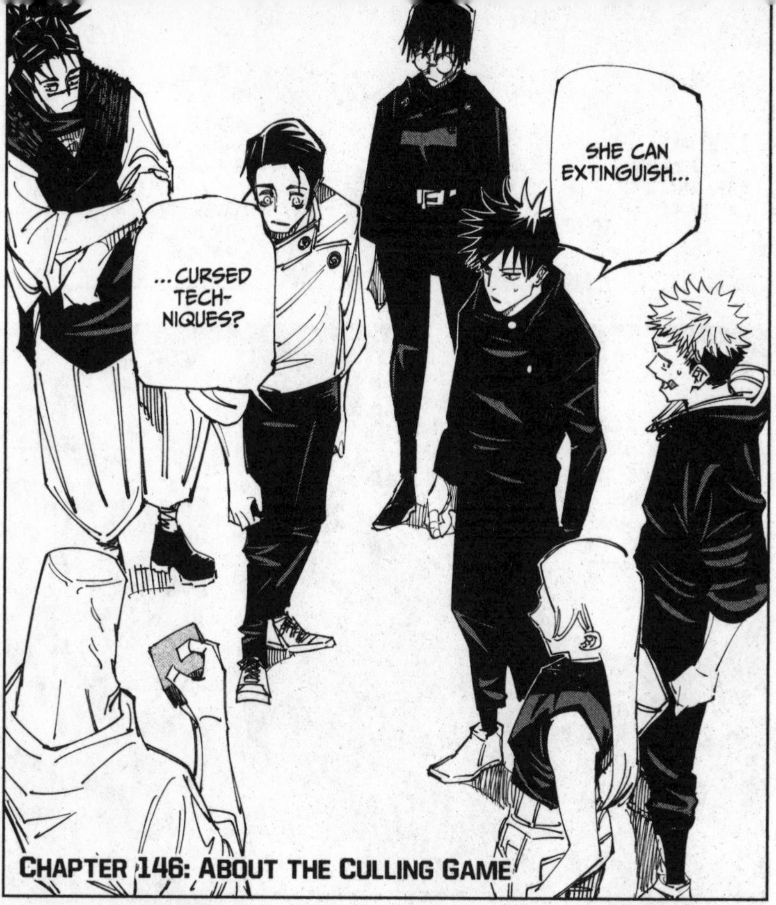
SHE CAN EXTINGUISH...
...CURSED TECHNIQUES?

Chapter 146: About the Culling Game

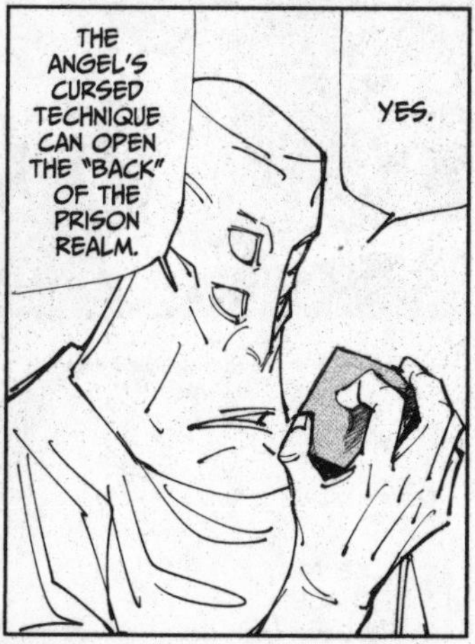
YES.
THE ANGEL'S CURSED TECHNIQUE CAN OPEN THE "BACK" OF THE PRISON REALM.

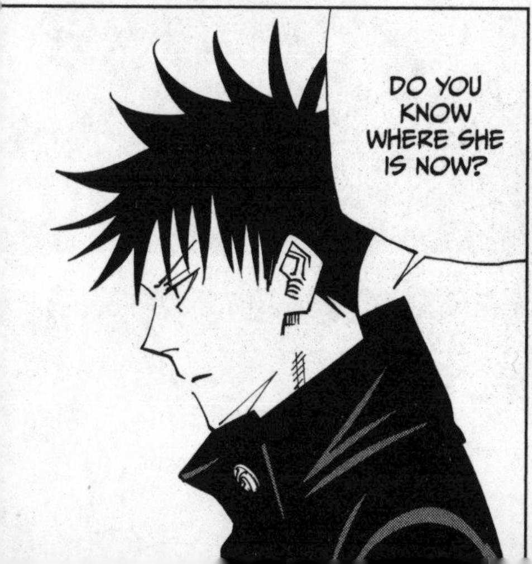
DO YOU KNOW WHERE SHE IS NOW?

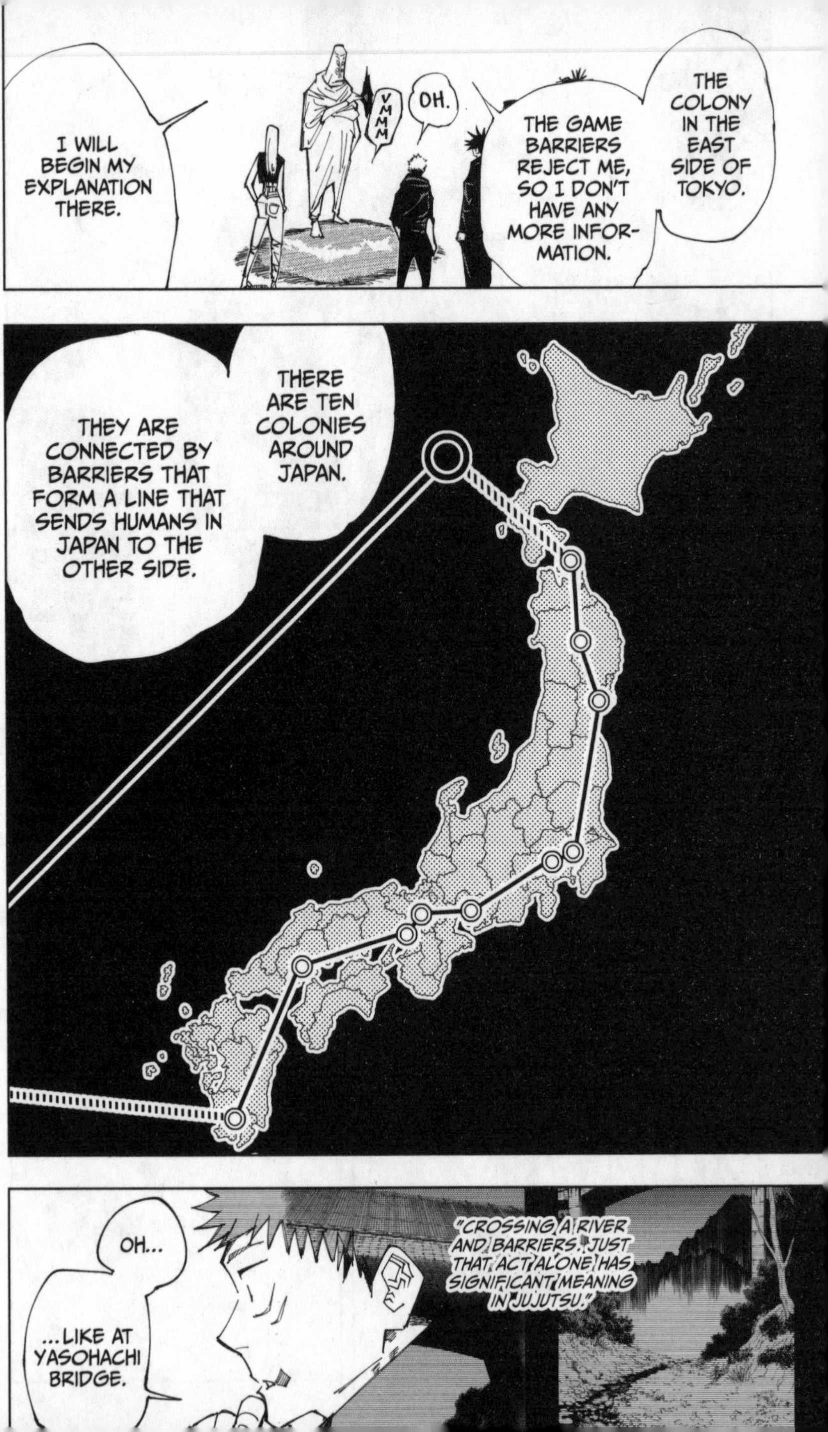
THE COLONY IN THE EAST SIDE OF TOKYO.
THE GAME BARRIERS REJECT ME, SO I DON'T HAVE ANY MORE INFORMATION.
OH.
VMMM
I WILL BEGIN MY EXPLANATION THERE.
THERE ARE TEN COLONIES AROUND JAPAN.
THEY ARE CONNECTED BY BARRIERS THAT FORM A LINE THAT SENDS HUMANS IN JAPAN TO THE OTHER SIDE.
"CROSSING A RIVER AND BARRIERS. JUST THAT ACT ALONE HAS SIGNIFICANT MEANING IN JUJUTSU."
OH...
...LIKE AT YASOHACHI BRIDGE.

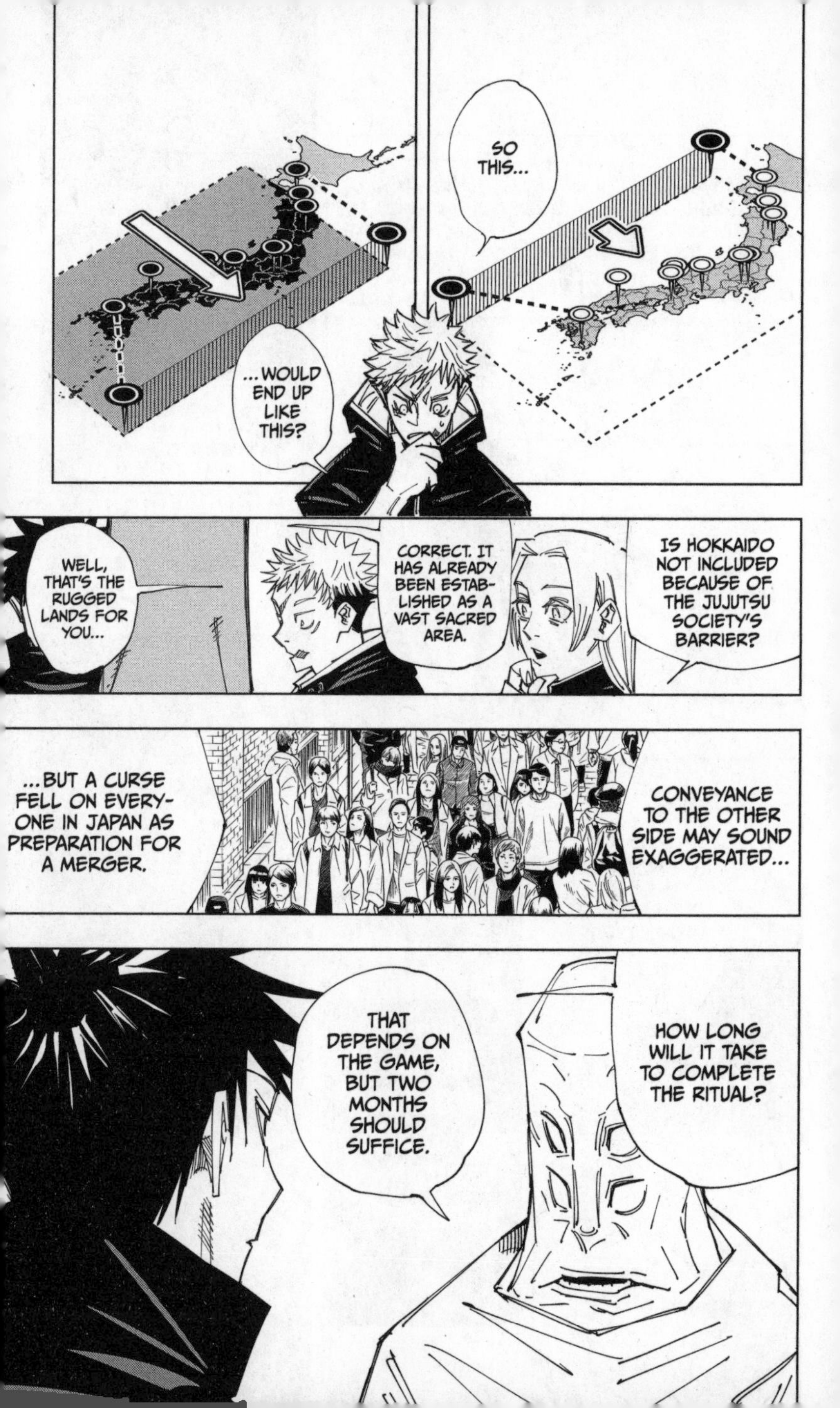
SO THIS...
...WOULD END UP LIKE THIS?
IS HOKKAIDO NOT INCLUDED BECAUSE OF THE JUJUTSU SOCIETY'S BARRIER?
CORRECT. IT HAS ALREADY BEEN ESTABLISHED AS A VAST SACRED AREA.
WELL, THAT'S THE RUGGED LANDS FOR YOU...
CONVEYANCE TO THE OTHER SIDE MAY SOUND EXAGGERATED...
...BUT A CURSE FELL ON EVERYONE IN JAPAN AS PREPARATION FOR A MERGER.
HOW LONG WILL IT TAKE TO COMPLETE THE RITUAL?
THAT DEPENDS ON THE GAME, BUT TWO MONTHS SHOULD SUFFICE.

1. After awakening a cursed technique, players must declare their participation in the culling game at a colony of their choice within 19 days.

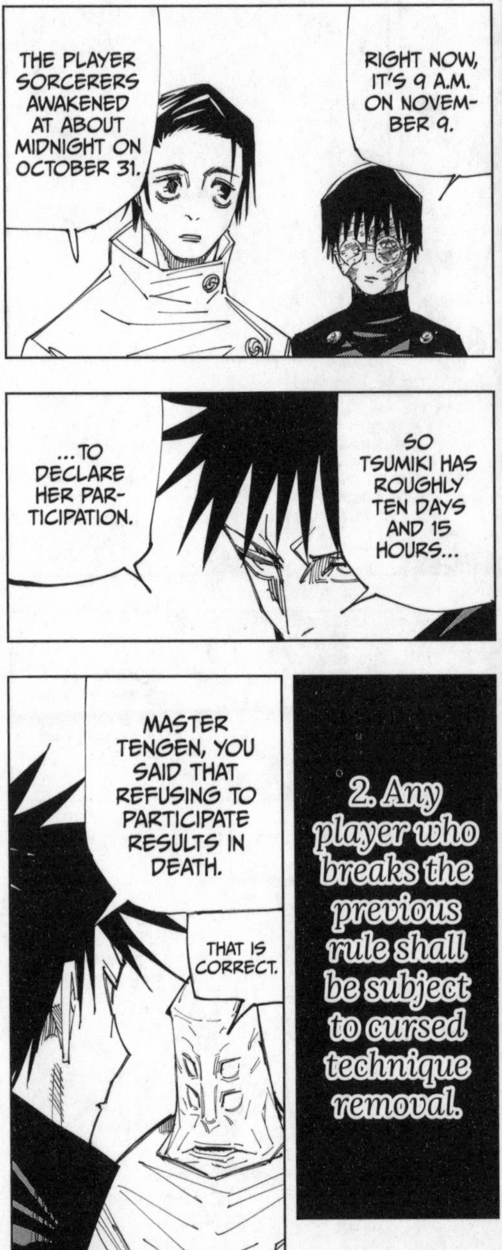

RIGHT NOW, IT'S 9 A.M. ON NOVEMBER 9.
THE PLAYER SORCERERS AWAKENED AT ABOUT MIDNIGHT ON OCTOBER 31.
SO TSUMIKI HAS ROUGHLY TEN DAYS AND 15 HOURS...
...TO DECLARE HER PARTICIPATION.
2. Any player who breaks the previous rule shall be subject to cursed technique removal.
MASTER TENGEN, YOU SAID THAT REFUSING TO PARTICIPATE RESULTS IN DEATH.
THAT IS CORRECT.

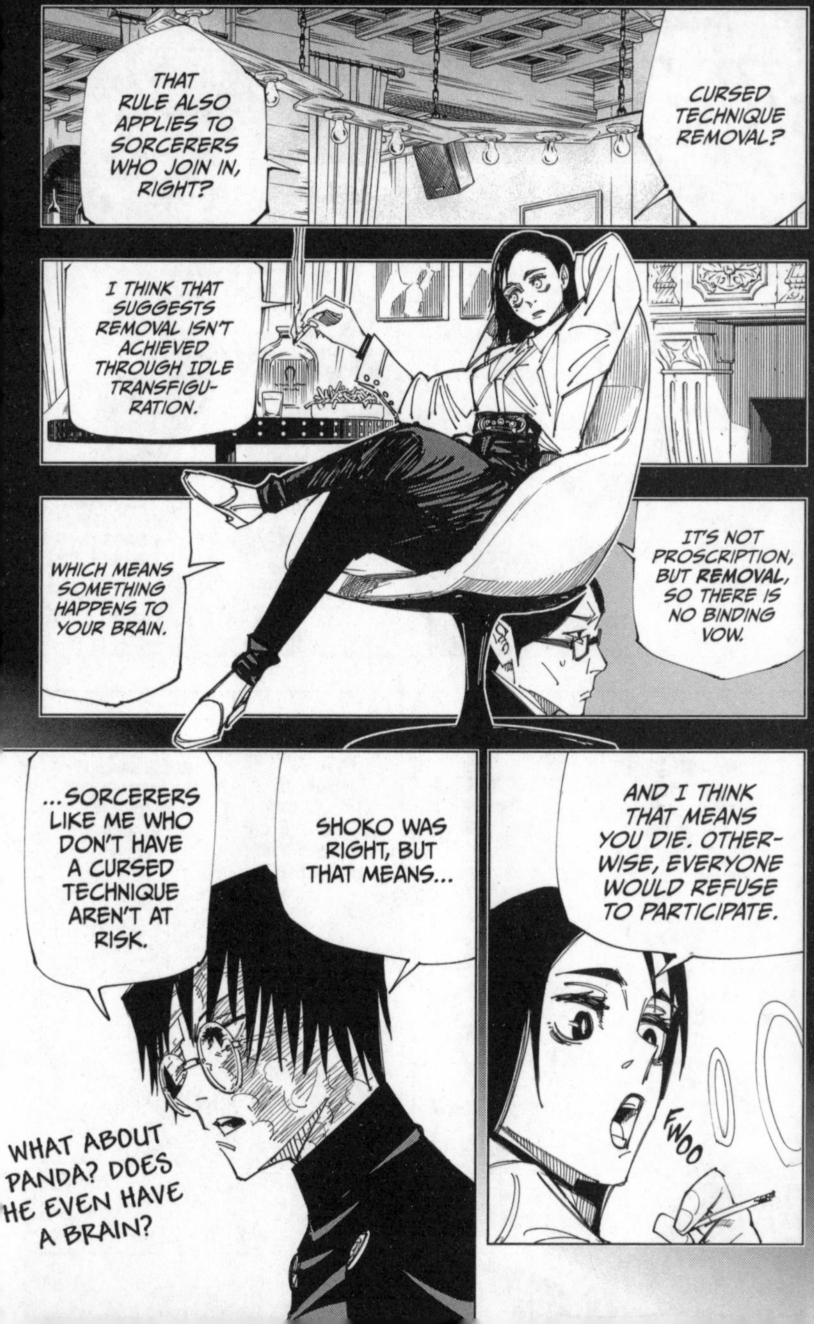
CURSED TECHNIQUE REMOVAL?
THAT RULE ALSO APPLIES TO SORCERERS WHO JOIN IN, RIGHT?
I THINK THAT SUGGESTS REMOVAL ISN'T ACHIEVED THROUGH IDLE TRANSFIGU-RATION.
IT'S NOT PROSCRIPTION, BUT **REMOVAL**, SO THERE IS NO BINDING VOW.
WHICH MEANS SOMETHING HAPPENS TO YOUR BRAIN.
AND I THINK THAT MEANS YOU DIE. OTHER-WISE, EVERYONE WOULD REFUSE TO PARTICIPATE.
FWOO
SHOKO WAS RIGHT, BUT THAT MEANS...
...SORCERERS LIKE ME WHO DON'T HAVE A CURSED TECHNIQUE AREN'T AT RISK.
WHAT ABOUT PANDA? DOES HE EVEN HAVE A BRAIN?

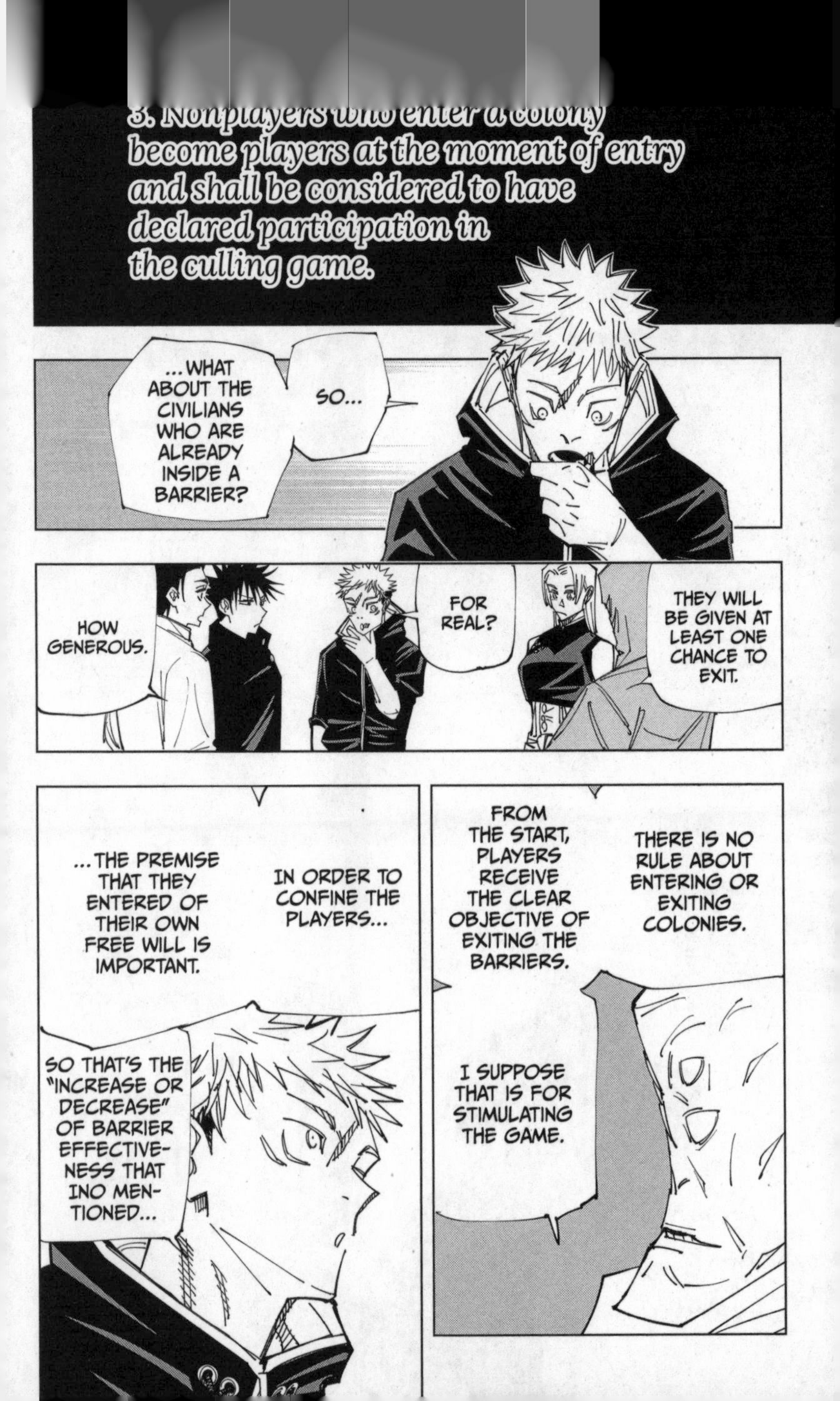
3. Nonplayers who enter a colony become players at the moment of entry and shall be considered to have declared participation in the culling game.
SO...
...WHAT ABOUT THE CIVILIANS WHO ARE ALREADY INSIDE A BARRIER?
THEY WILL BE GIVEN AT LEAST ONE CHANCE TO EXIT.
FOR REAL?
HOW GENEROUS.
THERE IS NO RULE ABOUT ENTERING OR EXITING COLONIES.
FROM THE START, PLAYERS RECEIVE THE CLEAR OBJECTIVE OF EXITING THE BARRIERS.
I SUPPOSE THAT IS FOR STIMULATING THE GAME.
IN ORDER TO CONFINE THE PLAYERS...
...THE PREMISE THAT THEY ENTERED OF THEIR OWN FREE WILL IS IMPORTANT.
SO THAT'S THE "INCREASE OR DECREASE" OF BARRIER EFFECTIVE-NESS THAT INO MEN-TIONED...

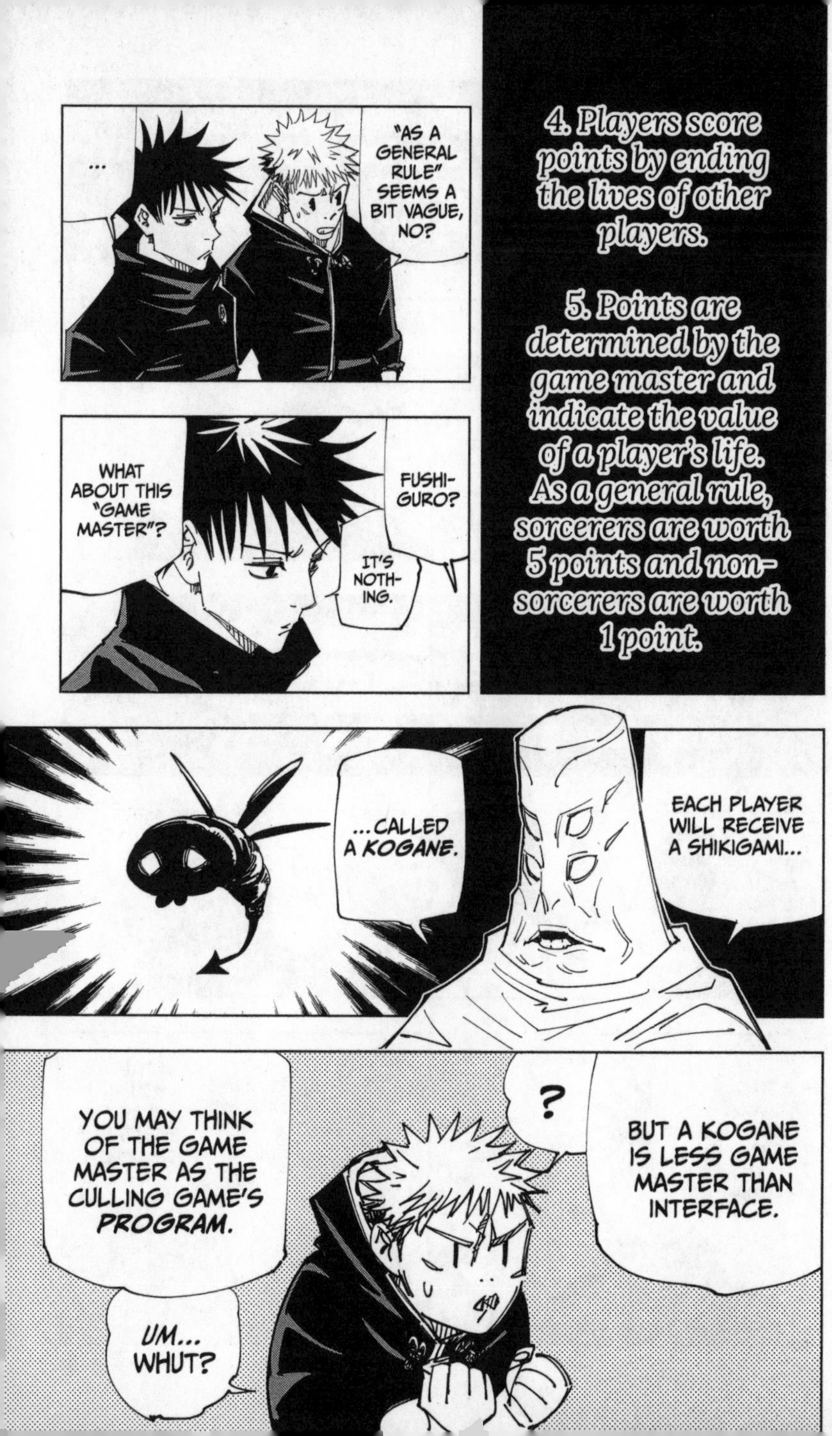
4. Players score points by ending the lives of other players.
5. Points are determined by the game master and indicate the value of a player's life. As a general rule, sorcerers are worth 5 points and non-sorcerers are worth 1 point.
"AS A GENERAL RULE" SEEMS A BIT VAGUE, NO?
...
FUSHI-GURO?
WHAT ABOUT THIS "GAME MASTER"?
IT'S NOTH-ING.
EACH PLAYER WILL RECEIVE A SHIKIGAMI...
...CALLED A KOGANE.
?
BUT A KOGANE IS LESS GAME MASTER THAN INTERFACE.
YOU MAY THINK OF THE GAME MASTER AS THE CULLING GAME'S PROGRAM.
UM... WHUT?

6. Players may expend 100 points to negotiate with the game master to add one new rule to the culling game. However, players cannot add their own life's value to the amount that can be spent.

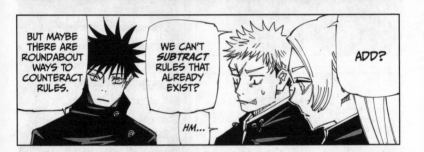

ADD?
WE CAN'T *SUBTRACT* RULES THAT ALREADY EXIST?
HM...
BUT MAYBE THERE ARE ROUNDABOUT WAYS TO COUNTERACT RULES.

7. In accordance with the previous rule, the game master must accept any proposed new rule unless it will have a marked and long-lasting effect on the culling game.

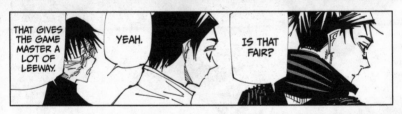

IS THAT FAIR?
YEAH.
THAT GIVES THE GAME MASTER A LOT OF LEEWAY.

ACTUALLY, YOU MAY EXPECT AN EQUITABLE DECISION.
THE PLAYERS ARE SUBJECT TO STRICT RULES.
SORCERY-WISE, KENJAKU IS DUE NO FURTHER BIAS.

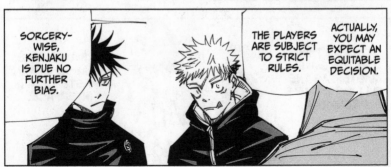

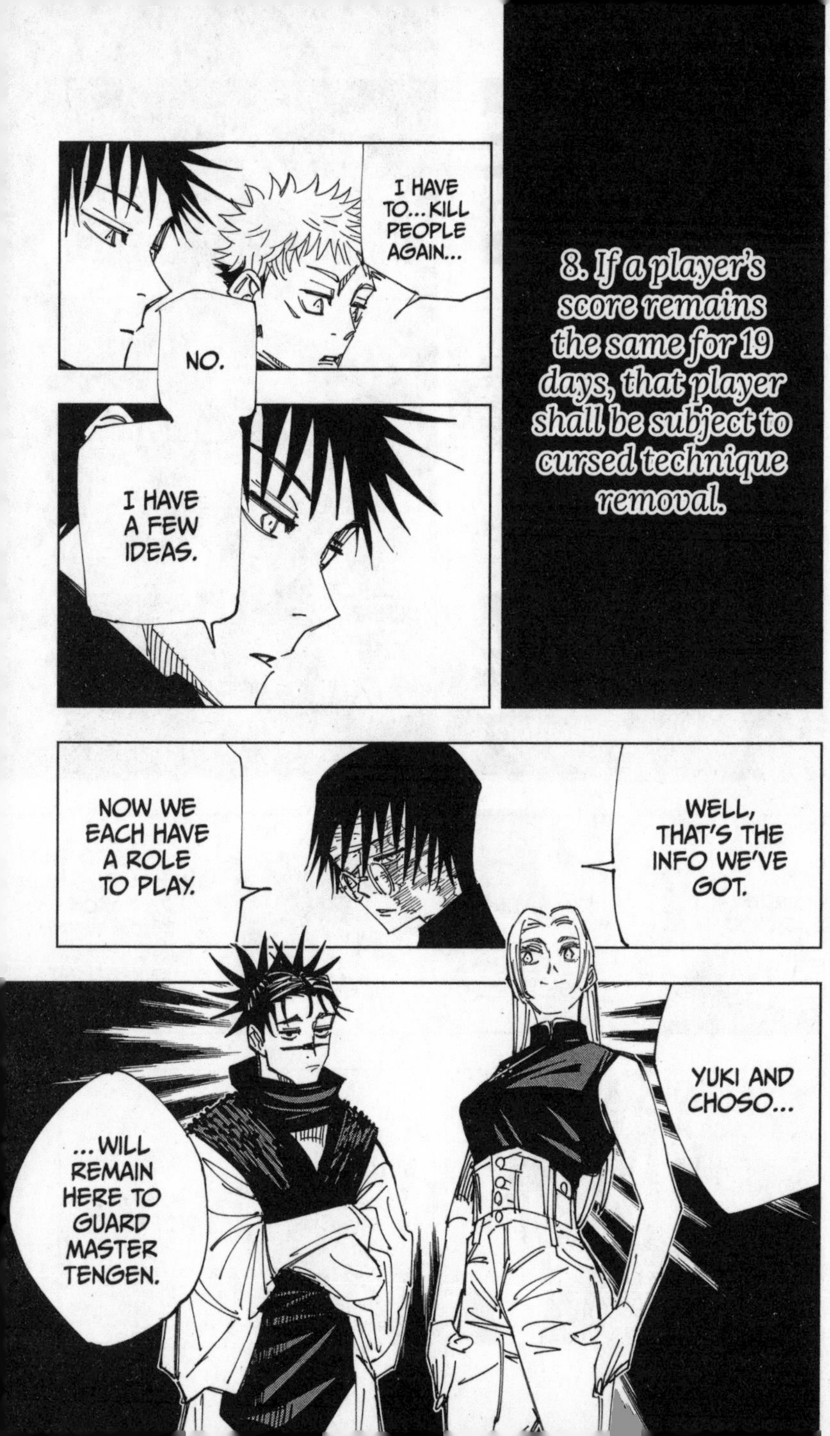
8. If a player's score remains the same for 19 days, that player shall be subject to cursed technique removal.
I HAVE TO... KILL PEOPLE AGAIN...
NO.
I HAVE A FEW IDEAS.
WELL, THAT'S THE INFO WE'VE GOT.
NOW WE EACH HAVE A ROLE TO PLAY.
YUKI AND CHOSO...
...WILL REMAIN HERE TO GUARD MASTER TENGEN.

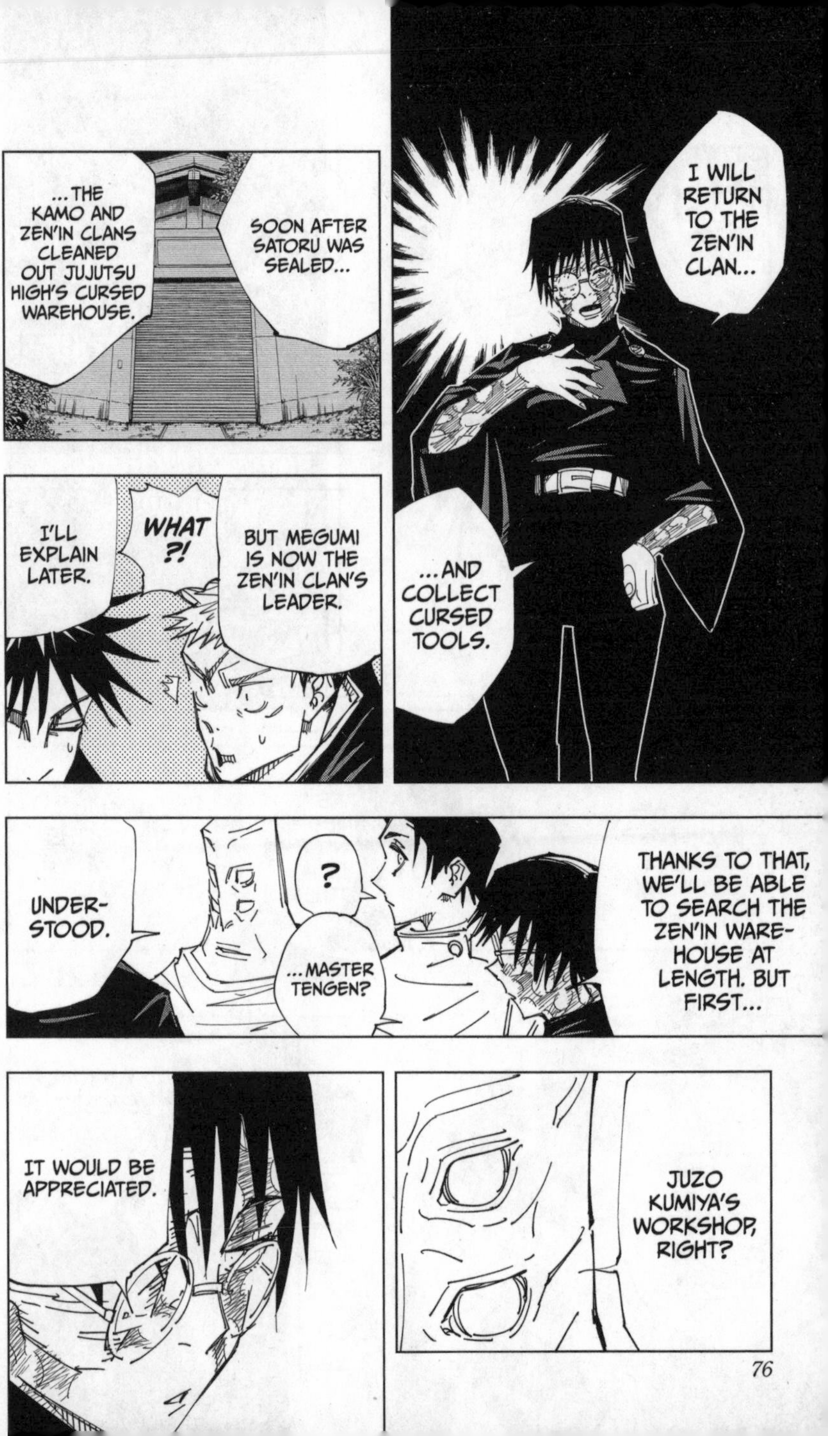

I WILL RETURN TO THE ZEN'IN CLAN...
...AND COLLECT CURSED TOOLS.
SOON AFTER SATORU WAS SEALED...
...THE KAMO AND ZEN'IN CLANS CLEANED OUT JUJUTSU HIGH'S CURSED WAREHOUSE.
BUT MEGUMI IS NOW THE ZEN'IN CLAN'S LEADER.
WHAT ?!
I'LL EXPLAIN LATER.
THANKS TO THAT, WE'LL BE ABLE TO SEARCH THE ZEN'IN WARE-HOUSE AT LENGTH. BUT FIRST...
?
...MASTER TENGEN?
UNDER-STOOD.
JUZO KUMIYA'S WORKSHOP, RIGHT?
IT WOULD BE APPRECIATED.

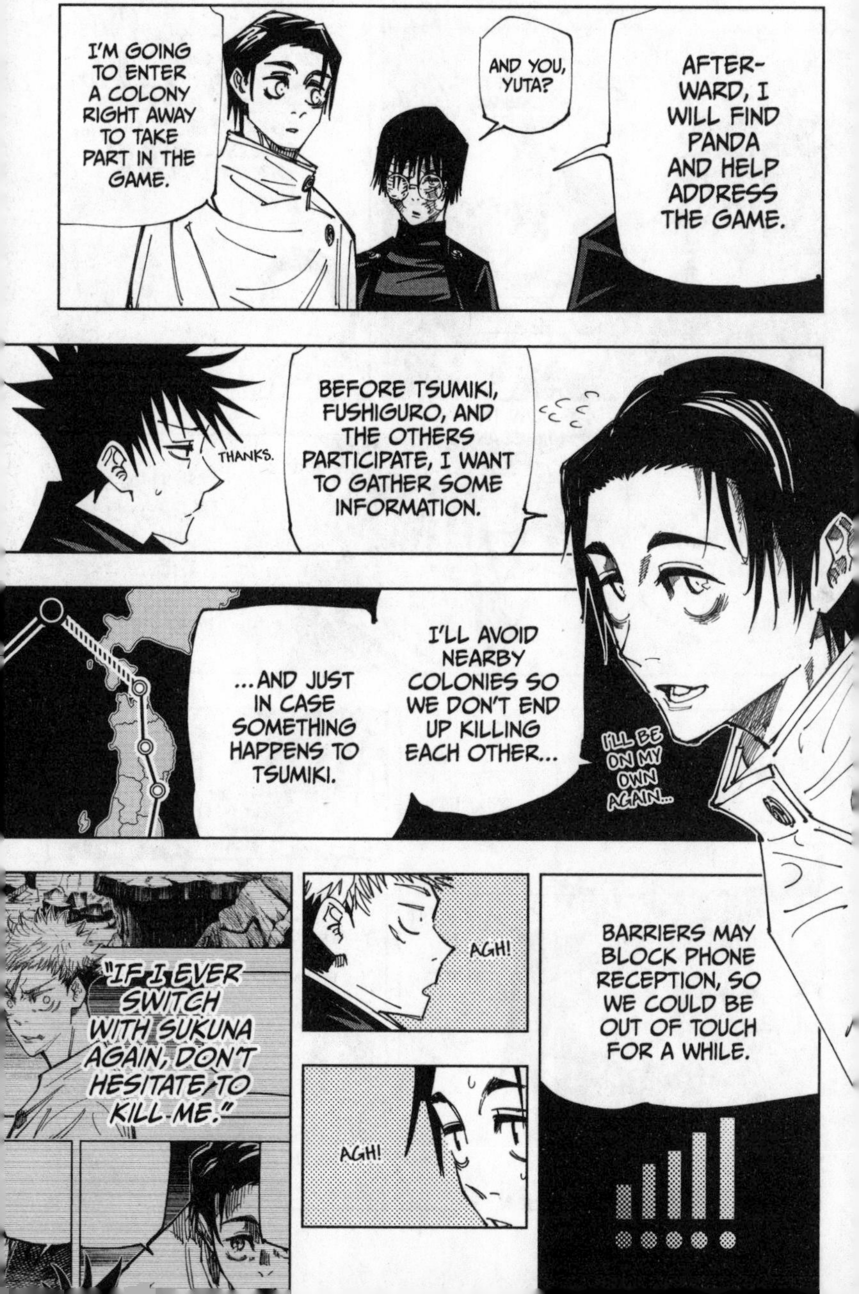
AFTER-WARD, I WILL FIND PANDA AND HELP ADDRESS THE GAME.
AND YOU, YUTA?
I'M GOING TO ENTER A COLONY RIGHT AWAY TO TAKE PART IN THE GAME.
BEFORE TSUMIKI, FUSHIGURO, AND THE OTHERS PARTICIPATE, I WANT TO GATHER SOME INFORMATION.
THANKS.
I'LL AVOID NEARBY COLONIES SO WE DON'T END UP KILLING EACH OTHER...
...AND JUST IN CASE SOMETHING HAPPENS TO TSUMIKI.
I'LL BE ON MY OWN AGAIN...
BARRIERS MAY BLOCK PHONE RECEPTION, SO WE COULD BE OUT OF TOUCH FOR A WHILE.
AGH!
AGH!
"IF I EVER SWITCH WITH SUKUNA AGAIN, DON'T HESITATE TO KILL ME."

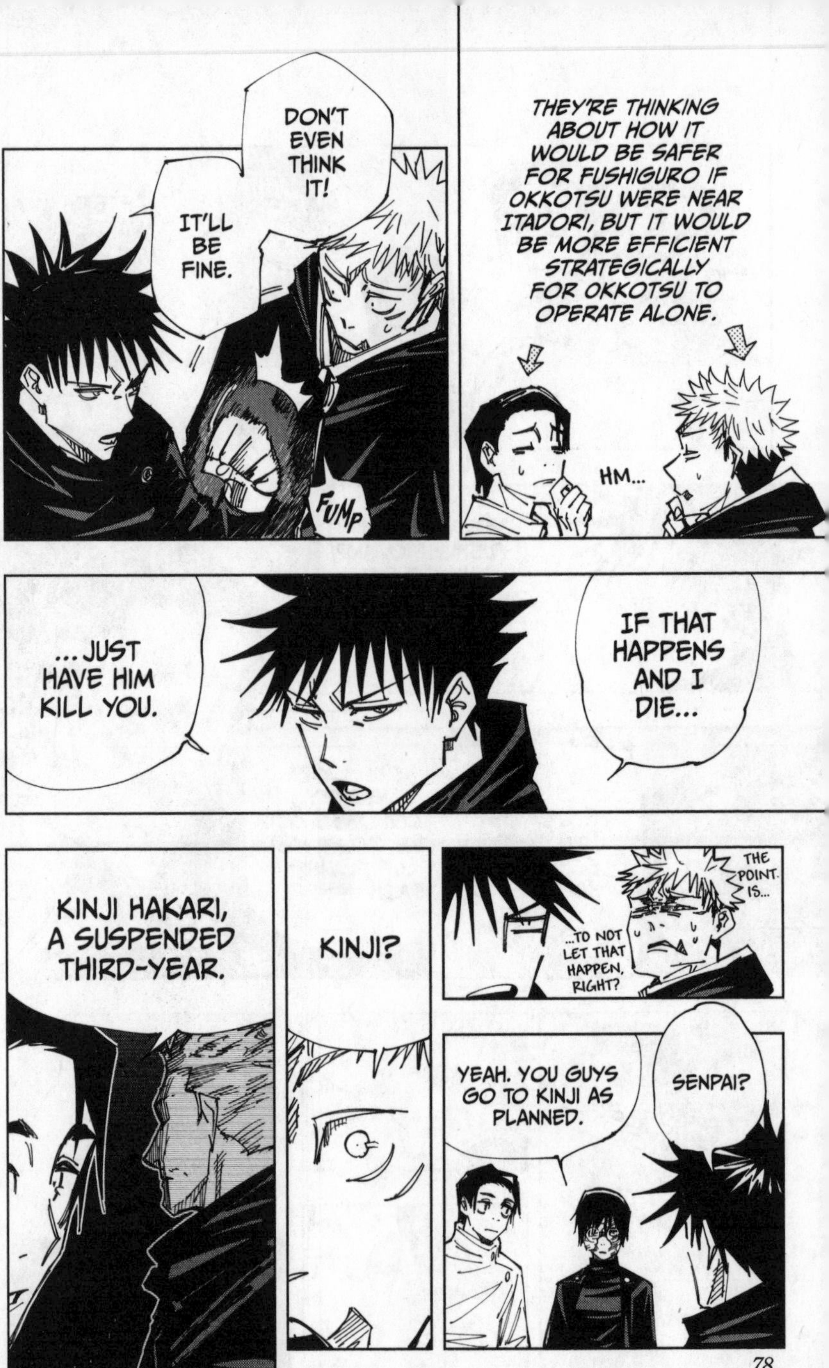
THEY'RE THINKING ABOUT HOW IT WOULD BE SAFER FOR FUSHIGURO IF OKKOTSU WERE NEAR ITADORI, BUT IT WOULD BE MORE EFFICIENT STRATEGICALLY FOR OKKOTSU TO OPERATE ALONE.
HM...
DON'T EVEN THINK IT!
IT'LL BE FINE.
FUMP
IF THAT HAPPENS AND I DIE...
...JUST HAVE HIM KILL YOU.
THE POINT IS...
...TO NOT LET THAT HAPPEN, RIGHT?
SENPAI?
YEAH. YOU GUYS GO TO KINJI AS PLANNED.
KINJI?
KINJI HAKARI, A SUSPENDED THIRD-YEAR.

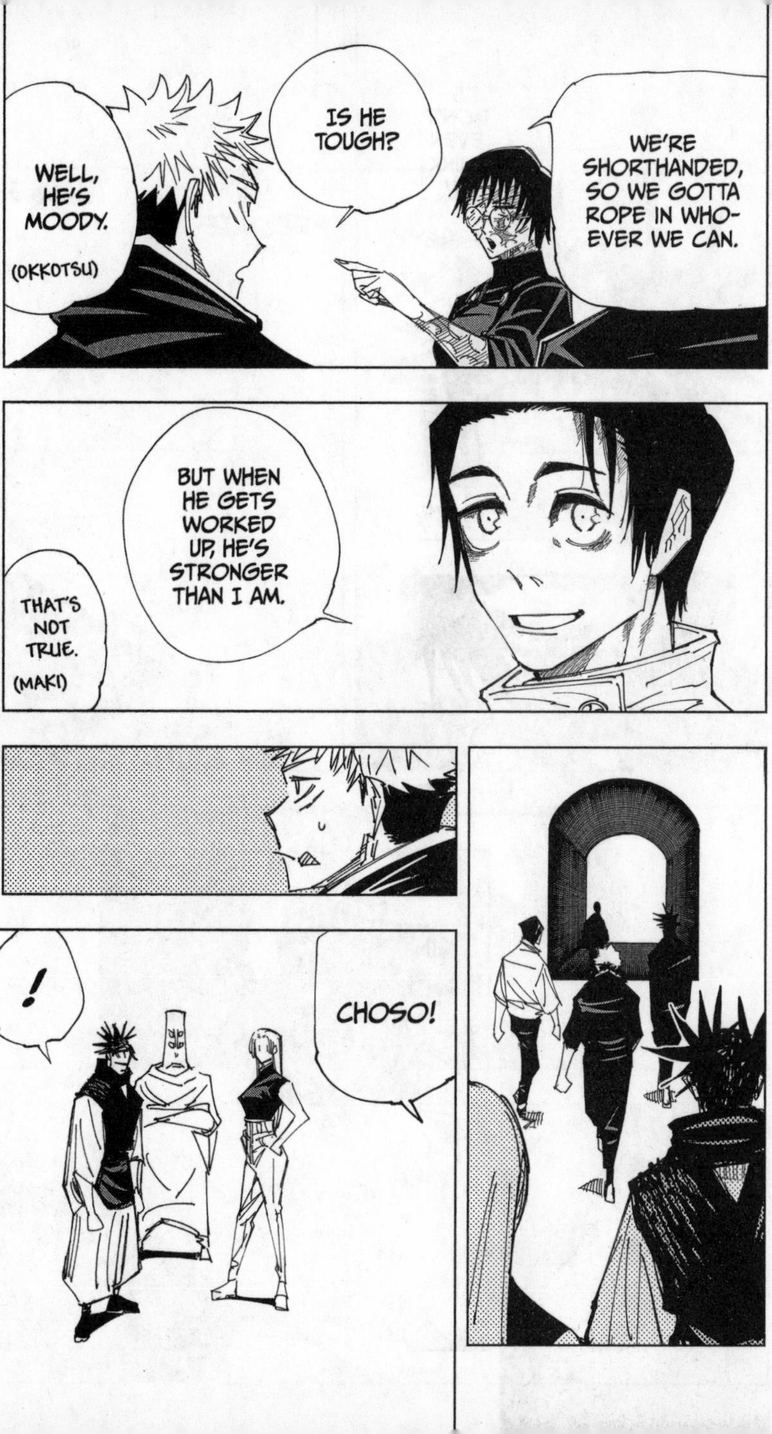
WE'RE SHORTHANDED, SO WE GOTTA ROPE IN WHO-EVER WE CAN.
IS HE TOUGH?
WELL, HE'S MOODY.
(OKKOTSU)
BUT WHEN HE GETS WORKED UP, HE'S STRONGER THAN I AM.
THAT'S NOT TRUE.
(MAKI)
CHOSO!
!

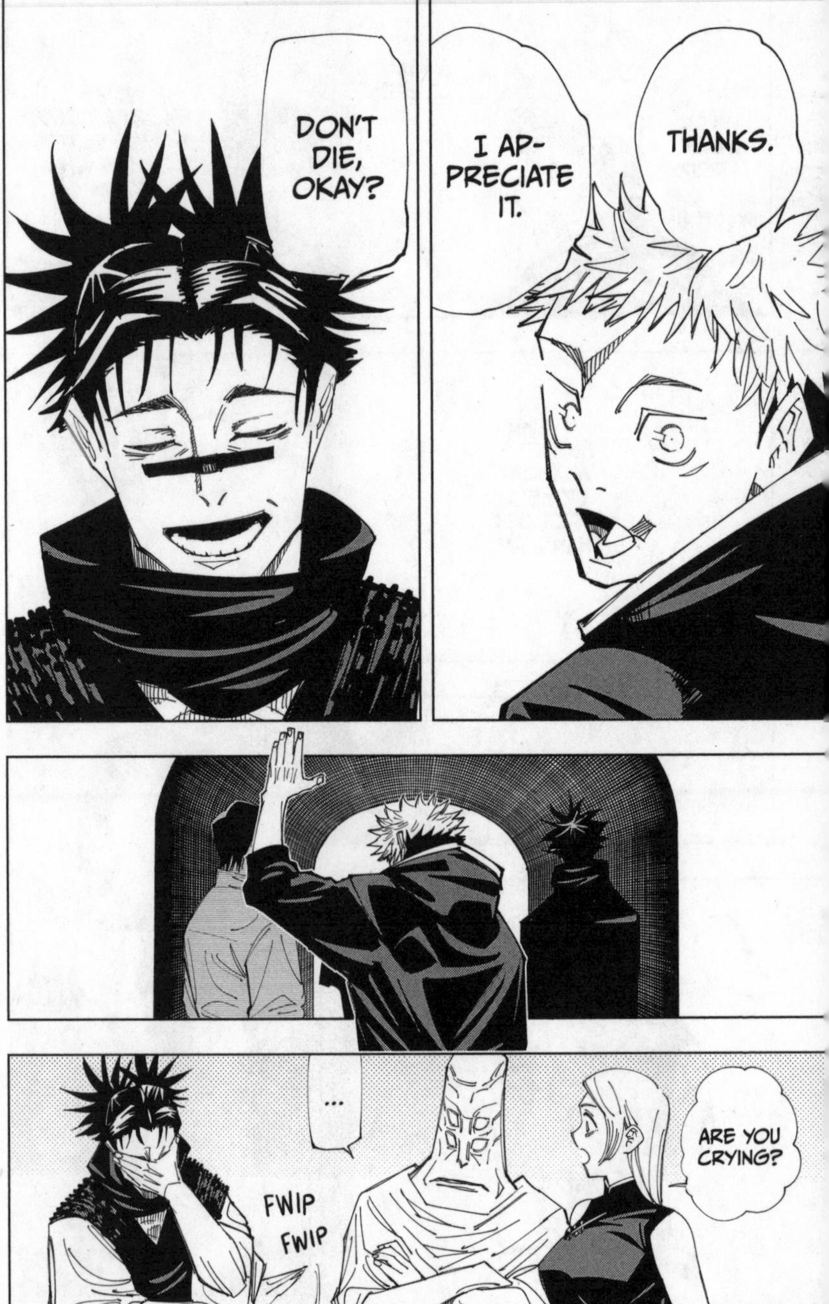
THANKS.
I AP-PRECIATE IT.
DON'T DIE, OKAY?
ARE YOU CRYING?
...
FWIP FWIP

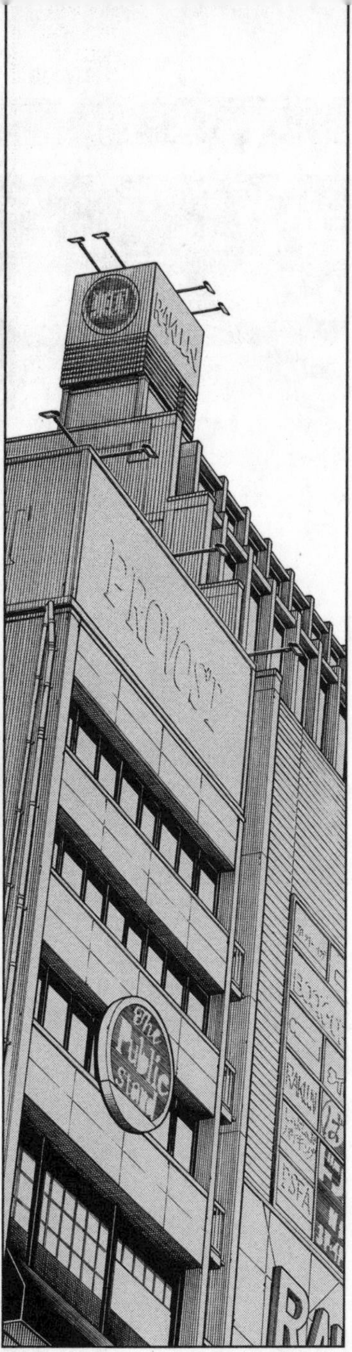
PROVOST
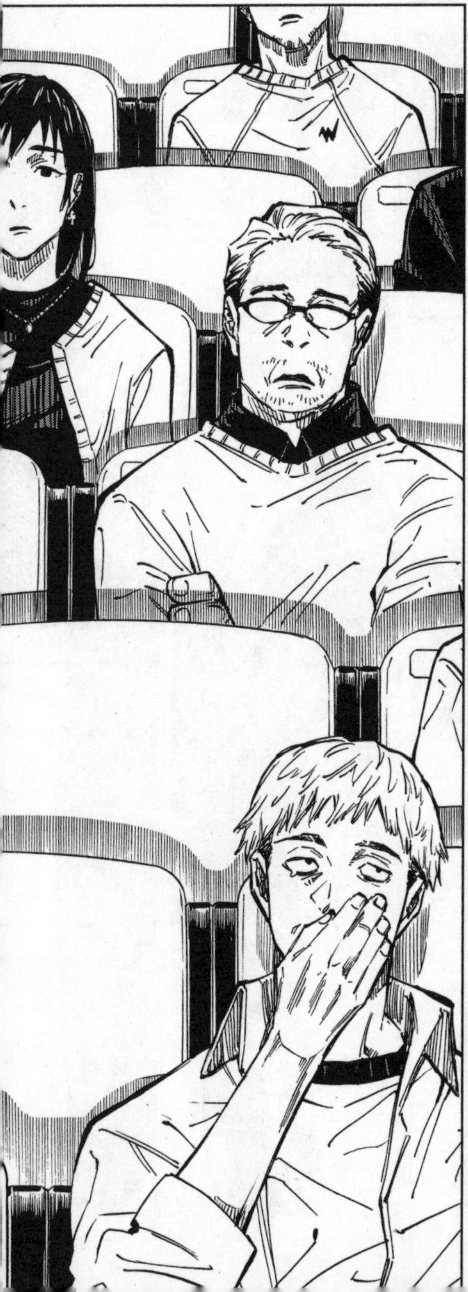

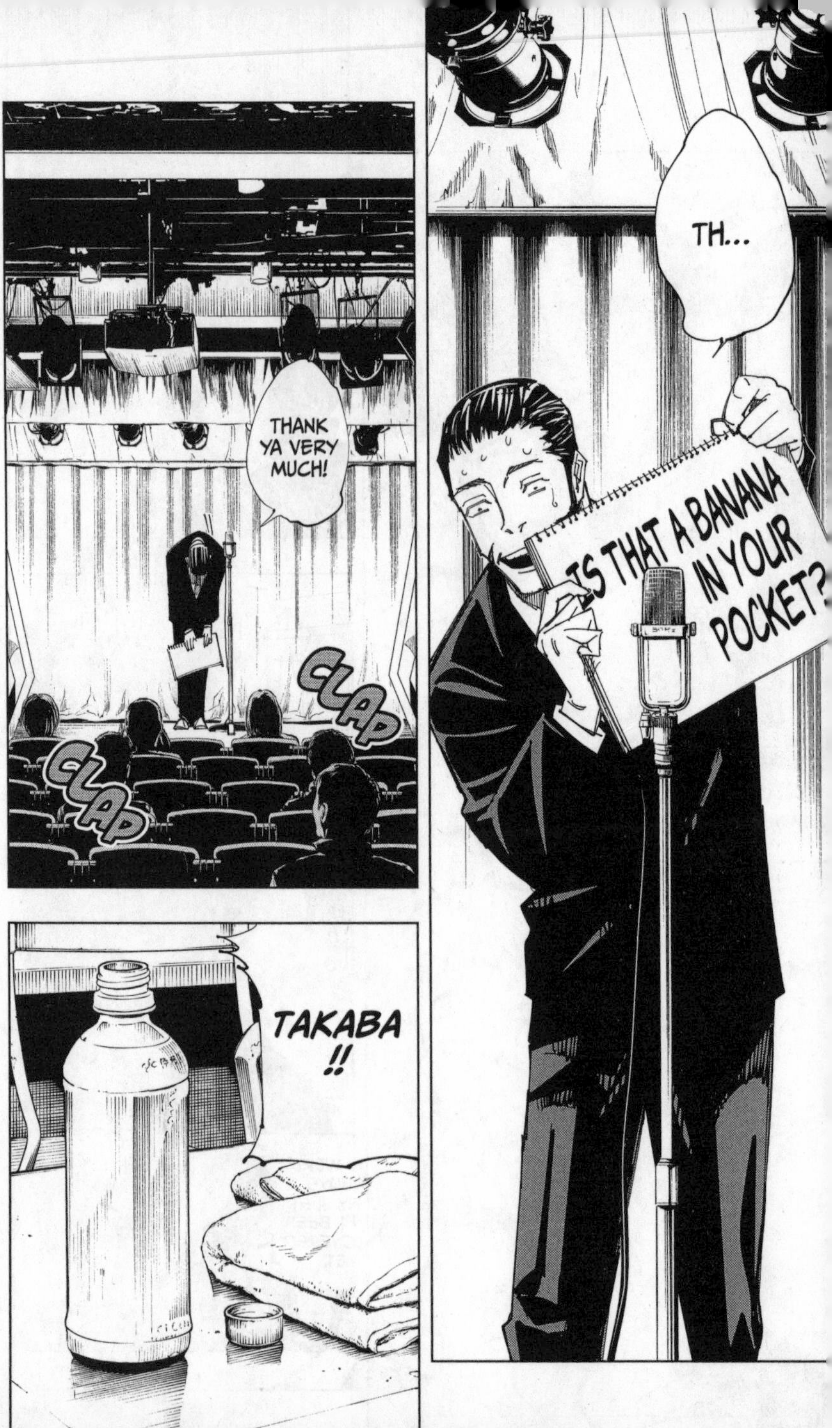
TH...
IS THAT A BANANA IN YOUR POCKET?
THANK YA VERY MUCH!
CLAP
CLAP
TAKABA!!

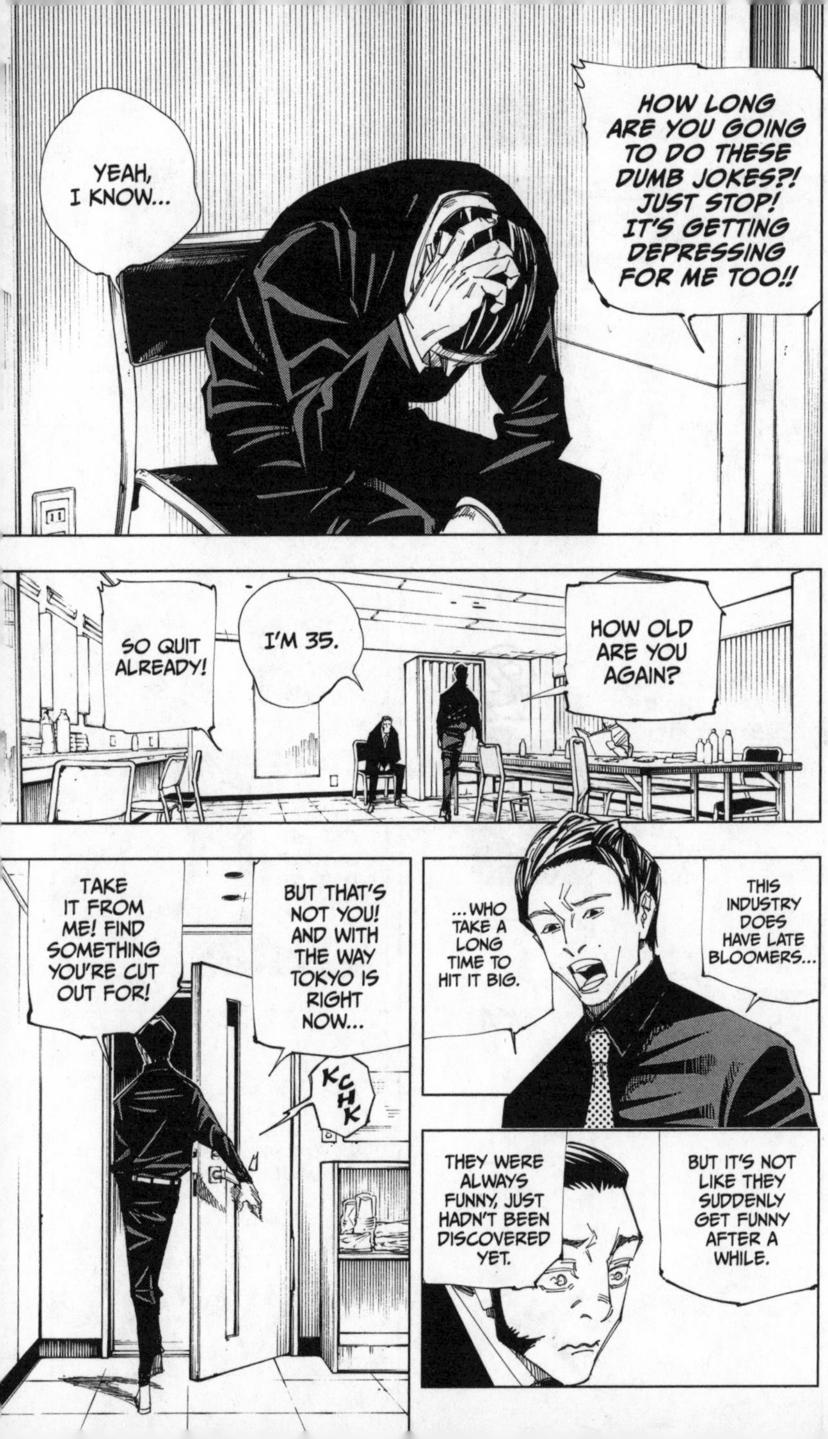
HOW LONG ARE YOU GOING TO DO THESE DUMB JOKES?! JUST STOP! IT'S GETTING DEPRESSING FOR ME TOO!!
YEAH, I KNOW...
HOW OLD ARE YOU AGAIN?
I'M 35.
SO QUIT ALREADY!
THIS INDUSTRY DOES HAVE LATE BLOOMERS...
...WHO TAKE A LONG TIME TO HIT IT BIG.
BUT IT'S NOT LIKE THEY SUDDENLY GET FUNNY AFTER A WHILE.
THEY WERE ALWAYS FUNNY, JUST HADN'T BEEN DISCOVERED YET.
BUT THAT'S NOT YOU! AND WITH THE WAY TOKYO IS RIGHT NOW...
TAKE IT FROM ME! FIND SOMETHING YOU'RE CUT OUT FOR!
KCHK

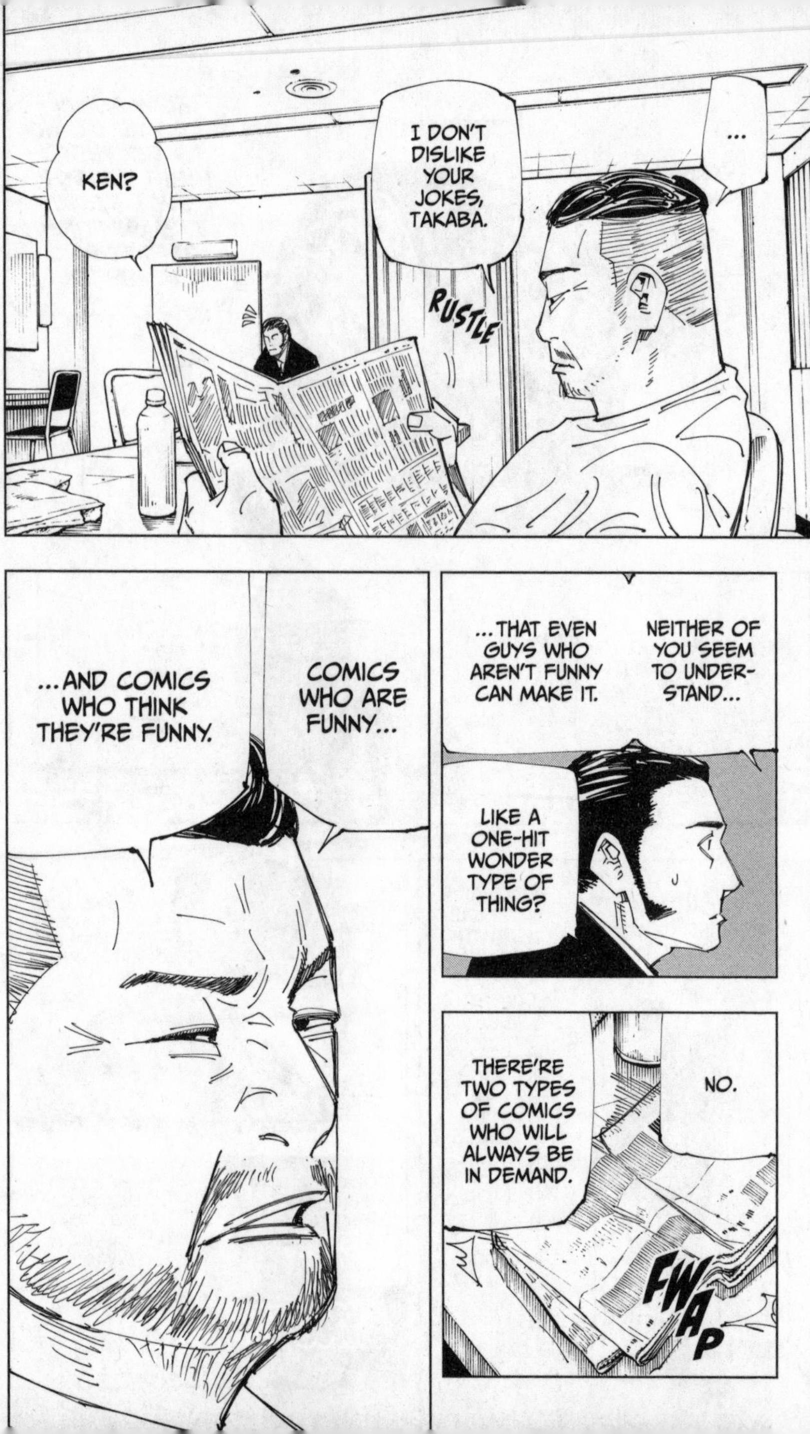
...
I DON'T DISLIKE YOUR JOKES, TAKABA.
RUSTLE
KEN?
NEITHER OF YOU SEEM TO UNDERSTAND...
...THAT EVEN GUYS WHO AREN'T FUNNY CAN MAKE IT.
LIKE A ONE-HIT WONDER TYPE OF THING?
NO.
THERE'RE TWO TYPES OF COMICS WHO WILL ALWAYS BE IN DEMAND.
FWAP
COMICS WHO ARE FUNNY...
...AND COMICS WHO THINK THEY'RE FUNNY.

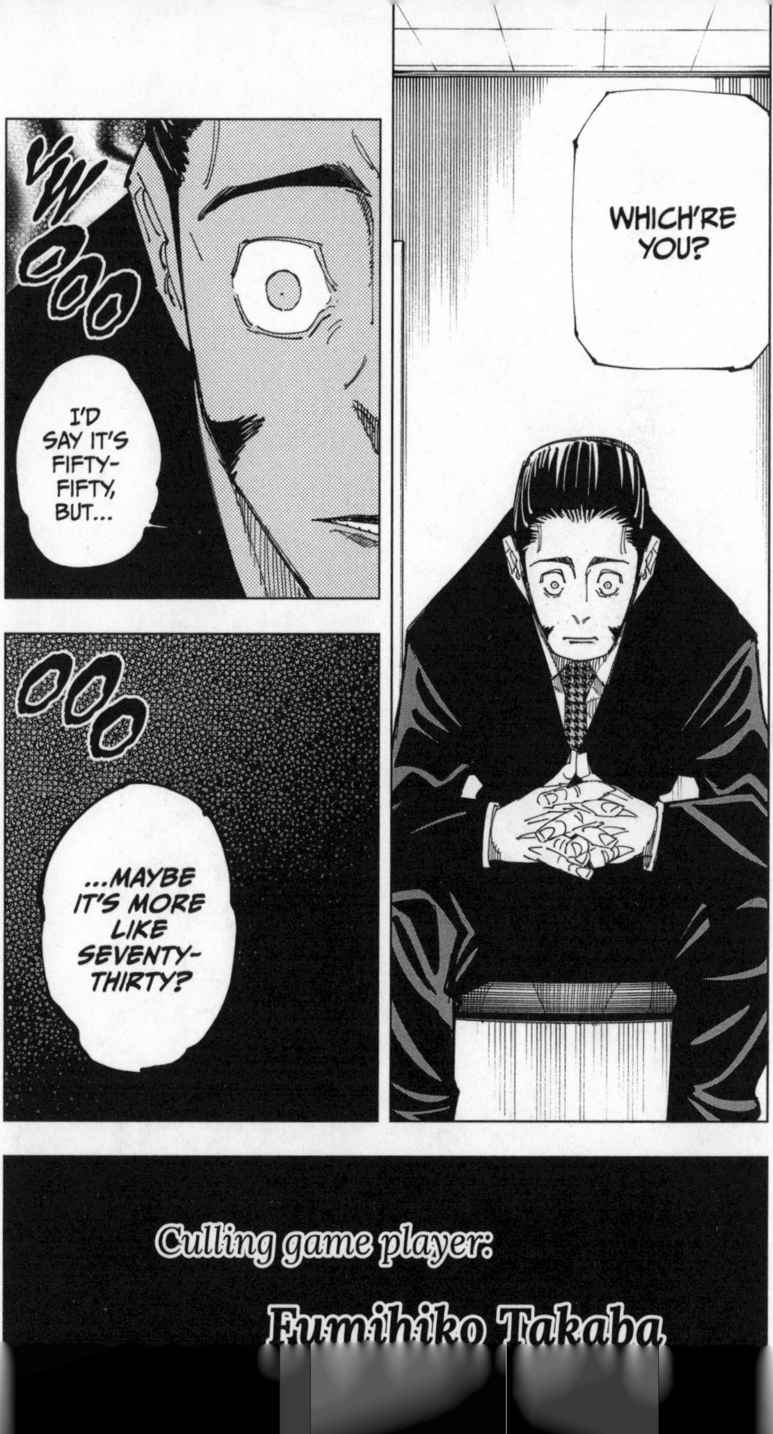
WHICH'RE YOU?
I'D SAY IT'S FIFTY-FIFTY, BUT...
...MAYBE IT'S MORE LIKE SEVENTY-THIRTY?
Culling game player:
Fumihiko Takaba

RANTA

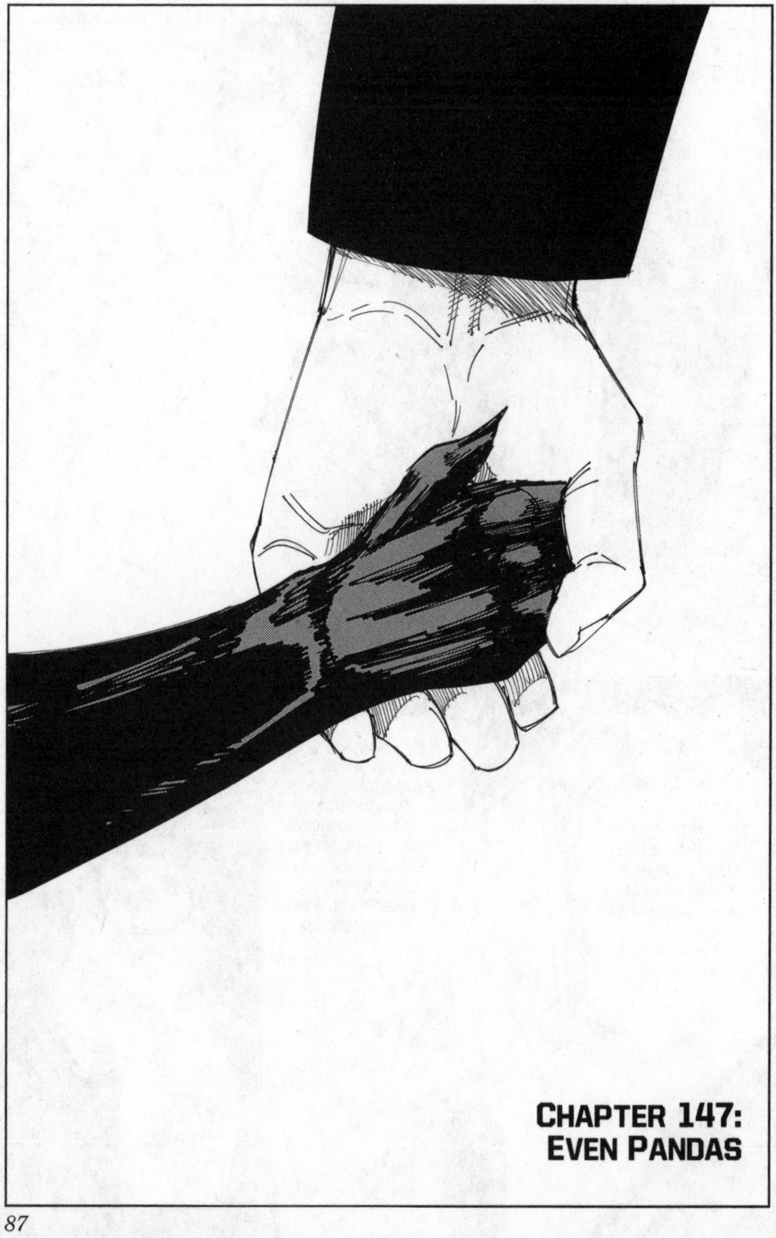

Chapter 147: Even Pandas

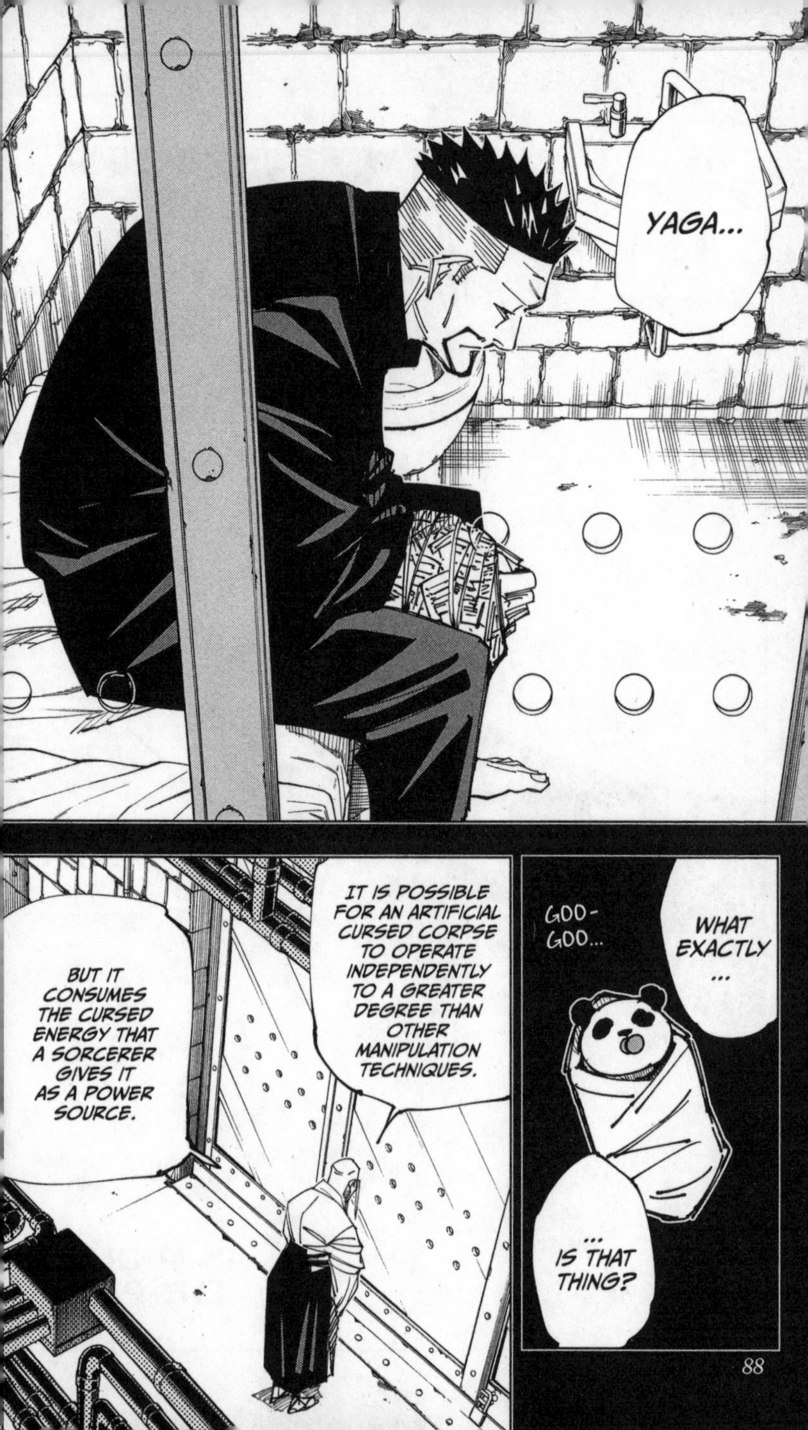
YAGA...
WHAT EXACTLY ...
GOO-GOO...
... IS THAT THING?
IT IS POSSIBLE FOR AN ARTIFICIAL CURSED CORPSE TO OPERATE INDEPENDENTLY TO A GREATER DEGREE THAN OTHER MANIPULATION TECHNIQUES.
BUT IT CONSUMES THE CURSED ENERGY THAT A SORCERER GIVES IT AS A POWER SOURCE.

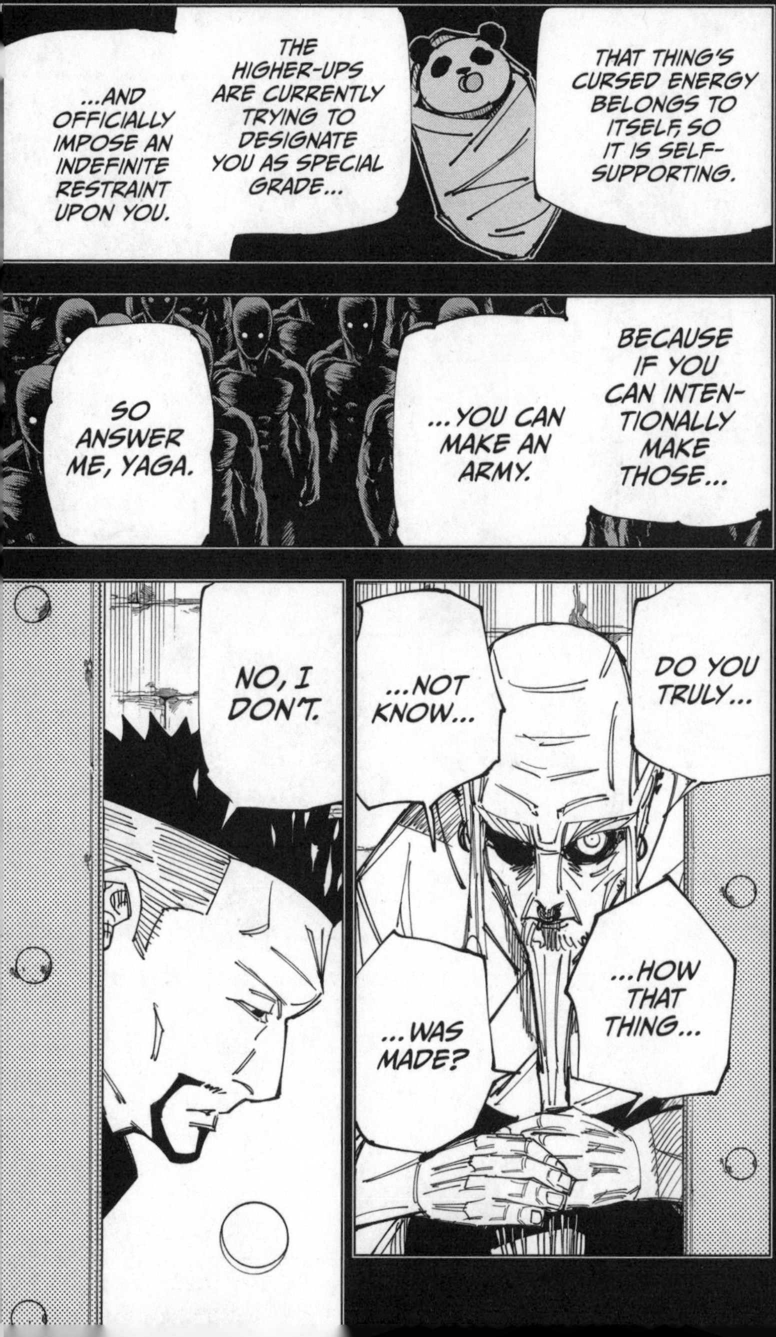
THAT THING'S CURSED ENERGY BELONGS TO ITSELF, SO IT IS SELF-SUPPORTING.
THE HIGHER-UPS ARE CURRENTLY TRYING TO DESIGNATE YOU AS SPECIAL GRADE...
...AND OFFICIALLY IMPOSE AN INDEFINITE RESTRAINT UPON YOU.
BECAUSE IF YOU CAN INTENTIONALLY MAKE THOSE...
...YOU CAN MAKE AN ARMY.
SO ANSWER ME, YAGA.
DO YOU TRULY...
...NOT KNOW...
...HOW THAT THING...
...WAS MADE?
NO, I DON'T.

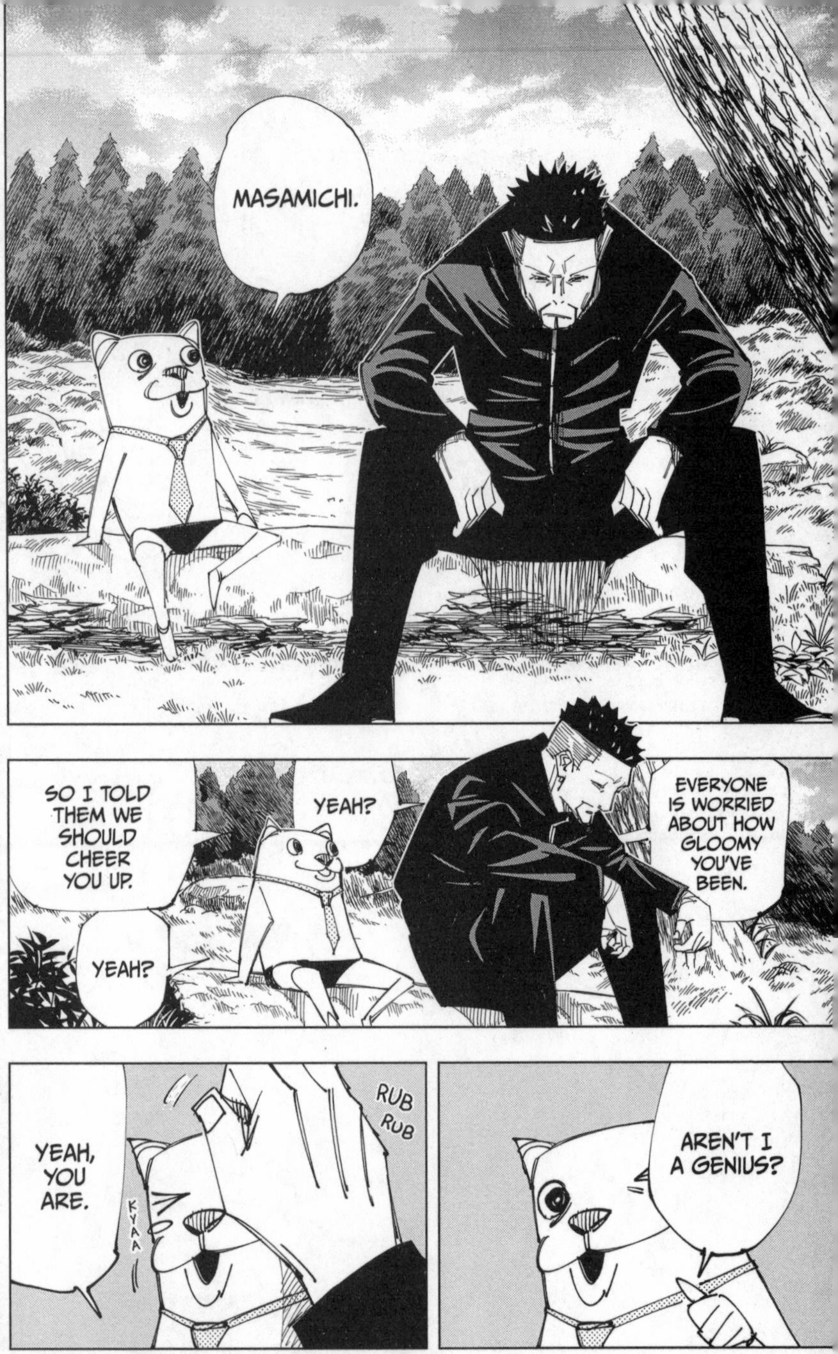

MASAMICHI.
EVERYONE IS WORRIED ABOUT HOW GLOOMY YOU'VE BEEN.
YEAH?
SO I TOLD THEM WE SHOULD CHEER YOU UP.
YEAH?
AREN'T I A GENIUS?
RUB RUB
YEAH, YOU ARE.
KYAA

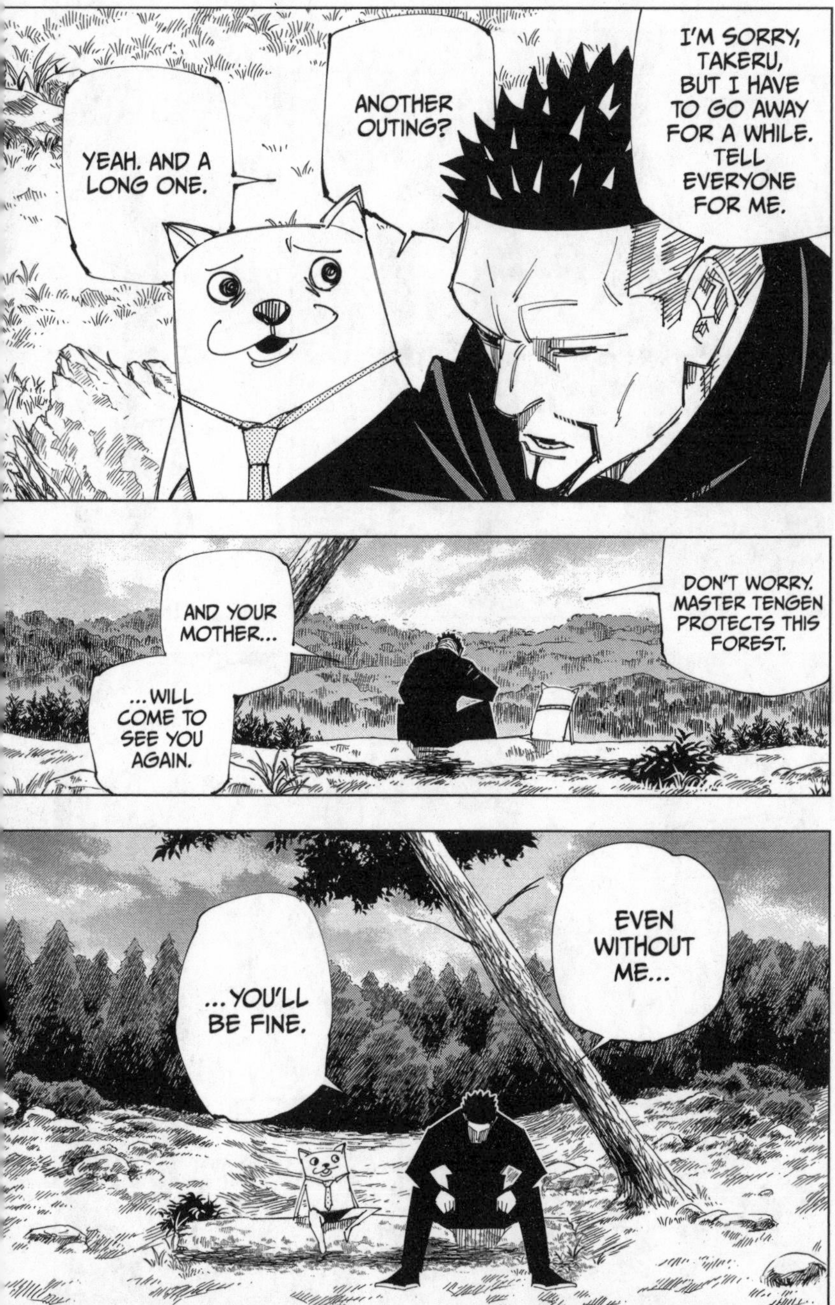
I'M SORRY, TAKERU, BUT I HAVE TO GO AWAY FOR A WHILE. TELL EVERYONE FOR ME.
ANOTHER OUTING?
YEAH. AND A LONG ONE.
DON'T WORRY. MASTER TENGEN PROTECTS THIS FOREST.
AND YOUR MOTHER...
...WILL COME TO SEE YOU AGAIN.
EVEN WITHOUT ME...
...YOU'LL BE FINE.

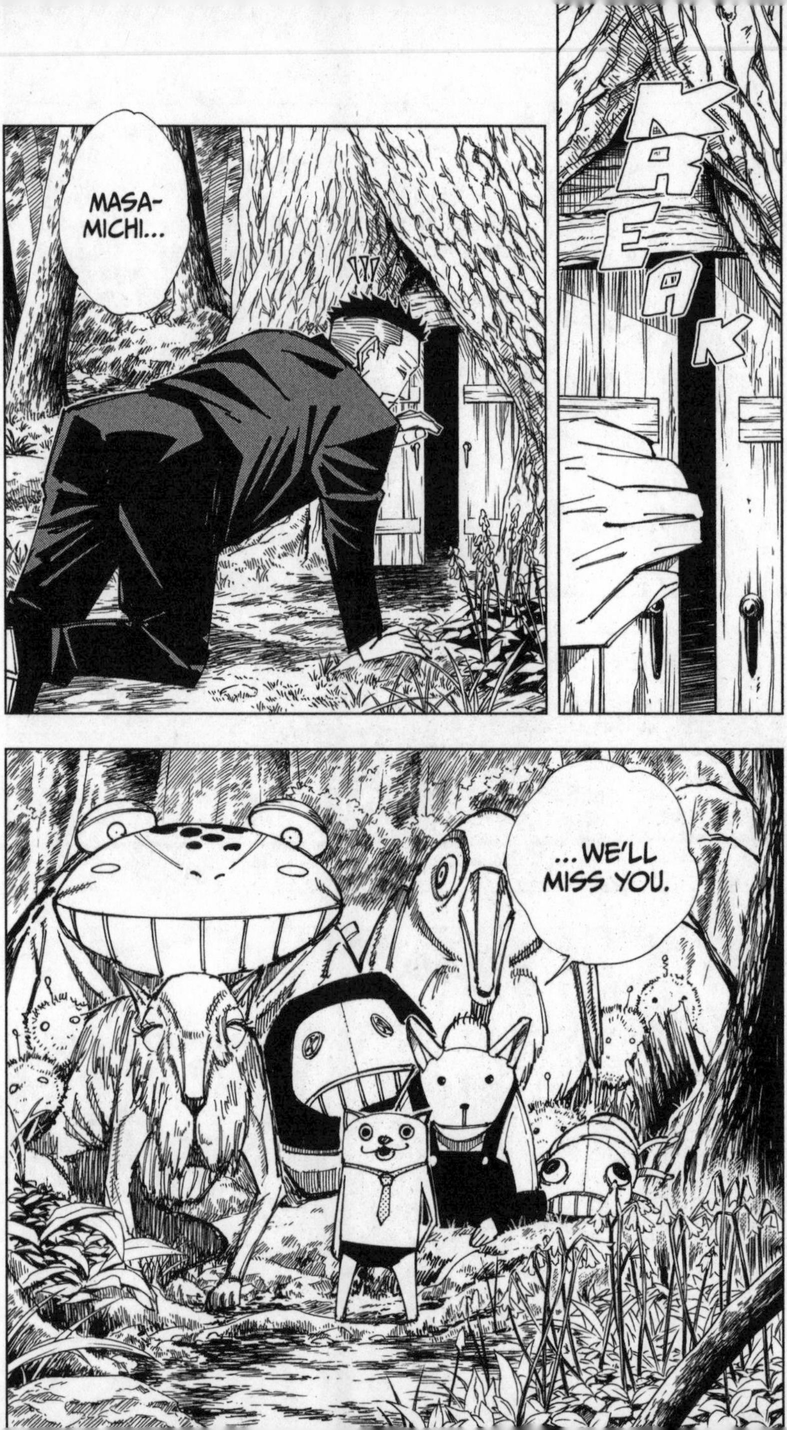
KREAK
MASA-MICHI...
...WE'LL MISS YOU.

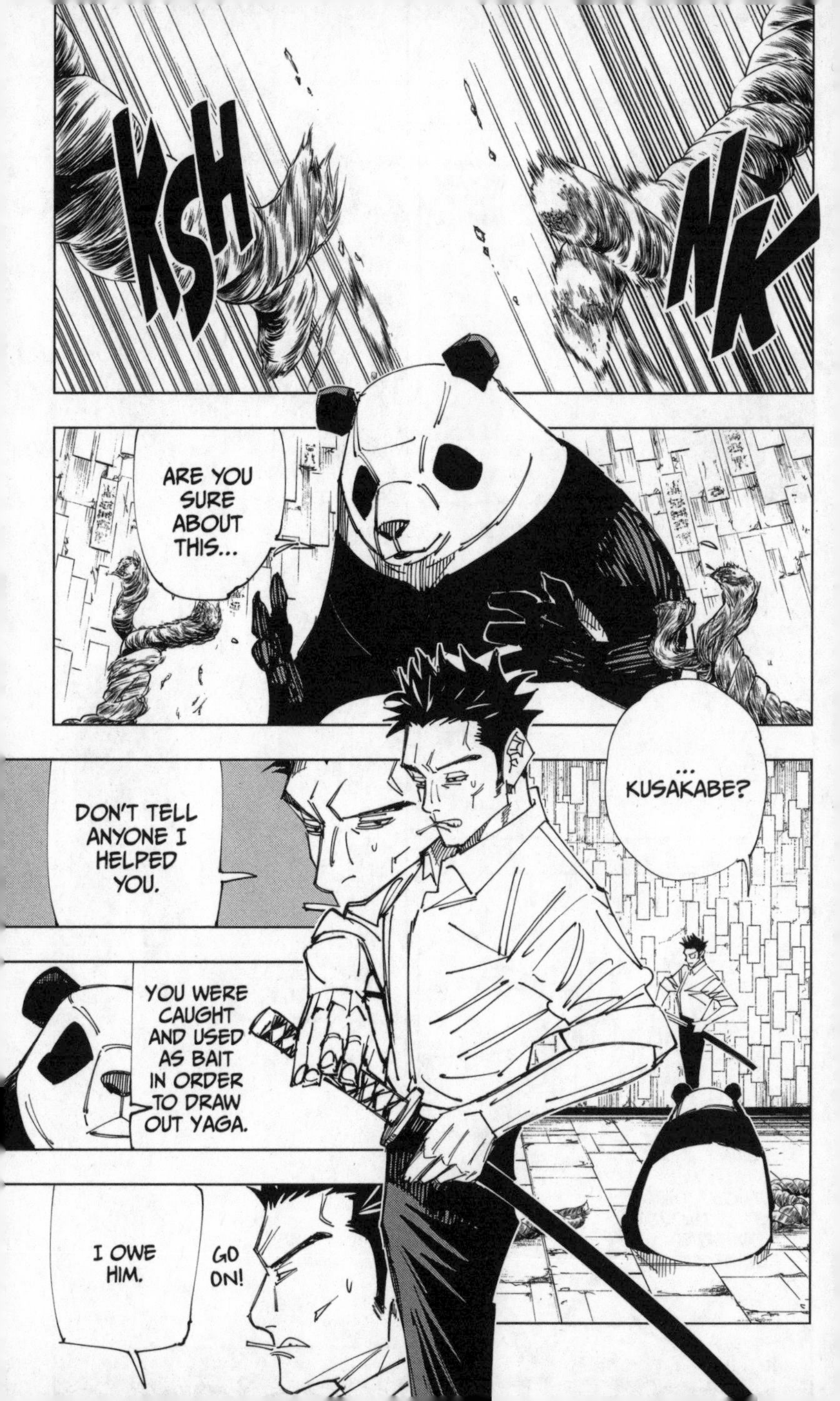

KSH
NK
ARE YOU SURE ABOUT THIS...
... KUSAKABE?
DON'T TELL ANYONE I HELPED YOU.
YOU WERE CAUGHT AND USED AS BAIT IN ORDER TO DRAW OUT YAGA.
GO ON!
I OWE HIM.

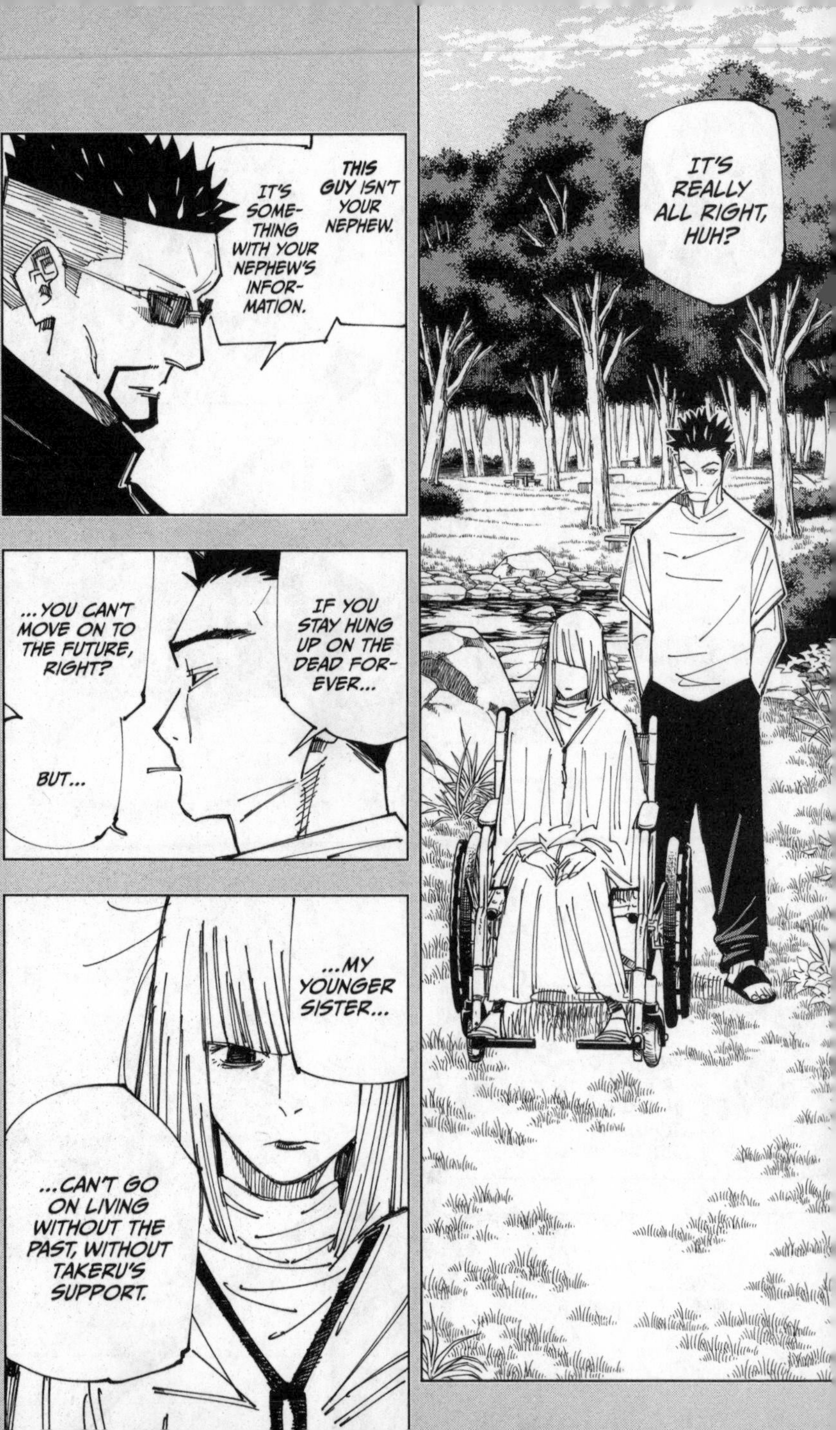
IT'S REALLY ALL RIGHT, HUH?
THIS GUY ISN'T YOUR NEPHEW.
IT'S SOMETHING WITH YOUR NEPHEW'S INFORMATION.
IF YOU STAY HUNG UP ON THE DEAD FOREVER...
...YOU CAN'T MOVE ON TO THE FUTURE, RIGHT?
BUT...
...MY YOUNGER SISTER...
...CAN'T GO ON LIVING WITHOUT THE PAST, WITHOUT TAKERU'S SUPPORT.

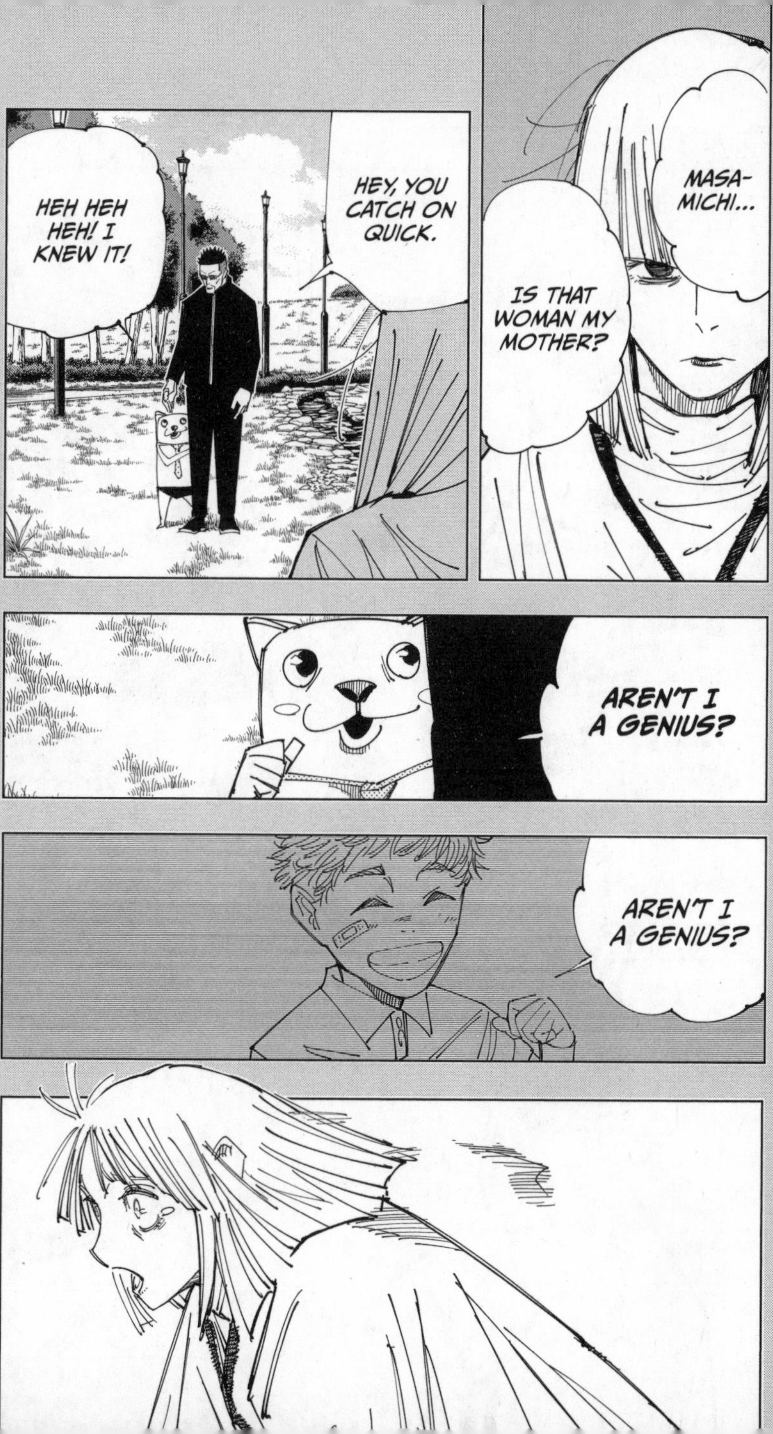
MASA-MICHI...
IS THAT WOMAN MY MOTHER?
HEY, YOU CATCH ON QUICK.
HEH HEH HEH! I KNEW IT!
AREN'T I A GENIUS?
AREN'T I A GENIUS?

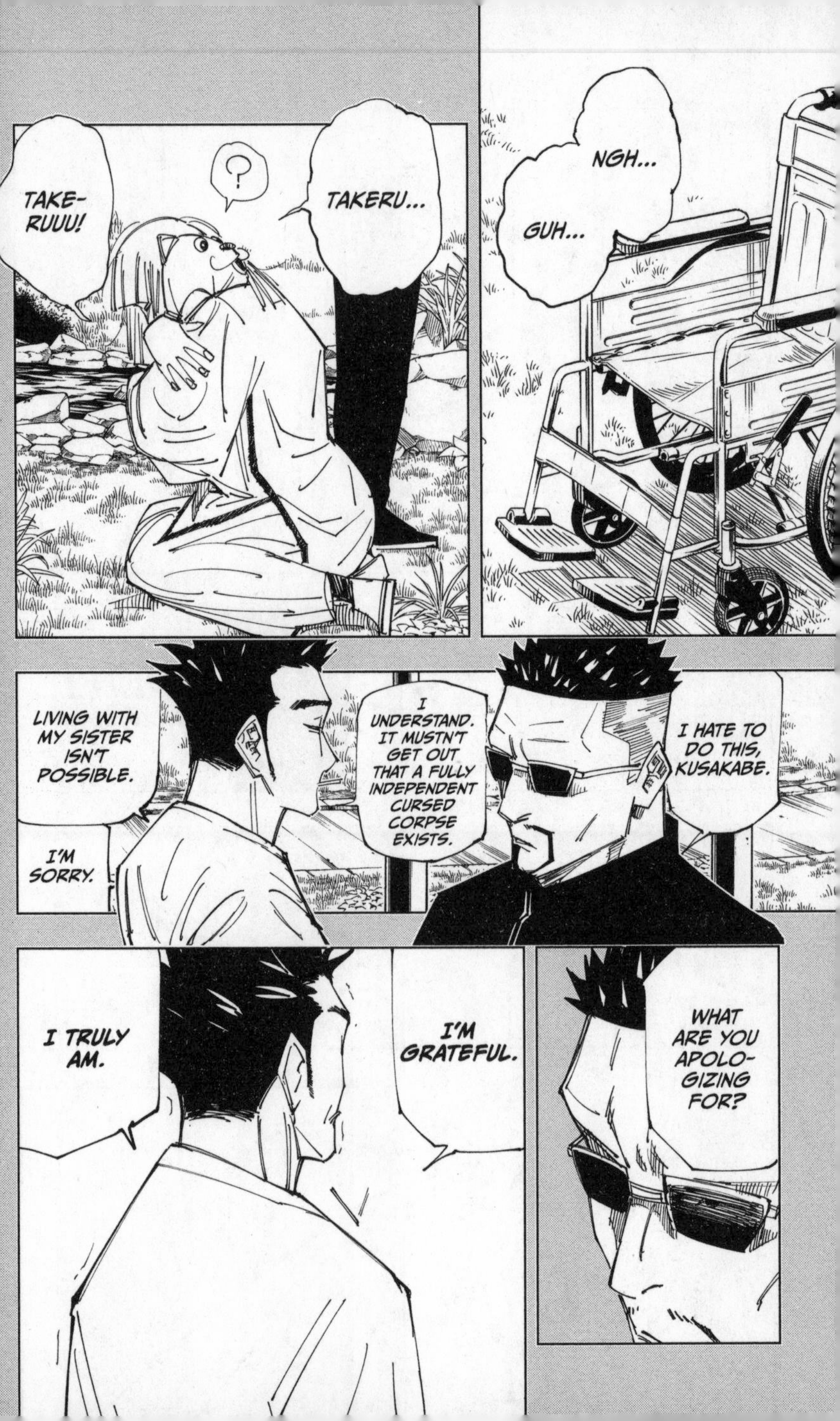
NGH...
GUH...
TAKERU...
?
TAKE-RUUU!
I HATE TO DO THIS, KUSAKABE.
I UNDERSTAND. IT MUSTN'T GET OUT THAT A FULLY INDEPENDENT CURSED CORPSE EXISTS.
LIVING WITH MY SISTER ISN'T POSSIBLE.
I'M SORRY.
WHAT ARE YOU APOLOGIZING FOR?
I'M GRATEFUL.
I TRULY AM.

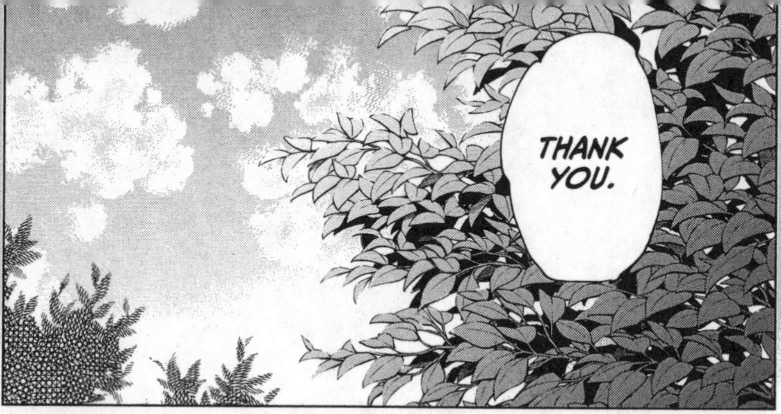
THANK YOU.
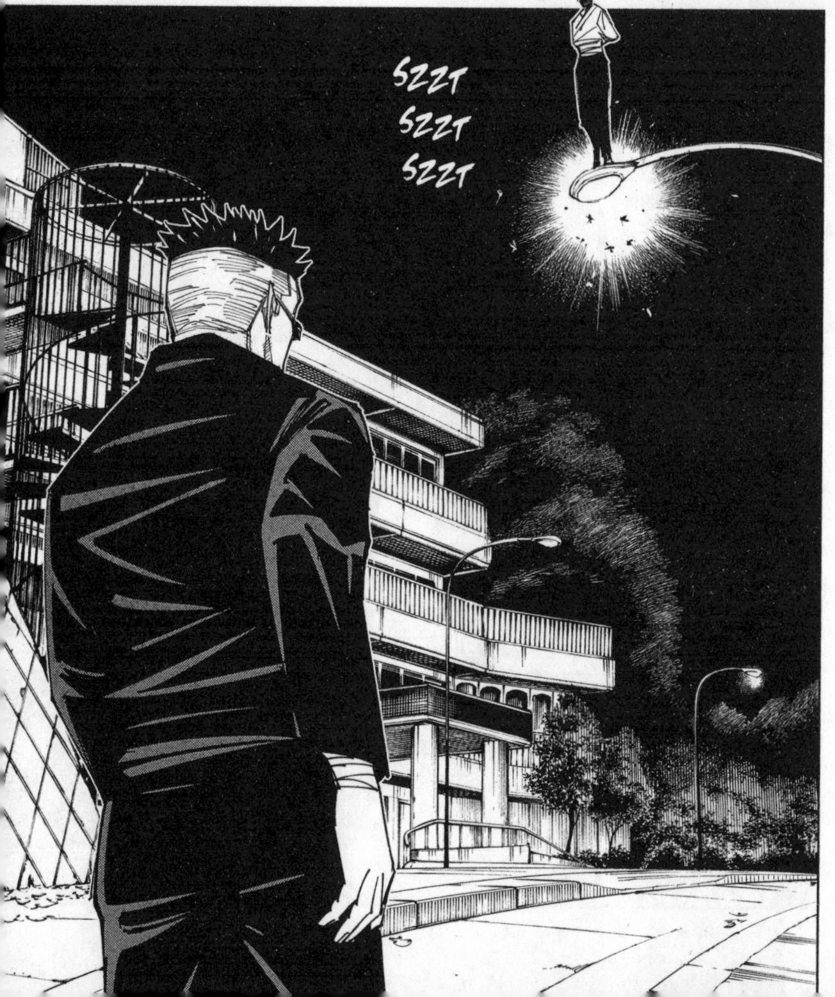
SZZT
SZZT
SZZT

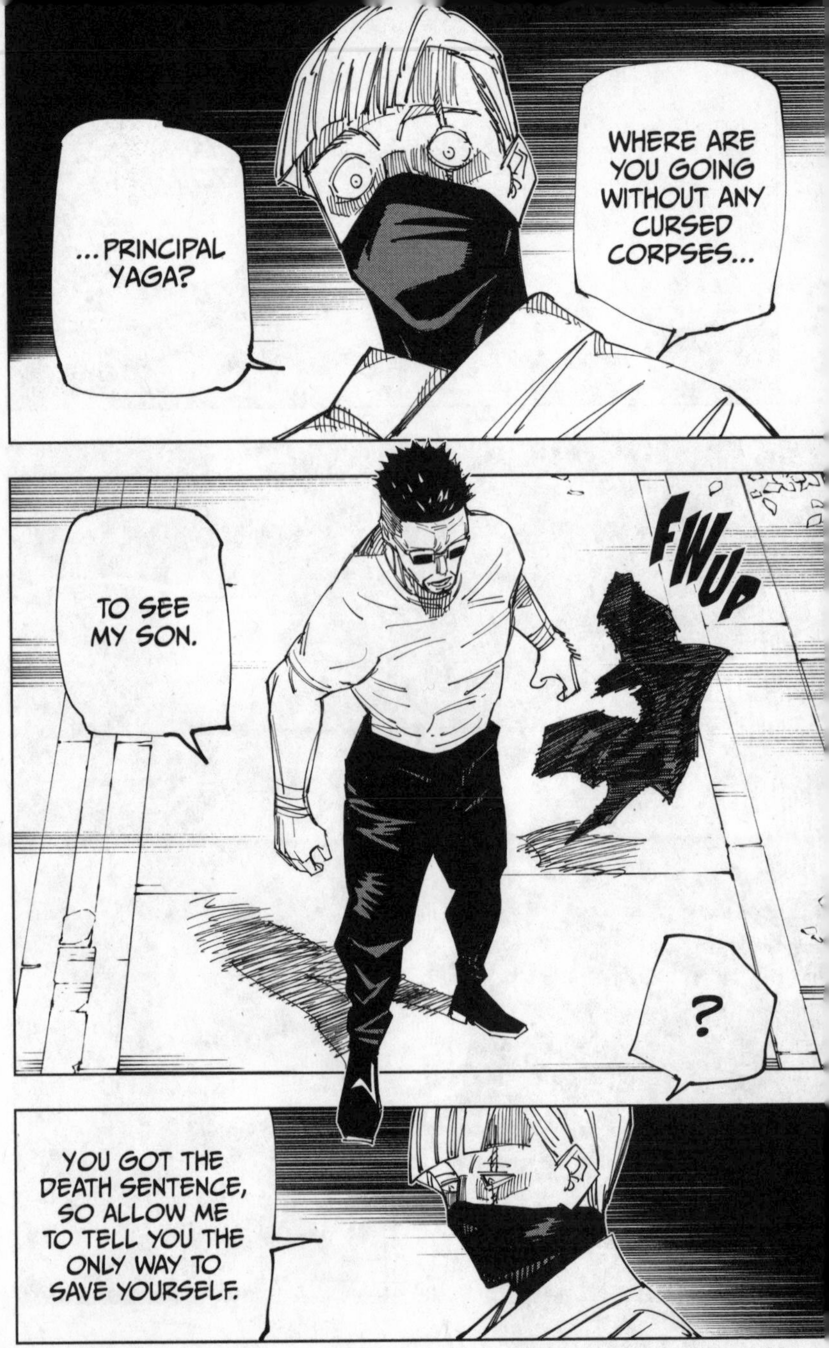
WHERE ARE YOU GOING WITHOUT ANY CURSED CORPSES...
...PRINCIPAL YAGA?
FWUP
TO SEE MY SON.
?
YOU GOT THE DEATH SENTENCE, SO ALLOW ME TO TELL YOU THE ONLY WAY TO SAVE YOURSELF.

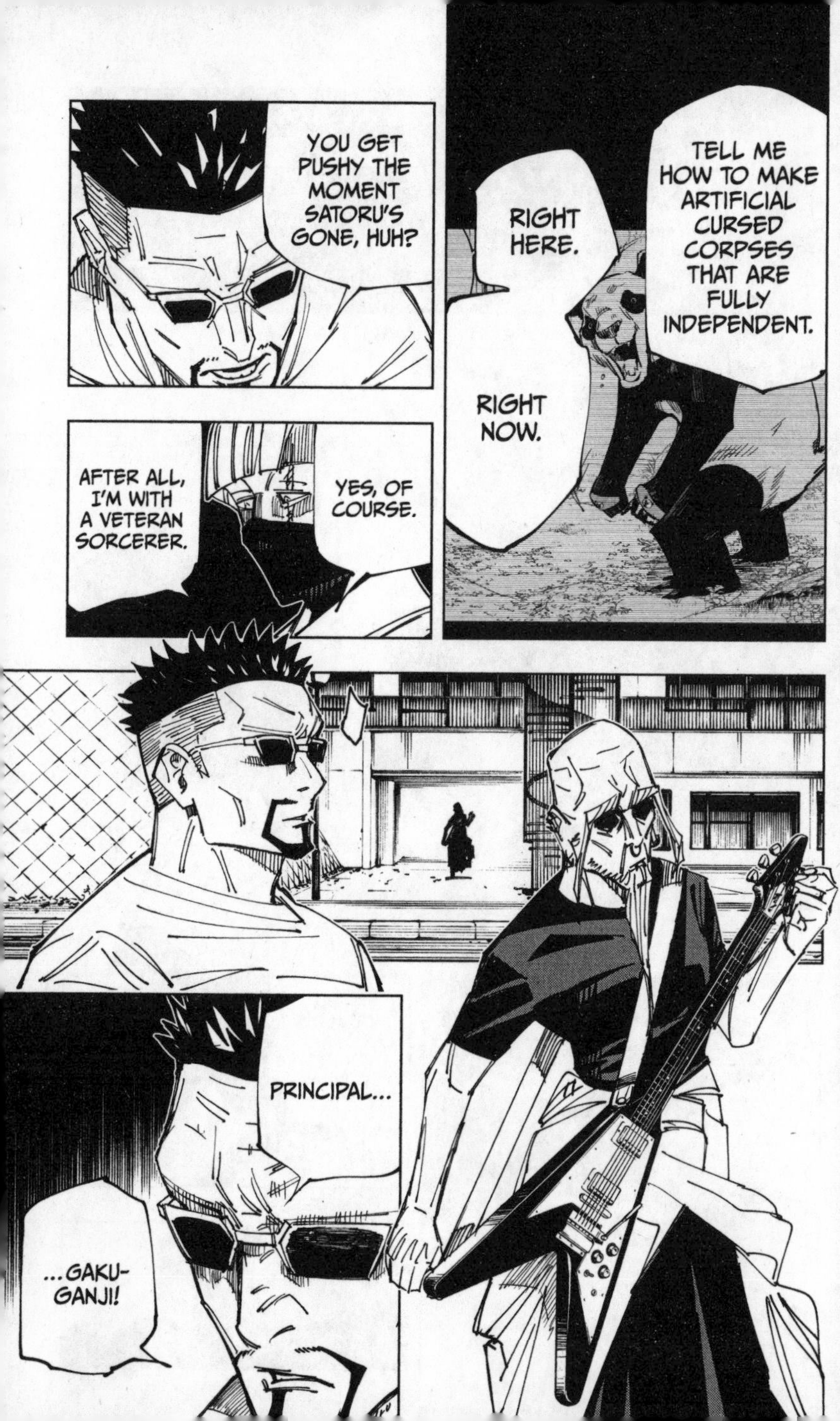
TELL ME HOW TO MAKE ARTIFICIAL CURSED CORPSES THAT ARE FULLY INDEPENDENT.
RIGHT HERE.
RIGHT NOW.
YOU GET PUSHY THE MOMENT SATORU'S GONE, HUH?
YES, OF COURSE.
AFTER ALL, I'M WITH A VETERAN SORCERER.
PRINCIPAL...
...GAKU-GANJI!

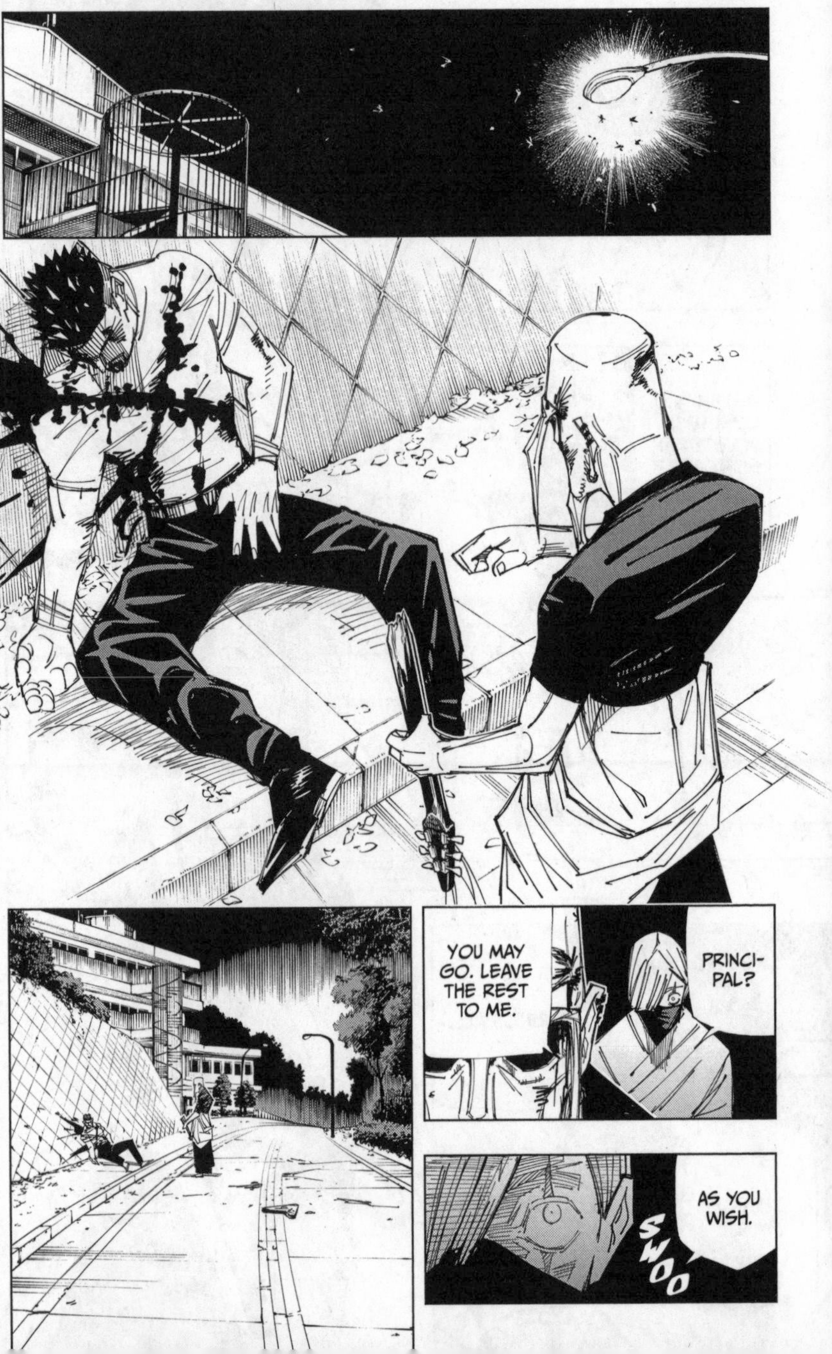
PRINCI-PAL?
YOU MAY GO. LEAVE THE REST TO ME.
AS YOU WISH.
SWOO

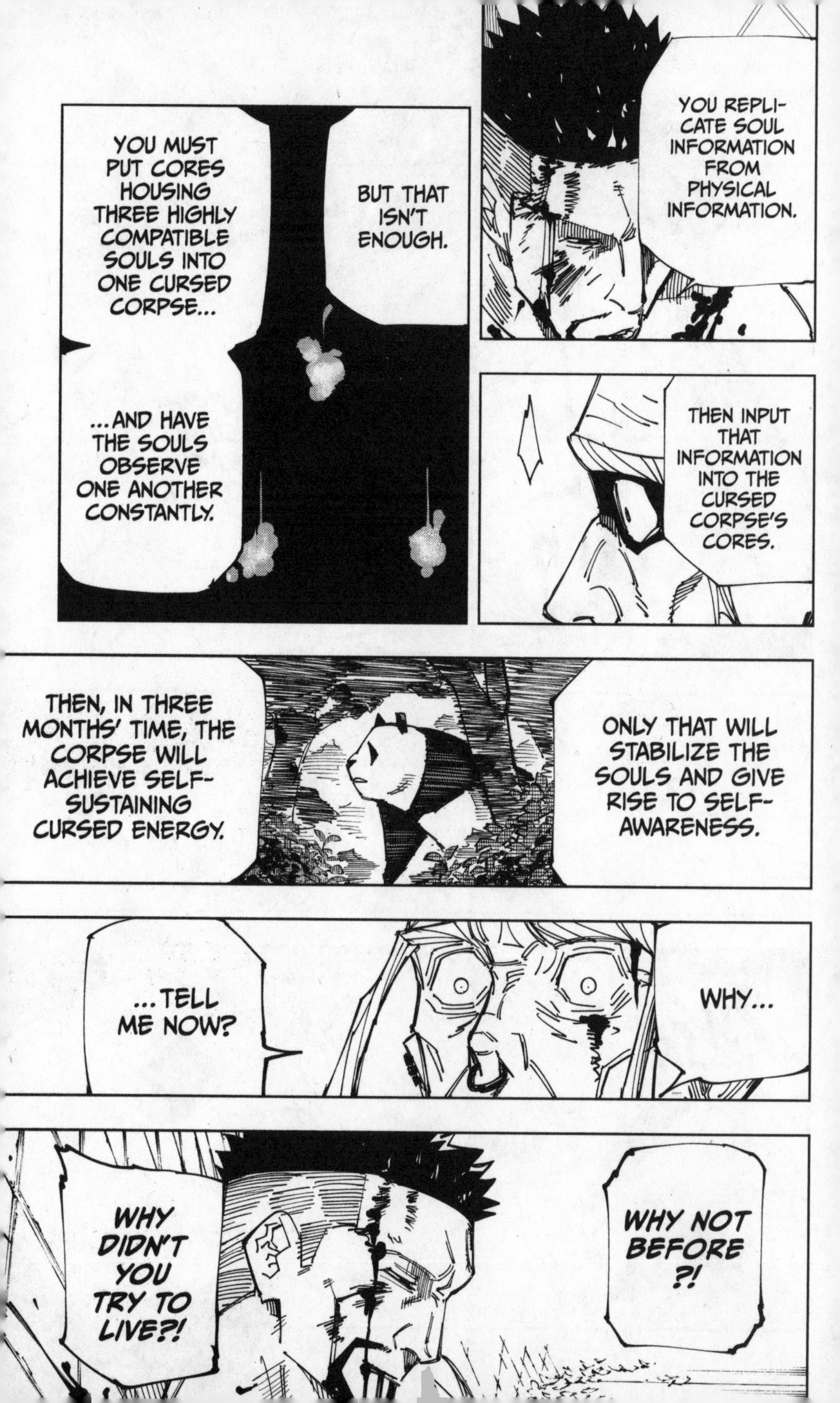
YOU REPLICATE SOUL INFORMATION FROM PHYSICAL INFORMATION.
THEN INPUT THAT INFORMATION INTO THE CURSED CORPSE'S CORES.
BUT THAT ISN'T ENOUGH.
YOU MUST PUT CORES HOUSING THREE HIGHLY COMPATIBLE SOULS INTO ONE CURSED CORPSE...
...AND HAVE THE SOULS OBSERVE ONE ANOTHER CONSTANTLY.
ONLY THAT WILL STABILIZE THE SOULS AND GIVE RISE TO SELF-AWARENESS.
THEN, IN THREE MONTHS' TIME, THE CORPSE WILL ACHIEVE SELF-SUSTAINING CURSED ENERGY.
WHY...
...TELL ME NOW?
WHY NOT BEFORE?!
WHY DIDN'T YOU TRY TO LIVE?!

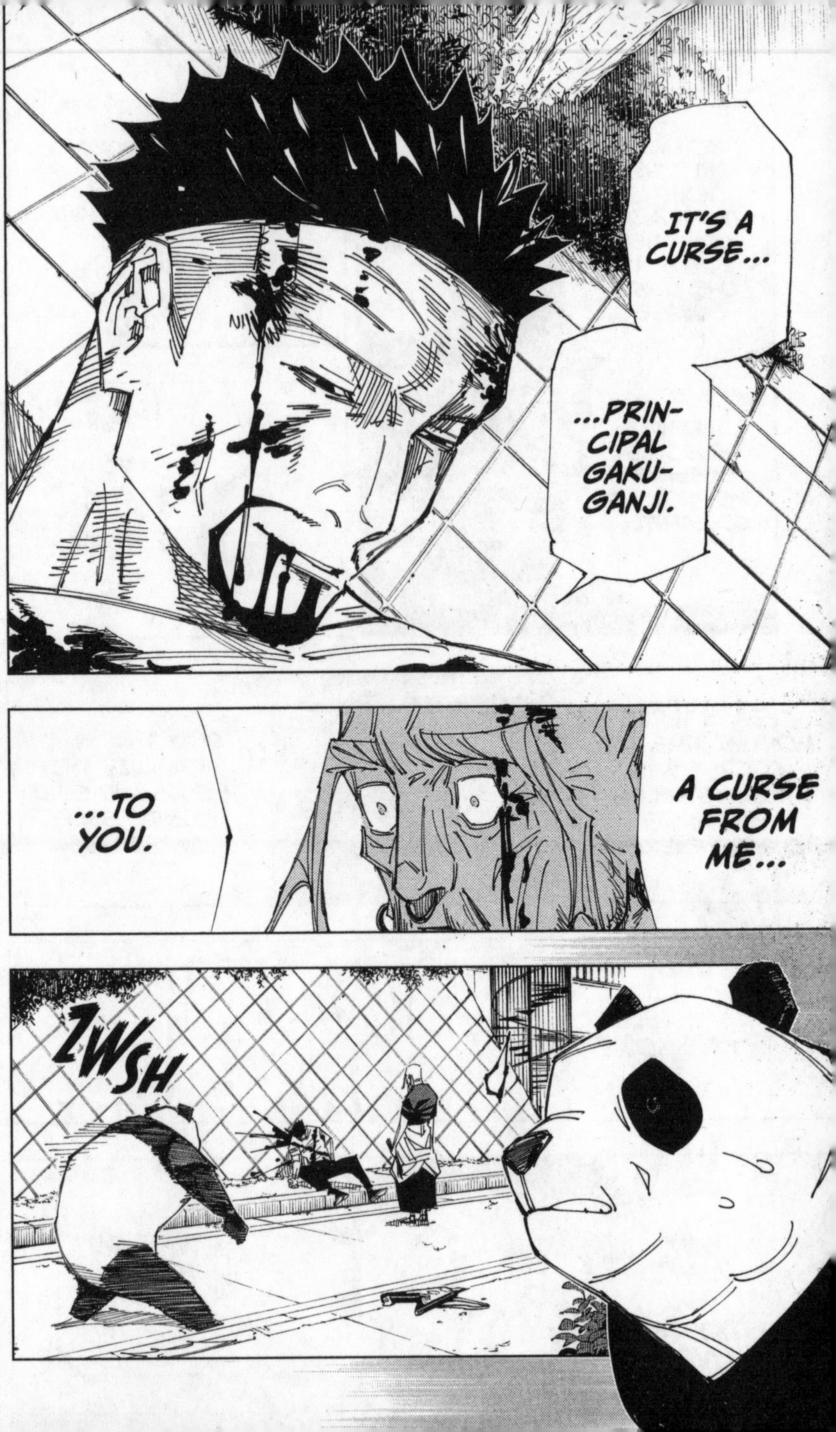
IT'S A CURSE...
...PRIN-CIPAL GAKU-GANJI.
A CURSE FROM ME...
...TO YOU.
ZWSH

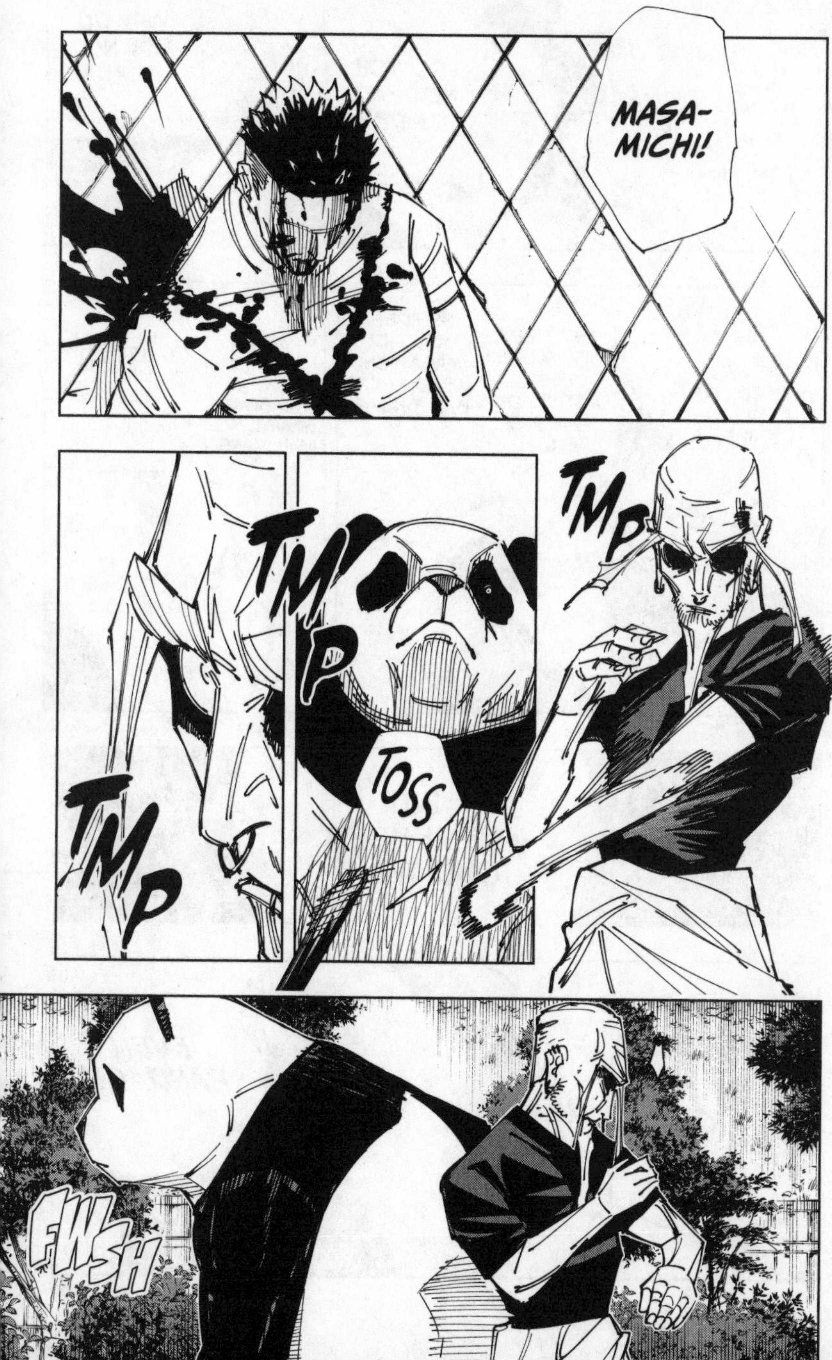
MASA-
MICHI!
TMP
TMP
TOSS
TMP
FWSH

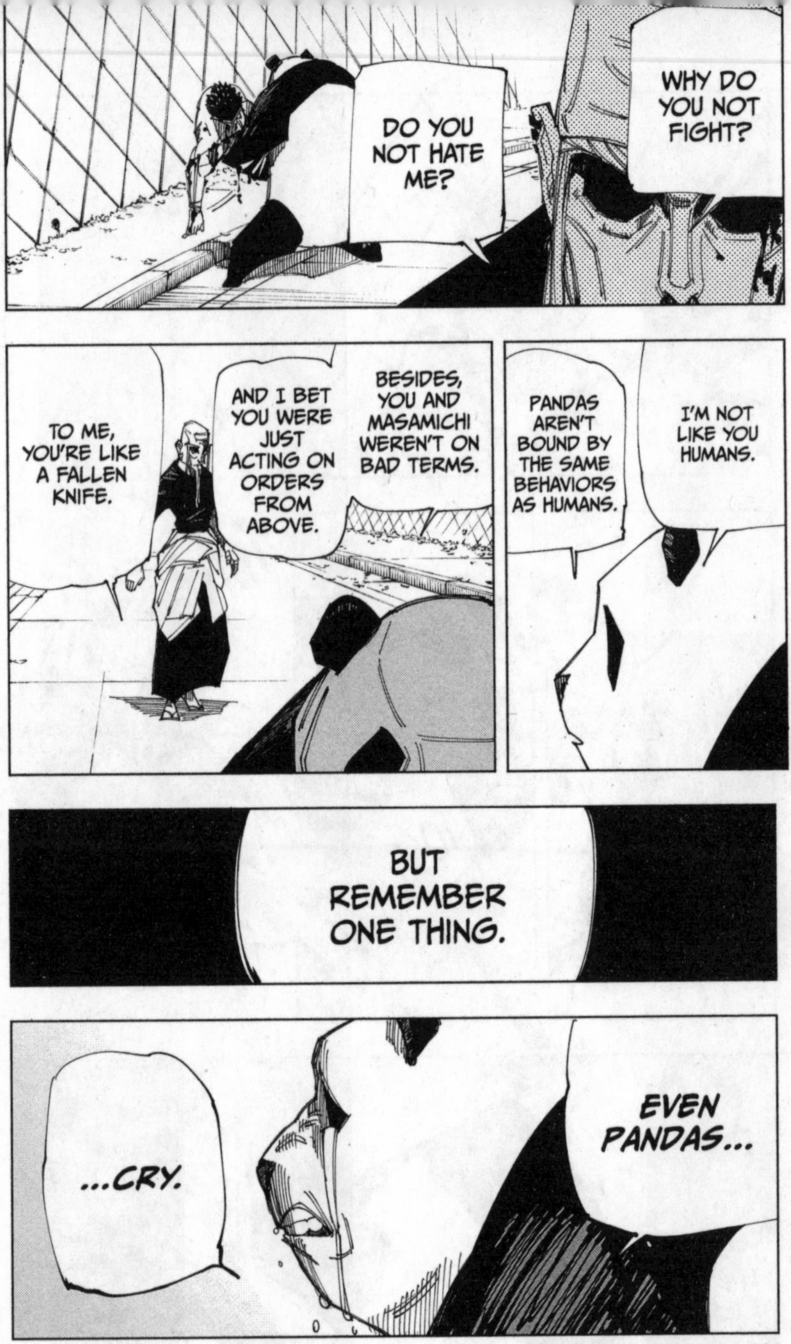
WHY DO YOU NOT FIGHT?
DO YOU NOT HATE ME?
I'M NOT LIKE YOU HUMANS.
PANDAS AREN'T BOUND BY THE SAME BEHAVIORS AS HUMANS.
BESIDES, YOU AND MASAMICHI WEREN'T ON BAD TERMS.
AND I BET YOU WERE JUST ACTING ON ORDERS FROM ABOVE.
TO ME, YOU'RE LIKE A FALLEN KNIFE.
BUT REMEMBER ONE THING.
EVEN PANDAS...
...CRY.

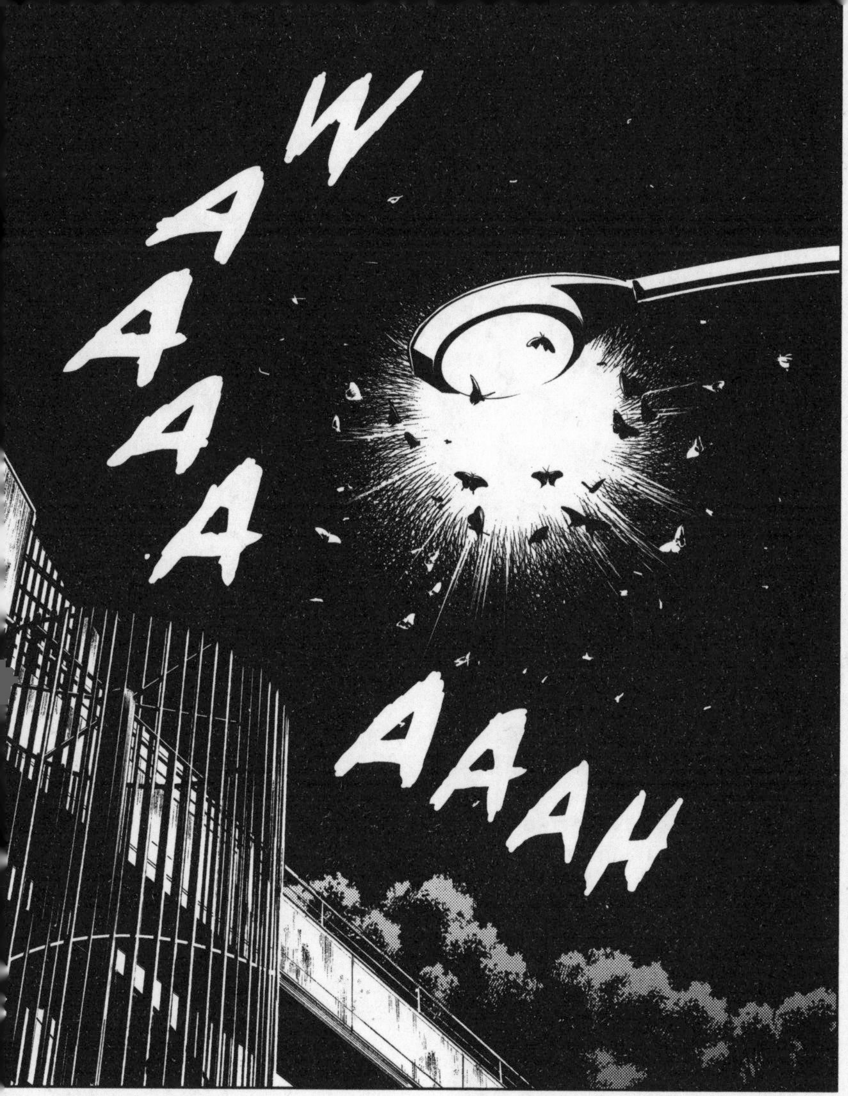
WAAAAAAAAH
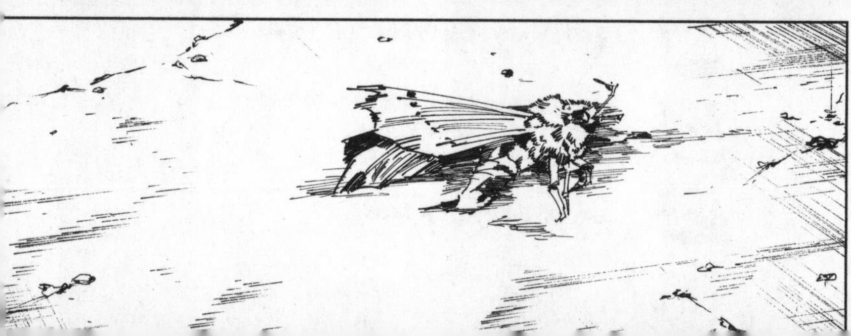

KUKURU UNIT (1) HEI REVIEW!!

• NOBITO

3.7 ⭐⭐⭐⭐⭐

 HE DOESN'T HAVE MUCH INTEREST IN US. BUT THAT SENSE OF DISTANCE IS JUST RIGHT.

 HE'S NEVER SOBER WHEN MAKING CONVERSATION.

 I WANTED HIM TO LIKE ME, SO I BOUGHT HIM SAKE AS A SOUVENIR. HE SEEMED PRETTY HAPPY. BUT DIDN'T REMEMBER MY FACE AFTERWARD.

• OGI ZEN'IN

1.0 ⭐⭐⭐⭐⭐

 HE ALWAYS SEEMS KIND OF ANGRY.

 HE SUDDENLY ORDERED US TO EMPTY THE CURSED WAREHOUSE. THAT WAS UNPLEASANT.

 HIS WIFE IS SUPER SCARY.

CHAPTER 148: PERFECT PREPARATION

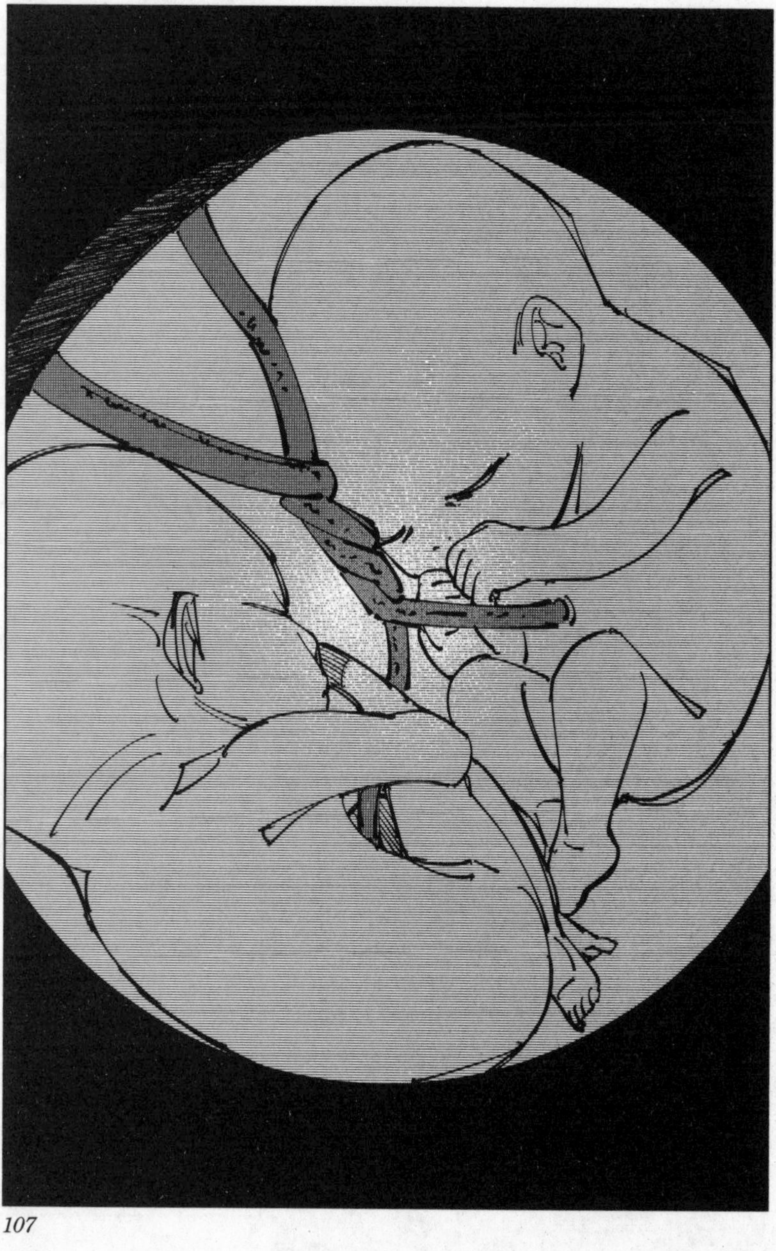

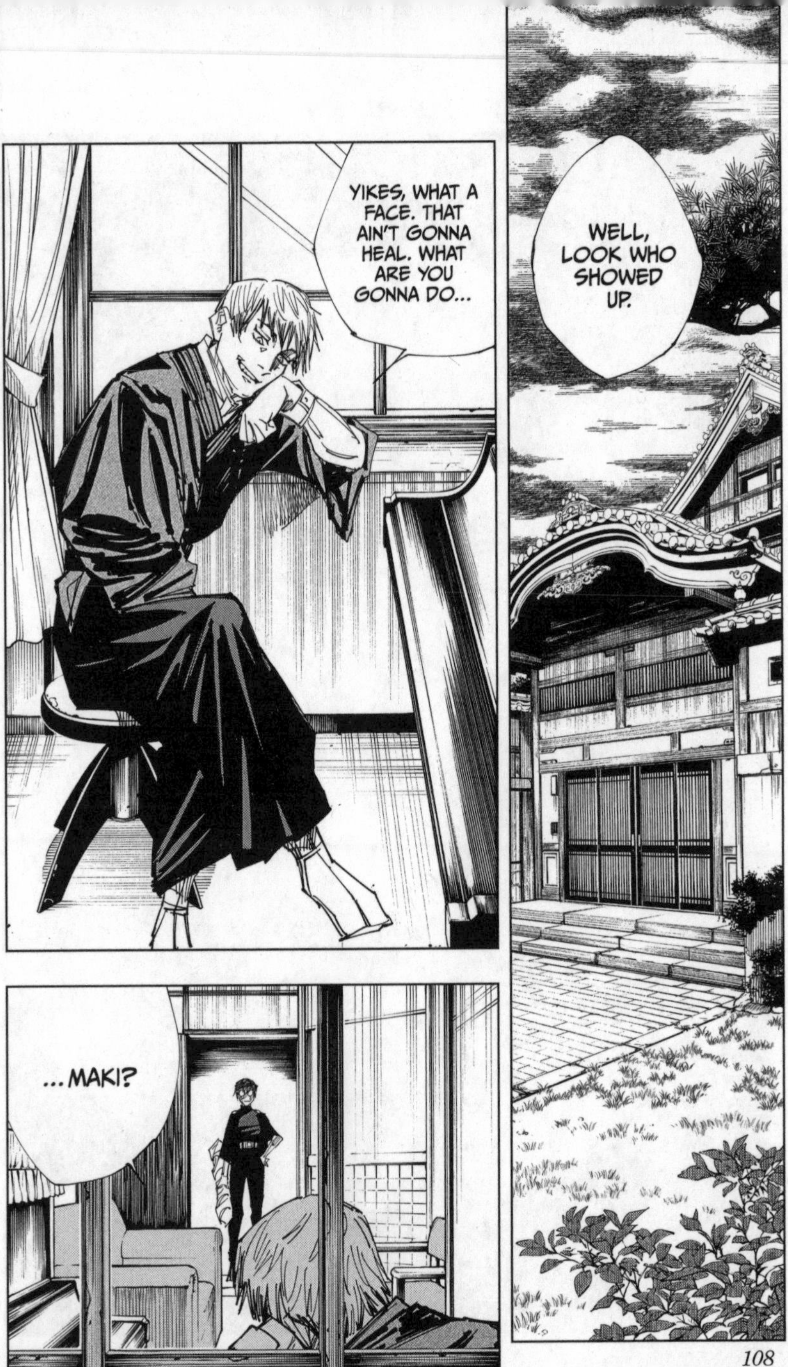
WELL, LOOK WHO SHOWED UP.
YIKES, WHAT A FACE. THAT AIN'T GONNA HEAL. WHAT ARE YOU GONNA DO...
...MAKI?

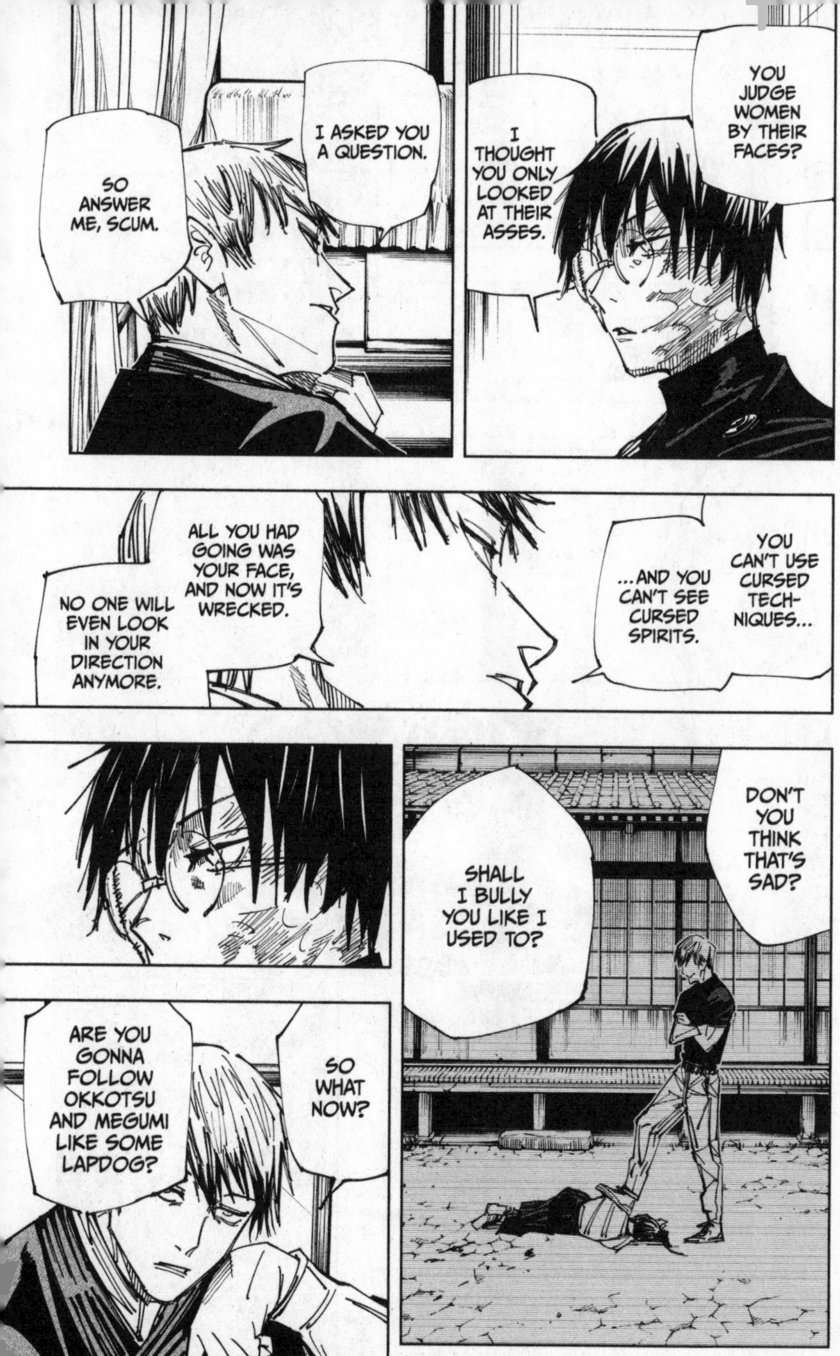
YOU JUDGE WOMEN BY THEIR FACES?
I THOUGHT YOU ONLY LOOKED AT THEIR ASSES.
I ASKED YOU A QUESTION.
SO ANSWER ME, SCUM.
YOU CAN'T USE CURSED TECH-NIQUES...
...AND YOU CAN'T SEE CURSED SPIRITS.
ALL YOU HAD GOING WAS YOUR FACE, AND NOW IT'S WRECKED.
NO ONE WILL EVEN LOOK IN YOUR DIRECTION ANYMORE.
DON'T YOU THINK THAT'S SAD?
SHALL I BULLY YOU LIKE I USED TO?
SO WHAT NOW?
ARE YOU GONNA FOLLOW OKKOTSU AND MEGUMI LIKE SOME LAPDOG?

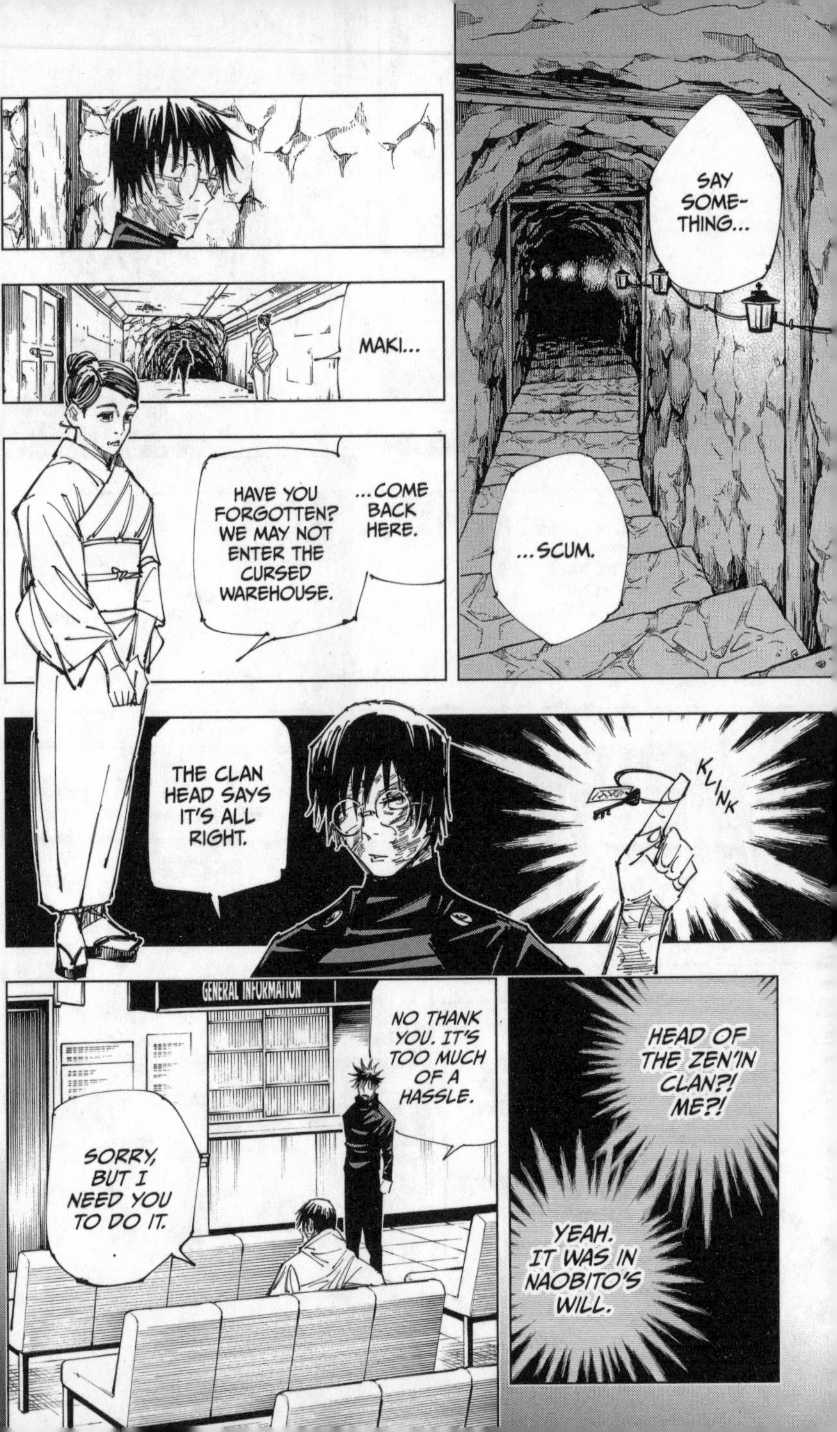
SAY SOMETHING...
...SCUM.
MAKI...
...COME BACK HERE.
HAVE YOU FORGOTTEN? WE MAY NOT ENTER THE CURSED WAREHOUSE.
KLINK
THE CLAN HEAD SAYS IT'S ALL RIGHT.
HEAD OF THE ZEN'IN CLAN?! ME?!
YEAH. IT WAS IN NAOBITO'S WILL.
GENERAL INFORMATION
NO THANK YOU. IT'S TOO MUCH OF A HASSLE.
SORRY, BUT I NEED YOU TO DO IT.

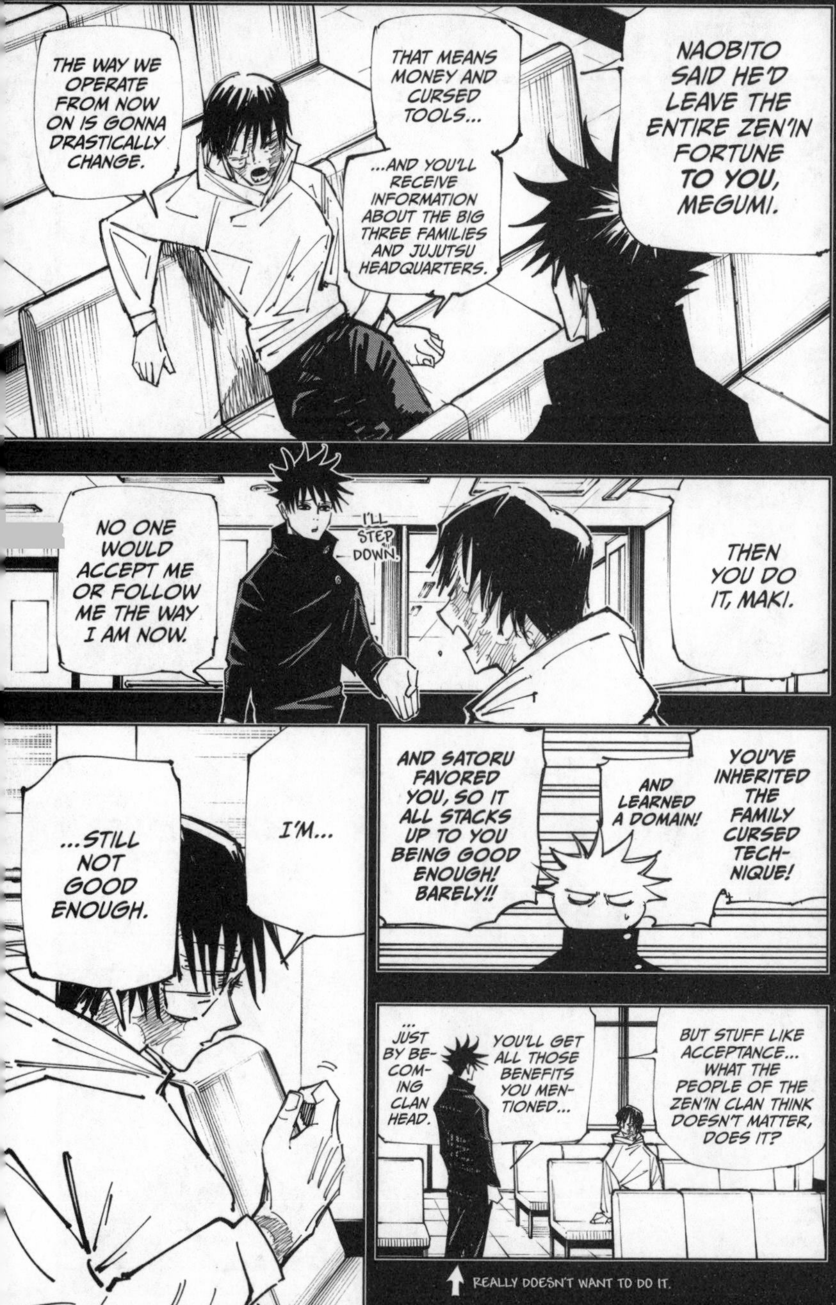
NAOBITO SAID HE'D LEAVE THE ENTIRE ZEN'IN FORTUNE TO YOU, MEGUMI.
THAT MEANS MONEY AND CURSED TOOLS...
...AND YOU'LL RECEIVE INFORMATION ABOUT THE BIG THREE FAMILIES AND JUJUTSU HEADQUARTERS.
THE WAY WE OPERATE FROM NOW ON IS GONNA DRASTICALLY CHANGE.
THEN YOU DO IT, MAKI.
I'LL STEP DOWN.
NO ONE WOULD ACCEPT ME OR FOLLOW ME THE WAY I AM NOW.
YOU'VE INHERITED THE FAMILY CURSED TECH-NIQUE!
AND LEARNED A DOMAIN!
AND SATORU FAVORED YOU, SO IT ALL STACKS UP TO YOU BEING GOOD ENOUGH! BARELY!!
BUT STUFF LIKE ACCEPTANCE... WHAT THE PEOPLE OF THE ZEN'IN CLAN THINK DOESN'T MATTER, DOES IT?
YOU'LL GET ALL THOSE BENEFITS YOU MEN-TIONED...
...JUST BY BE-COM-ING CLAN HEAD.
I'M...
...STILL NOT GOOD ENOUGH.

↑ REALLY DOESN'T WANT TO DO IT.

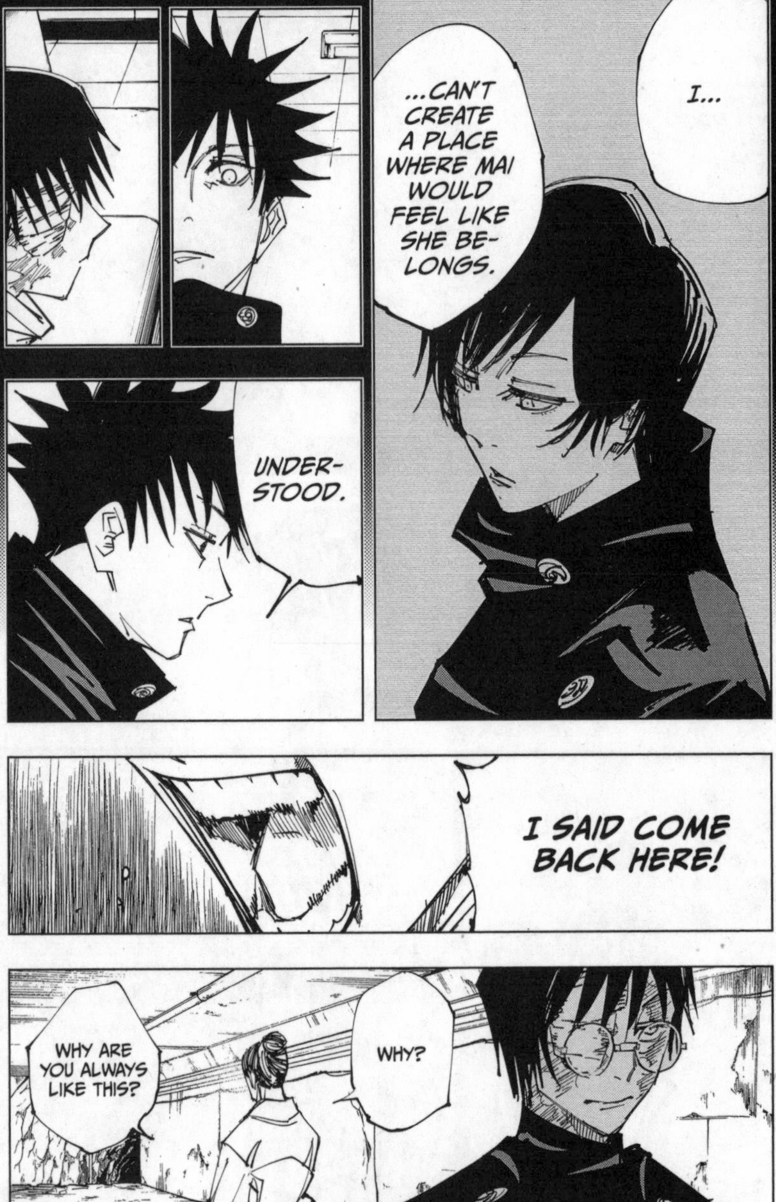
I...
...CAN'T CREATE A PLACE WHERE MAI WOULD FEEL LIKE SHE BE-LONGS.
UNDER-STOOD.
I SAID COME BACK HERE!
WHY?
WHY ARE YOU ALWAYS LIKE THIS?

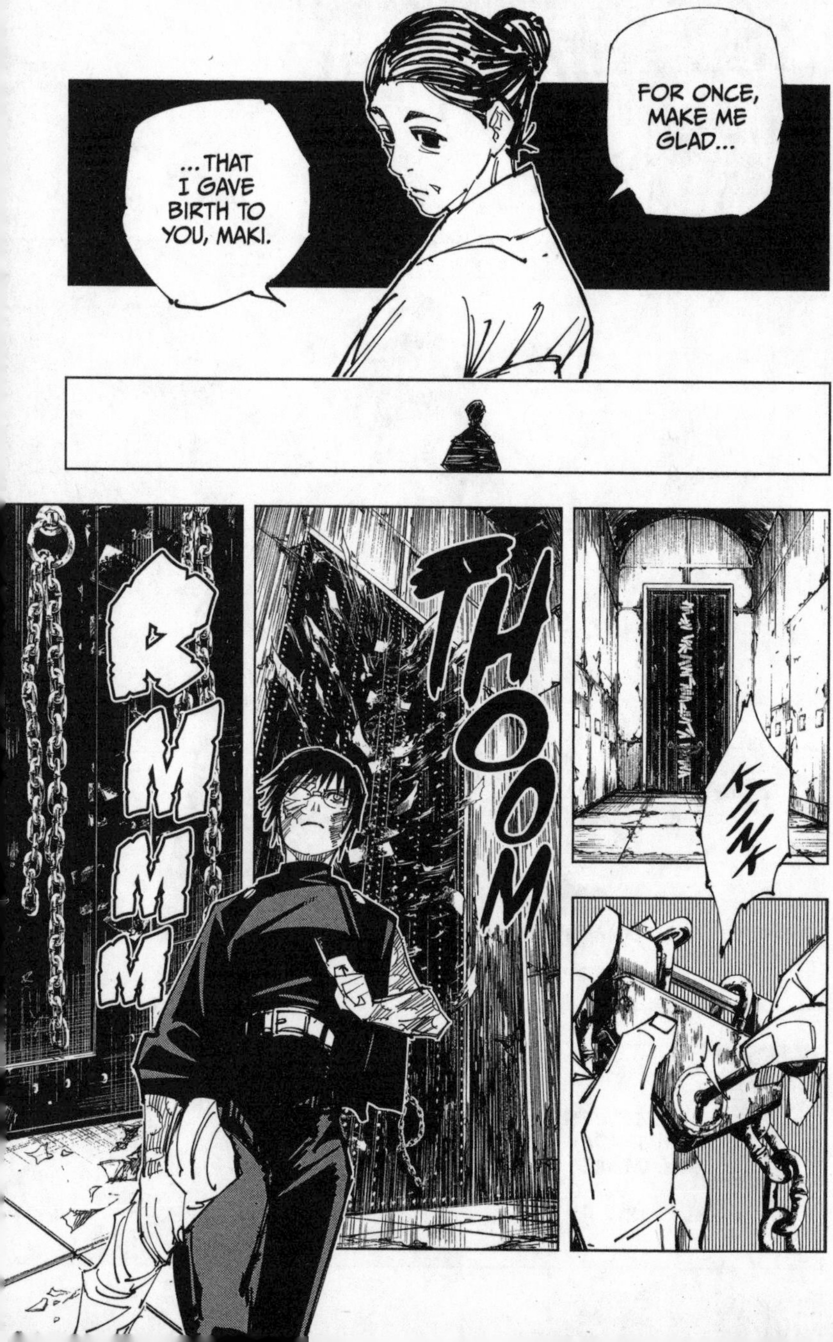
FOR ONCE, MAKE ME GLAD...
...THAT I GAVE BIRTH TO YOU, MAKI.
KLINK
THOOM
RMMM

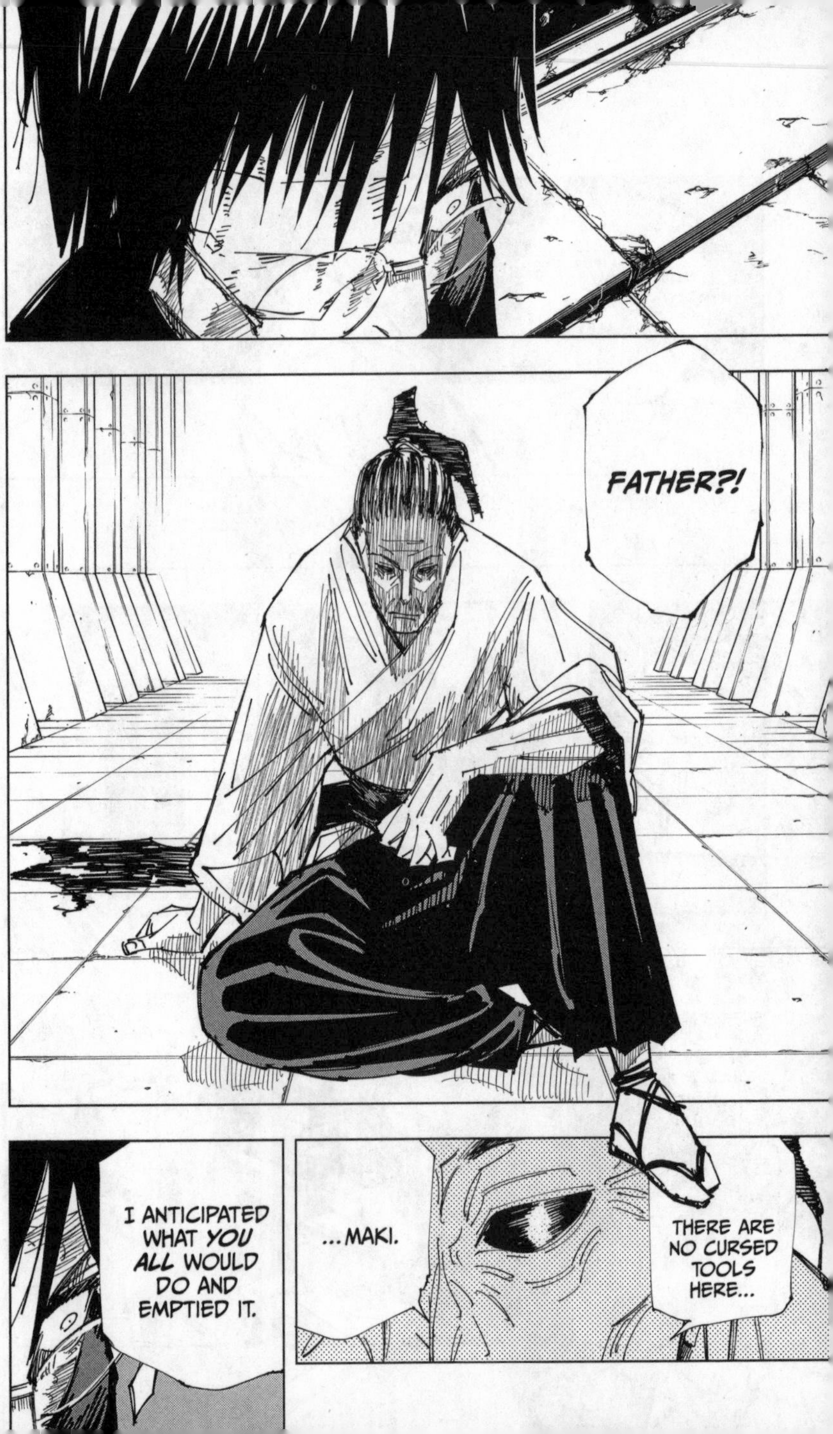
FATHER?!
THERE ARE NO CURSED TOOLS HERE...
...MAKI.
I ANTICIPATED WHAT YOU ALL WOULD DO AND EMPTIED IT.

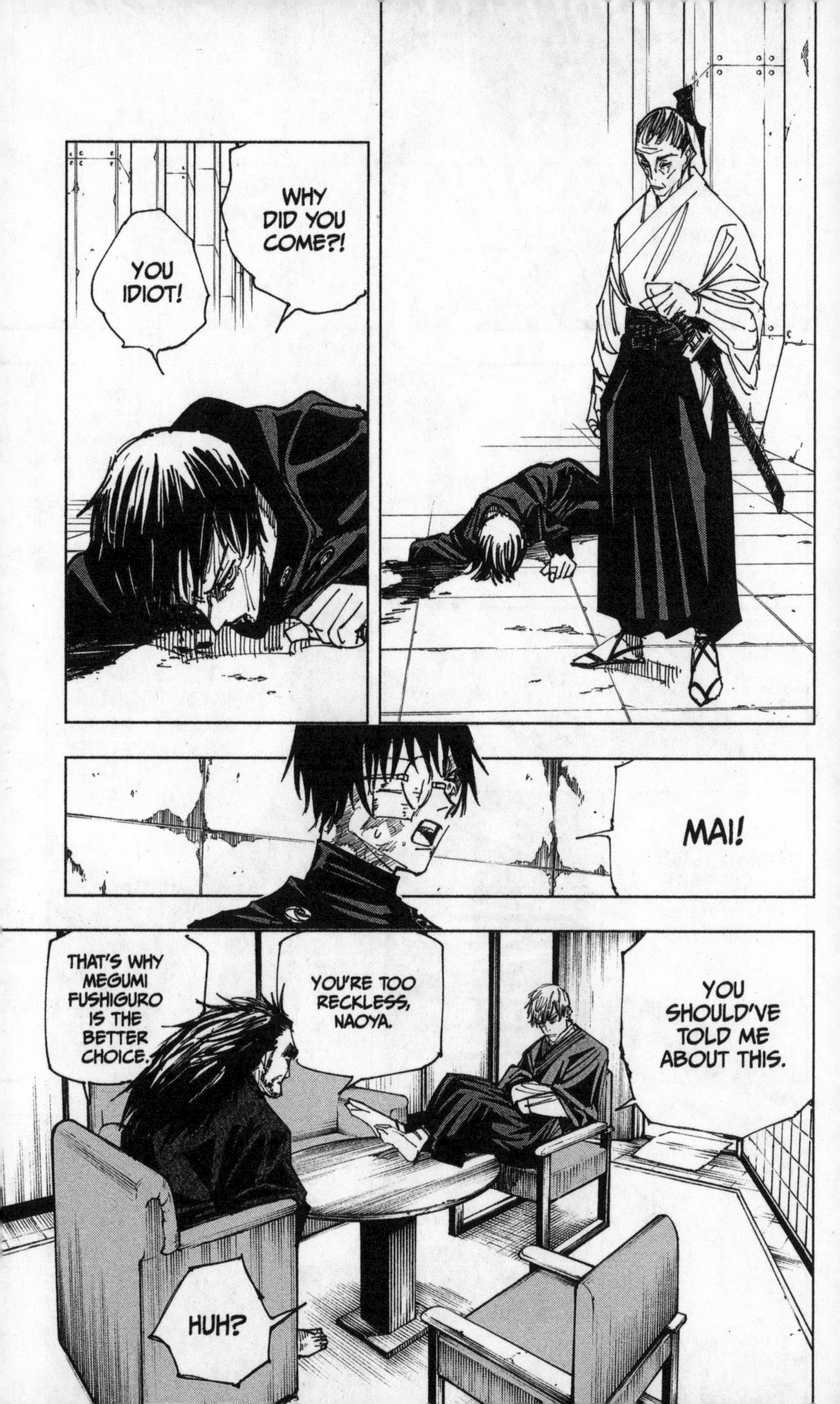
WHY DID YOU COME?!
YOU IDIOT!
MAI!
YOU SHOULD'VE TOLD ME ABOUT THIS.
YOU'RE TOO RECKLESS, NAOYA.
THAT'S WHY MEGUMI FUSHIGURO IS THE BETTER CHOICE.
HUH?

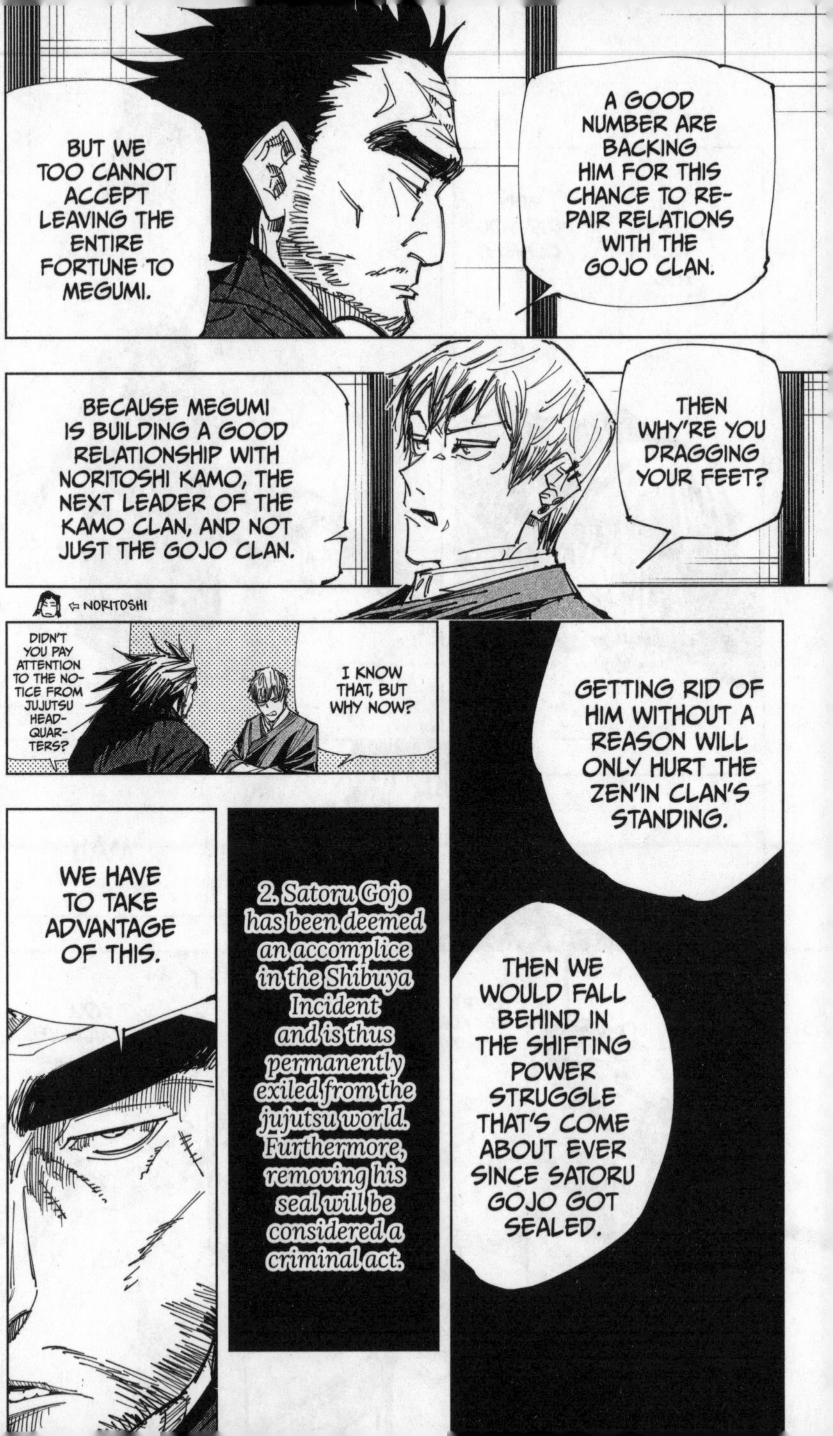

A GOOD NUMBER ARE BACKING HIM FOR THIS CHANCE TO RE-PAIR RELATIONS WITH THE GOJO CLAN.
BUT WE TOO CANNOT ACCEPT LEAVING THE ENTIRE FORTUNE TO MEGUMI.
THEN WHY'RE YOU DRAGGING YOUR FEET?
BECAUSE MEGUMI IS BUILDING A GOOD RELATIONSHIP WITH NORITOSHI KAMO, THE NEXT LEADER OF THE KAMO CLAN, AND NOT JUST THE GOJO CLAN.
⇦ NORITOSHI
GETTING RID OF HIM WITHOUT A REASON WILL ONLY HURT THE ZEN'IN CLAN'S STANDING.
THEN WE WOULD FALL BEHIND IN THE SHIFTING POWER STRUGGLE THAT'S COME ABOUT EVER SINCE SATORU GOJO GOT SEALED.
DIDN'T YOU PAY ATTENTION TO THE NO-TICE FROM JUJUTSU HEAD-QUAR-TERS?
I KNOW THAT, BUT WHY NOW?
2. Satoru Gojo has been deemed an accomplice in the Shibuya Incident and is thus permanently exiled from the jujutsu world. Furthermore, removing his seal will be considered a criminal act.
WE HAVE TO TAKE ADVANTAGE OF THIS.

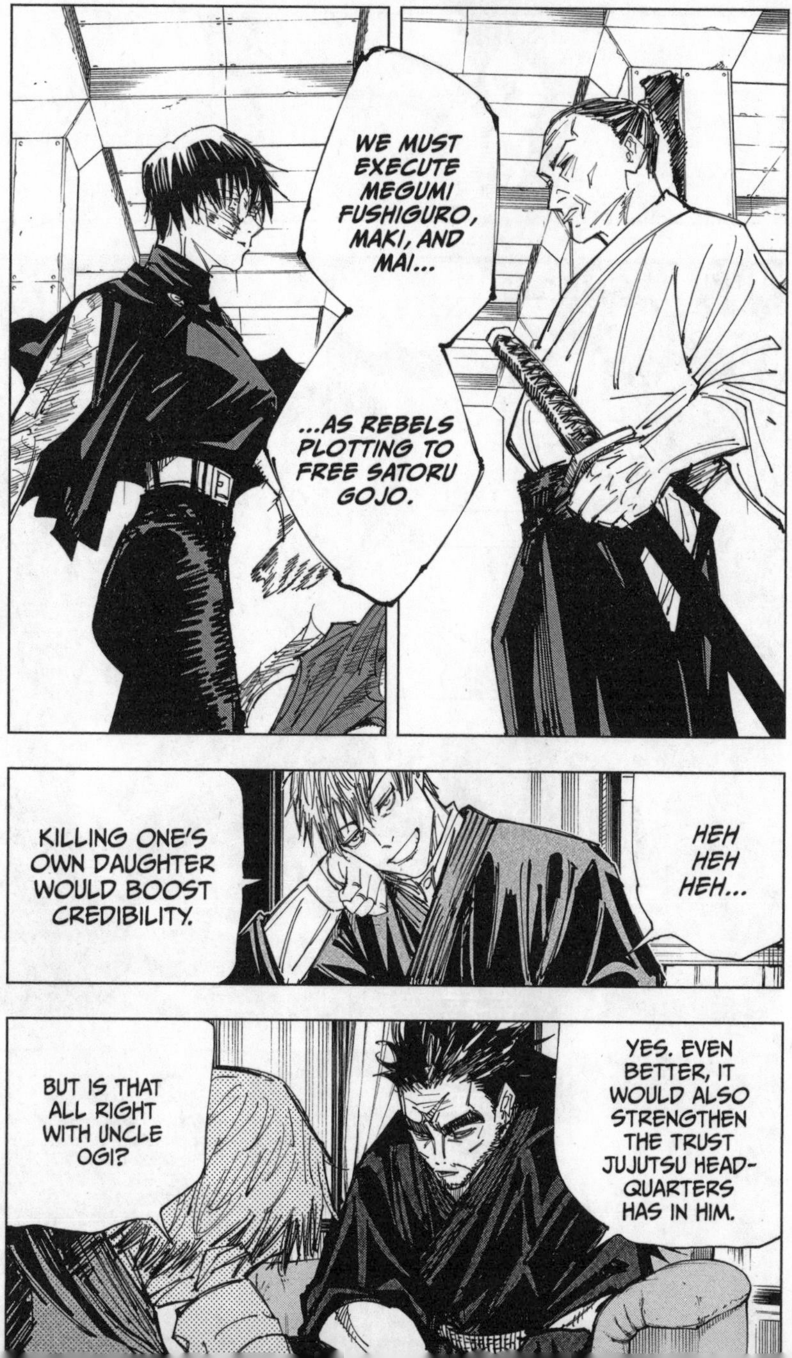
WE MUST EXECUTE MEGUMI FUSHIGURO, MAKI, AND MAI...
...AS REBELS PLOTTING TO FREE SATORU GOJO.
HEH HEH HEH...
KILLING ONE'S OWN DAUGHTER WOULD BOOST CREDIBILITY.
YES. EVEN BETTER, IT WOULD ALSO STRENGTHEN THE TRUST JUJUTSU HEAD-QUARTERS HAS IN HIM.
BUT IS THAT ALL RIGHT WITH UNCLE OGI?

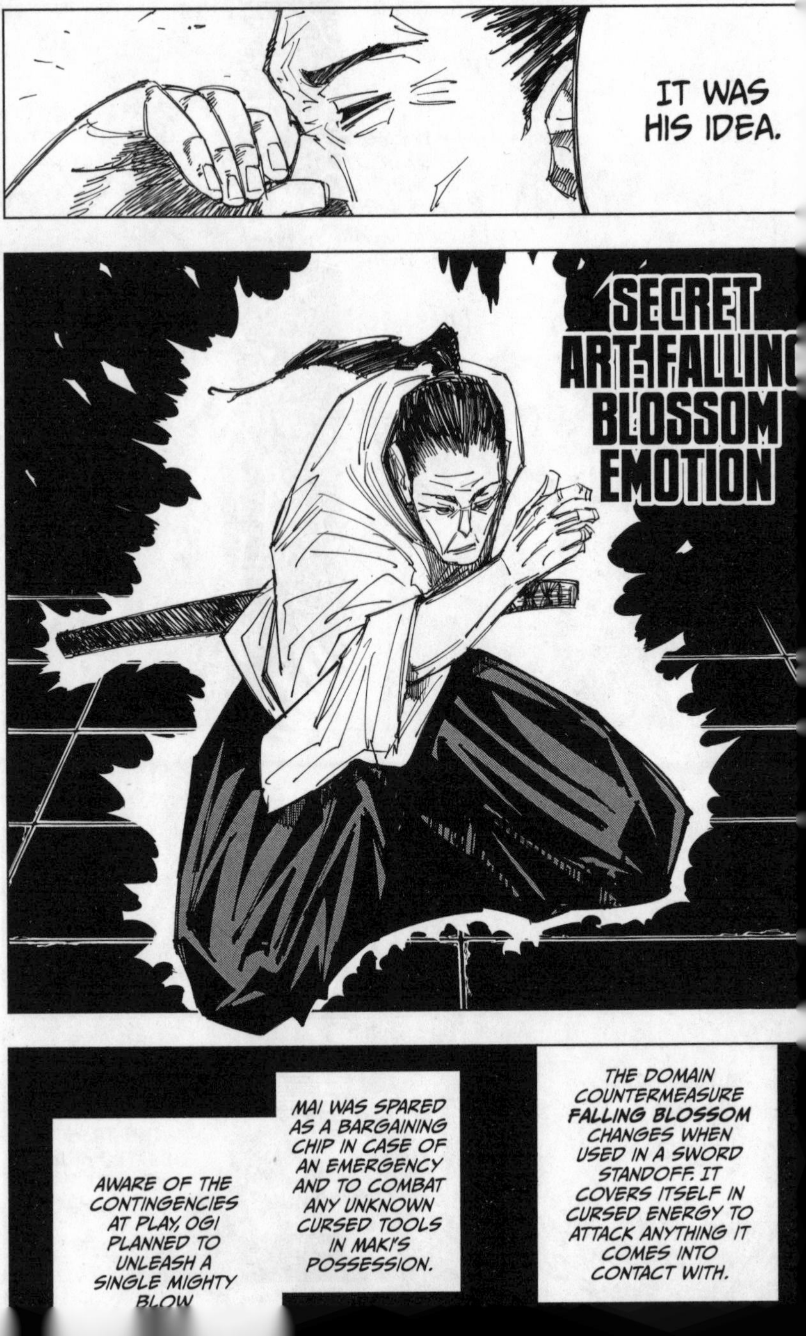

IT WAS HIS IDEA.
SECRET ART: FALLIN
BLOSSOM EMOTION
THE DOMAIN COUNTERMEASURE FALLING BLOSSOM CHANGES WHEN USED IN A SWORD STANDOFF. IT COVERS ITSELF IN CURSED ENERGY TO ATTACK ANYTHING IT COMES INTO CONTACT WITH.
MAI WAS SPARED AS A BARGAINING CHIP IN CASE OF AN EMERGENCY AND TO COMBAT ANY UNKNOWN CURSED TOOLS IN MAKI'S POSSESSION.
AWARE OF THE CONTINGENCIES AT PLAY, OGI PLANNED TO UNLEASH A SINGLE MIGHTY BLOW

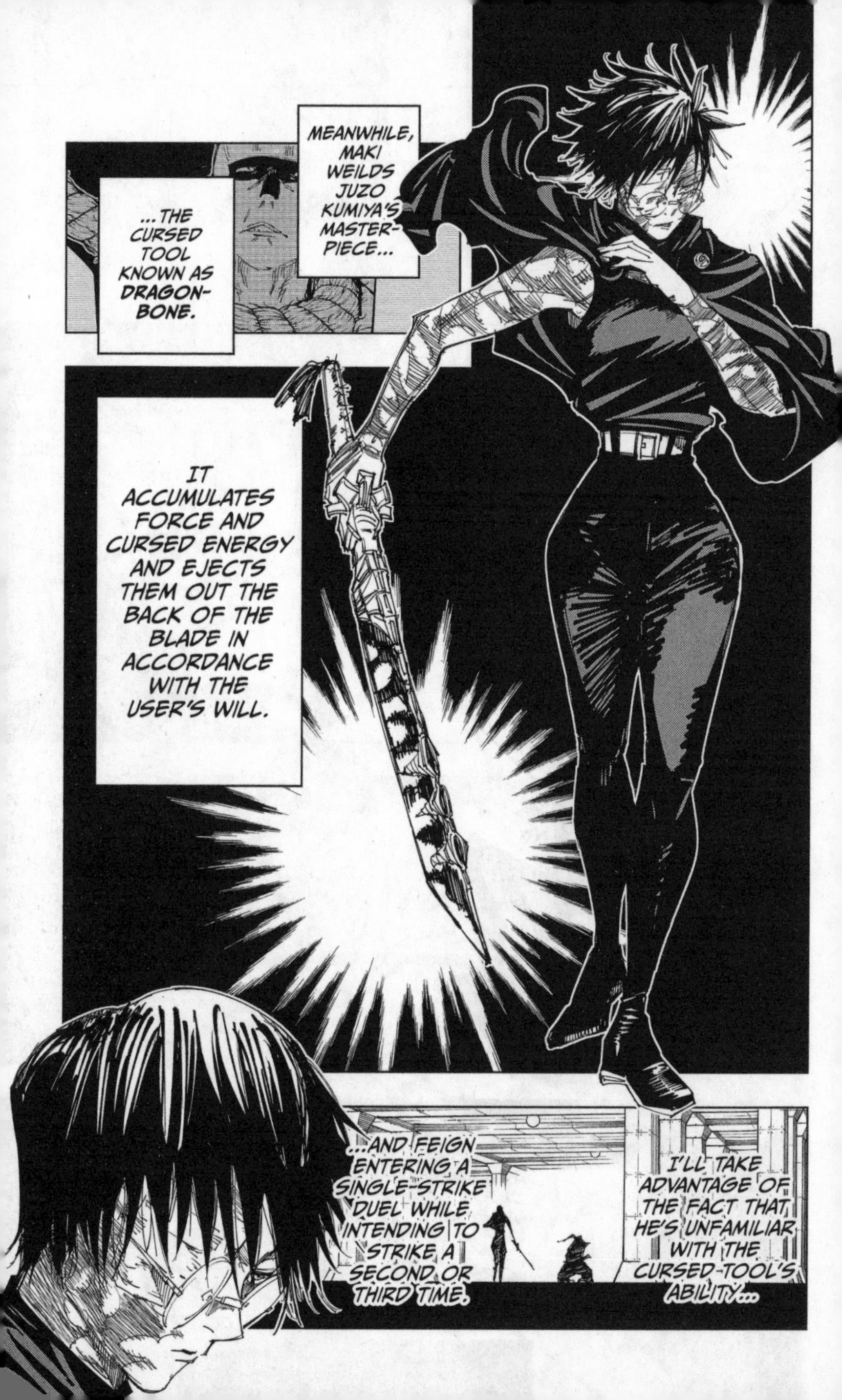
MEANWHILE, MAKI WEILDS JUZO KUMIYA'S MASTER-PIECE...
...THE CURSED TOOL KNOWN AS DRAGON-BONE.
IT ACCUMULATES FORCE AND CURSED ENERGY AND EJECTS THEM OUT THE BACK OF THE BLADE IN ACCORDANCE WITH THE USER'S WILL.
I'LL TAKE ADVANTAGE OF THE FACT THAT HE'S UNFAMILIAR WITH THE CURSED-TOOL'S ABILITY...
...AND FEIGN ENTERING A SINGLE-STRIKE DUEL WHILE INTENDING TO STRIKE A SECOND OR THIRD TIME.

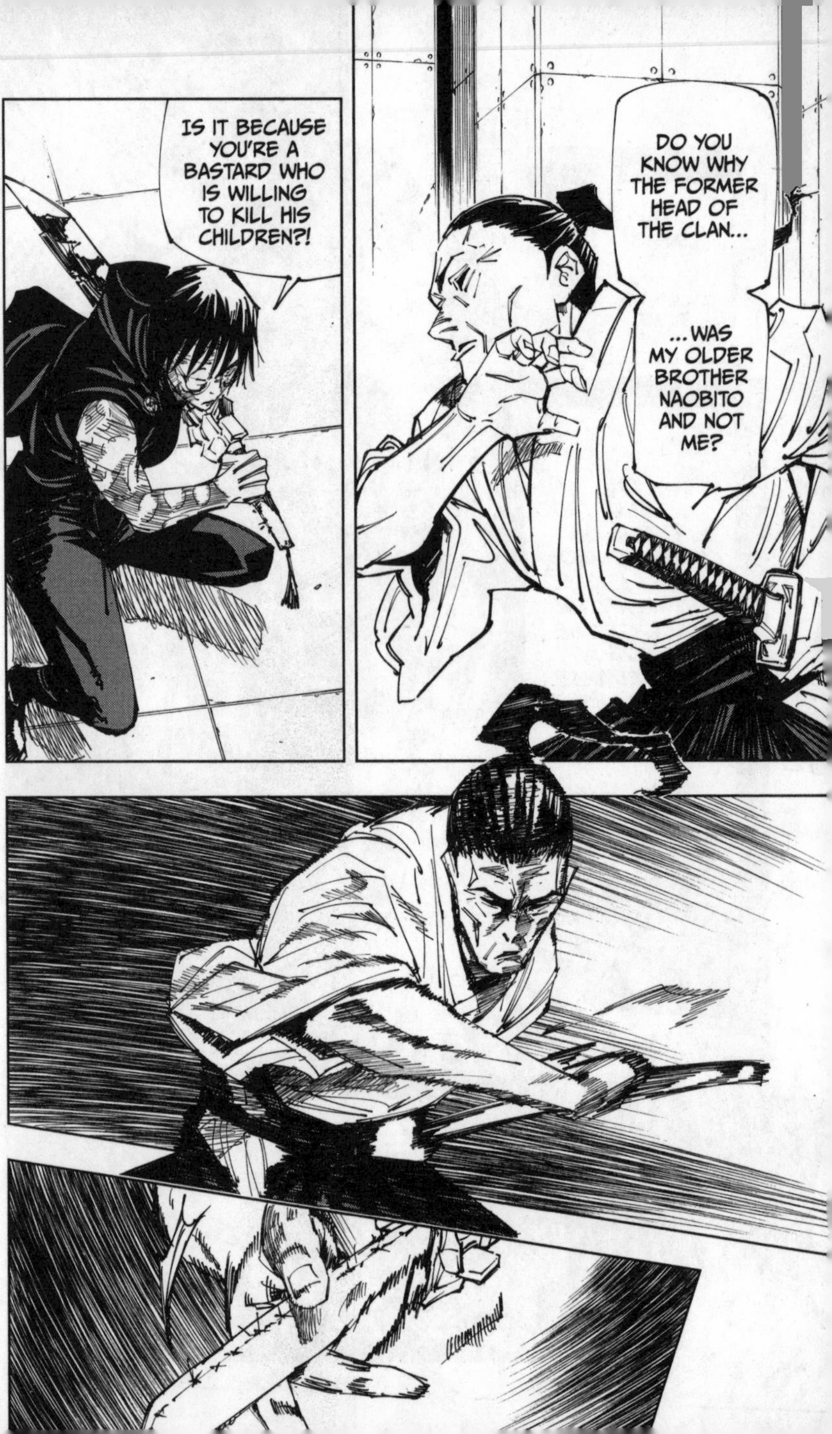
DO YOU KNOW WHY THE FORMER HEAD OF THE CLAN...
...WAS MY OLDER BROTHER NAOBITO AND NOT ME?
IS IT BECAUSE YOU'RE A BASTARD WHO IS WILLING TO KILL HIS CHILDREN?!

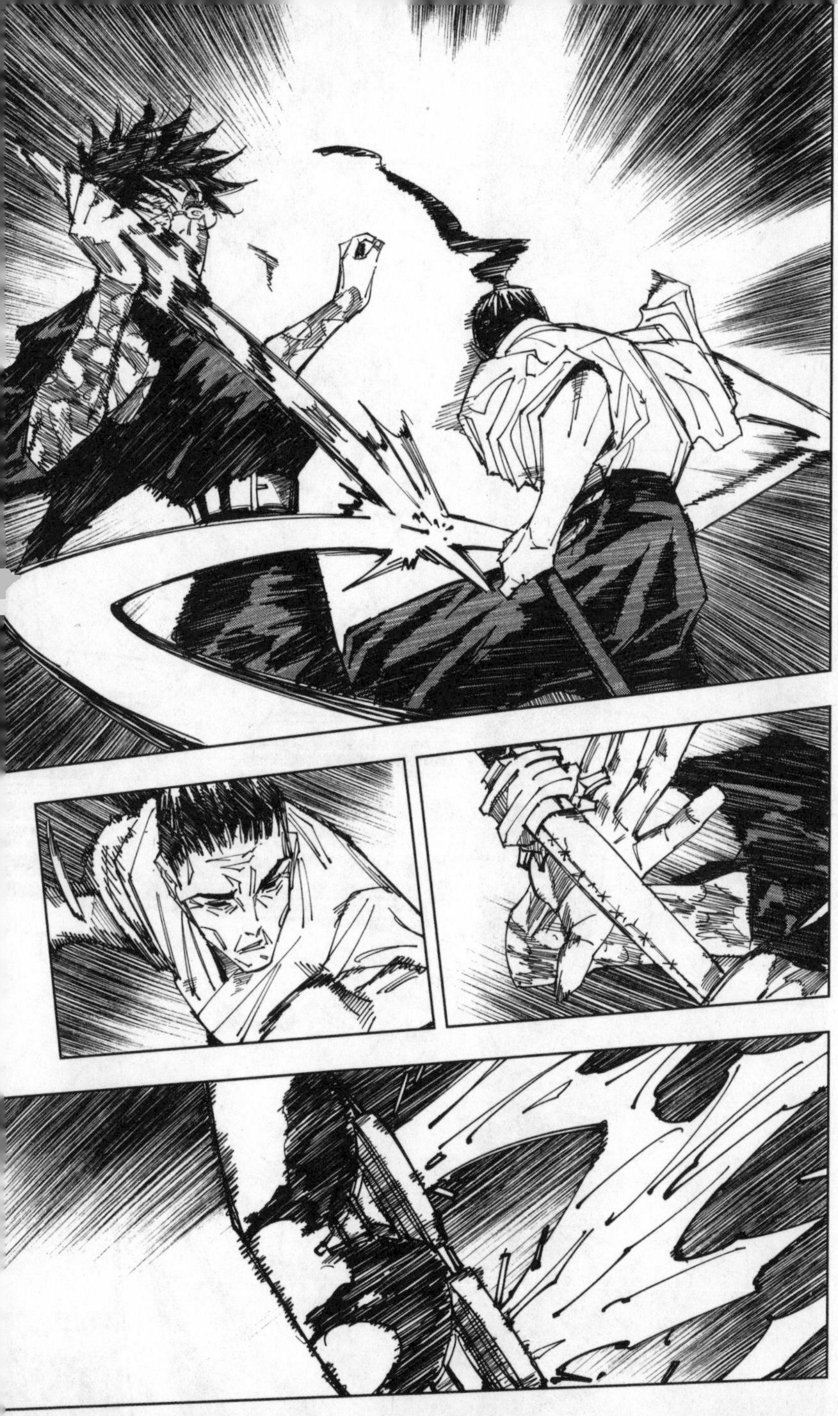

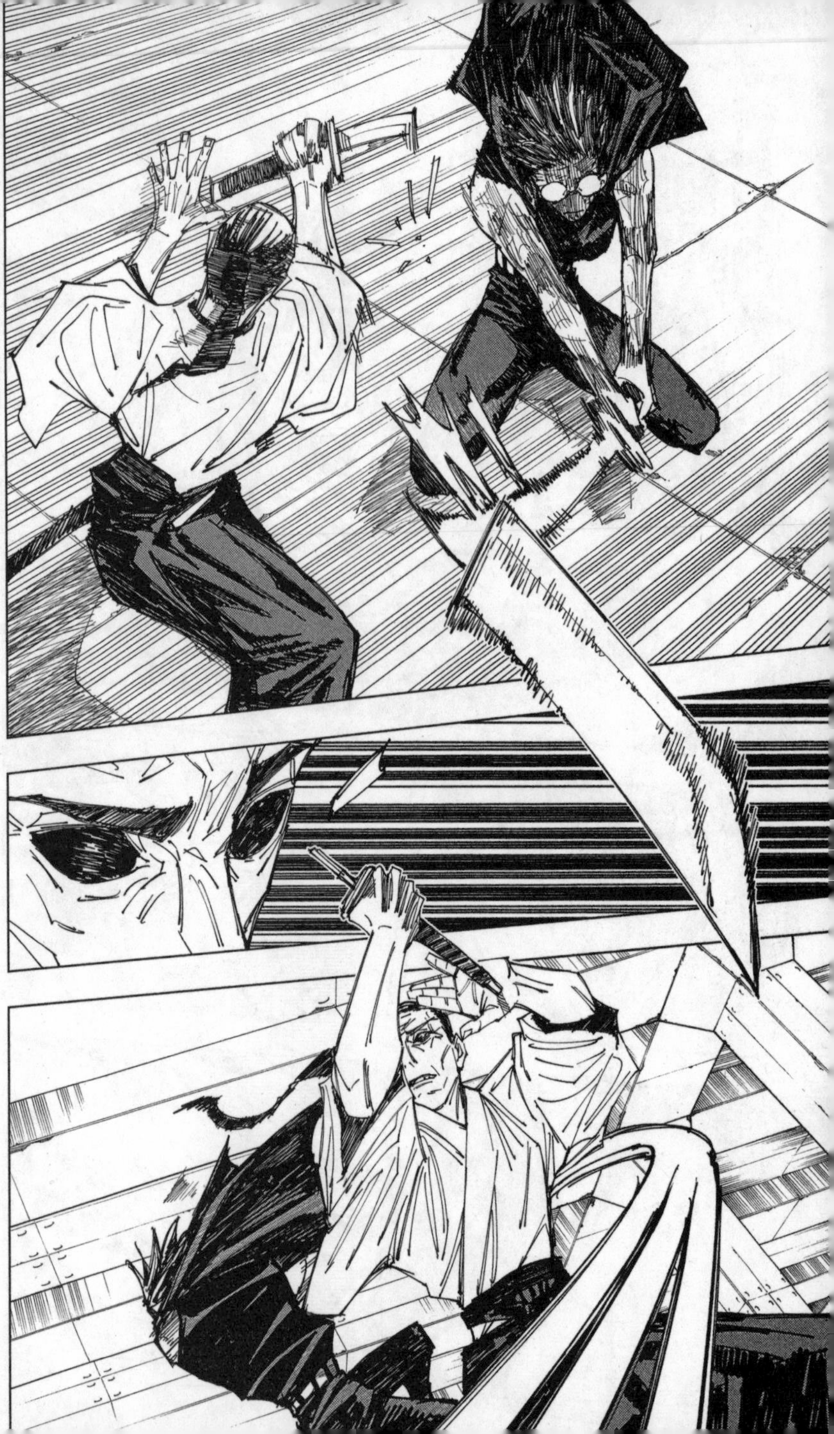

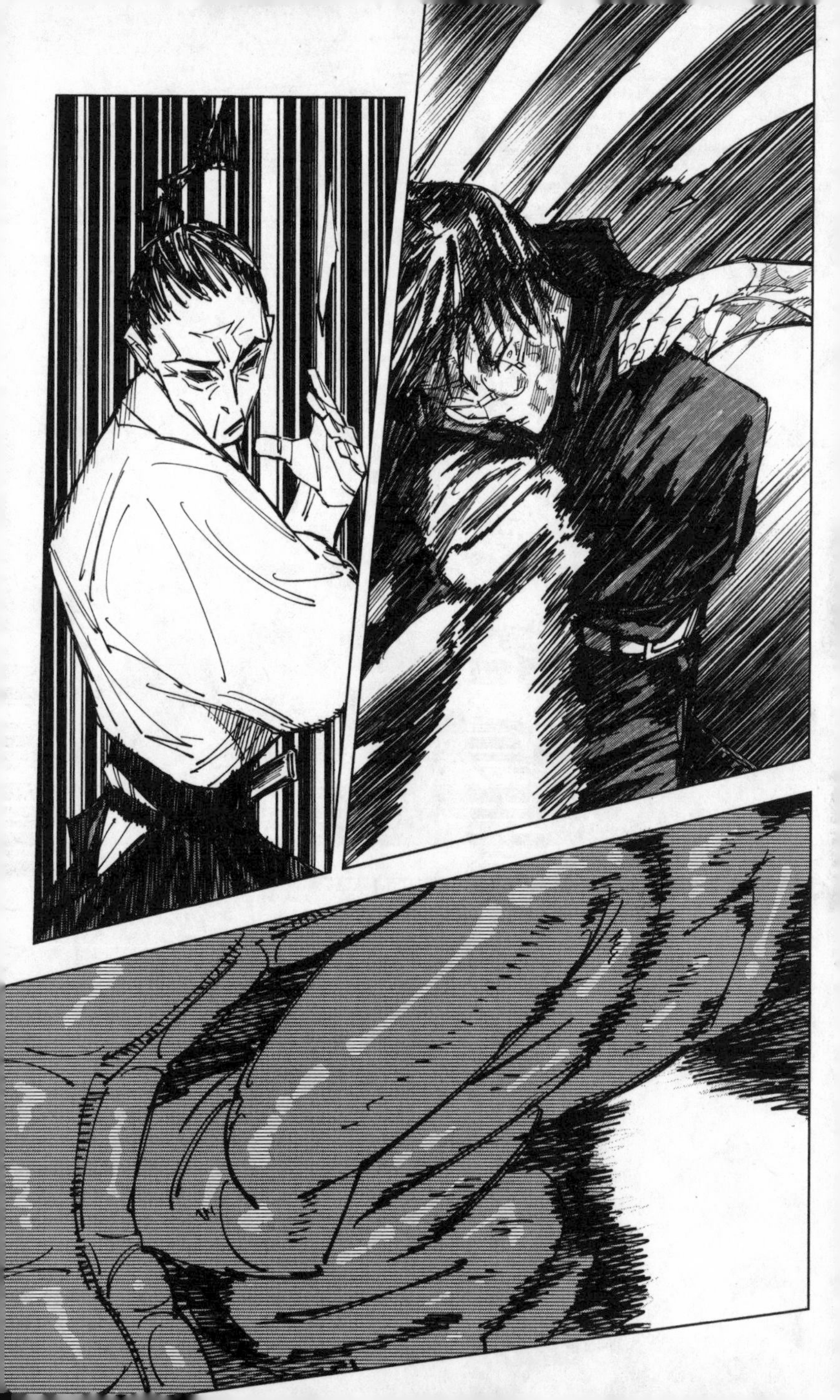

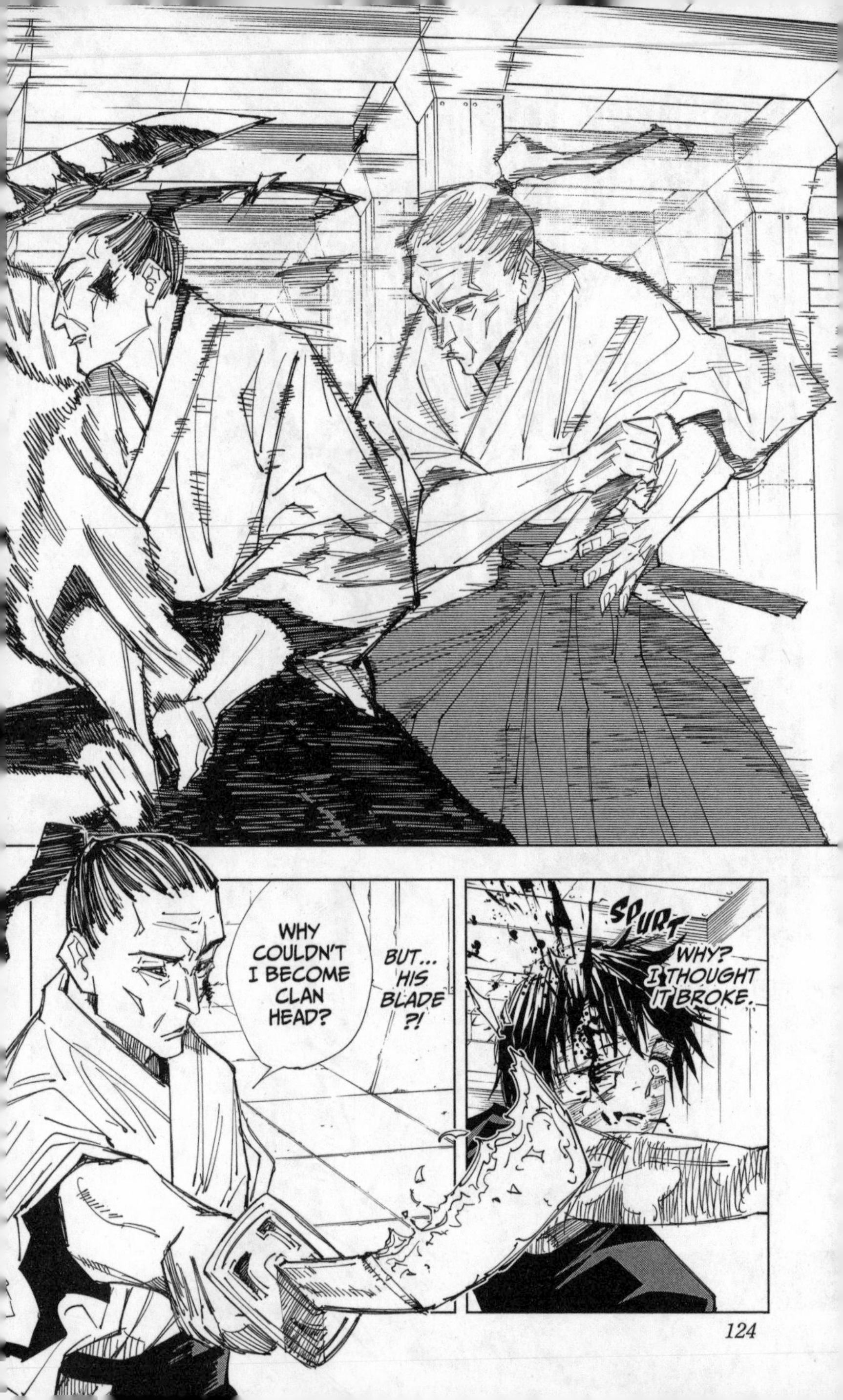
SPURT
WHY? I THOUGHT IT BROKE.
BUT... HIS BLADE ?!
WHY COULDN'T I BECOME CLAN HEAD?

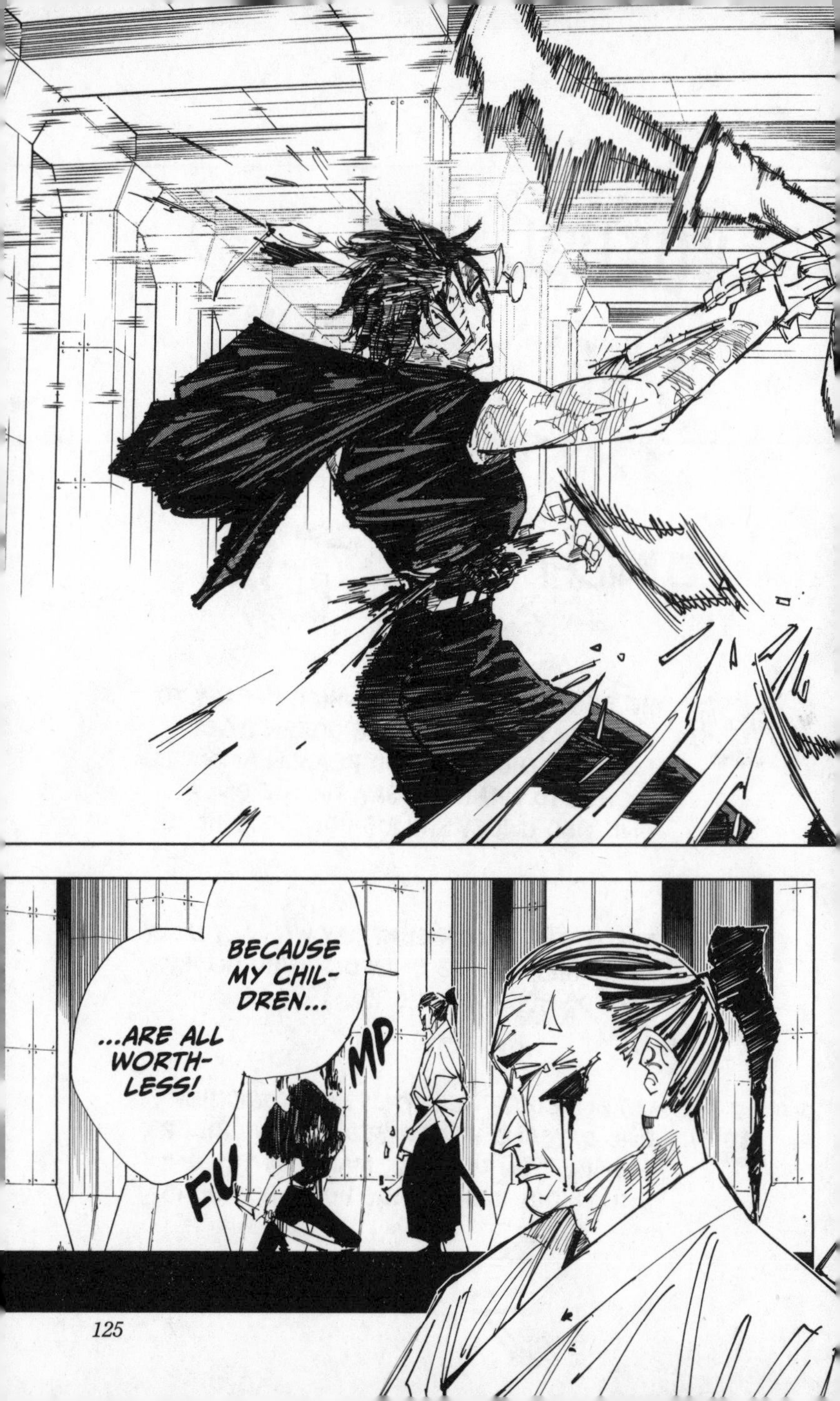

BECAUSE MY CHIL- DREN...
...ARE ALL WORTH- LESS!
FU
MP

KUKURU UNIT ② HEI REVIEW!!

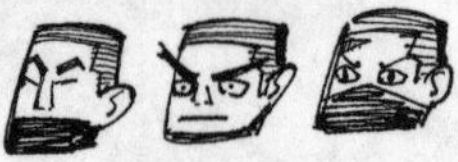

• JINICHI

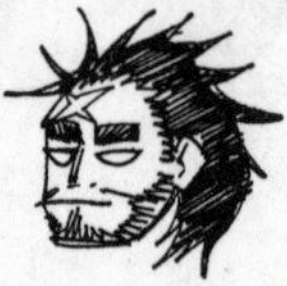

4.8 ☆☆☆☆☆

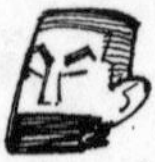

HE SEEMS UNFRIENDLY, WHICH IS EASY TO MISUNDERSTAND, BUT HE DOESN'T GET ANGRY WITHOUT A GOOD REASON AND WILL LISTEN TO WHAT YOU SAY. I'M THE ONLY ONE WHO UNDERSTANDS HOW GOOD HE IS.

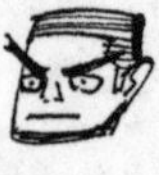

THE WATERMELON THAT DAY WAS ACTUALLY FROM HIM. I'M THE ONLY ONE WHO UNDERSTANDS HOW GOOD HE IS.

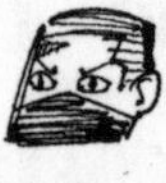

WE ENDED UP WEIGHTLIFTING TOGETHER ONE DAY, AND HE PRAISED MY QUADRICEPS, SAYING, "YOU'RE HUGE, MAN." I'M THE ONLY ONE WHO UNDERSTANDS HOW GOOD HE IS.

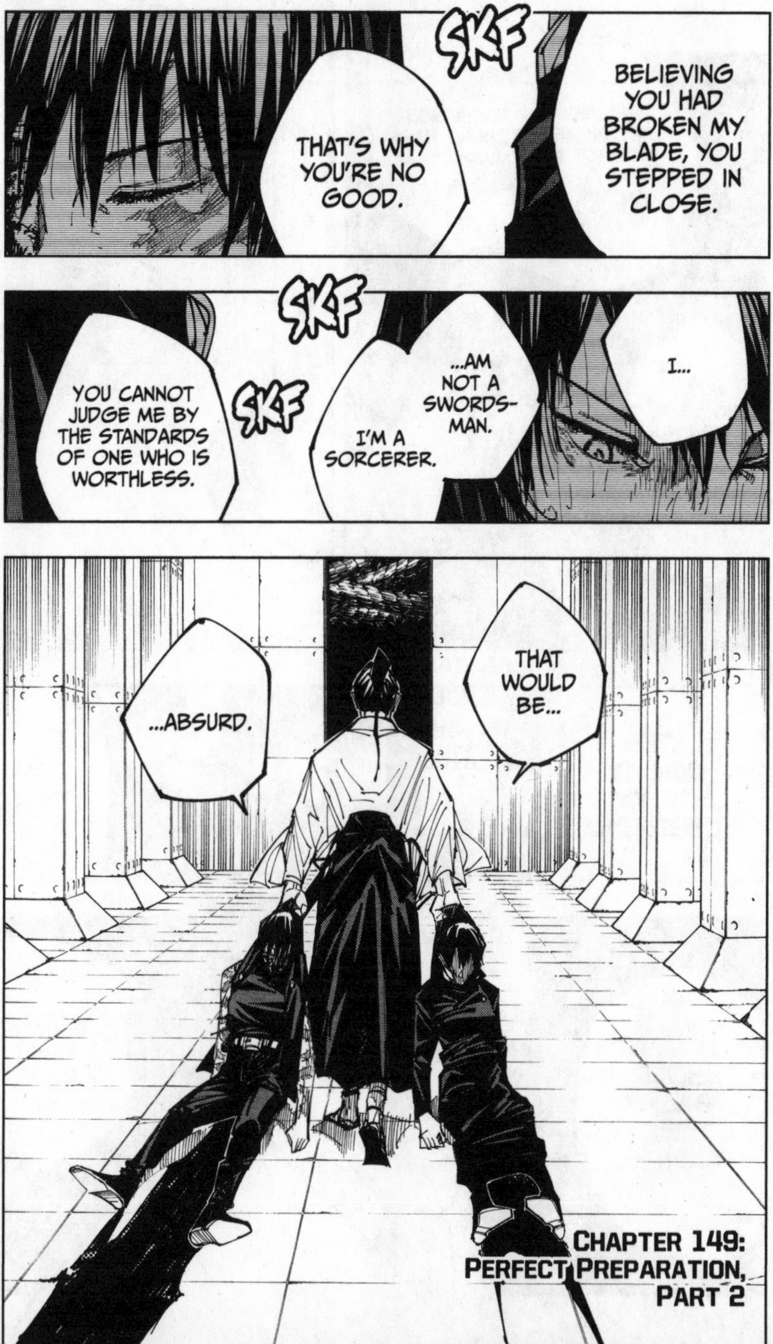
BELIEVING YOU HAD BROKEN MY BLADE, YOU STEPPED IN CLOSE.
SKF
THAT'S WHY YOU'RE NO GOOD.
I...
...AM NOT A SWORDS-MAN.
I'M A SORCERER.
SKF
SKF
YOU CANNOT JUDGE ME BY THE STANDARDS OF ONE WHO IS WORTHLESS.
THAT WOULD BE...
...ABSURD.

CHAPTER 149: PERFECT PREPARATION, PART 2

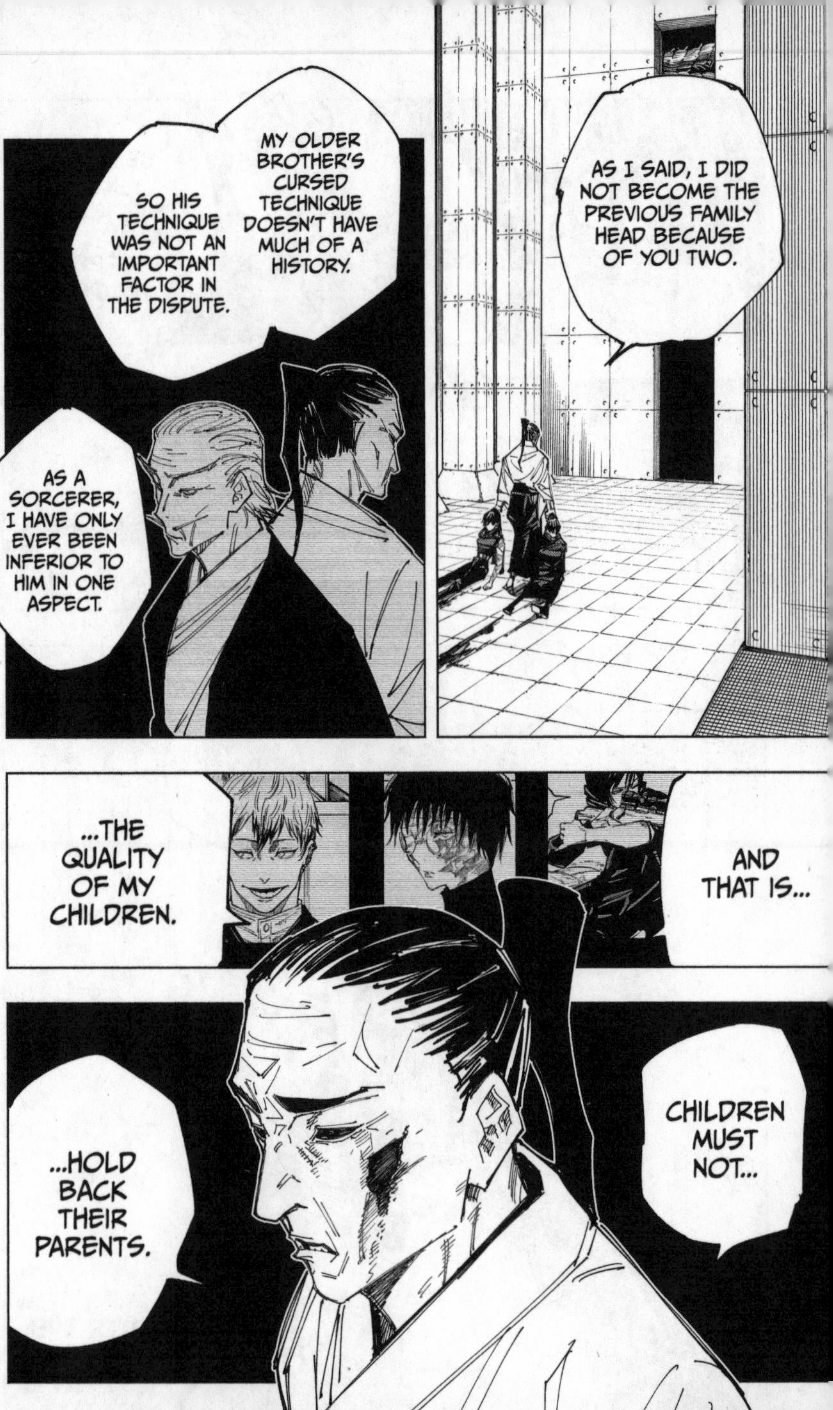
AS I SAID, I DID NOT BECOME THE PREVIOUS FAMILY HEAD BECAUSE OF YOU TWO.
MY OLDER BROTHER'S CURSED TECHNIQUE DOESN'T HAVE MUCH OF A HISTORY.
SO HIS TECHNIQUE WAS NOT AN IMPORTANT FACTOR IN THE DISPUTE.
AS A SORCERER, I HAVE ONLY EVER BEEN INFERIOR TO HIM IN ONE ASPECT.
AND THAT IS...
...THE QUALITY OF MY CHILDREN.
CHILDREN MUST NOT...
...HOLD BACK THEIR PARENTS.

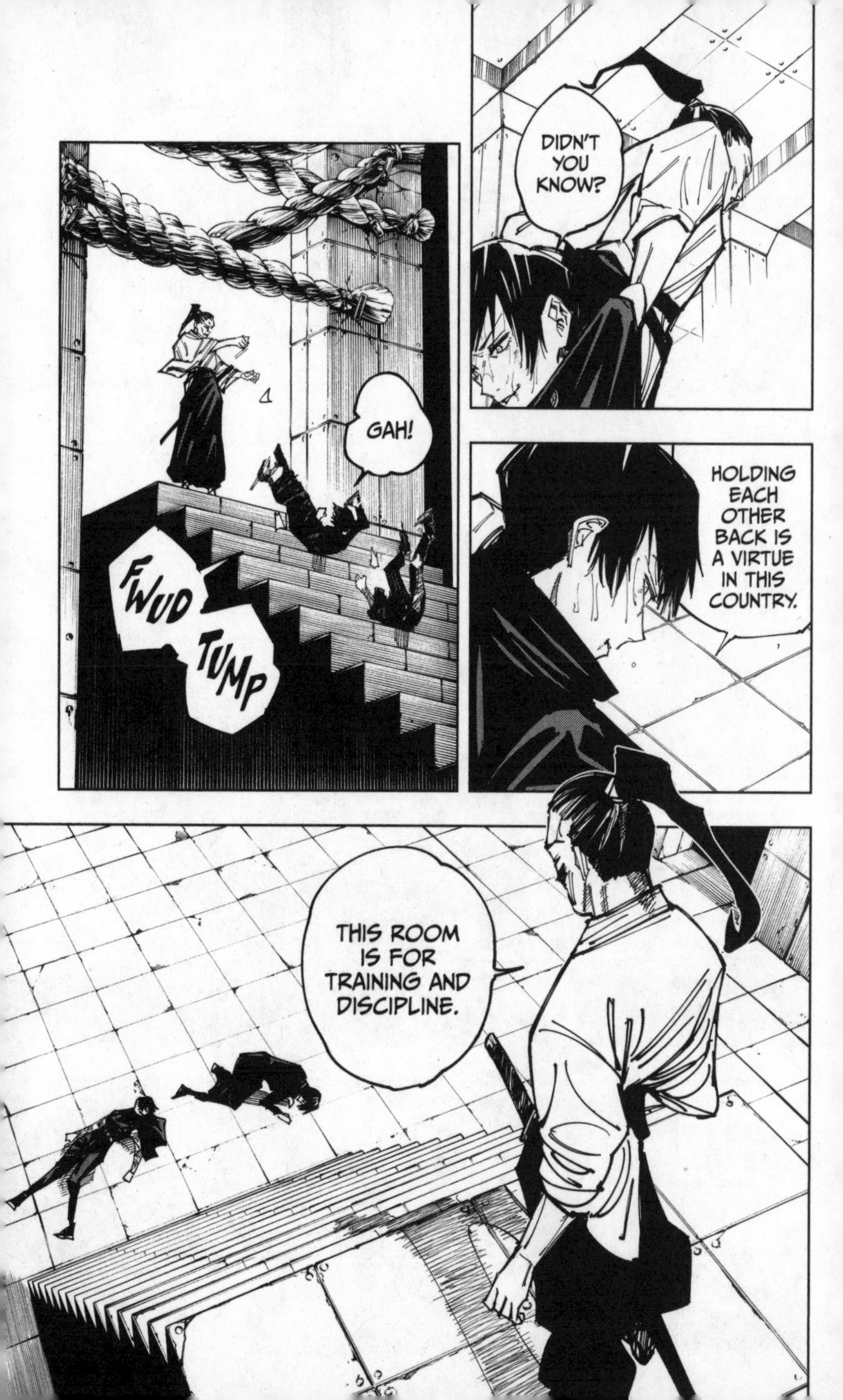
DIDN'T YOU KNOW?
HOLDING EACH OTHER BACK IS A VIRTUE IN THIS COUNTRY.
GAH!
FWUD
TUMP
THIS ROOM IS FOR TRAINING AND DISCIPLINE.

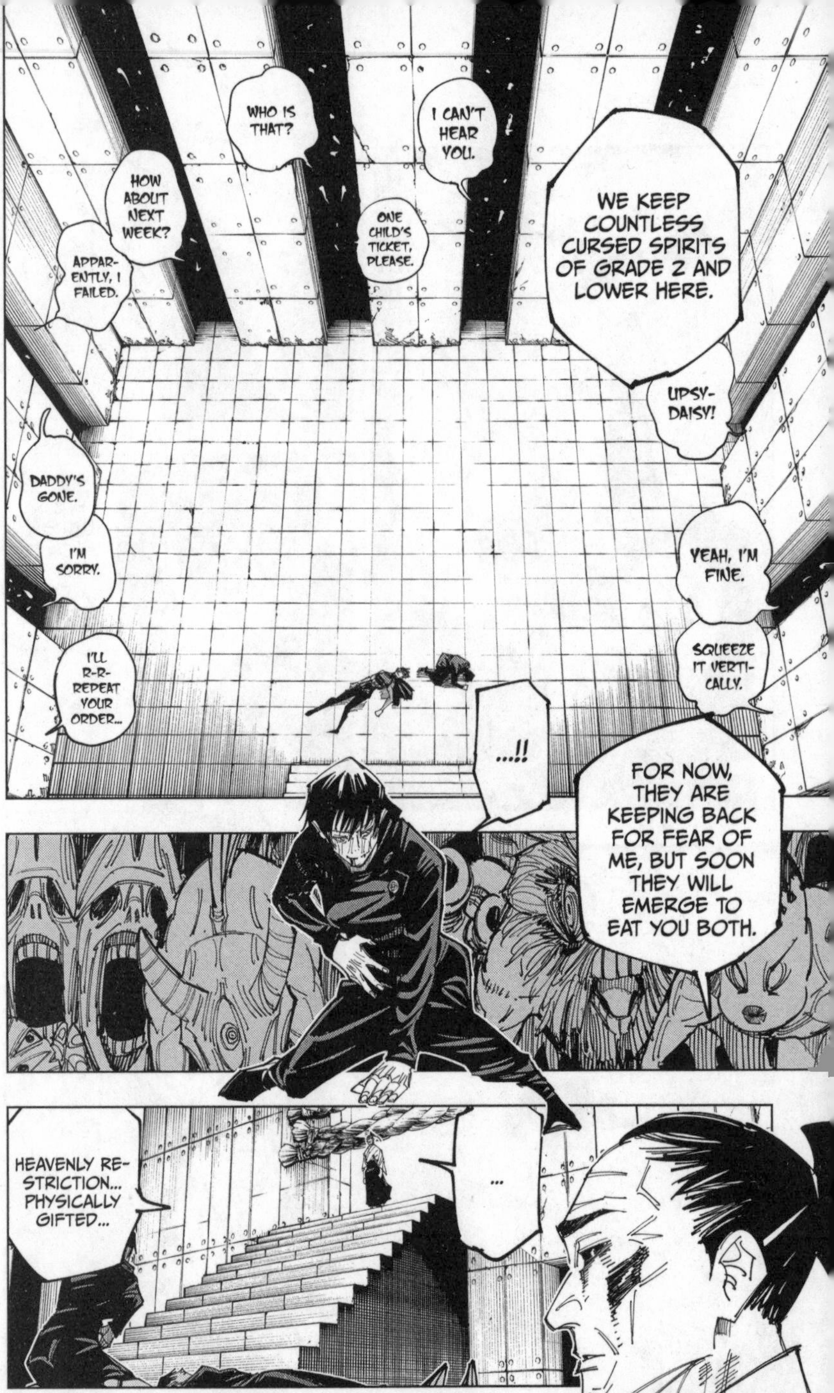
WE KEEP COUNTLESS CURSED SPIRITS OF GRADE 2 AND LOWER HERE.
I CAN'T HEAR YOU.
WHO IS THAT?
ONE CHILD'S TICKET, PLEASE.
HOW ABOUT NEXT WEEK?
APPAR-ENTLY, I FAILED.
UPSY-DAISY!
DADDY'S GONE.
YEAH, I'M FINE.
I'M SORRY.
SQUEEZE IT VERTI-CALLY.
I'LL R-R-REPEAT YOUR ORDER...
FOR NOW, THEY ARE KEEPING BACK FOR FEAR OF ME, BUT SOON THEY WILL EMERGE TO EAT YOU BOTH.
...!!
...
HEAVENLY RE-STRICTION... PHYSICALLY GIFTED...

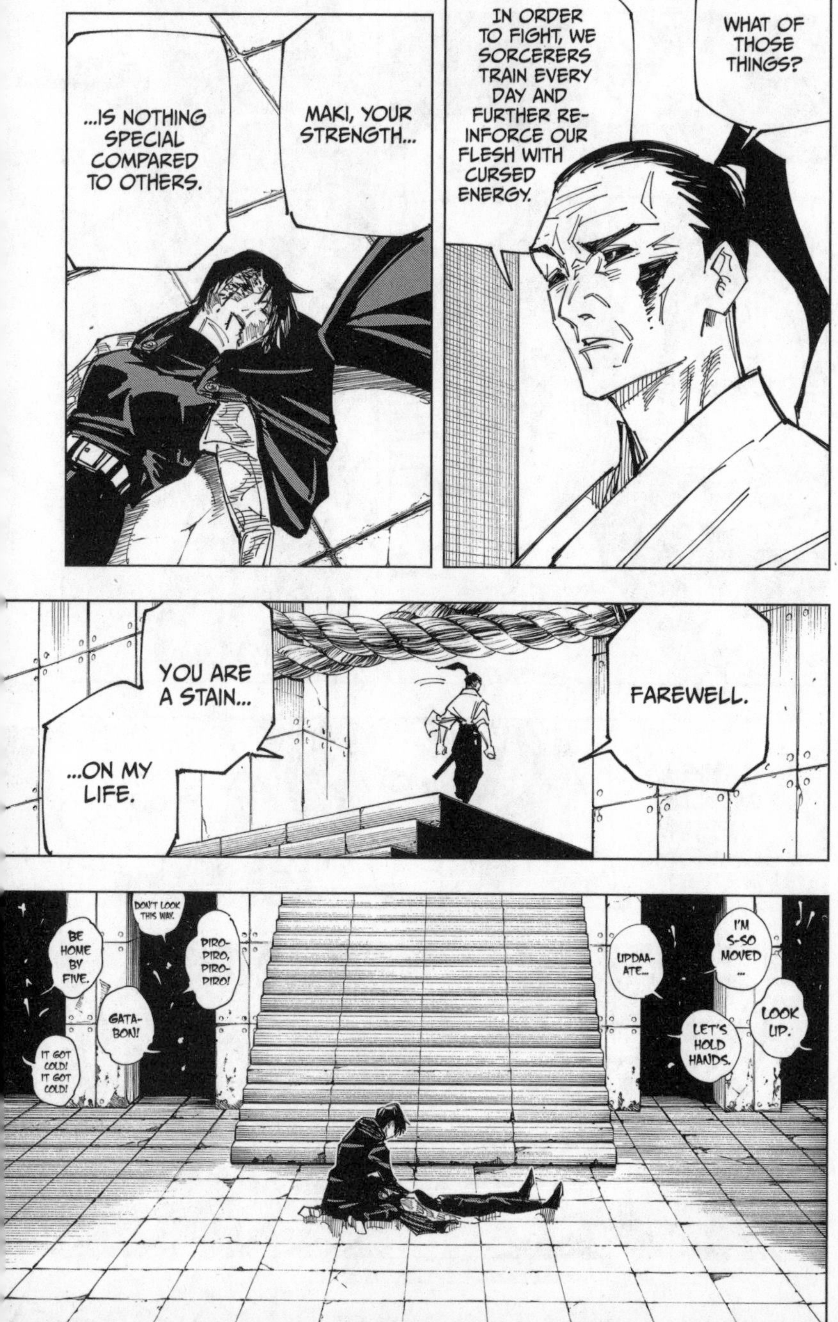
WHAT OF THOSE THINGS?
IN ORDER TO FIGHT, WE SORCERERS TRAIN EVERY DAY AND FURTHER RE-INFORCE OUR FLESH WITH CURSED ENERGY.
MAKI, YOUR STRENGTH...
...IS NOTHING SPECIAL COMPARED TO OTHERS.
FAREWELL.
YOU ARE A STAIN...
...ON MY LIFE.
I'M S-SO MOVED ...
LOOK UP.
LET'S HOLD HANDS.
UPDAAATE...
DON'T LOOK THIS WAY.
PIRO-PIRO, PIRO-PIRO!
BE HOME BY FIVE.
GATA-BON!
IT GOT COLD! IT GOT COLD!

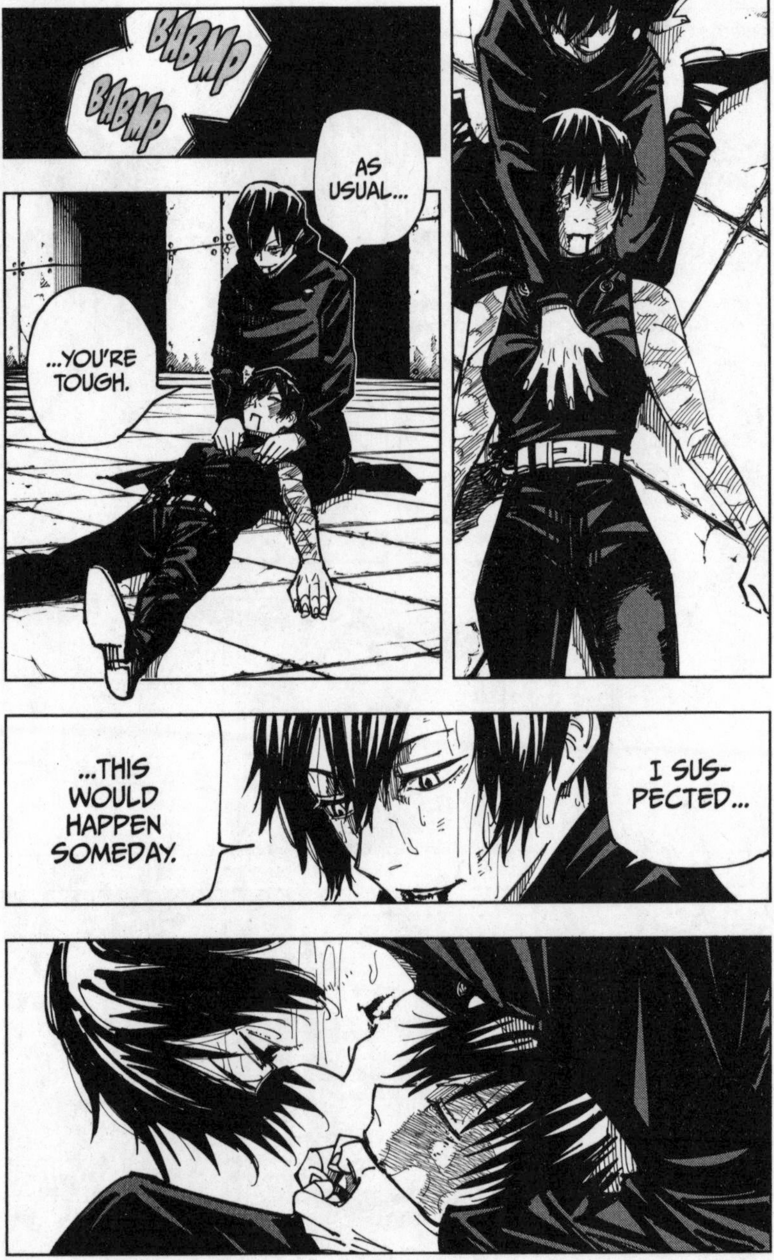
BABMP
BABMP
AS USUAL...
...YOU'RE TOUGH.
I SUS-PECTED...
...THIS WOULD HAPPEN SOMEDAY.

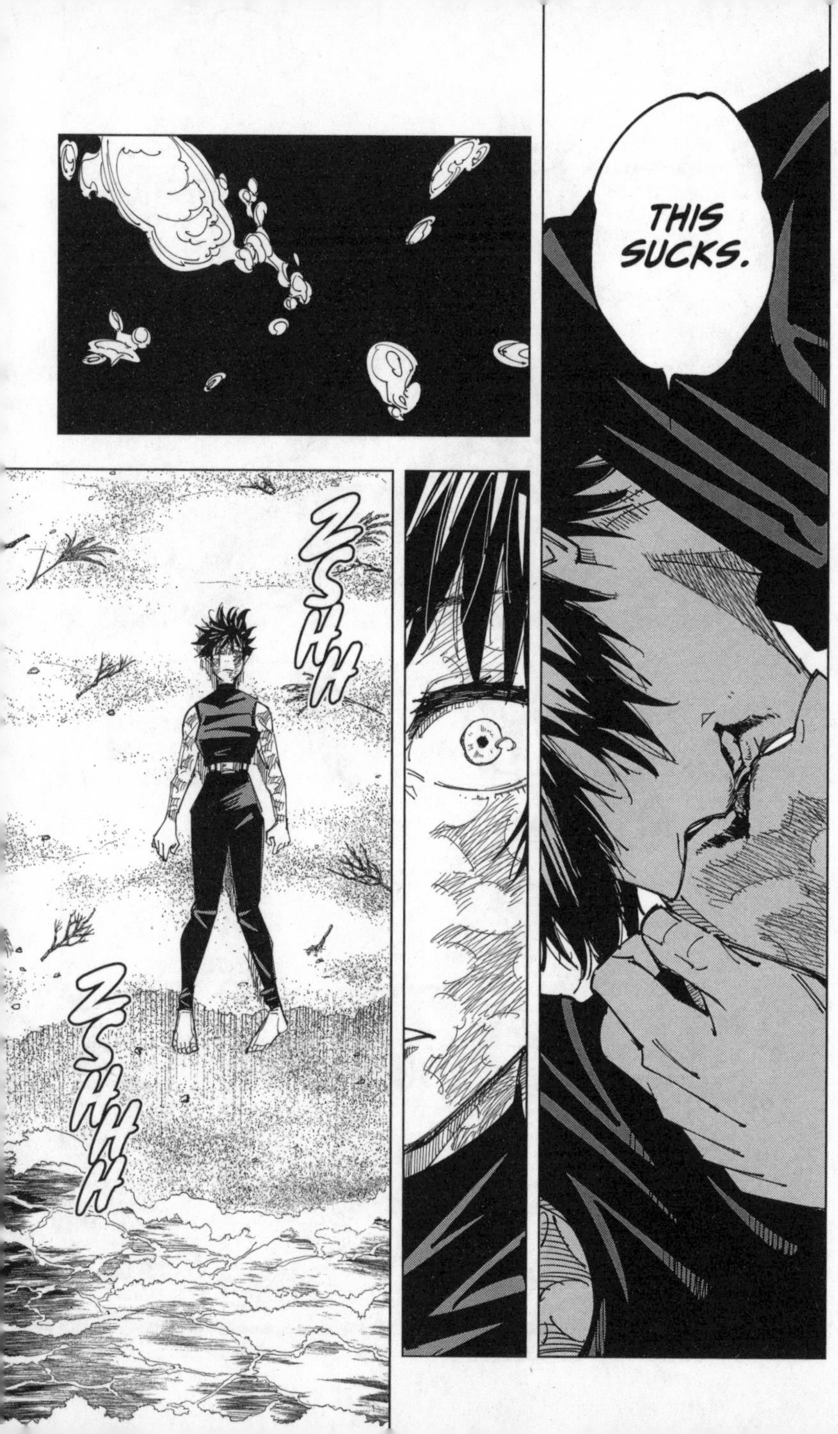
THIS SUCKS.
ZSHH
ZSHHH

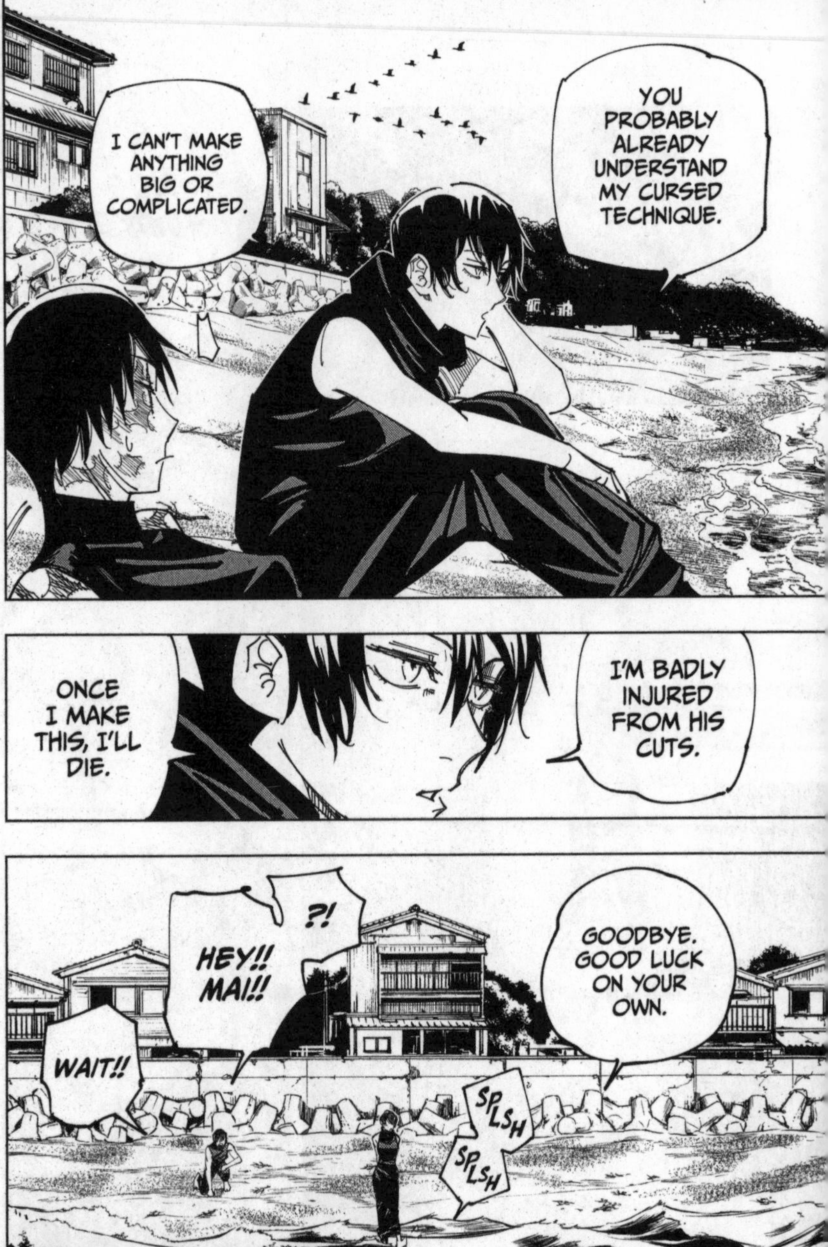
YOU PROBABLY ALREADY UNDERSTAND MY CURSED TECHNIQUE.
I CAN'T MAKE ANYTHING BIG OR COMPLICATED.
I'M BADLY INJURED FROM HIS CUTS.
ONCE I MAKE THIS, I'LL DIE.
GOODBYE. GOOD LUCK ON YOUR OWN.
SPLSH
SPLSH
?!
HEY!! MAI!!
WAIT!!

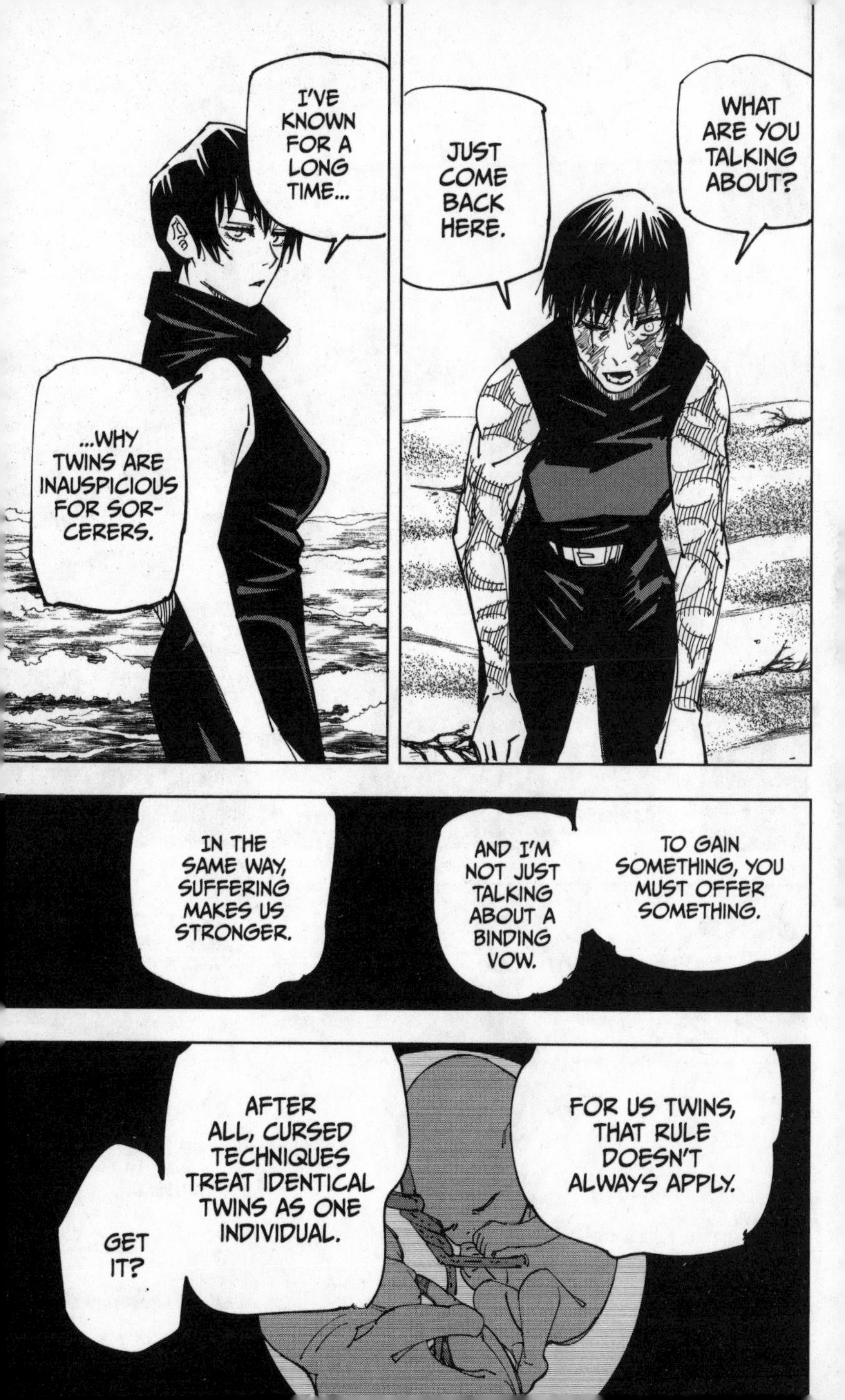
WHAT ARE YOU TALKING ABOUT?
JUST COME BACK HERE.
I'VE KNOWN FOR A LONG TIME...
...WHY TWINS ARE INAUSPICIOUS FOR SOR-CERERS.
TO GAIN SOMETHING, YOU MUST OFFER SOMETHING.
AND I'M NOT JUST TALKING ABOUT A BINDING VOW.
IN THE SAME WAY, SUFFERING MAKES US STRONGER.
FOR US TWINS, THAT RULE DOESN'T ALWAYS APPLY.
AFTER ALL, CURSED TECHNIQUES TREAT IDENTICAL TWINS AS ONE INDIVIDUAL.
GET IT?

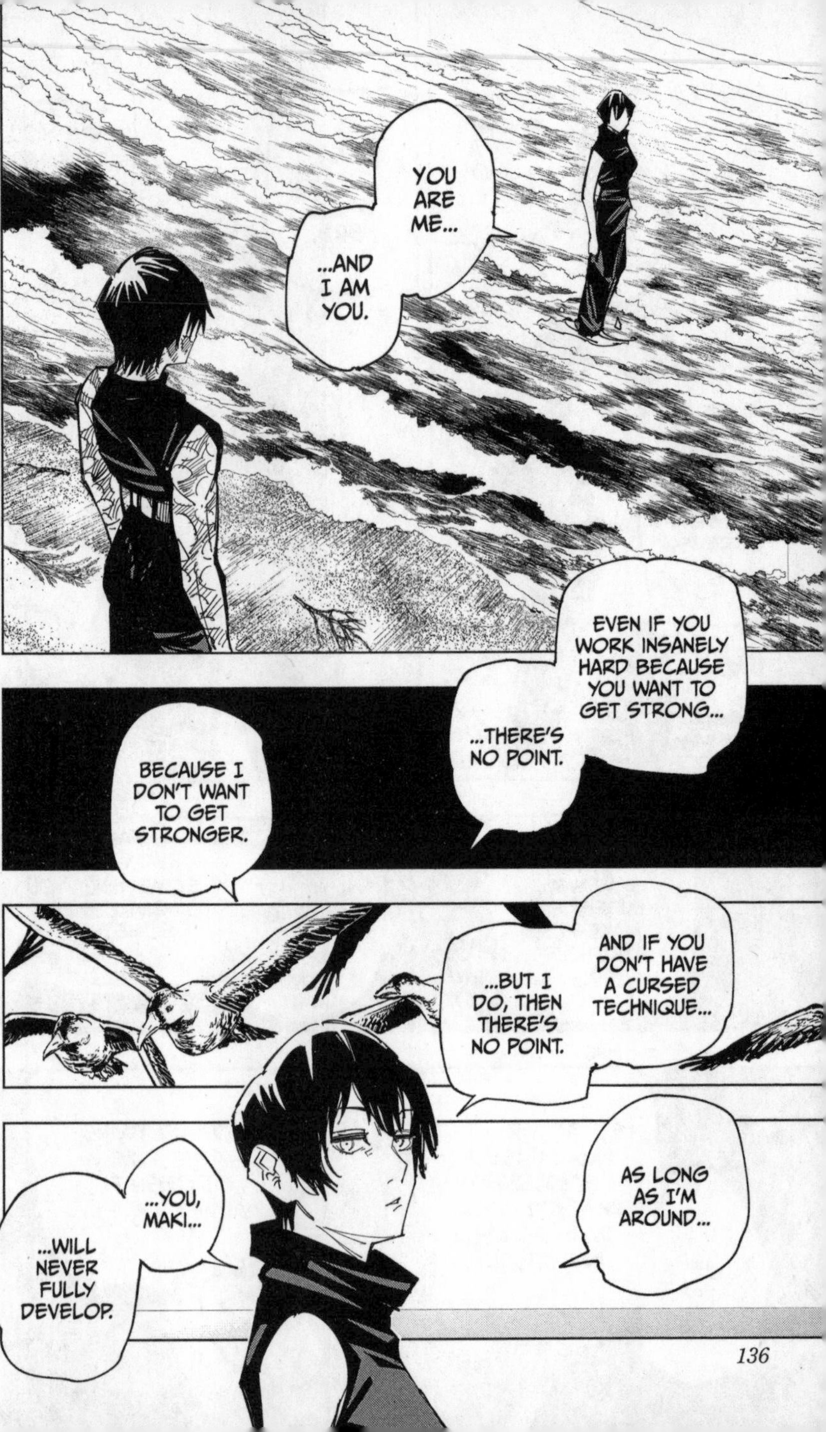
YOU ARE ME...
...AND I AM YOU.
EVEN IF YOU WORK INSANELY HARD BECAUSE YOU WANT TO GET STRONG...
...THERE'S NO POINT.
BECAUSE I DON'T WANT TO GET STRONGER.
AND IF YOU DON'T HAVE A CURSED TECHNIQUE...
...BUT I DO, THEN THERE'S NO POINT.
AS LONG AS I'M AROUND...
...YOU, MAKI...
...WILL NEVER FULLY DEVELOP.

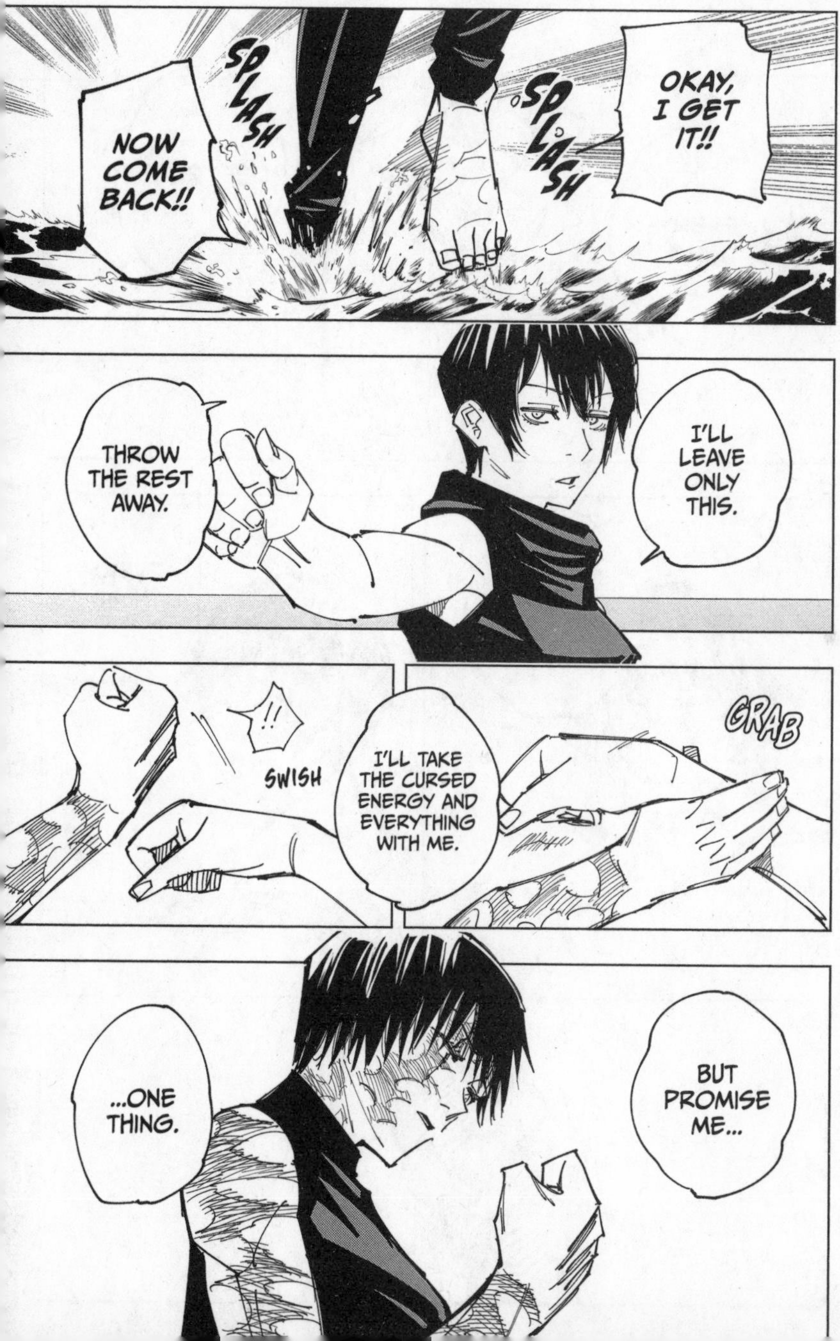
OKAY, I GET IT!!
SPLASH
SPLASH
NOW COME BACK!!
I'LL LEAVE ONLY THIS.
THROW THE REST AWAY.
GRAB
I'LL TAKE THE CURSED ENERGY AND EVERYTHING WITH ME.
!!
SWISH
BUT PROMISE ME...
...ONE THING.

...EVERY-THING.

DESTROY...

...BIG SISTER.

EVERY-THING...

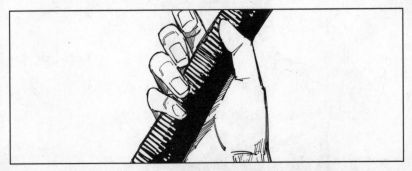

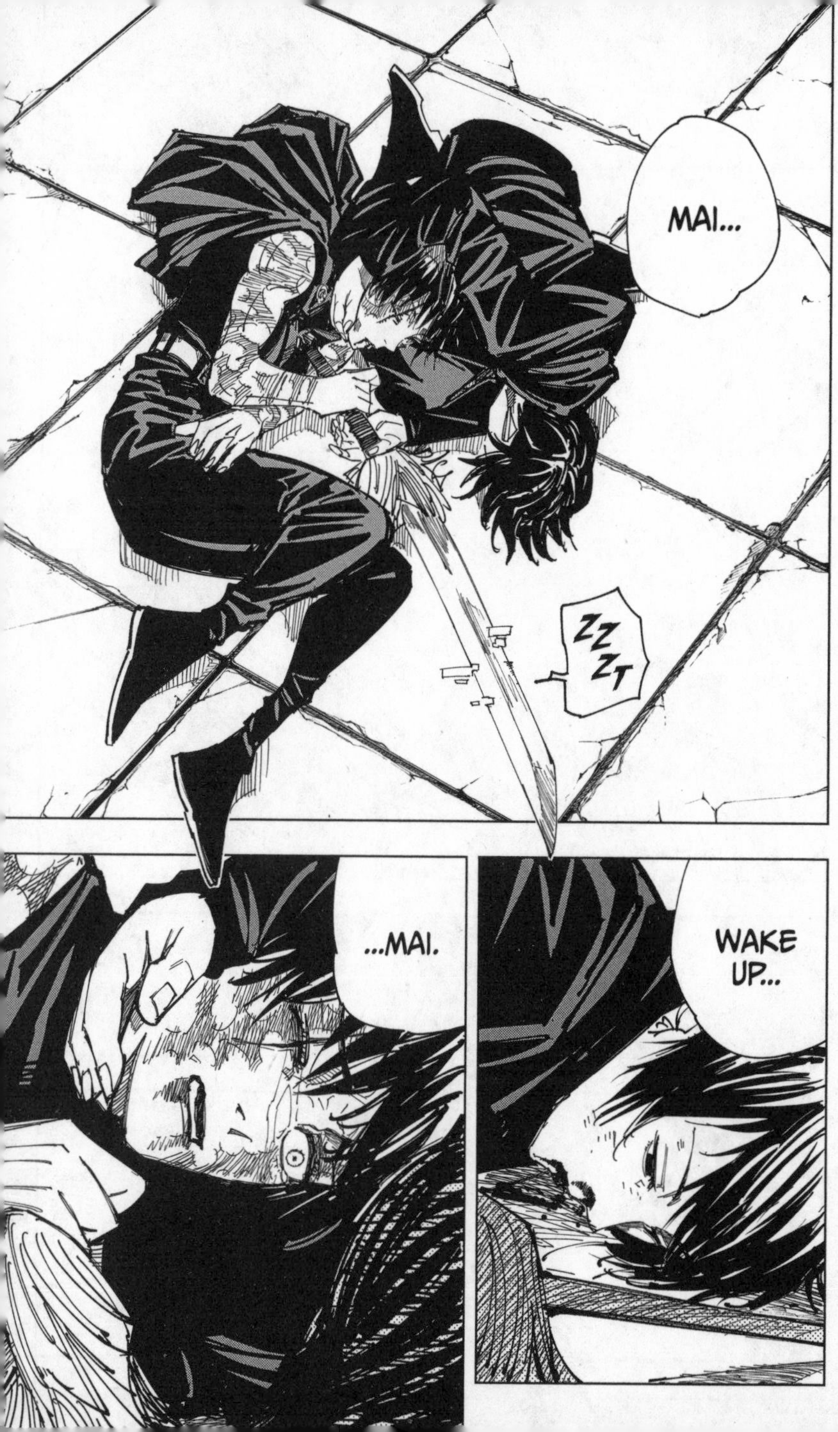
MAI...
ZZZZT
WAKE UP...
...MAI.

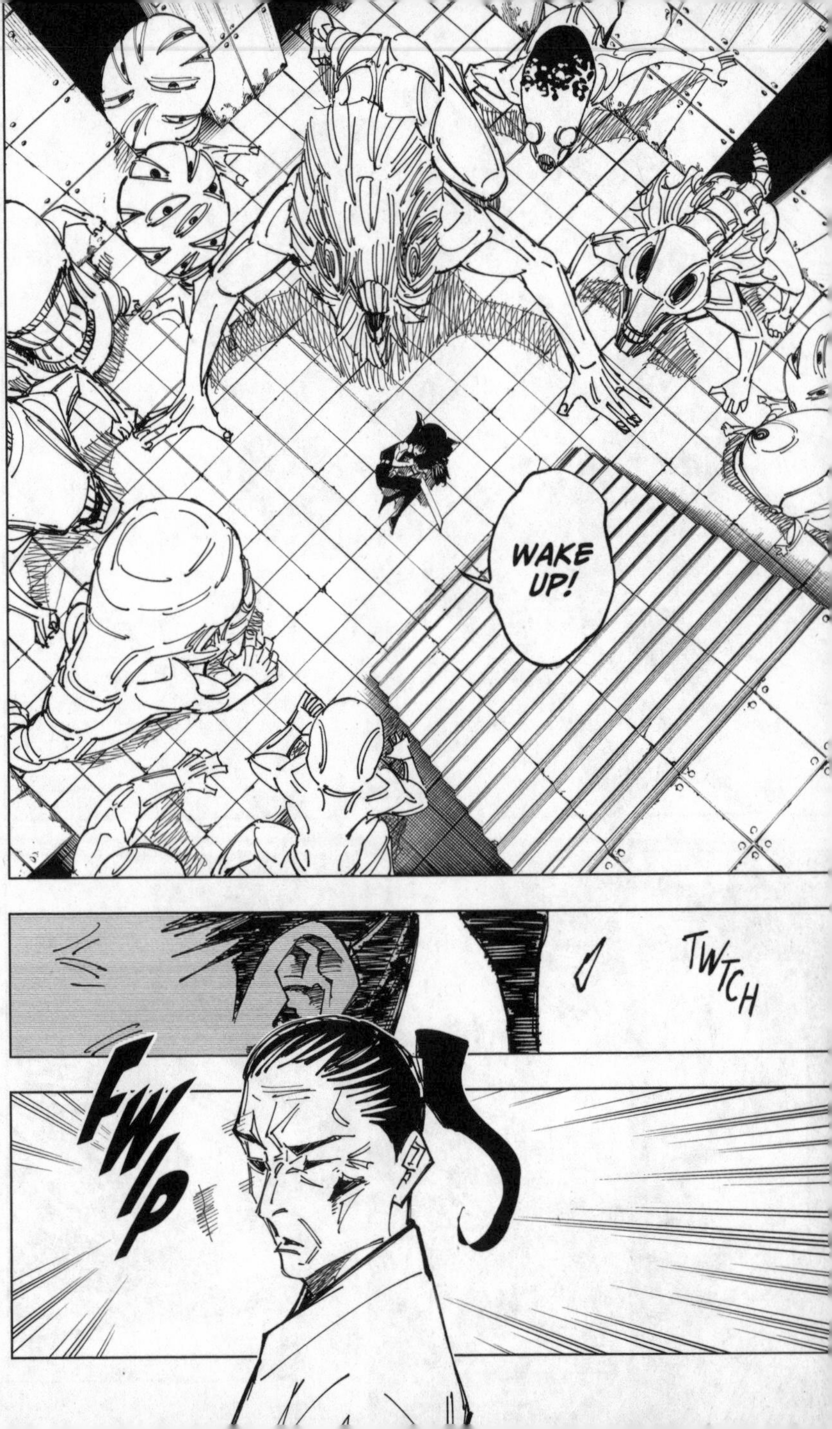
WAKE UP!
TWTCH
FWIP

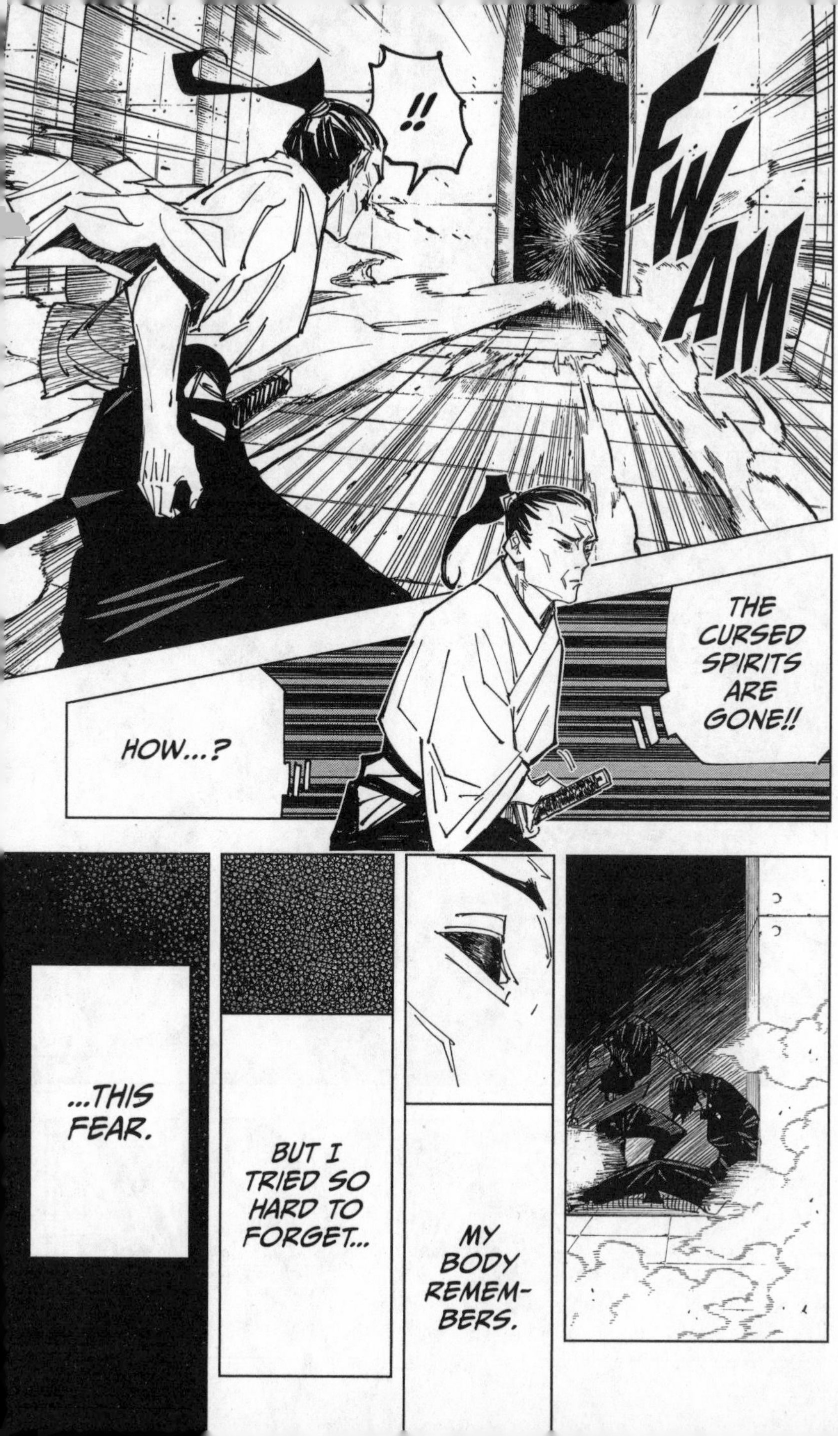
FWAM
!!
THE CURSED SPIRITS ARE GONE!!
HOW...?
MY BODY REMEMBERS.
BUT I TRIED SO HARD TO FORGET...
...THIS FEAR.

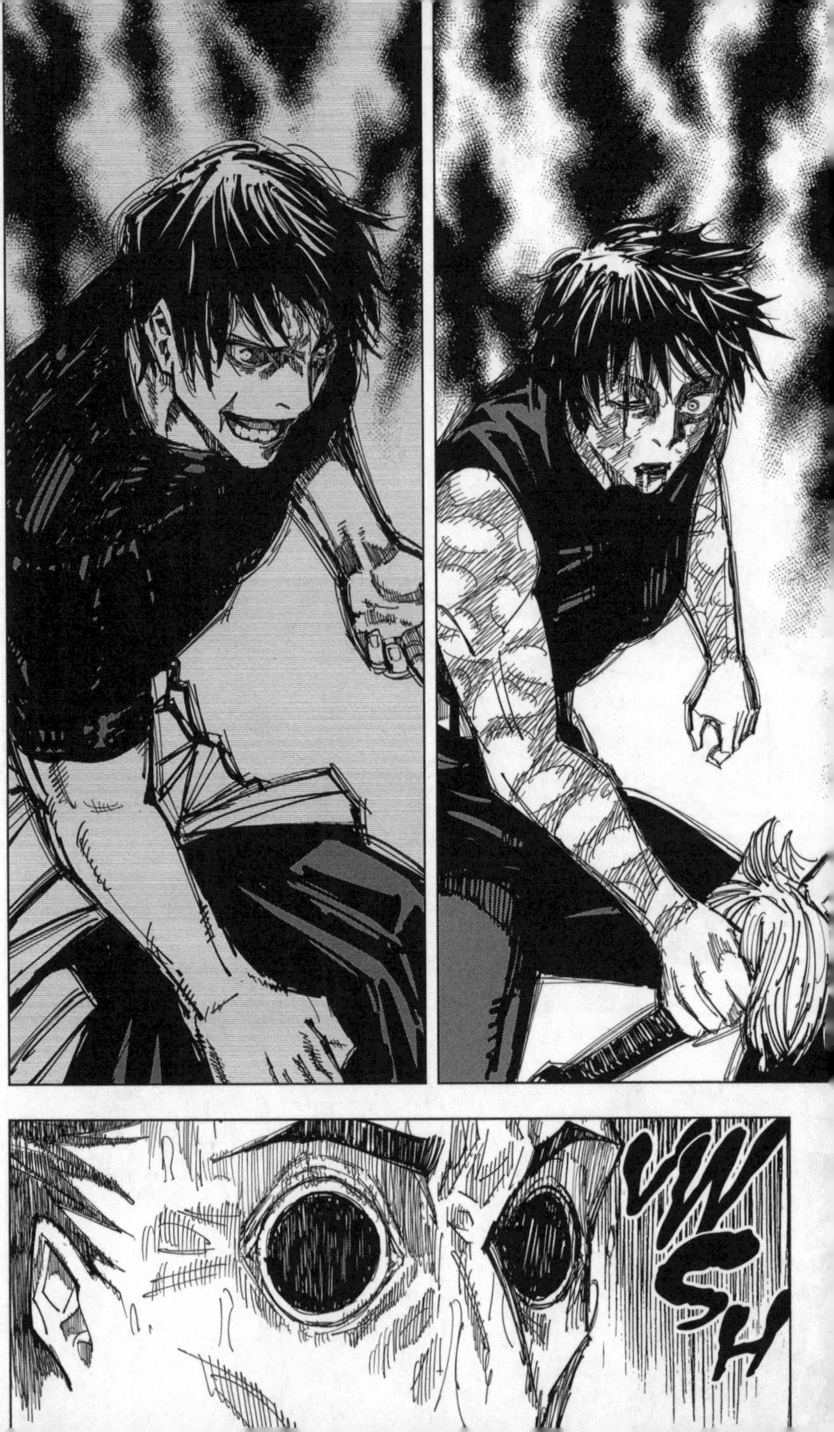
WSH

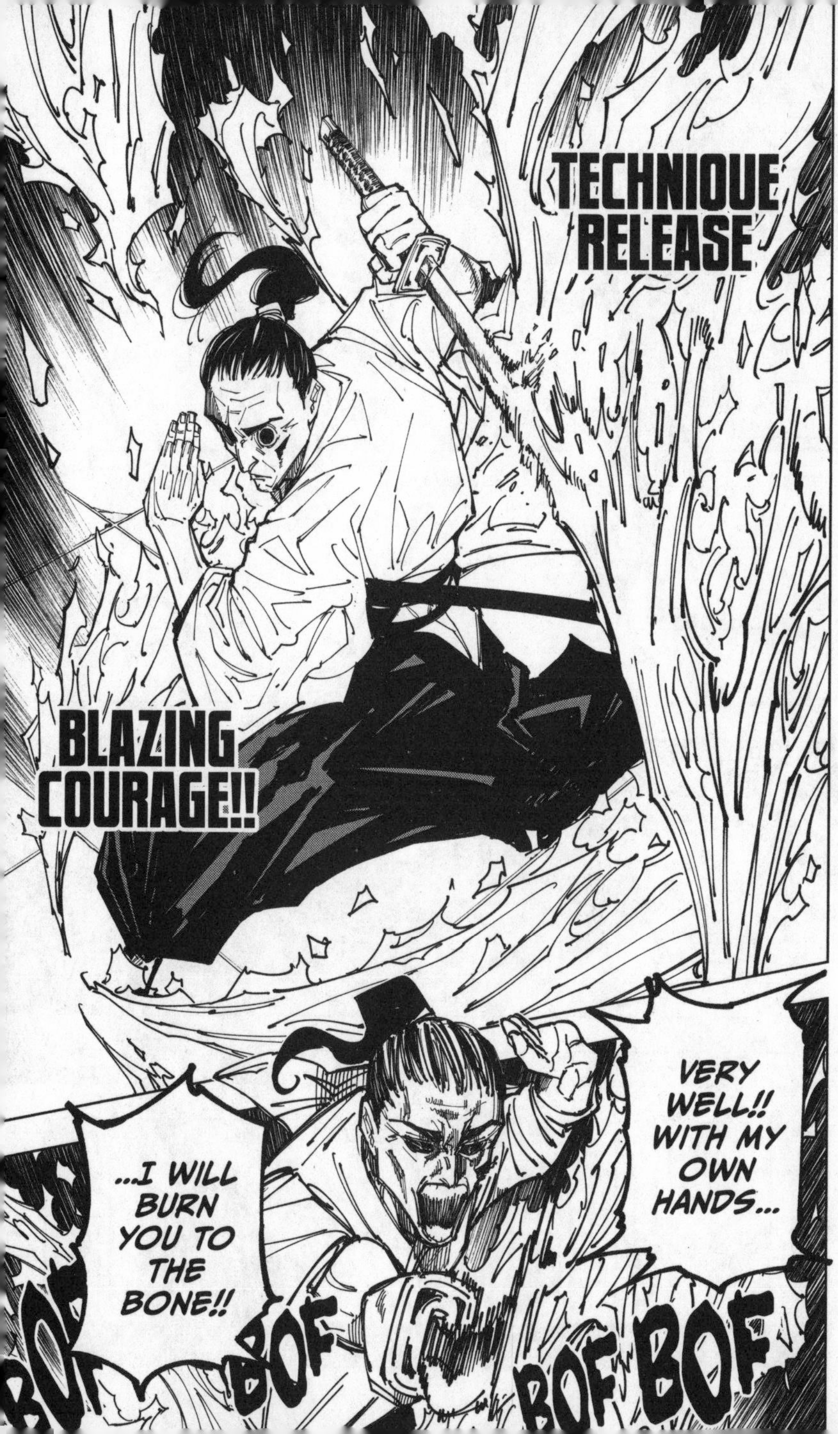
TECHNIQUE RELEASE
BLAZING COURAGE!!
VERY WELL!! WITH MY OWN HANDS...
...I WILL BURN YOU TO THE BONE!!
BOF BOF
BOF

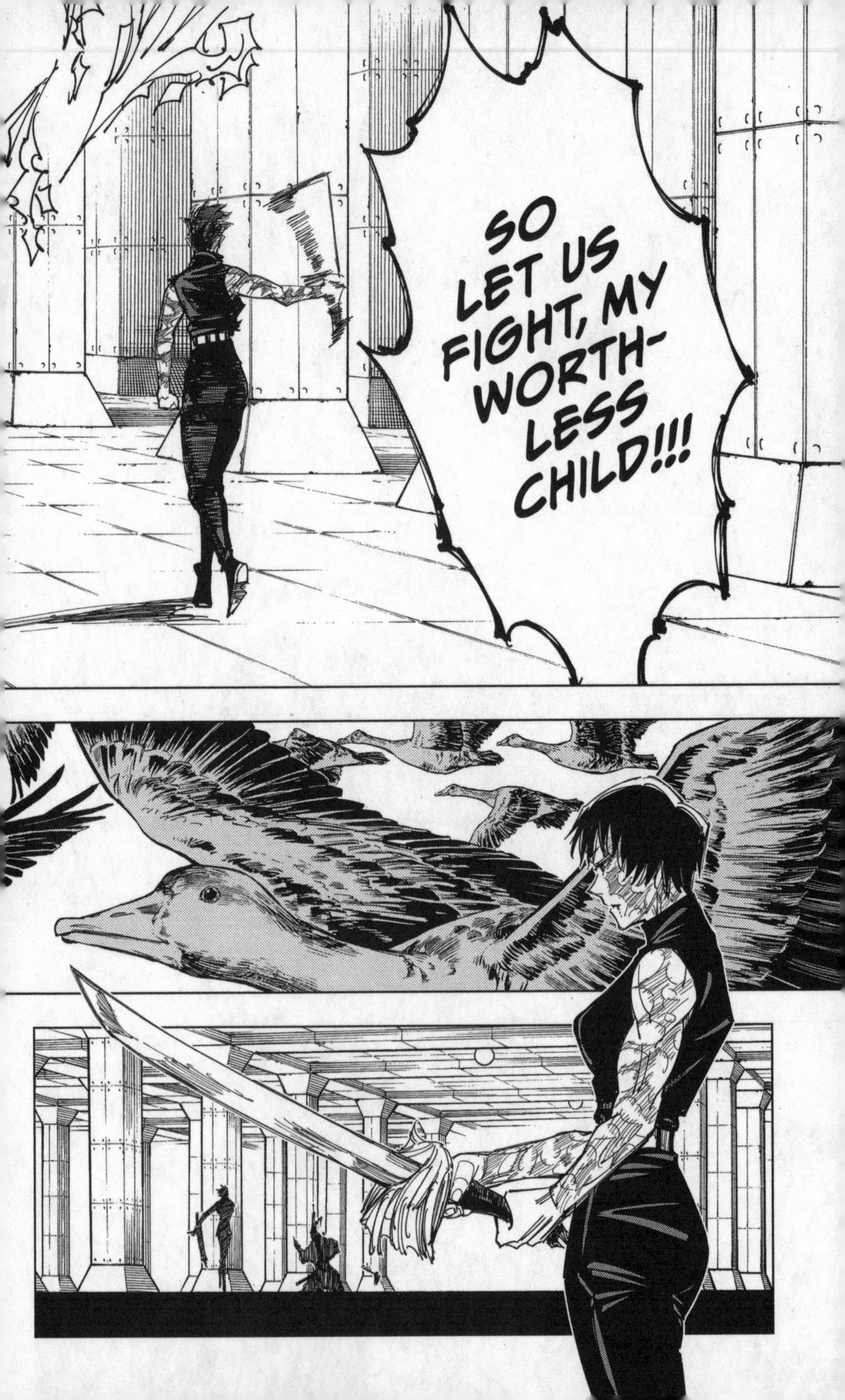
SO LET US FIGHT, MY WORTH-LESS CHILD!!!

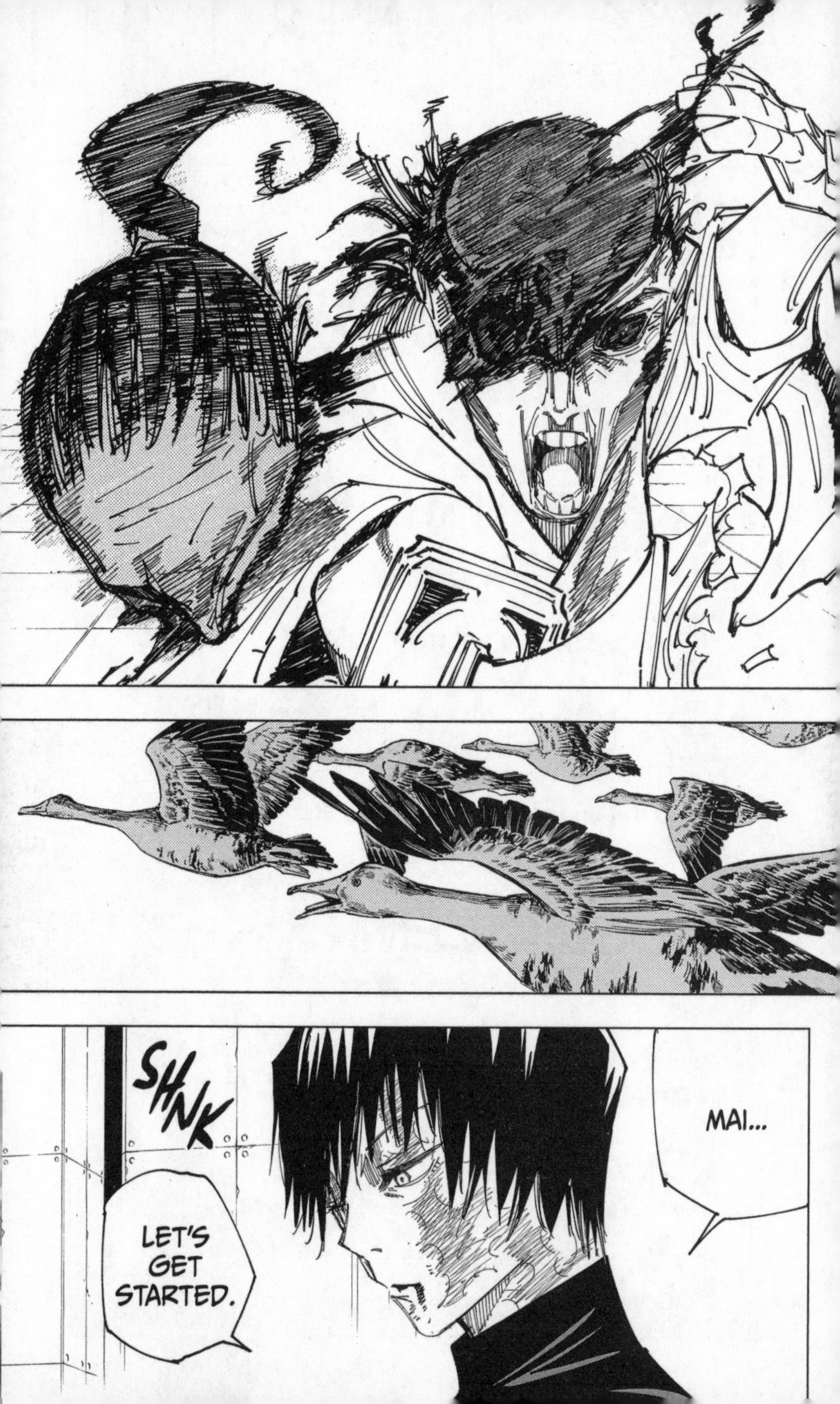
MAI...
SHNK
LET'S GET STARTED.

KUKURU UNIT ③
HEI REVIEW!!

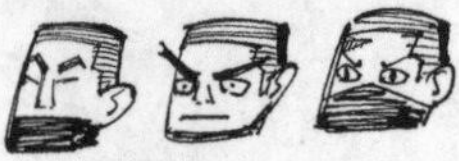

• RANTA ZEN'IN

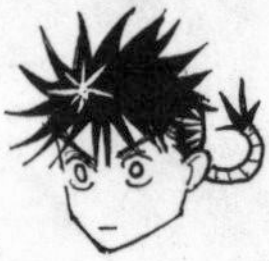

5.0 ☆☆☆☆☆

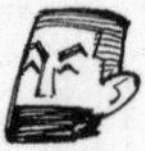

HE'S VERY POLITE TO US.

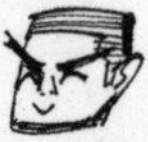

HE'LL EVEN CLEAN THE DOJO BEFORE WE DO.

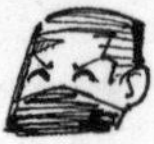

I WANT HIM TO EAT HIS FILL OF MEAT.

• CHOJURO ZEN'IN

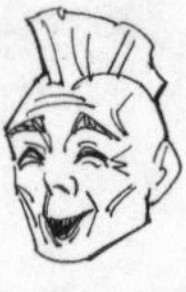

3.1 ☆☆☆★★

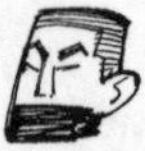

HE'S BEEN ANCIENT EVER SINCE I WAS A KID. I'VE NEVER SEEN HIM TALK.

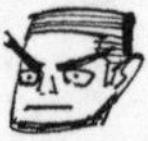

HOW OLD IS HE?

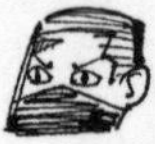

SERIOUSLY. HOW OLD?!

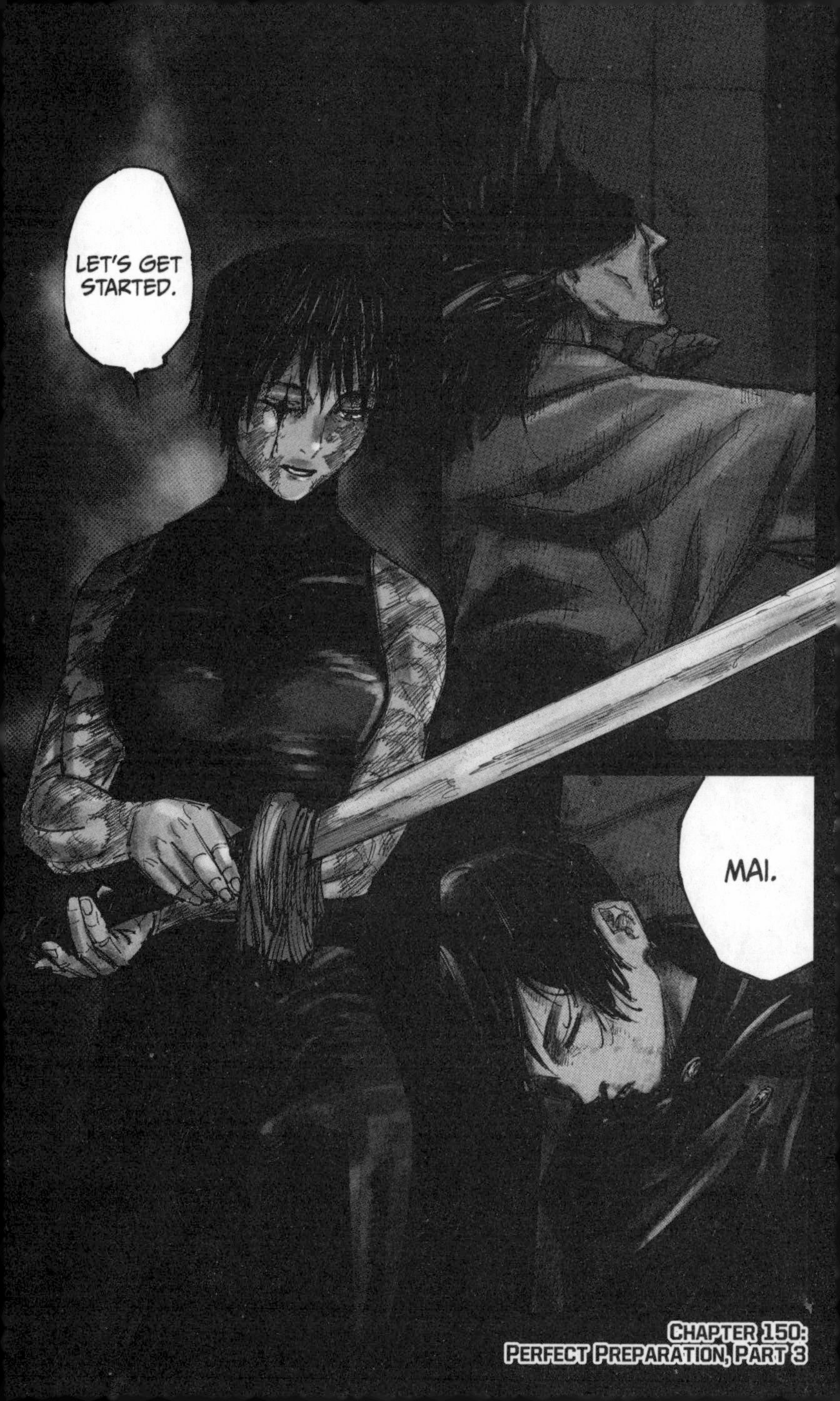
MAI.
LET'S GET STARTED.

Chapter 150: Perfect Preparation, Part 3

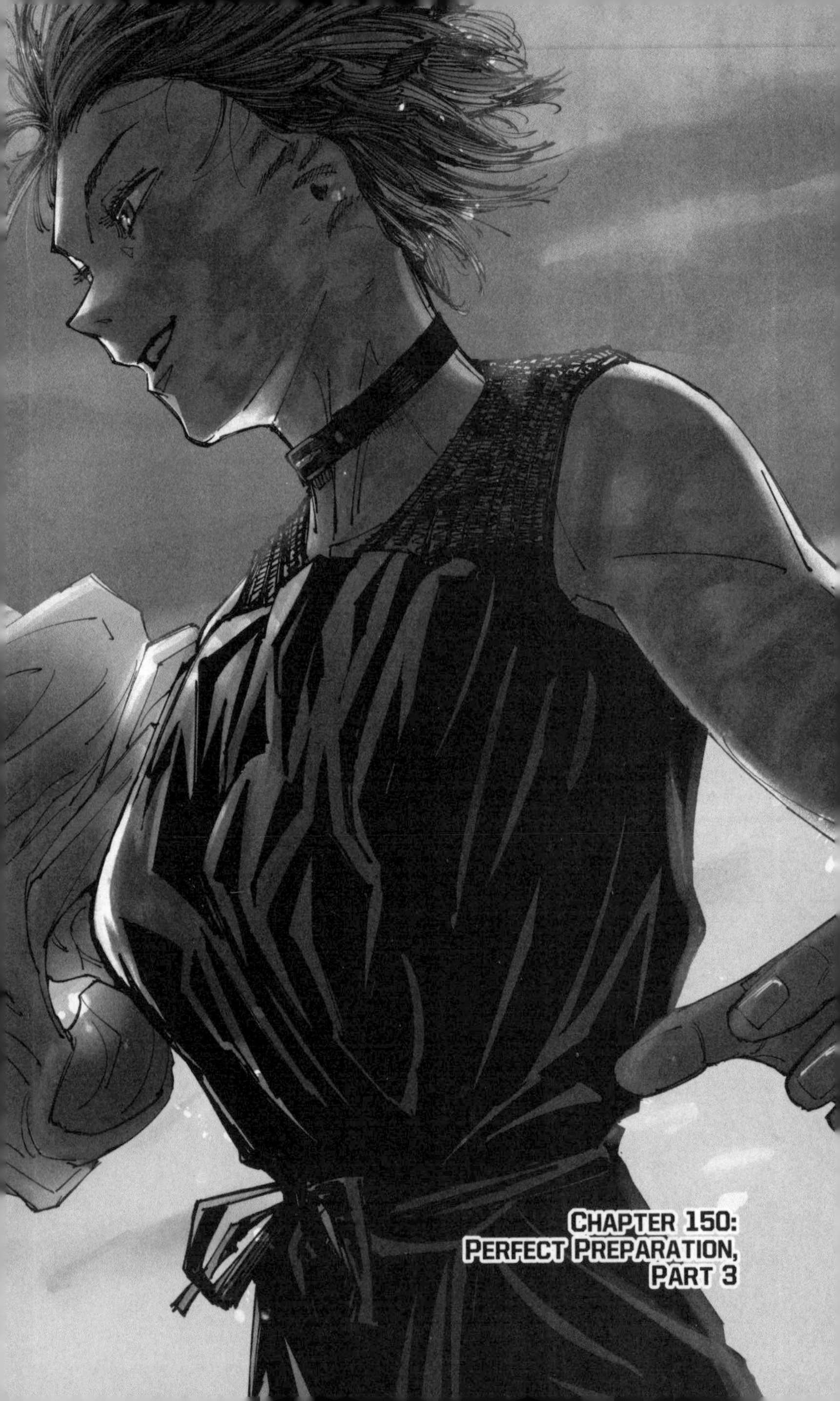
Chapter 150:
Perfect Preparation,
Part 3

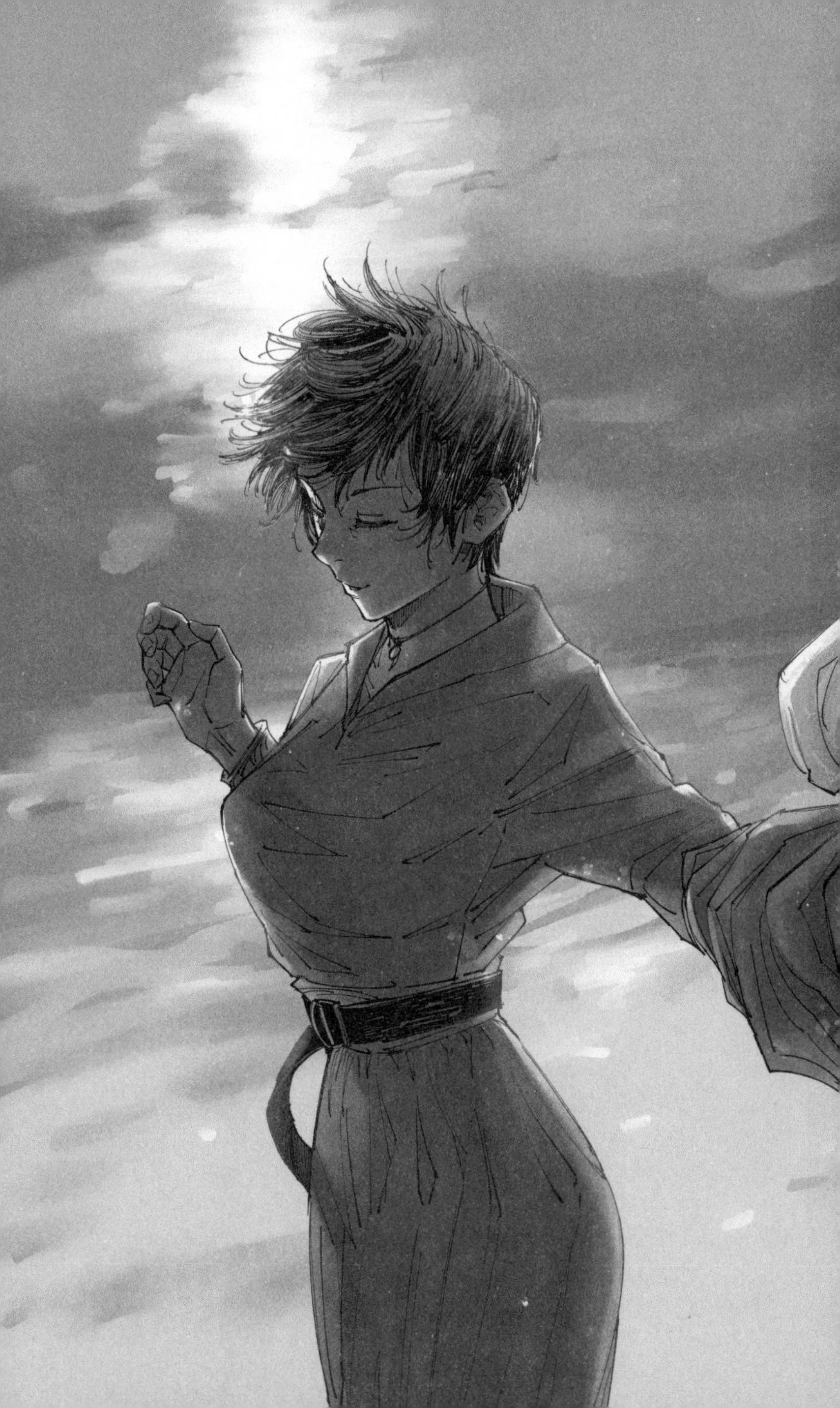

JUJUTSU KAISEN

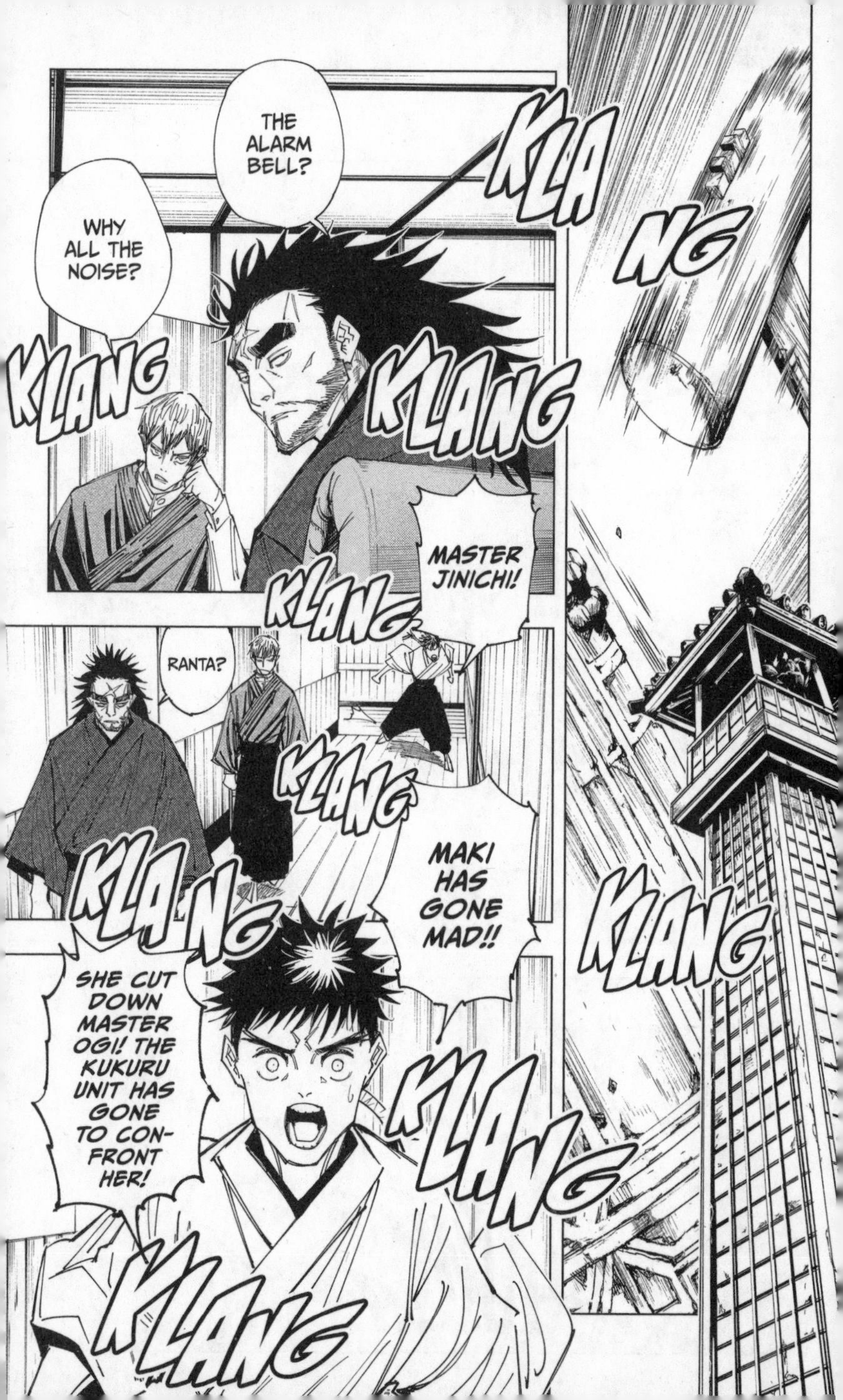
KLANG
KLANG
THE ALARM BELL?
WHY ALL THE NOISE?
KLANG
KLANG
MASTER JINICHI!
KLANG
KLANG
RANTA?
KLANG
MAKI HAS GONE MAD!!
SHE CUT DOWN MASTER OGI! THE KUKURU UNIT HAS GONE TO CON-FRONT HER!
KLANG
KLANG

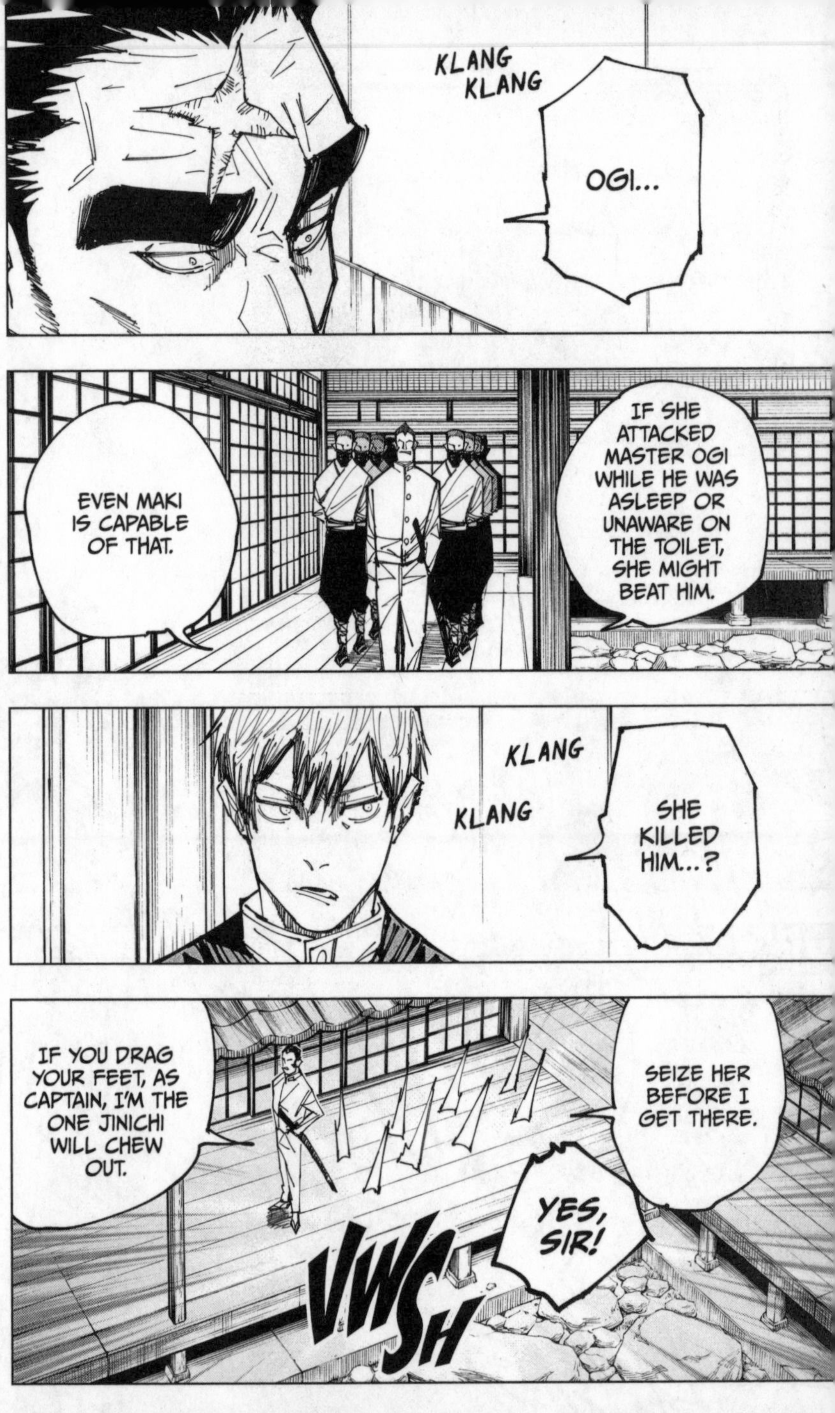
KLANG
KLANG
OGI...
IF SHE ATTACKED MASTER OGI WHILE HE WAS ASLEEP OR UNAWARE ON THE TOILET, SHE MIGHT BEAT HIM.
EVEN MAKI IS CAPABLE OF THAT.
KLANG
KLANG
SHE KILLED HIM...?
SEIZE HER BEFORE I GET THERE.
IF YOU DRAG YOUR FEET, AS CAPTAIN, I'M THE ONE JINICHI WILL CHEW OUT.
YES, SIR!
VWSH

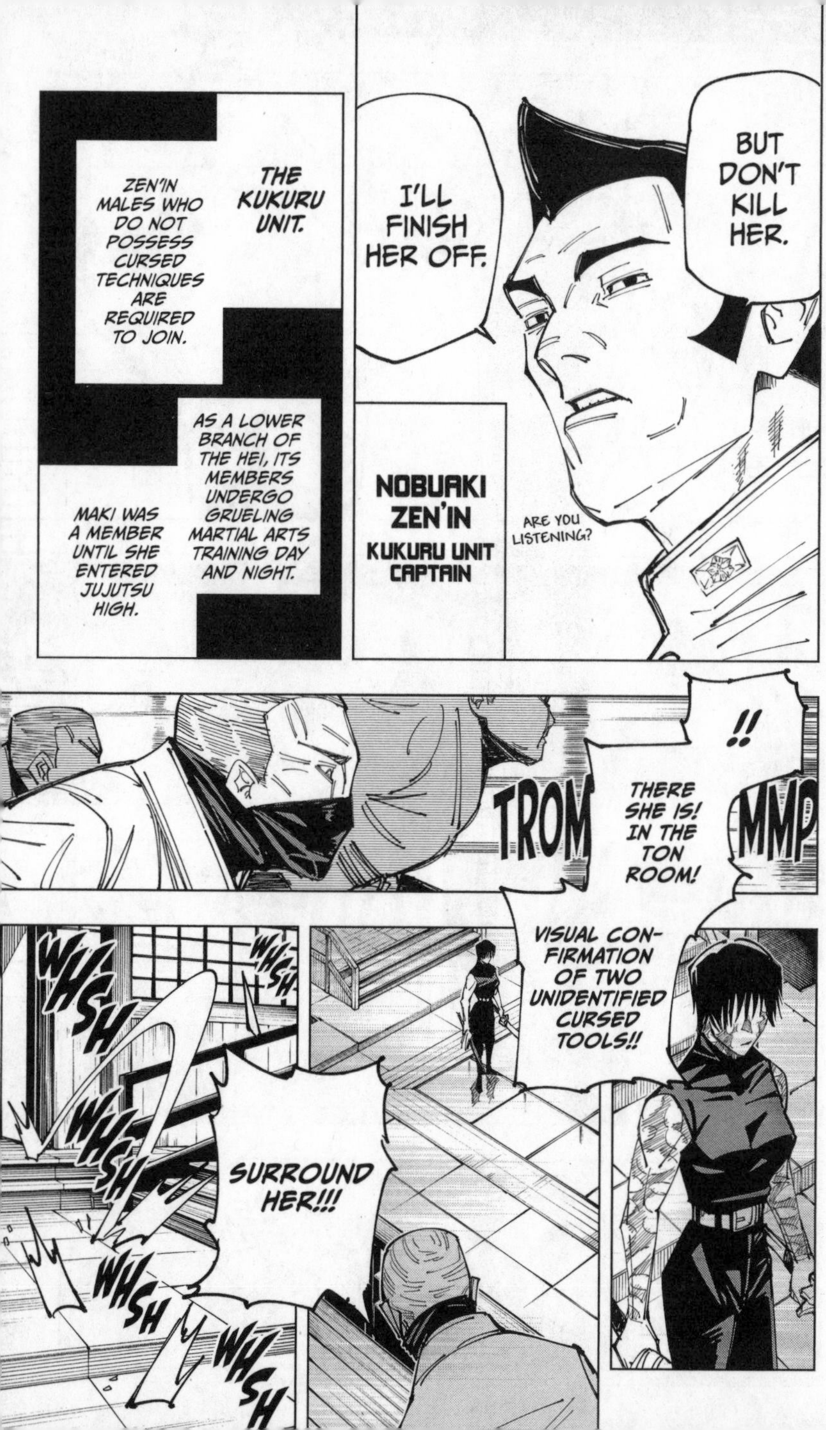
BUT DON'T KILL HER.
I'LL FINISH HER OFF.
NOBUAKI ZEN'IN
KUKURU UNIT CAPTAIN
ARE YOU LISTENING?
THE KUKURU UNIT.
ZEN'IN MALES WHO DO NOT POSSESS CURSED TECHNIQUES ARE REQUIRED TO JOIN.
AS A LOWER BRANCH OF THE HEI, ITS MEMBERS UNDERGO GRUELING MARTIAL ARTS TRAINING DAY AND NIGHT.
MAKI WAS A MEMBER UNTIL SHE ENTERED JUJUTSU HIGH.
!!
TROMMMP
THERE SHE IS! IN THE TON ROOM!
VISUAL CONFIRMATION OF TWO UNIDENTIFIED CURSED TOOLS!!
SURROUND HER!!!
WHSH
WHSH
WHSH
WHSH
WHSH

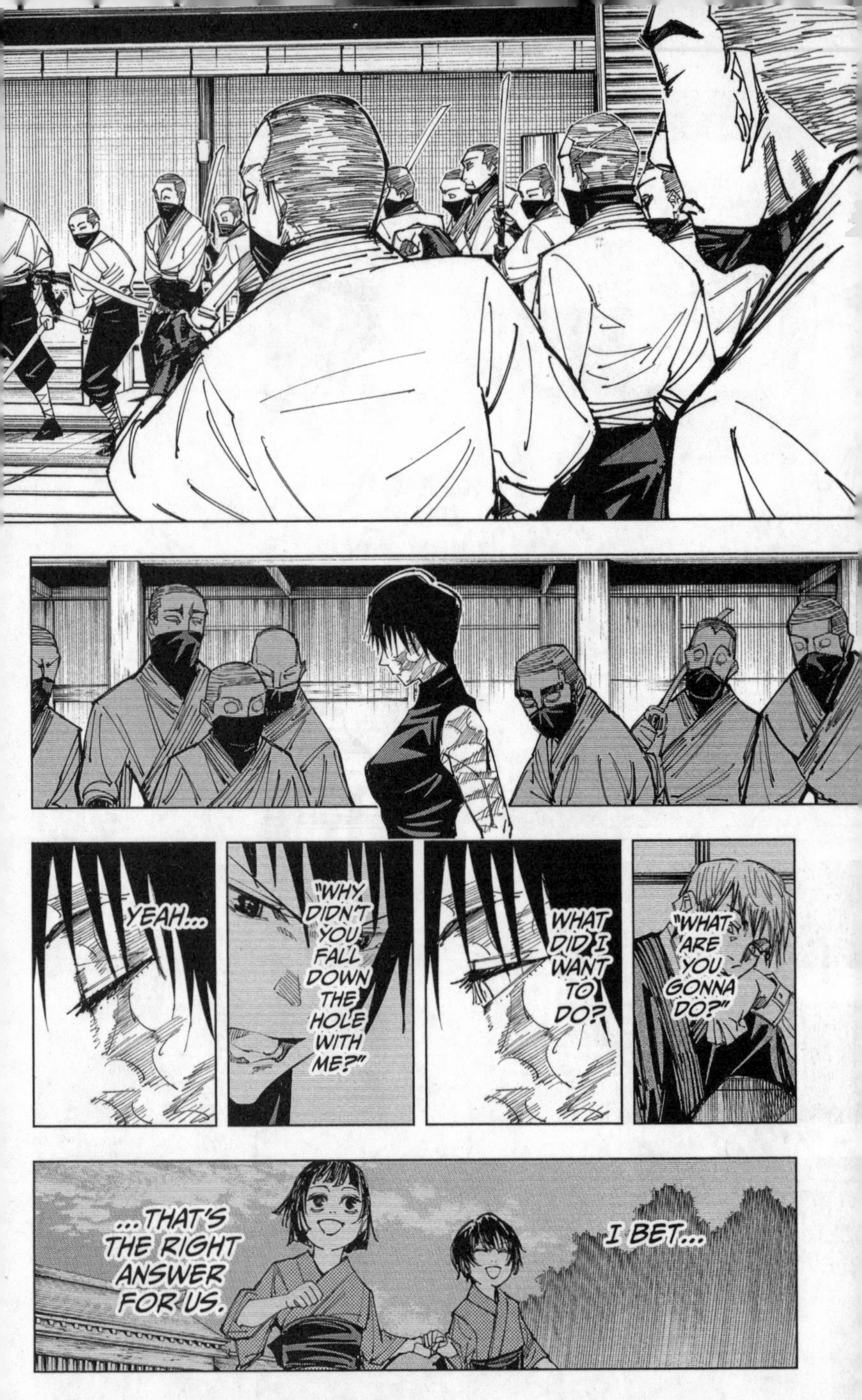
"WHAT ARE YOU GONNA DO?"
WHAT DID I WANT TO DO?
"WHY DIDN'T YOU FALL DOWN THE HOLE WITH ME?"
YEAH...
I BET...
...THAT'S THE RIGHT ANSWER FOR US.

ATTACK!!

I'M SORRY.

I'M SORRY, MAI.

"BUT PROMISE ME..."

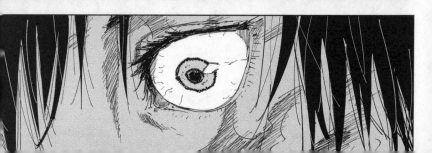

"DESTROY EVERYTHING."

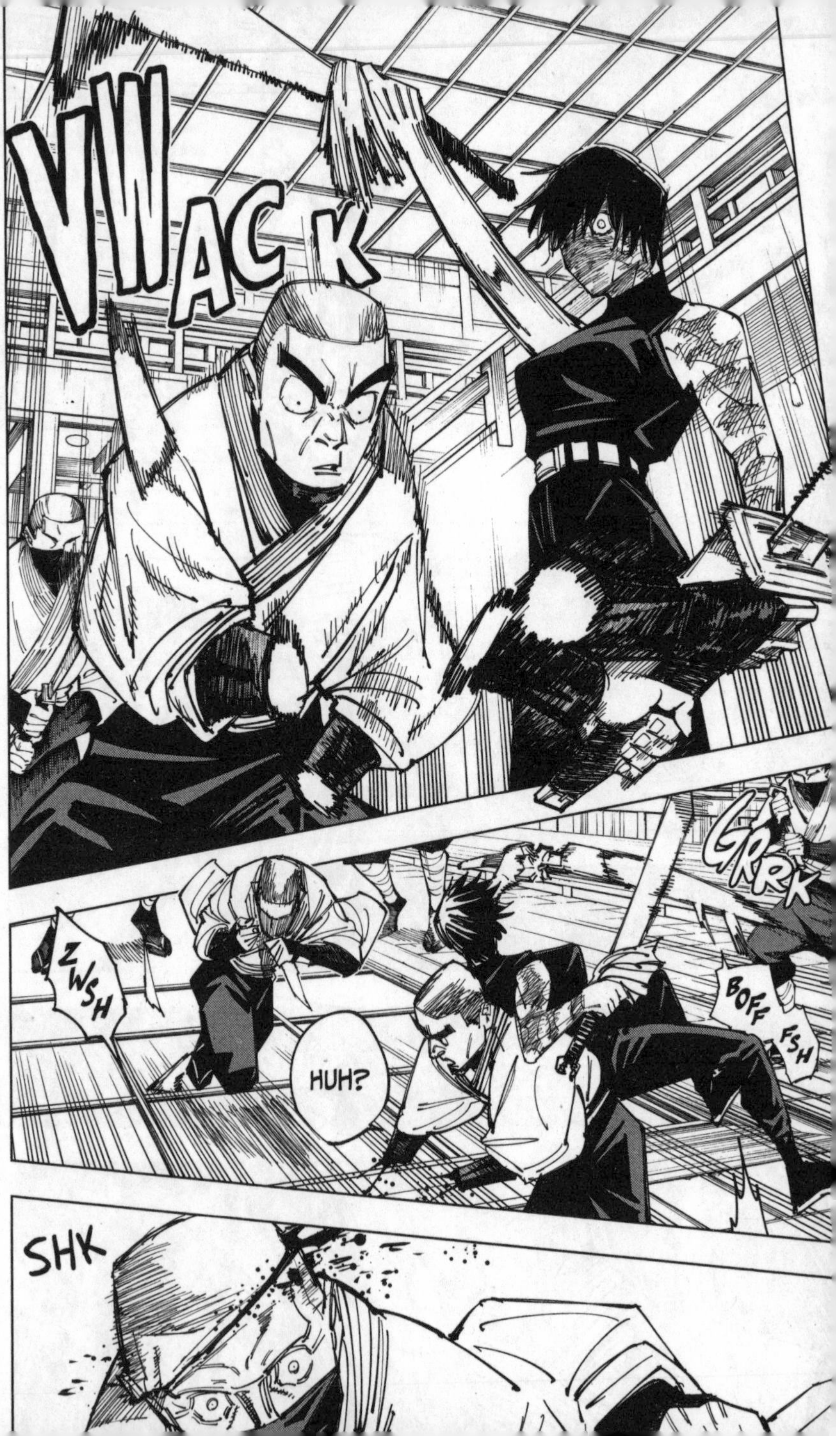
VWACK
GRRK
BOFF
FSH
HUH?
ZWSH
SHK

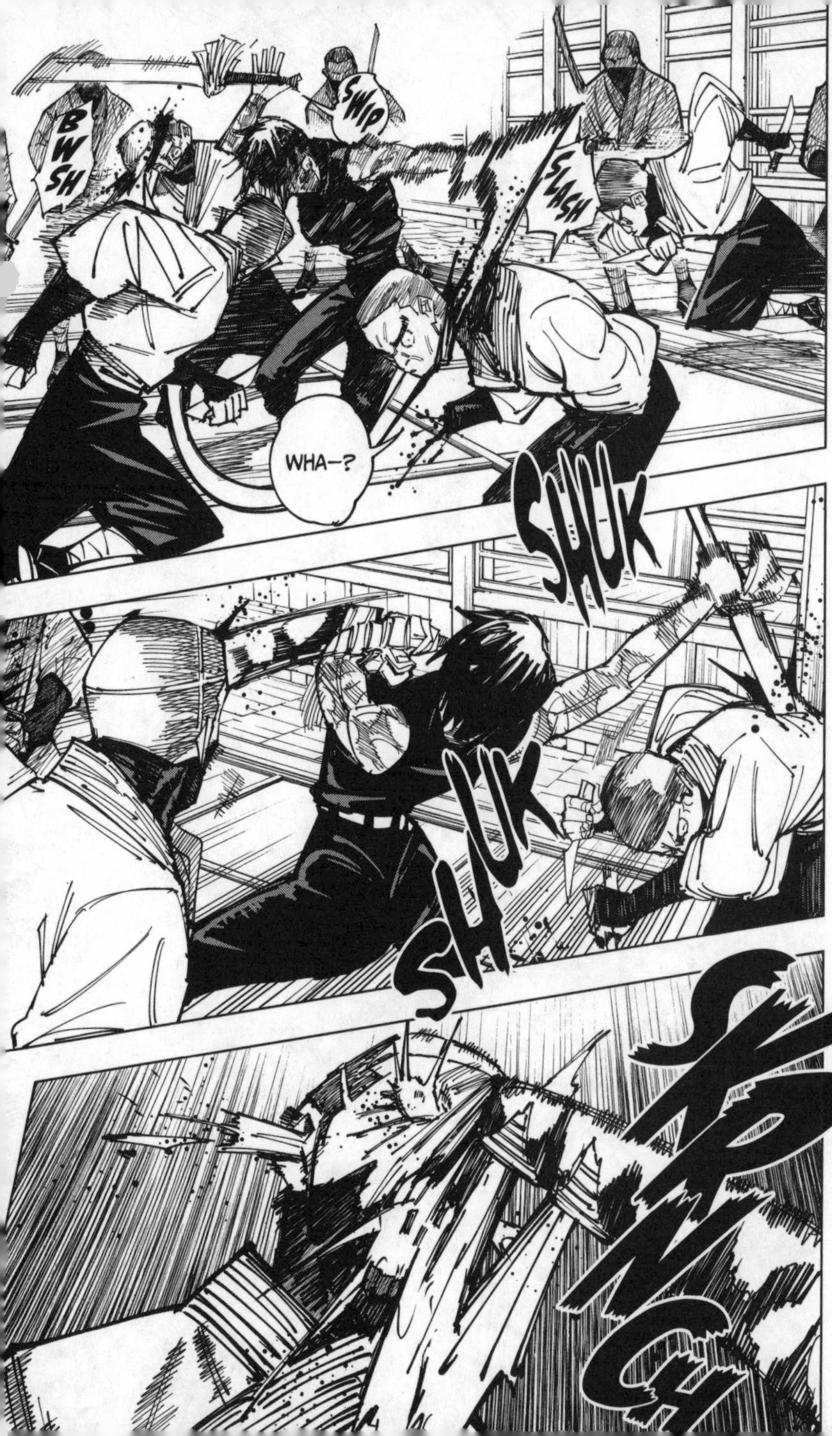
SLASH
SWIP
BWSH
WHA-?
SHUK
SHUK
SKRNCH

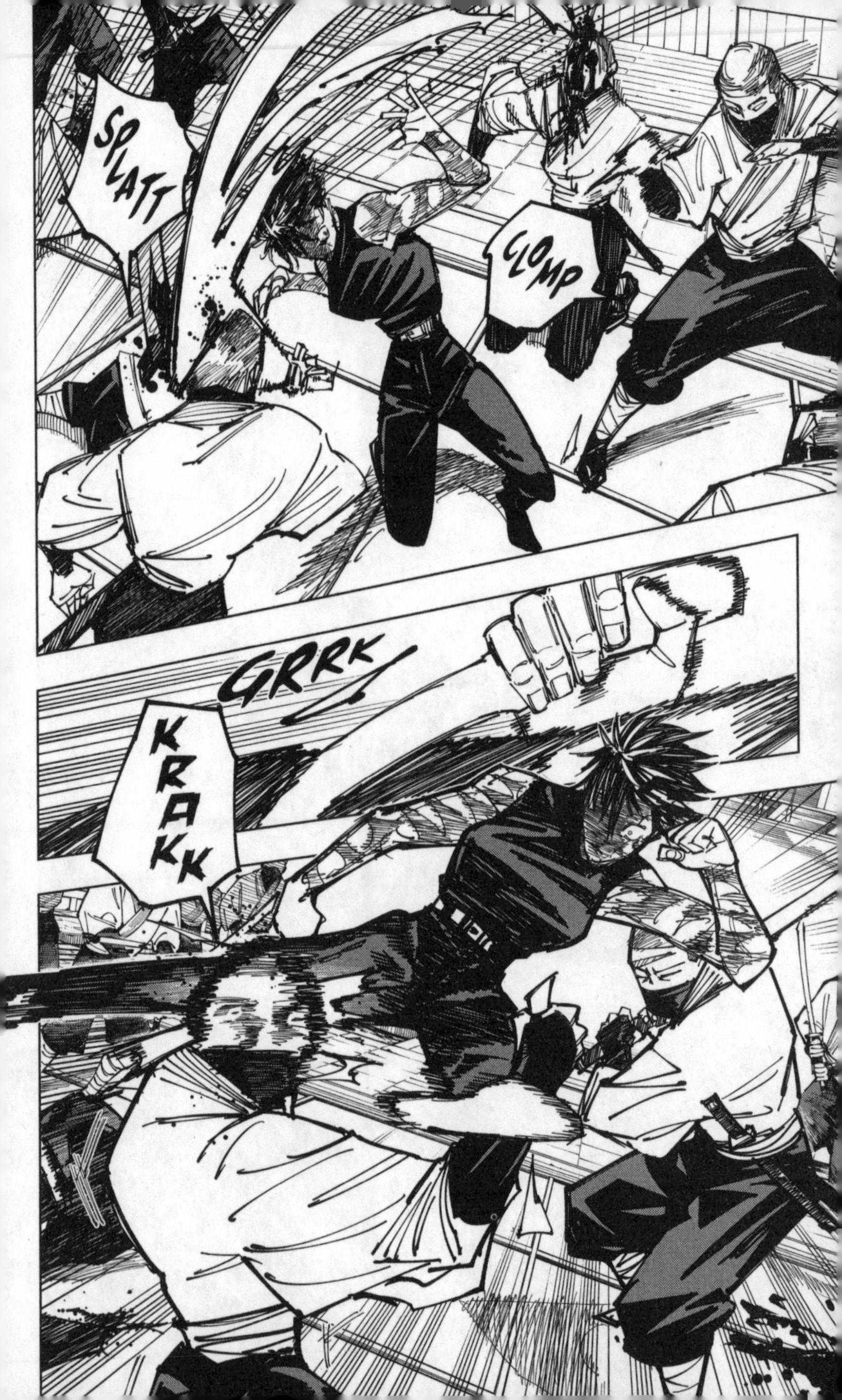
CLOMP
SPLATT
GRRK
KRAKK

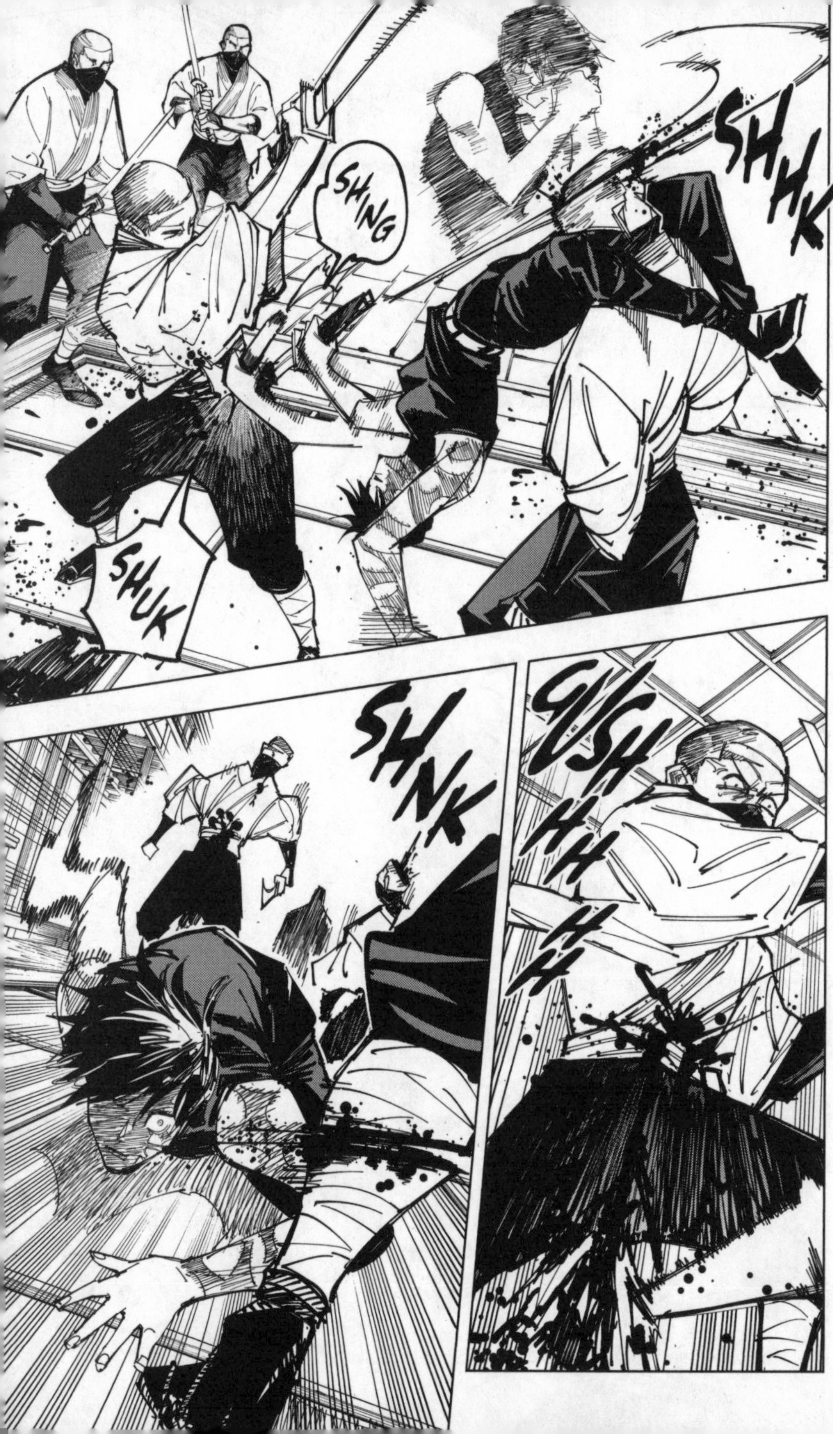
SHHK
SHING
SHUK
GUSHHHHHH
SHNK

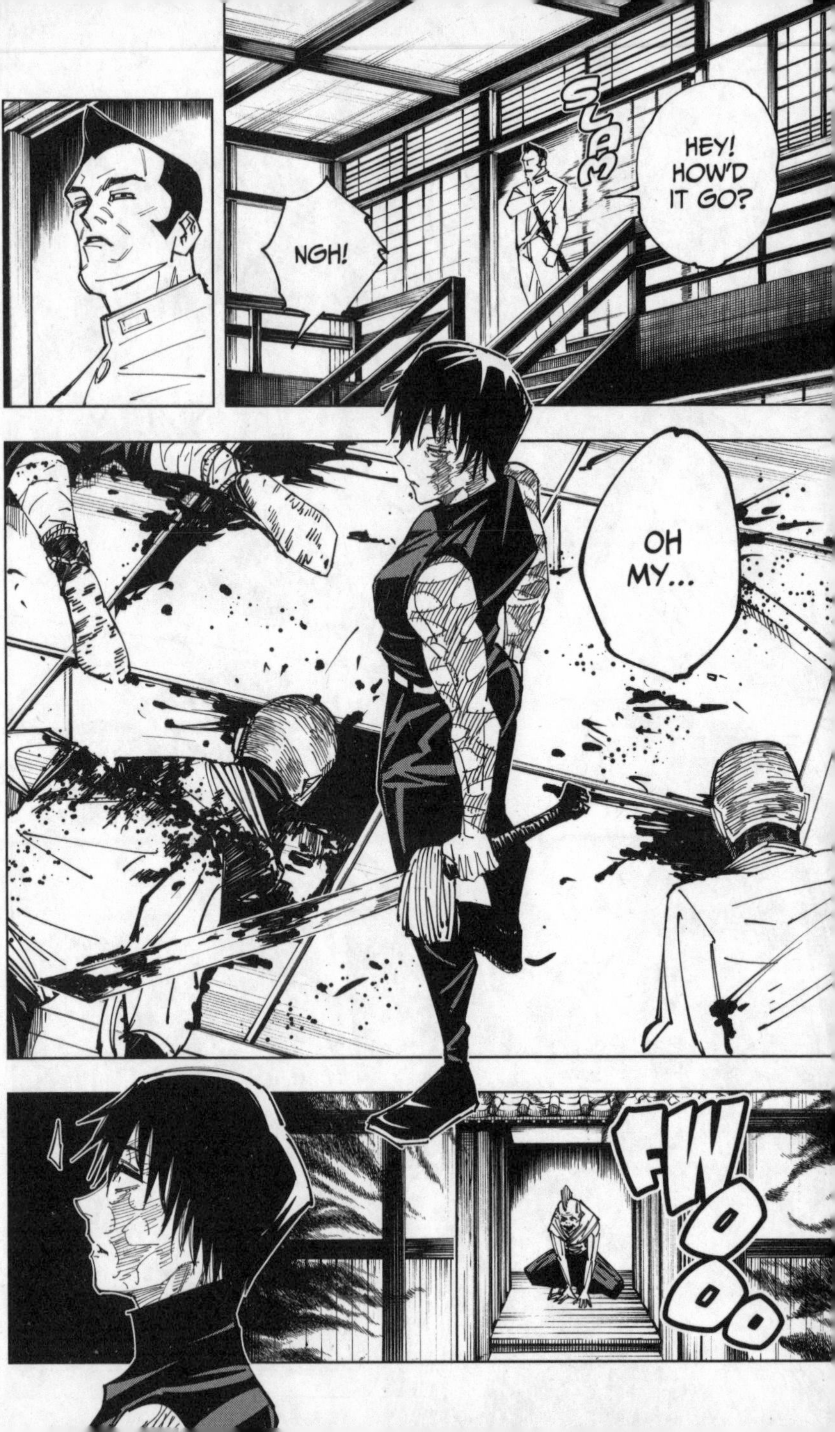
SLAM
HEY! HOW'D IT GO?
NGH!
OH MY...
FWOOO

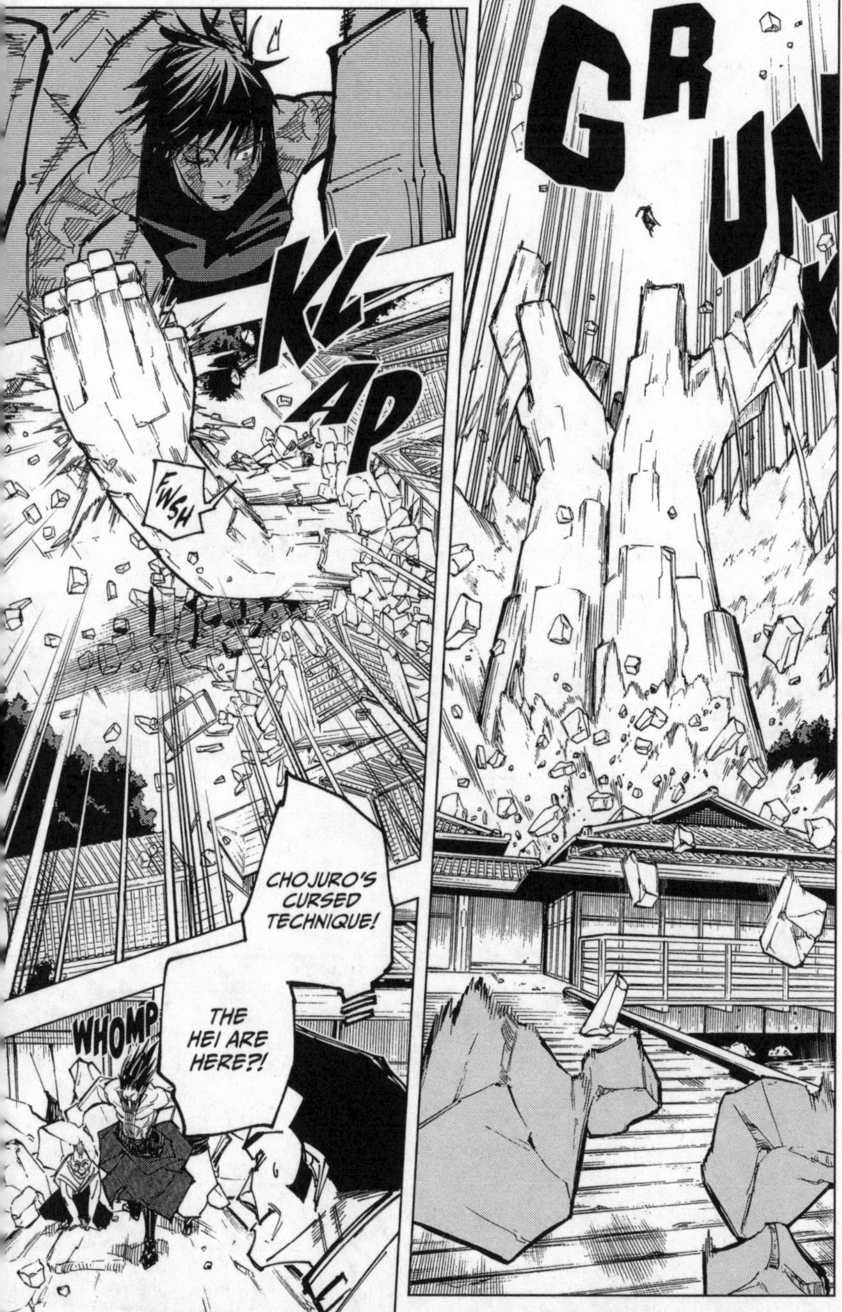
GRUNK
KLAP
FWSH
CHOJURO'S CURSED TECHNIQUE!
THE HEI ARE HERE?!
WHOMP

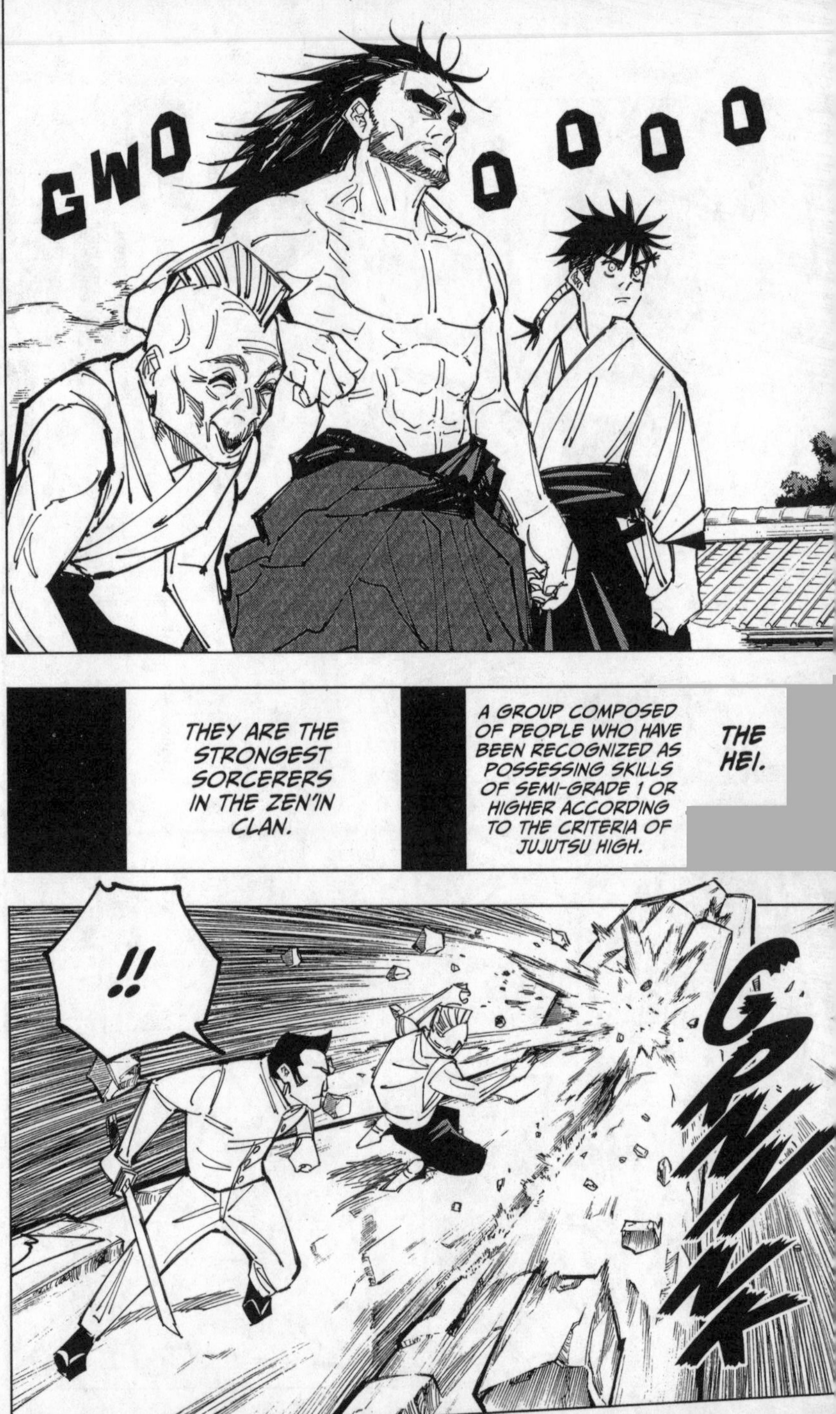
GWO OOOO
THE HEI.
A GROUP COMPOSED OF PEOPLE WHO HAVE BEEN RECOGNIZED AS POSSESSING SKILLS OF SEMI-GRADE 1 OR HIGHER ACCORDING TO THE CRITERIA OF JUJUTSU HIGH.
THEY ARE THE STRONGEST SORCERERS IN THE ZEN'IN CLAN.
!!
GRNNNK

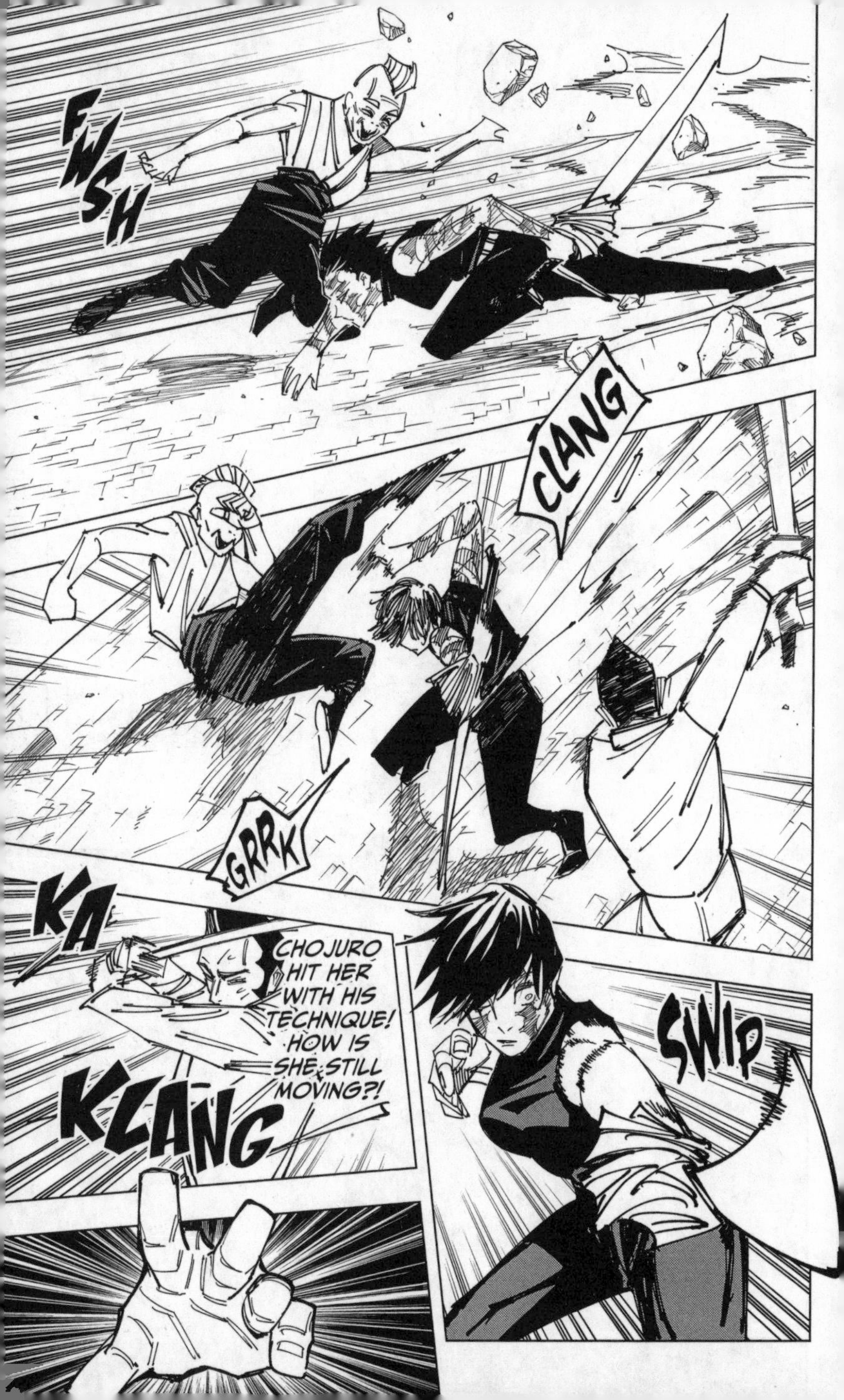
FWSH
CLANG
GRRK
SWIP
KA
CHOJURO HIT HER WITH HIS TECHNIQUE! HOW IS SHE STILL MOVING?!
KLANG

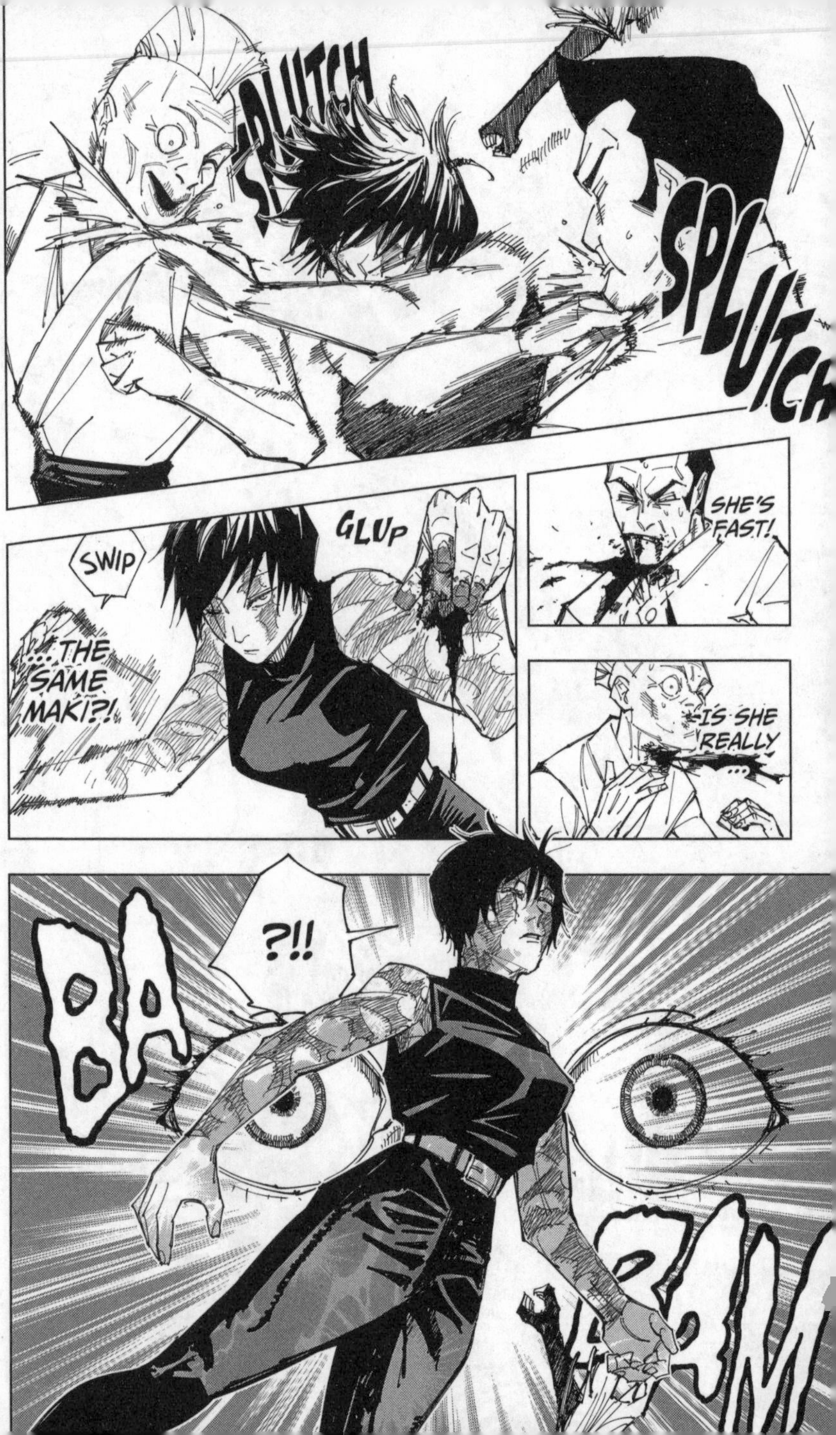
SPLUTCH
SPLUTCH
SHE'S FAST!
IS SHE REALLY ...
GLUP
SWIP
...THE SAME MAKI?!
?!!
BA

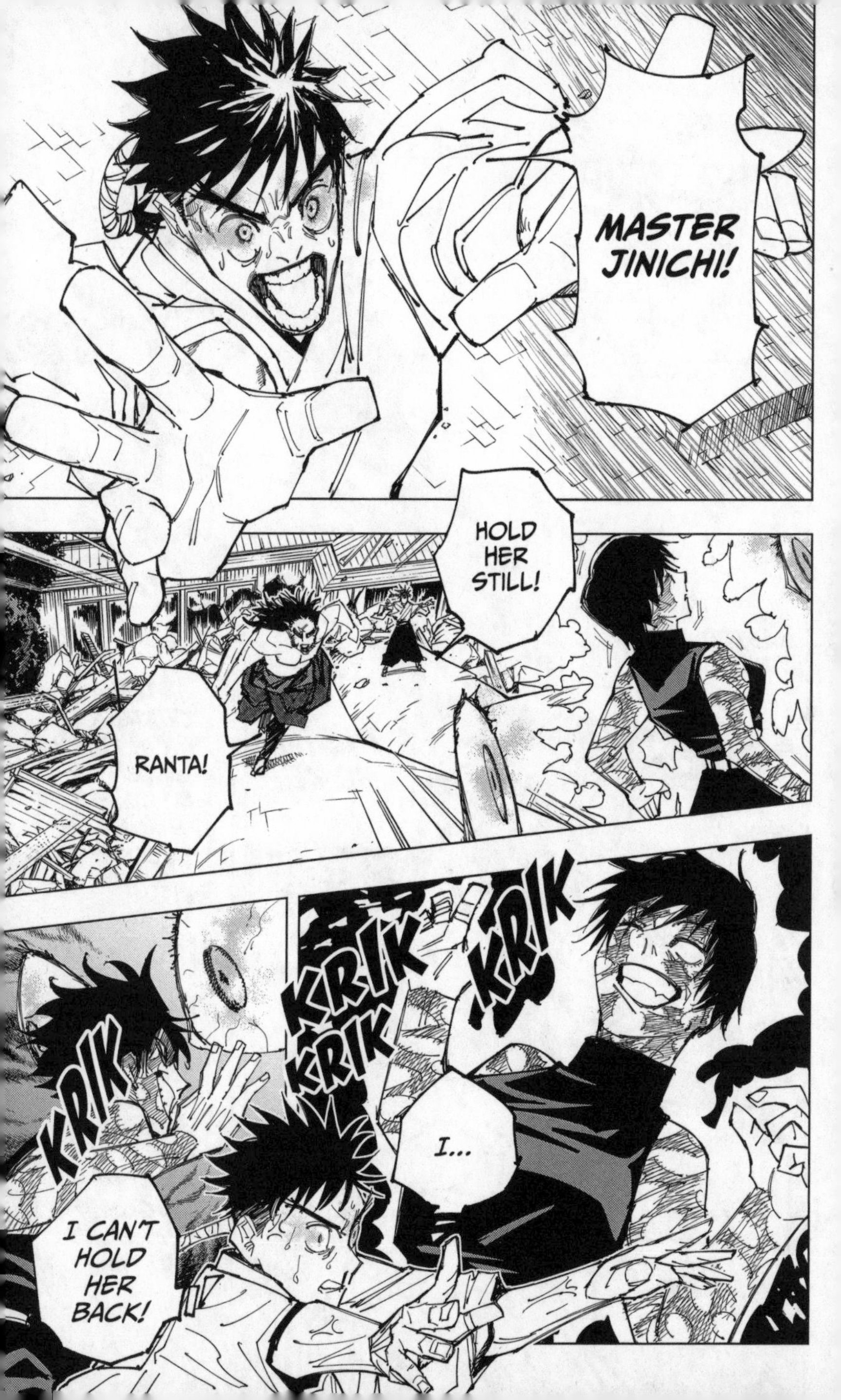
MASTER JINICHI!
HOLD HER STILL!
RANTA!
KRIK
KRIK
KRIK
KRIK
I...
I CAN'T HOLD HER BACK!

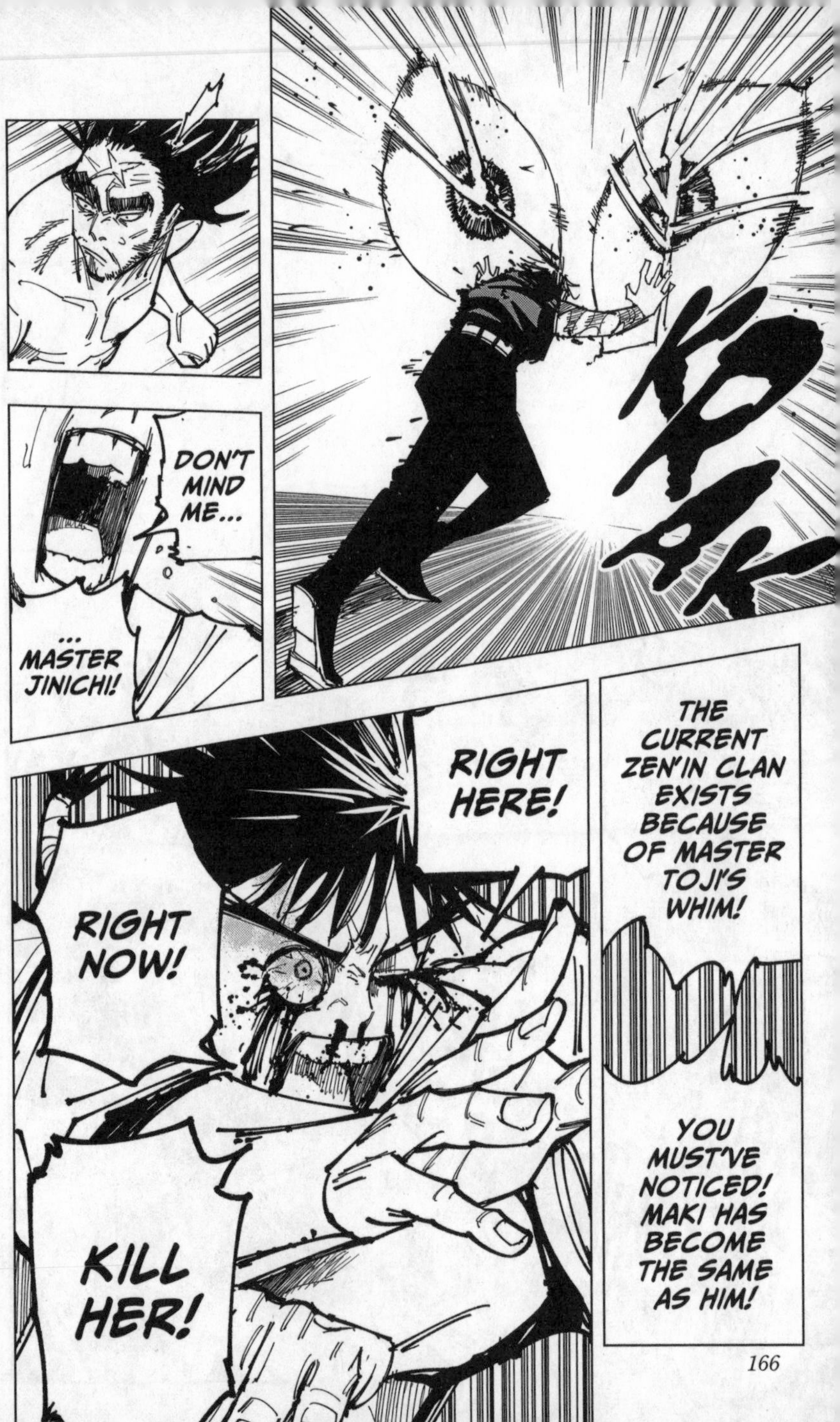
KRAK
DON'T MIND ME...
...MASTER JINICHI!
THE CURRENT ZEN'IN CLAN EXISTS BECAUSE OF MASTER TOJI'S WHIM!
YOU MUST'VE NOTICED! MAKI HAS BECOME THE SAME AS HIM!
RIGHT HERE!
RIGHT NOW!
KILL HER!

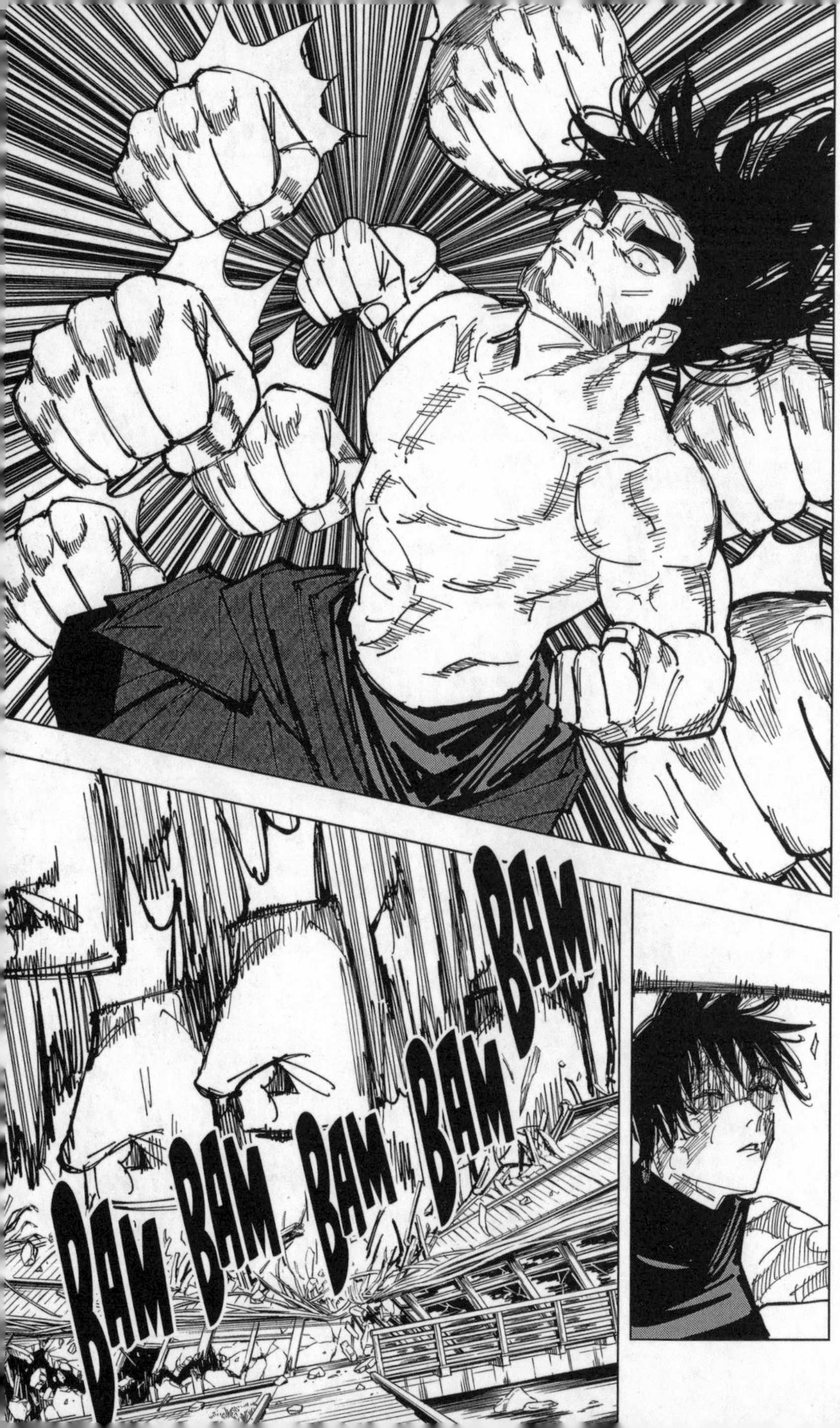

BAM BAM BAM BAM BAM

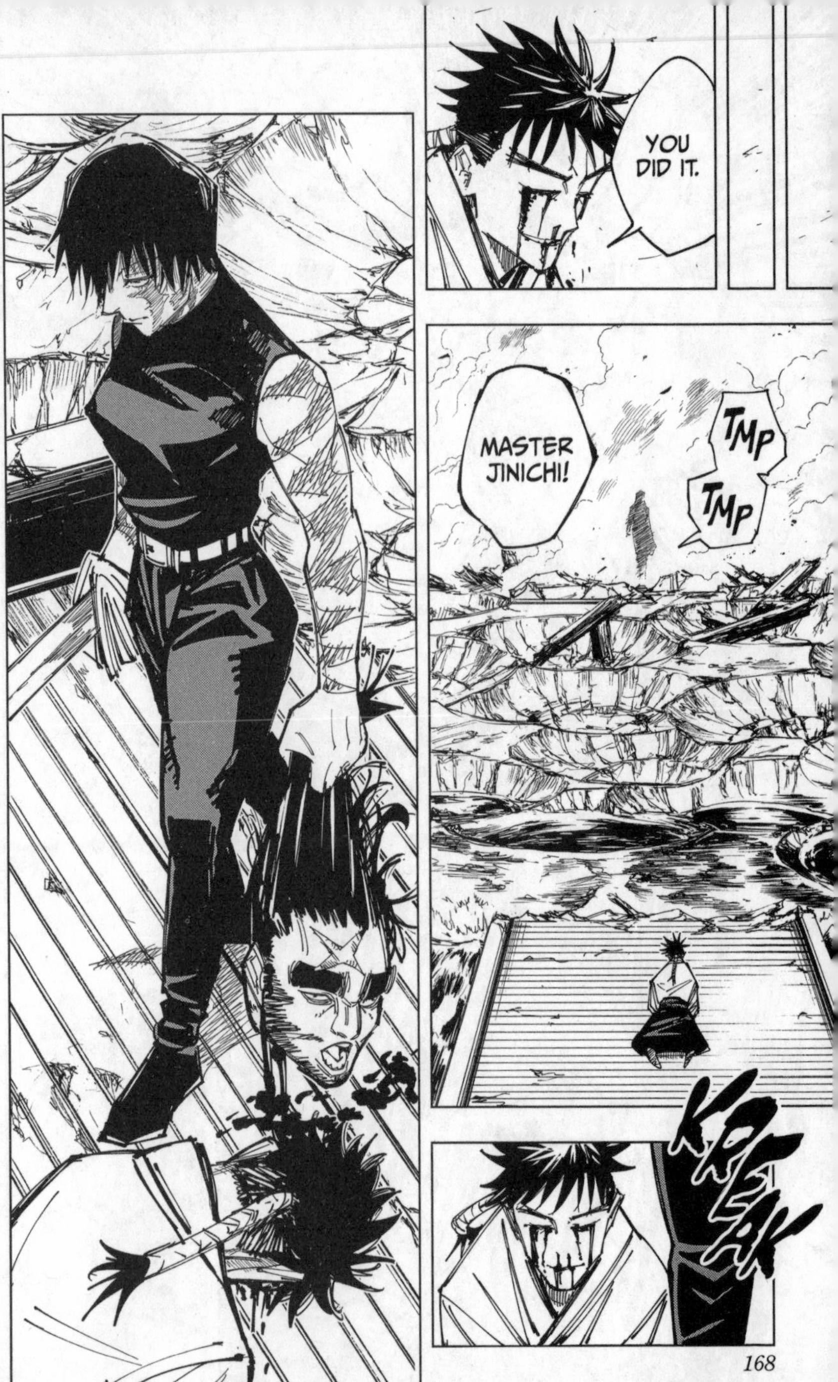
YOU DID IT.
TMP
TMP
MASTER JINICHI!

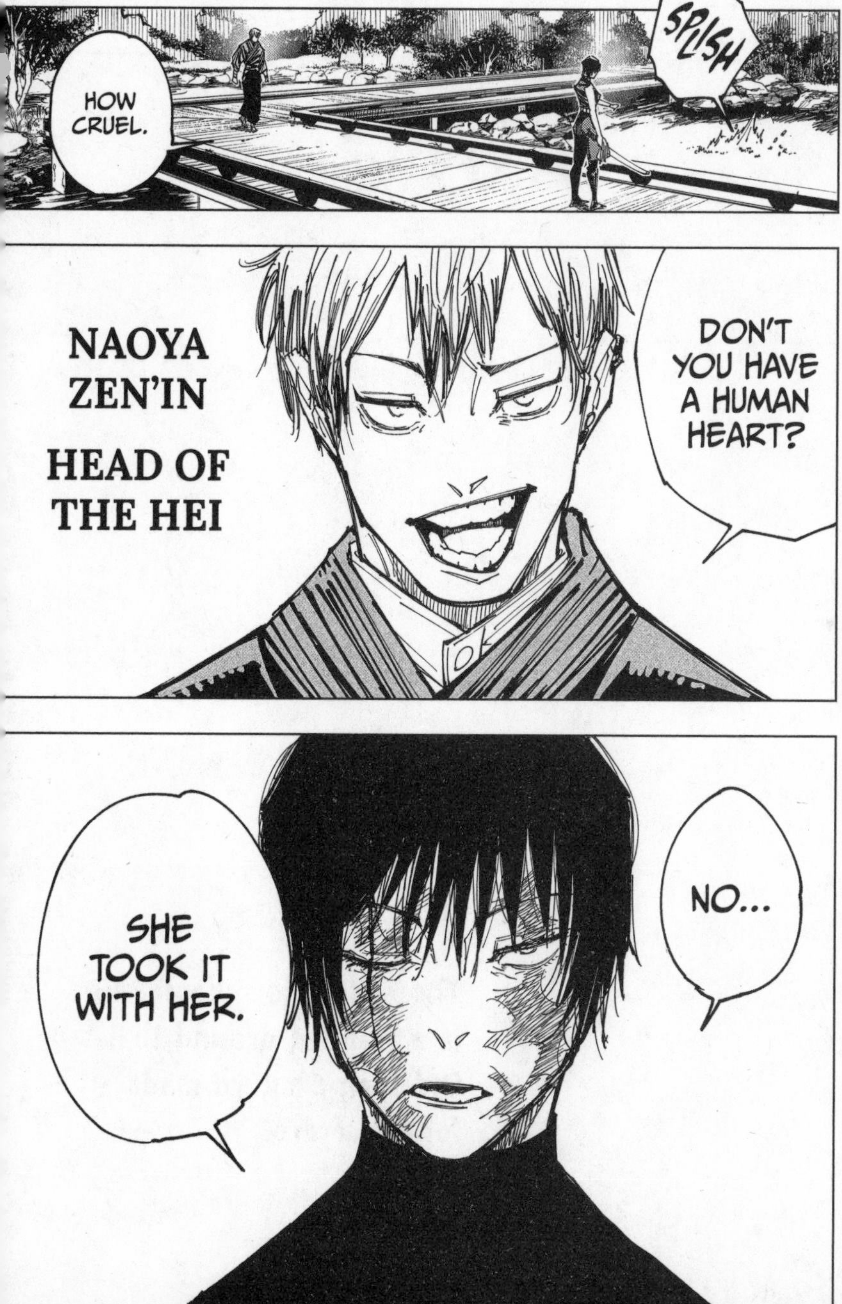
SPLISH
HOW CRUEL.
DON'T YOU HAVE A HUMAN HEART?
NAOYA ZEN'IN
HEAD OF THE HEI
NO...
SHE TOOK IT WITH HER.

The setting for chapter 151 is a training ground that Old Man Chojuro made for sorcerers.

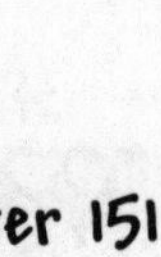

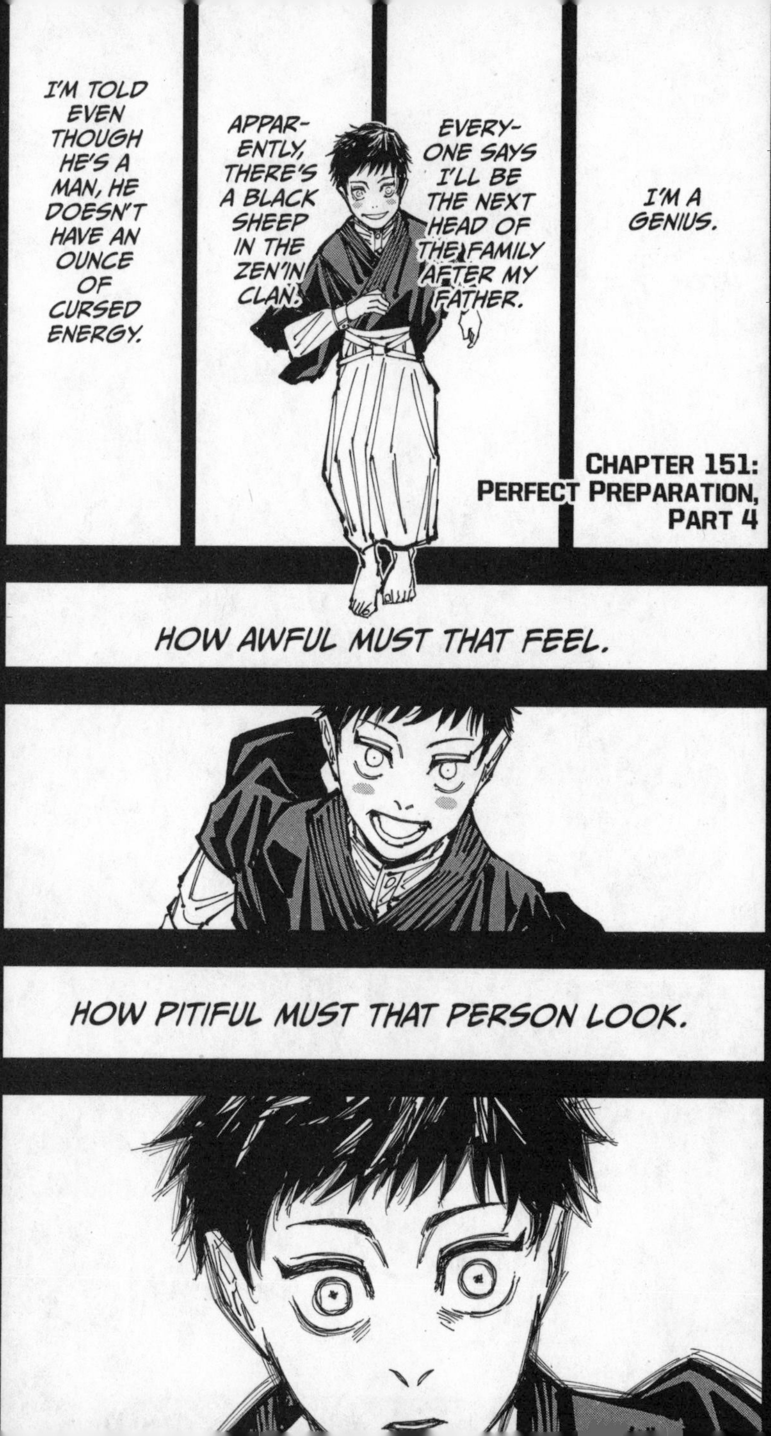
I'M A GENIUS.
CHAPTER 151: PERFECT PREPARATION, PART 4
EVERYONE SAYS I'LL BE THE NEXT HEAD OF THE FAMILY AFTER MY FATHER.
APPARENTLY, THERE'S A BLACK SHEEP IN THE ZEN'IN CLAN.
I'M TOLD EVEN THOUGH HE'S A MAN, HE DOESN'T HAVE AN OUNCE OF CURSED ENERGY.
HOW AWFUL MUST THAT FEEL.
HOW PITIFUL MUST THAT PERSON LOOK.

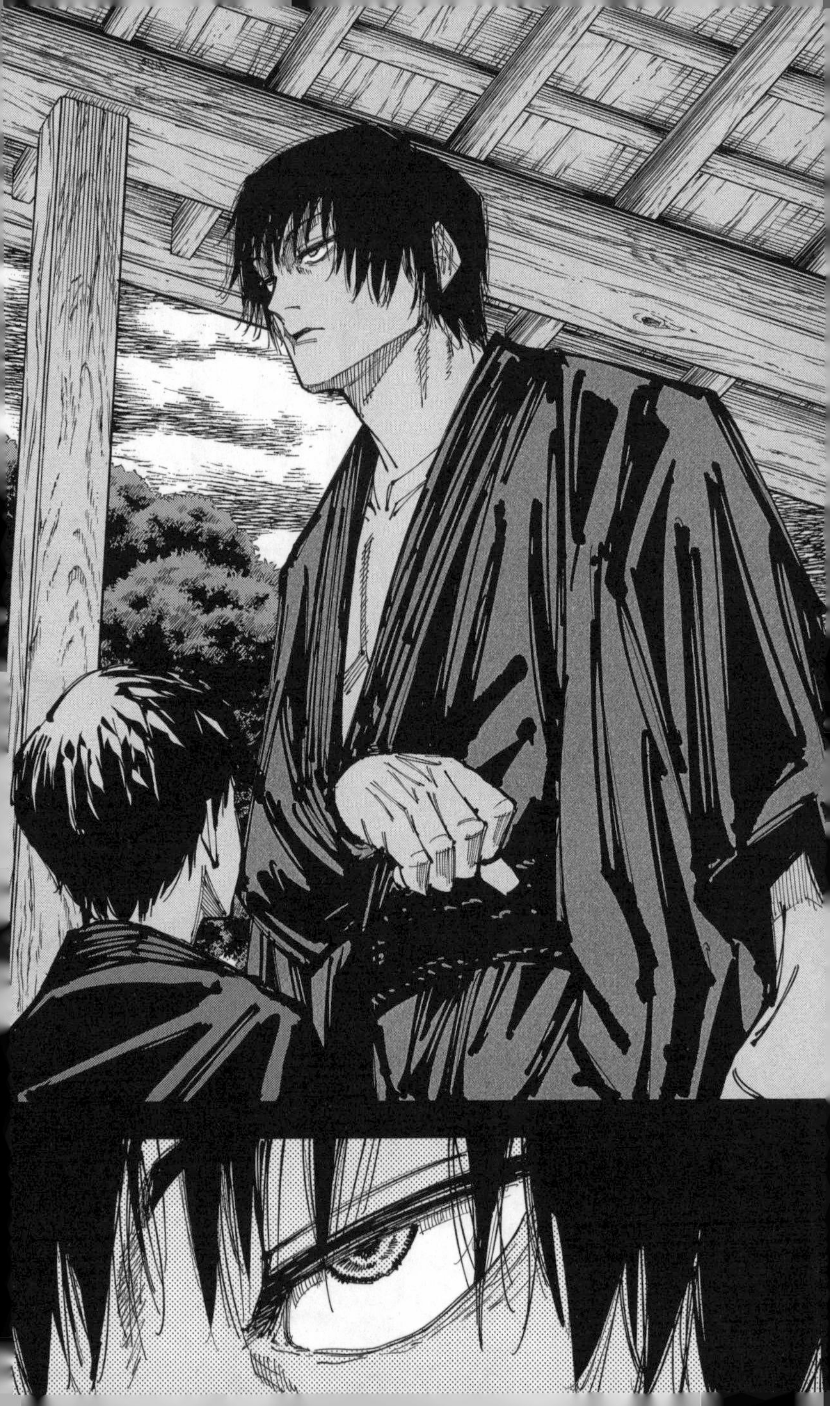

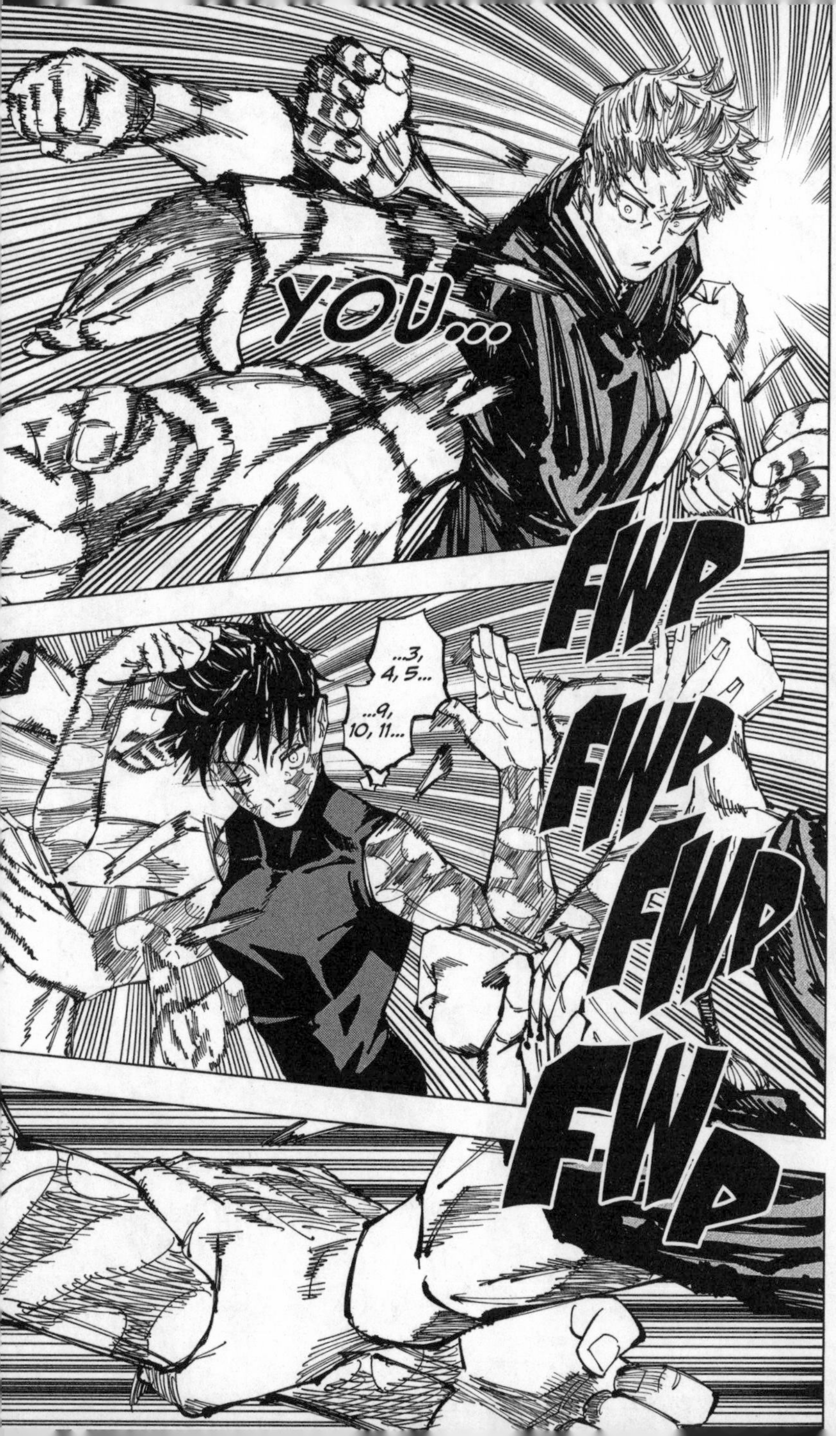
YOU...
FWP
FWP
FWP
FWP
...3, 4, 5...
...9, 10, 11...

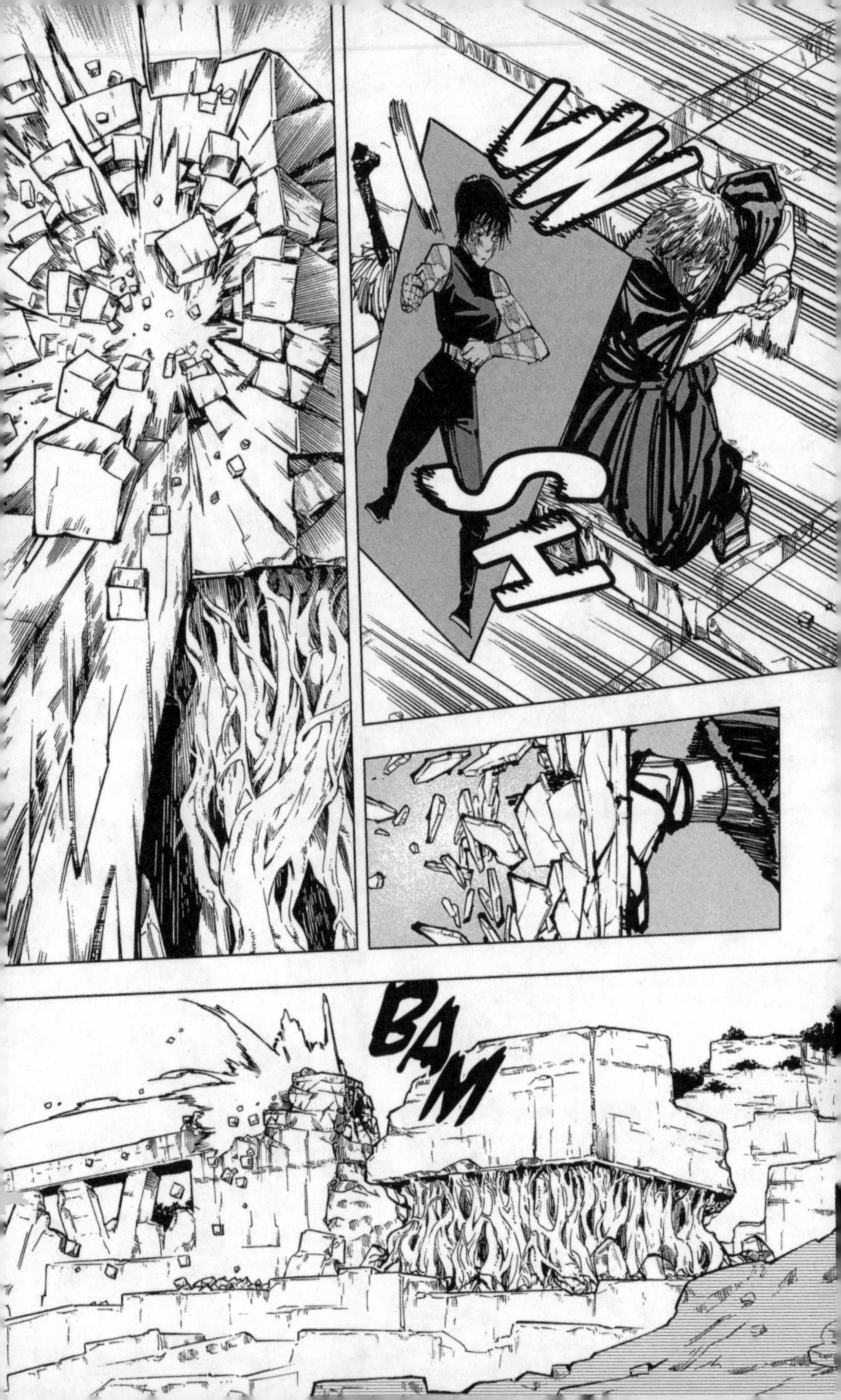
WHOOSH
BAM

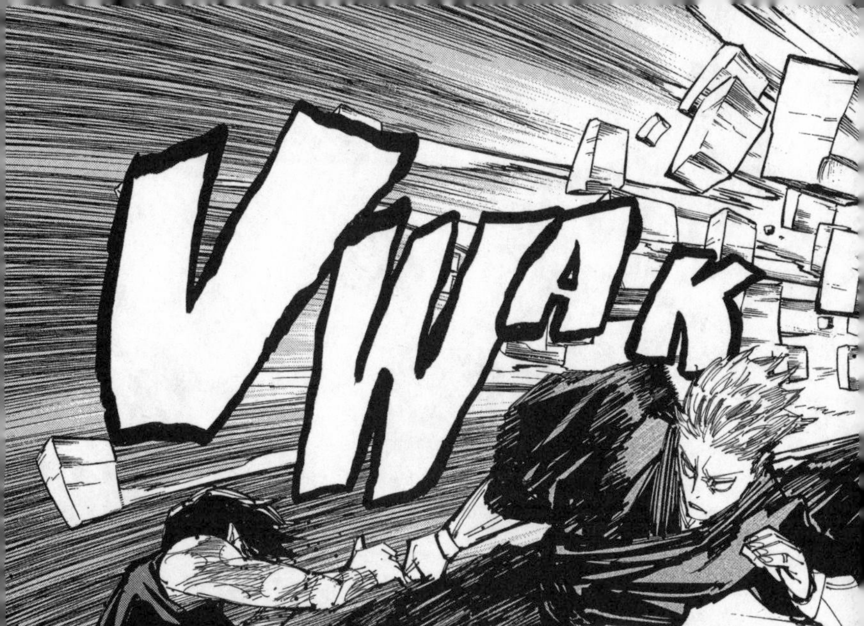
WHAK

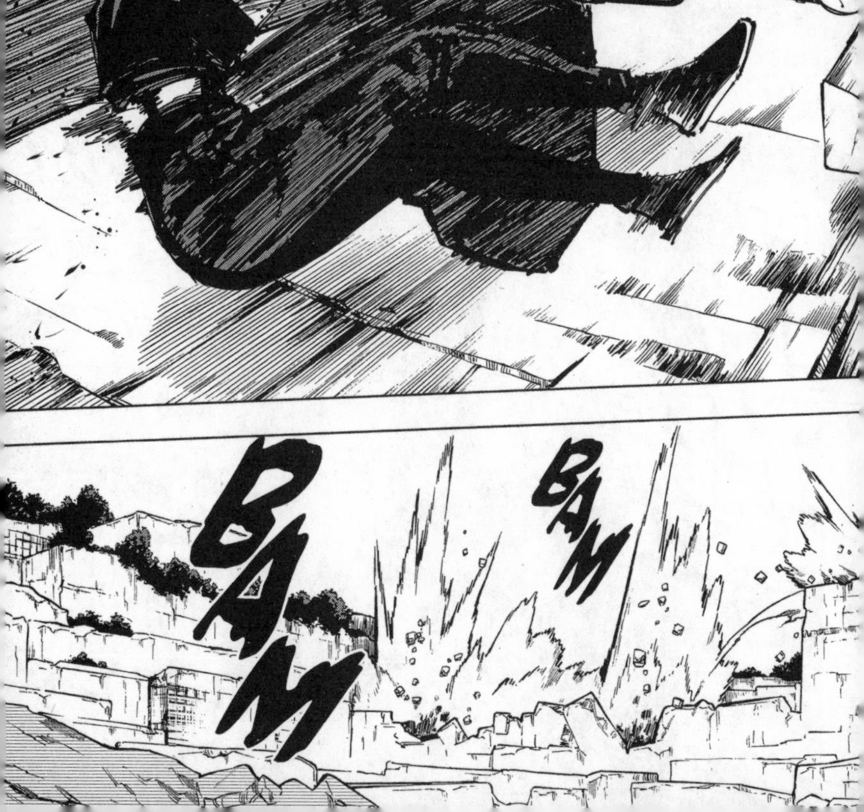
BAM
BAM

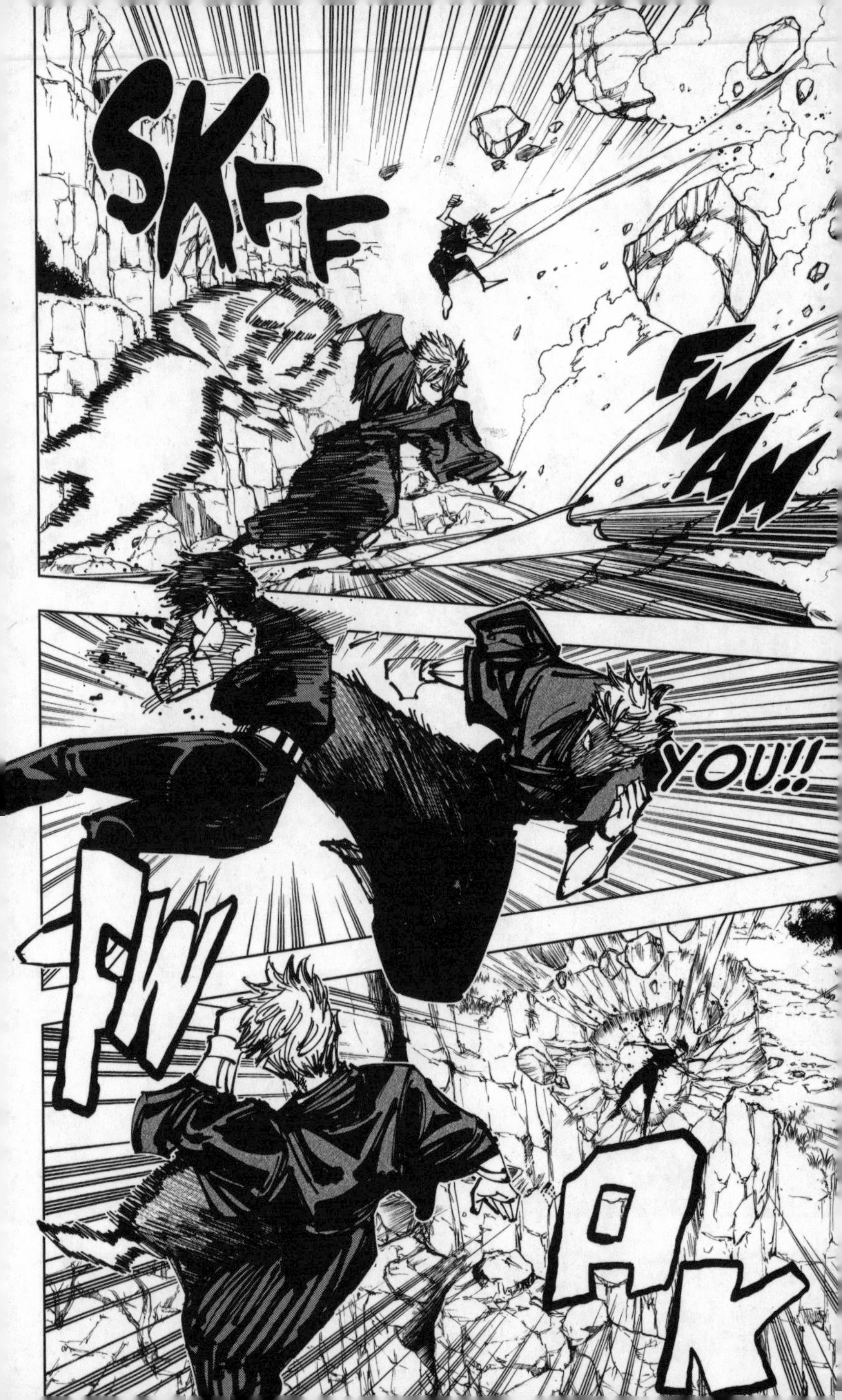
FWAM
SKFF
YOU!!
FWAK

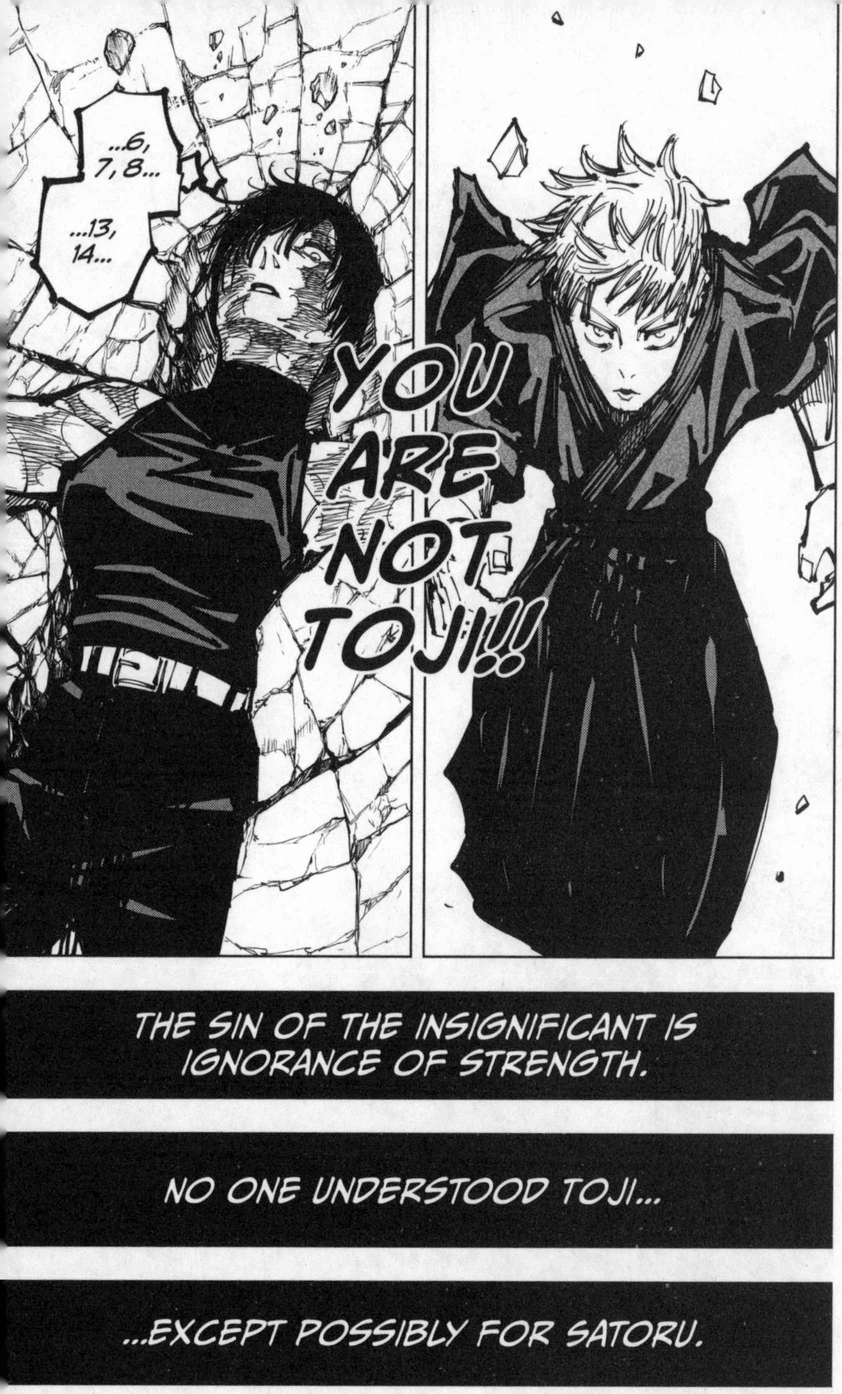
YOU ARE NOT TOJI!!!
...6, 7, 8...
...13, 14...

THE SIN OF THE INSIGNIFICANT IS IGNORANCE OF STRENGTH.

NO ONE UNDERSTOOD TOJI...

...EXCEPT POSSIBLY FOR SATORU.

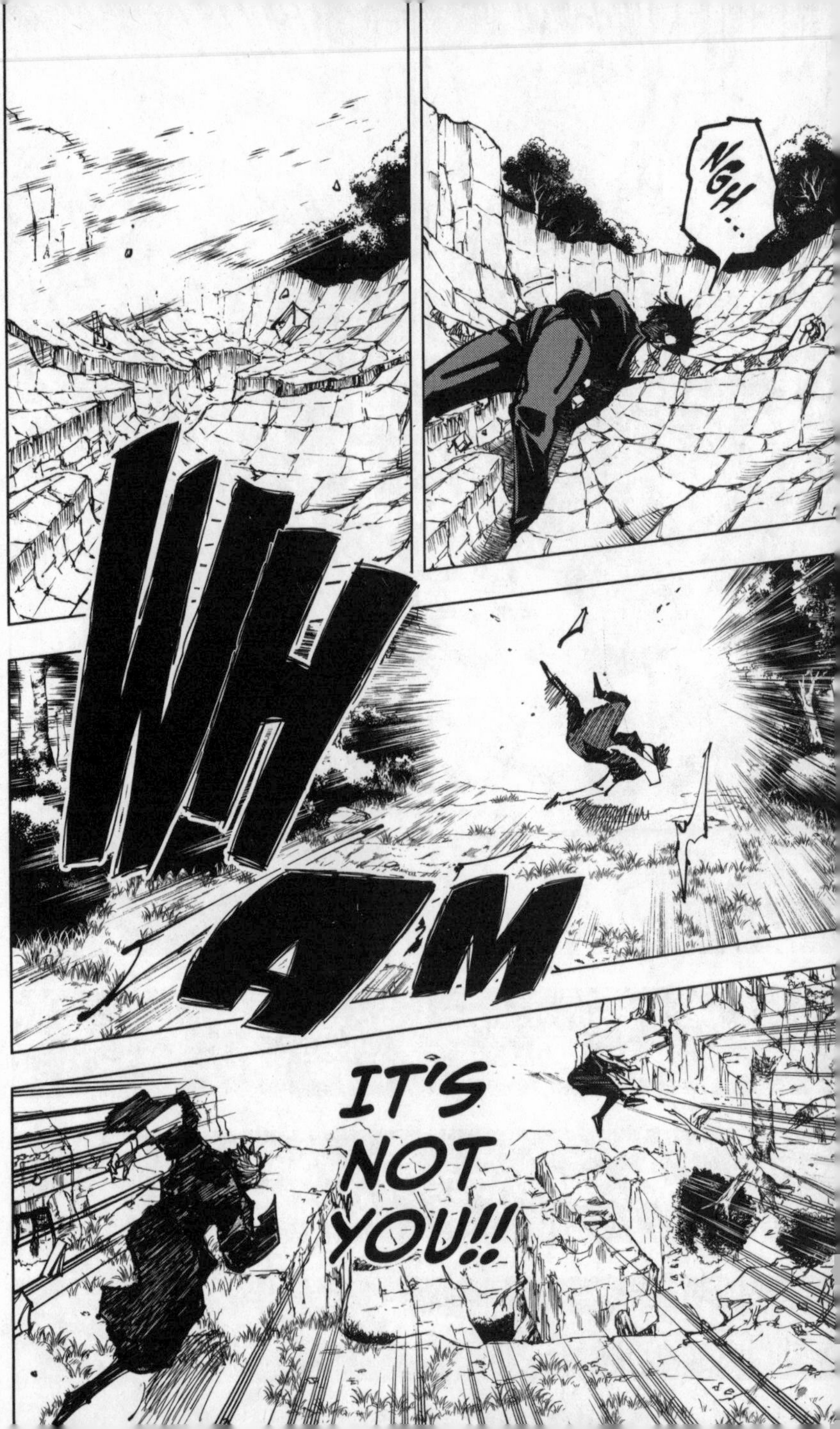
NGH...
WHAM
IT'S NOT YOU!!

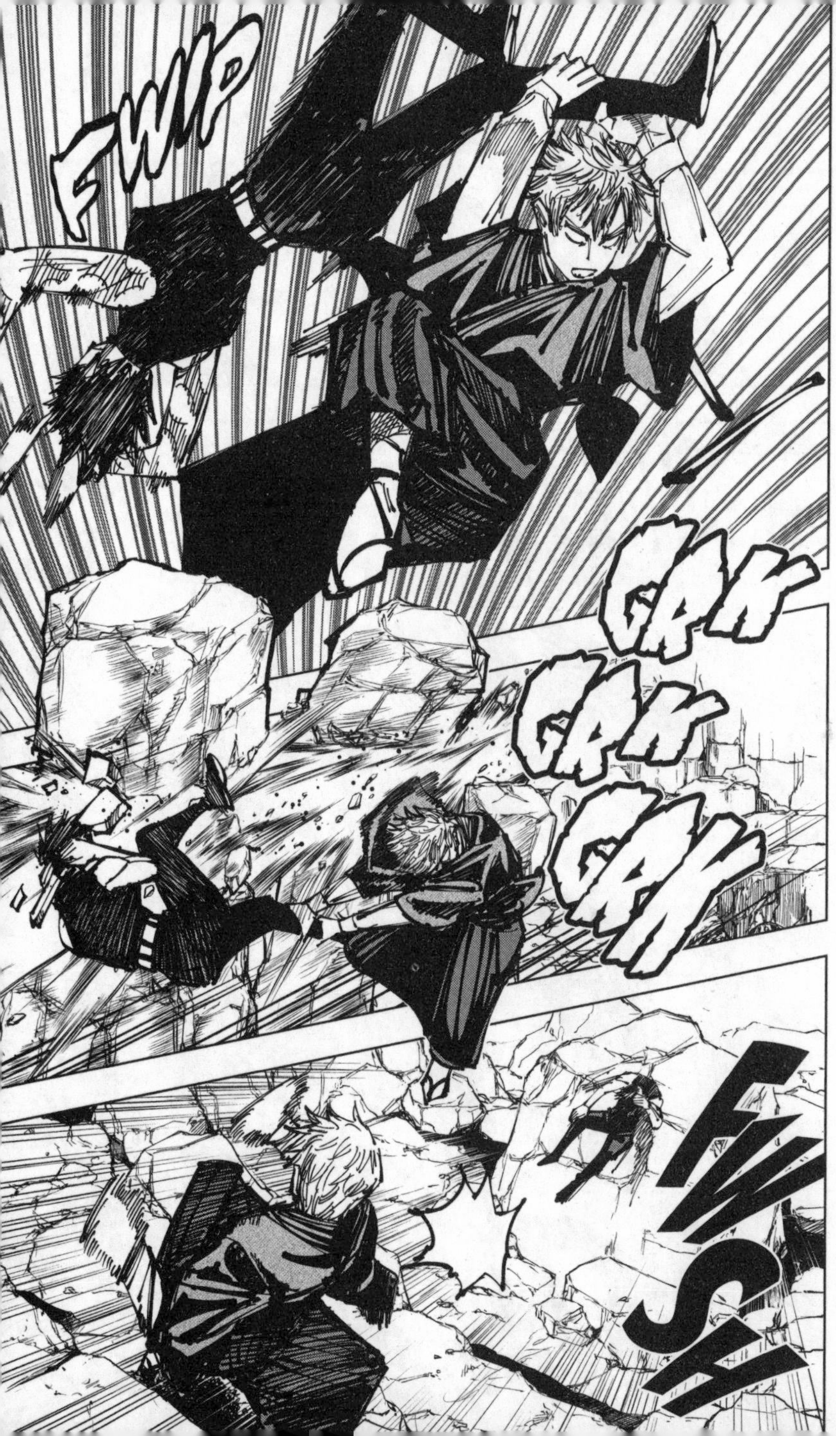
FWIP
CRK
CRK
CRK
FWSH

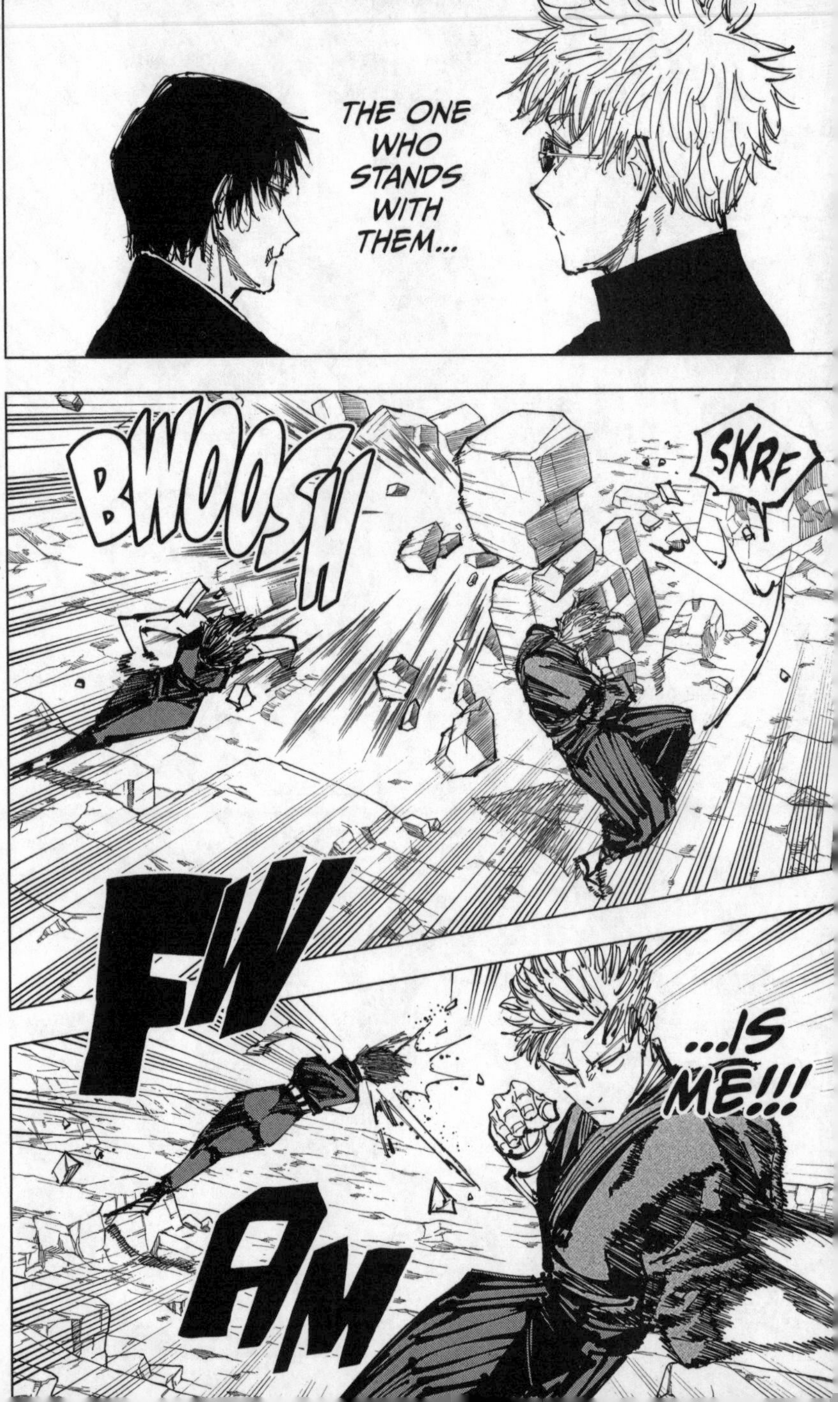
THE ONE WHO STANDS WITH THEM...
SKRF
BWOOSH
...IS ME!!!
FWAM

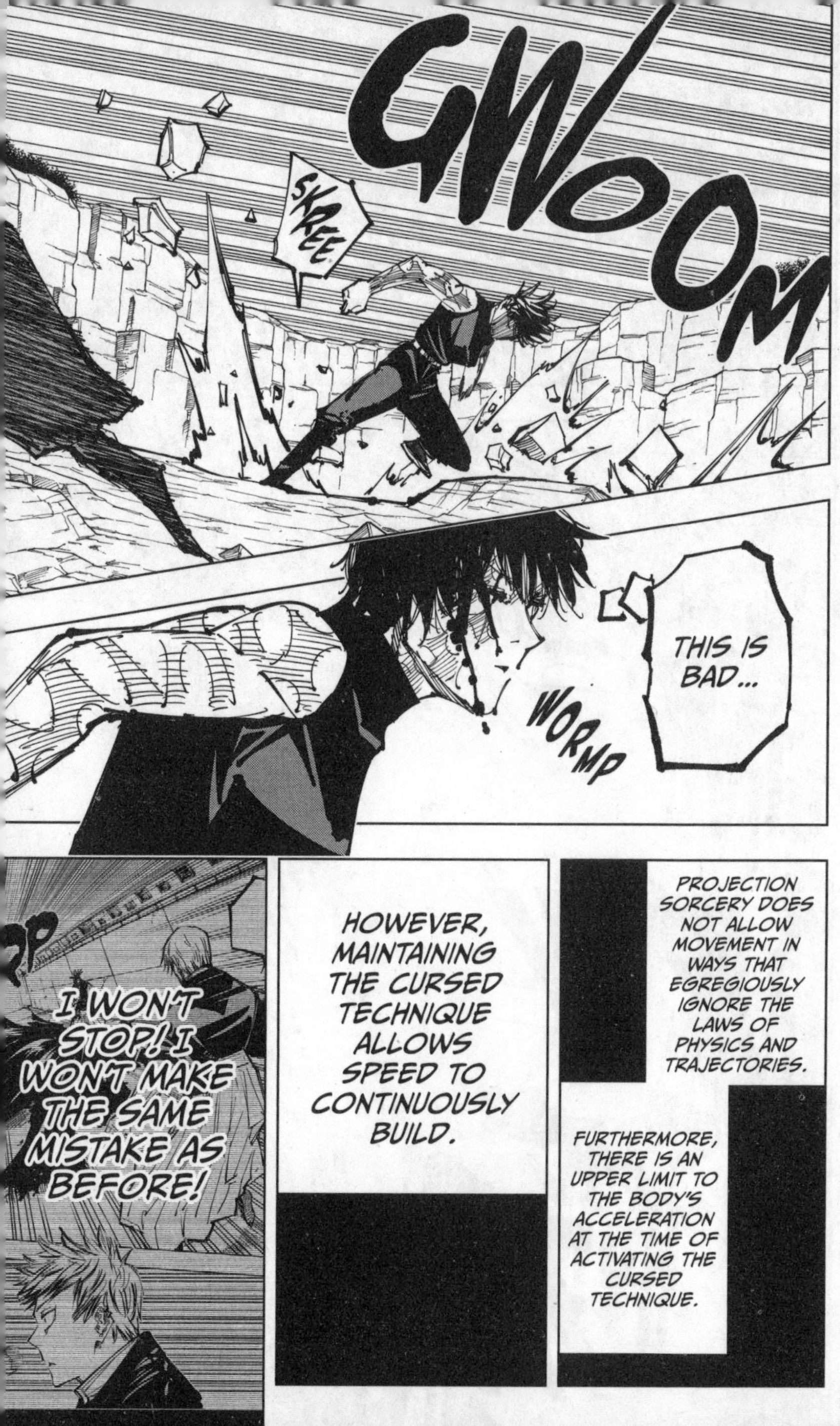
GWOOM
SKREE
THIS IS BAD...
WORMP
PROJECTION SORCERY DOES NOT ALLOW MOVEMENT IN WAYS THAT EGREGIOUSLY IGNORE THE LAWS OF PHYSICS AND TRAJECTORIES.
FURTHERMORE, THERE IS AN UPPER LIMIT TO THE BODY'S ACCELERATION AT THE TIME OF ACTIVATING THE CURSED TECHNIQUE.
HOWEVER, MAINTAINING THE CURSED TECHNIQUE ALLOWS SPEED TO CONTINUOUSLY BUILD.
I WON'T STOP! I WON'T MAKE THE SAME MISTAKE AS BEFORE!

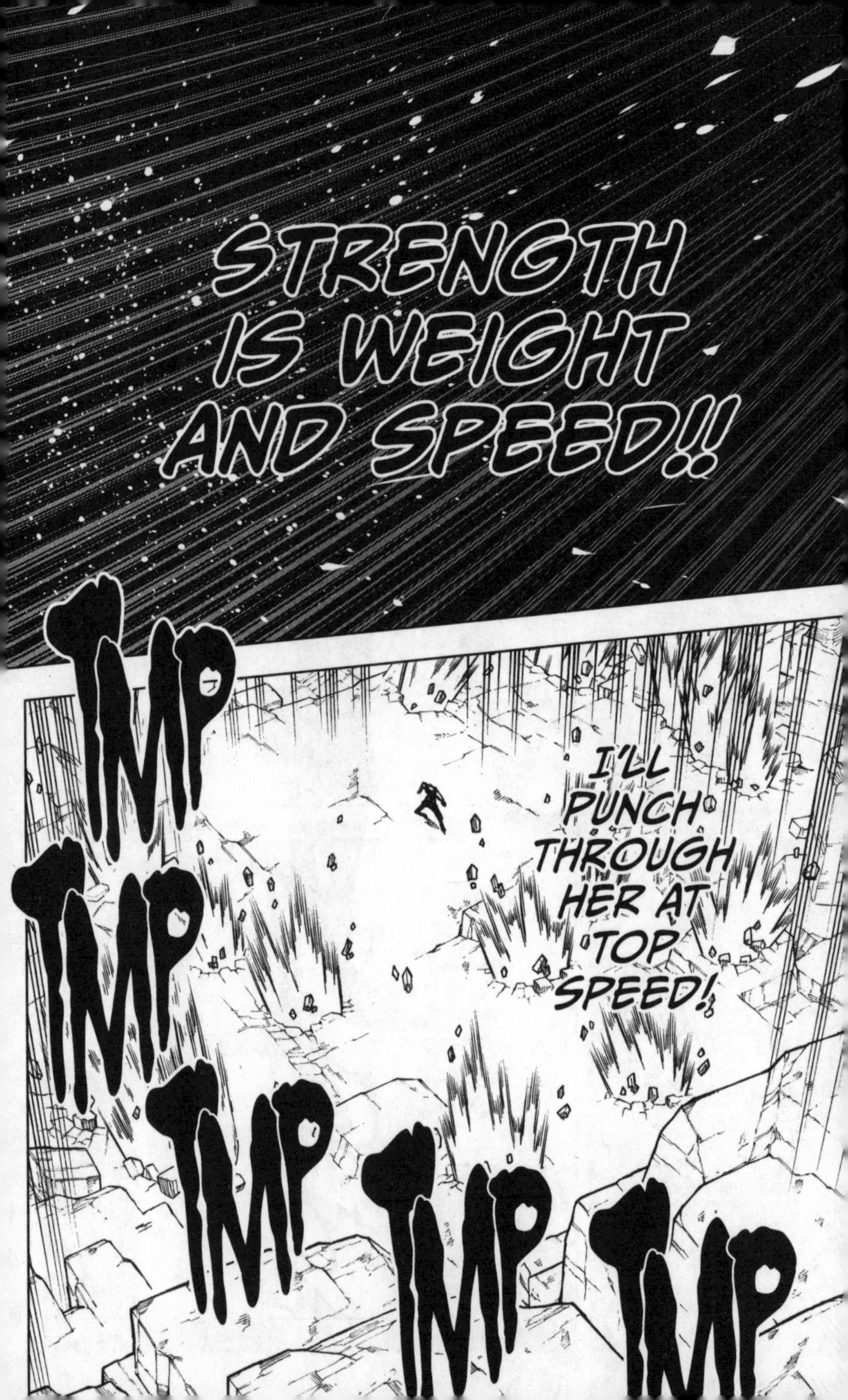
STRENGTH IS WEIGHT AND SPEED!!
I'LL PUNCH THROUGH HER AT TOP SPEED!
TMP
TMP
TMP
TMP
TMP

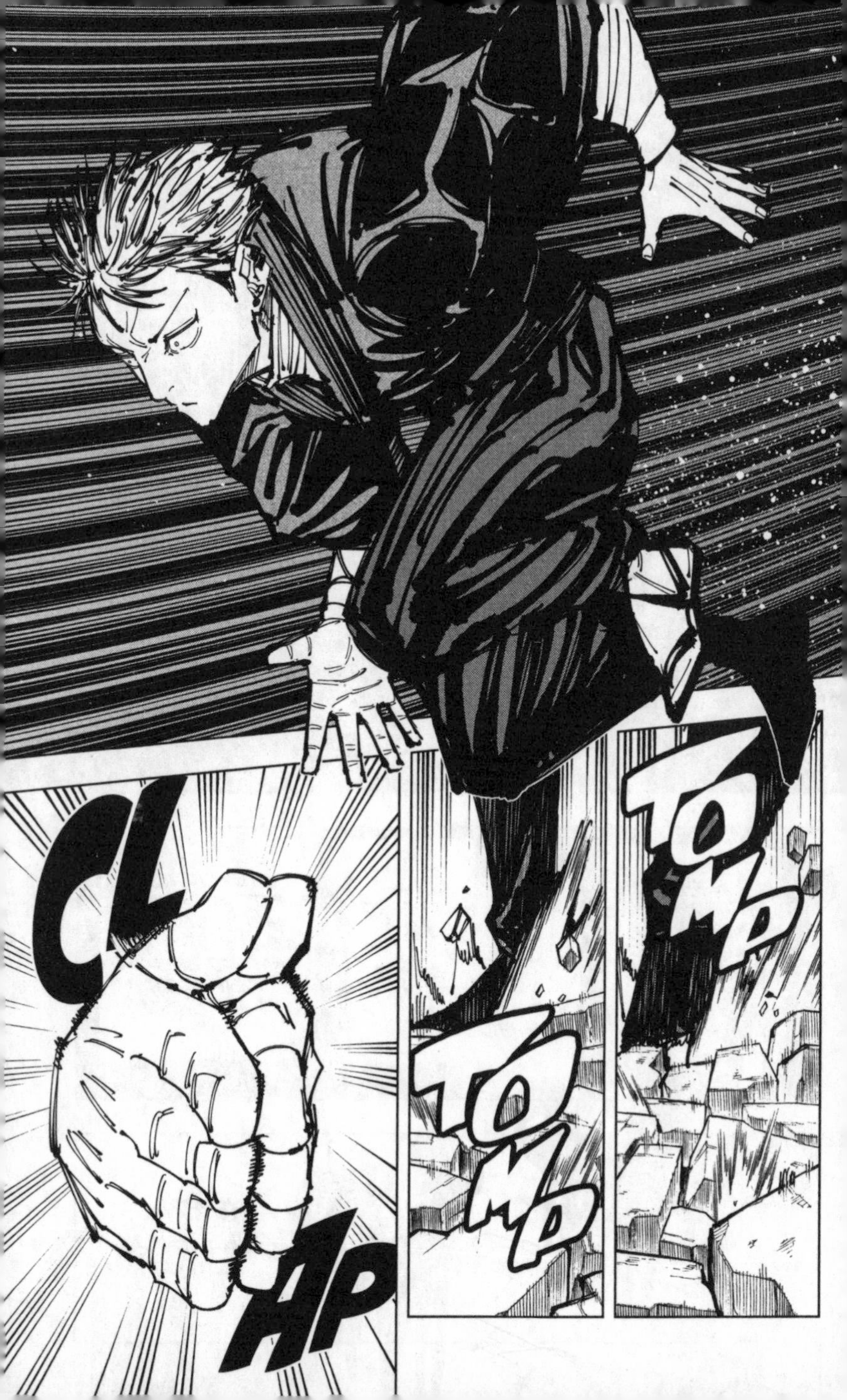
TOMP
TOMP
CLAP

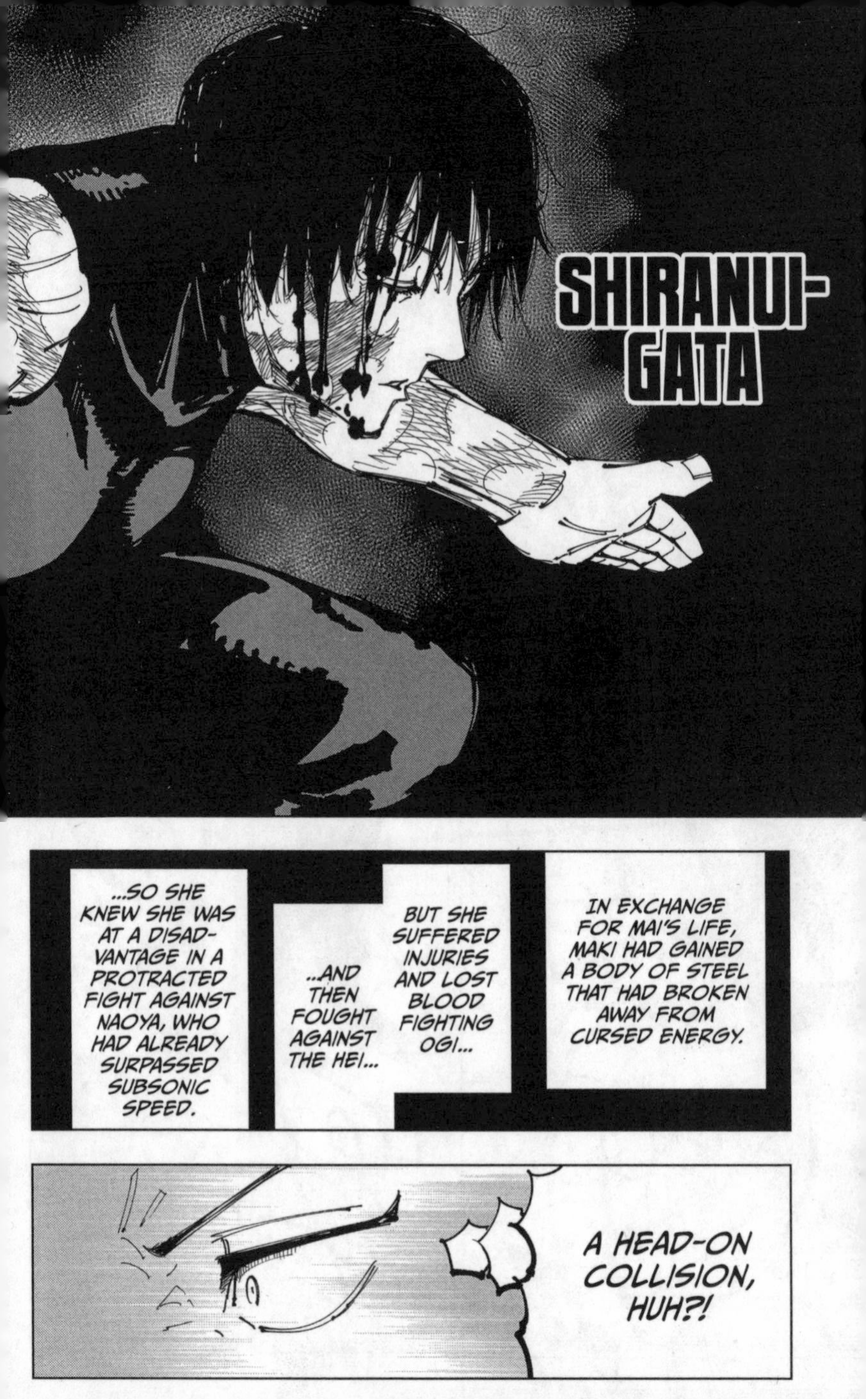
SHIRANUI-GATA
IN EXCHANGE FOR MAI'S LIFE, MAKI HAD GAINED A BODY OF STEEL THAT HAD BROKEN AWAY FROM CURSED ENERGY.
BUT SHE SUFFERED INJURIES AND LOST BLOOD FIGHTING OGI...
...AND THEN FOUGHT AGAINST THE HEI...
...SO SHE KNEW SHE WAS AT A DISAD-VANTAGE IN A PROTRACTED FIGHT AGAINST NAOYA, WHO HAD ALREADY SURPASSED SUBSONIC SPEED.
A HEAD-ON COLLISION, HUH?!

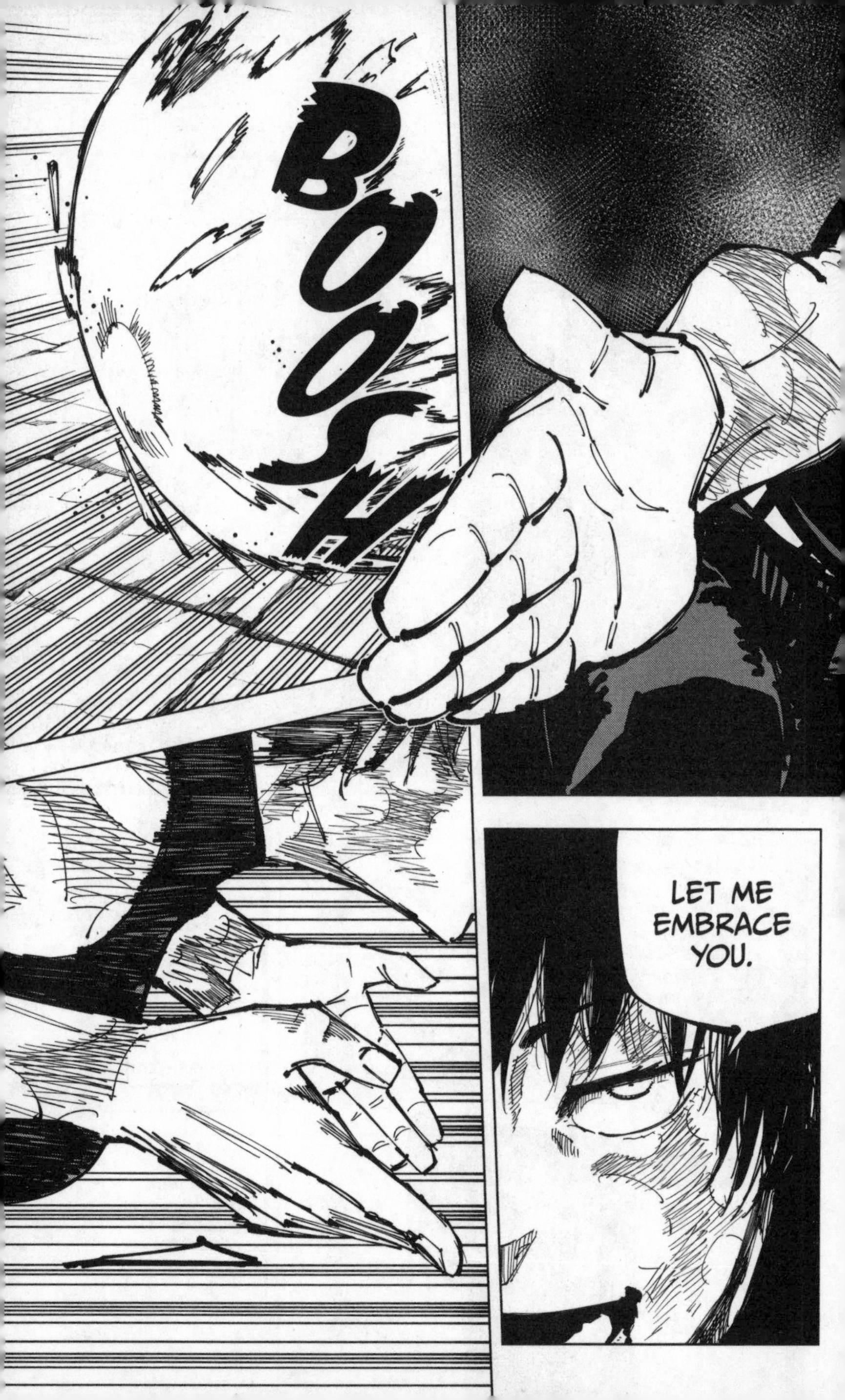
BOOSH
LET ME EMBRACE YOU.

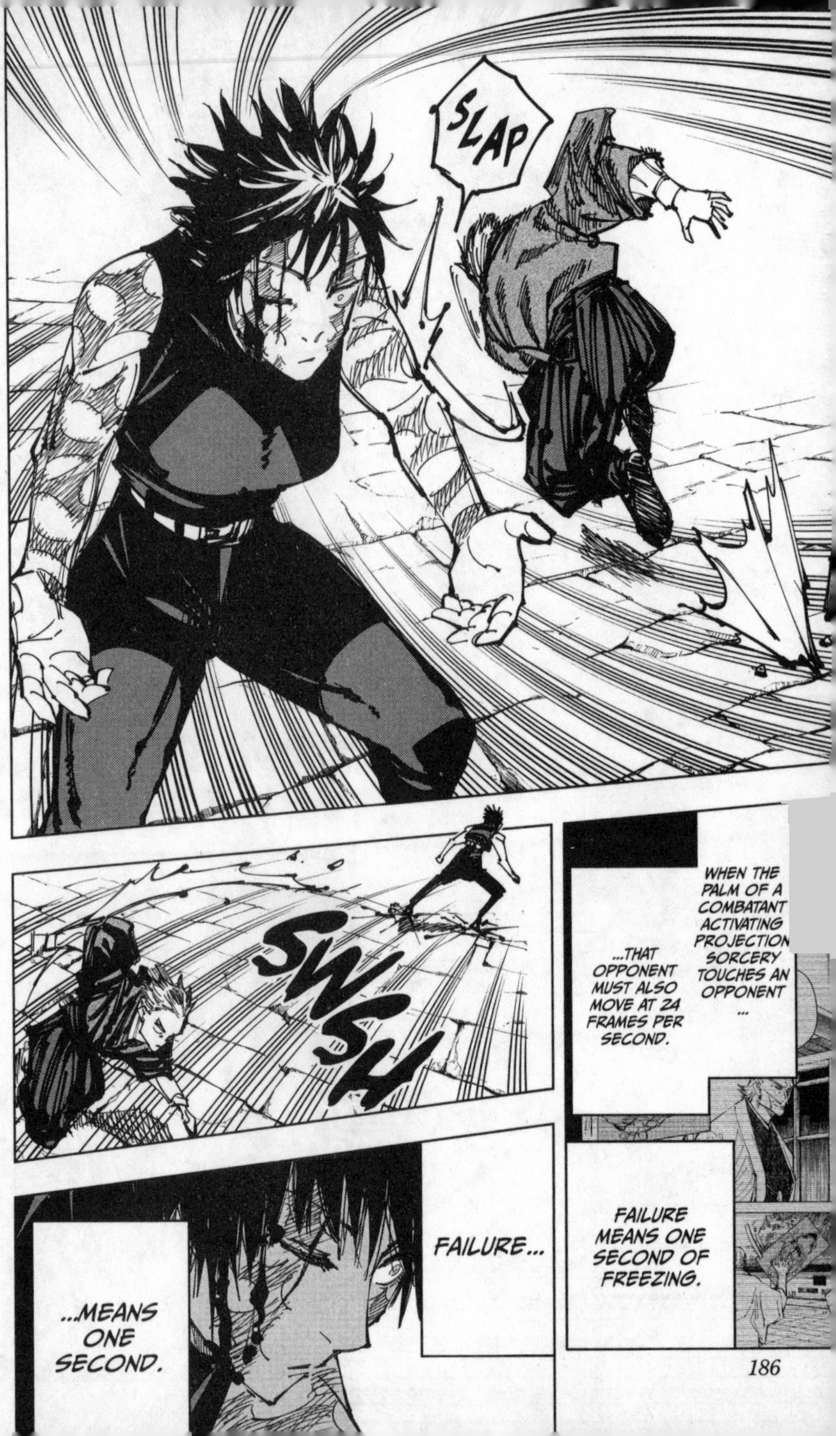
SLAP
WHEN THE PALM OF A COMBATANT ACTIVATING PROJECTION SORCERY TOUCHES AN OPPONENT...
...THAT OPPONENT MUST ALSO MOVE AT 24 FRAMES PER SECOND.
SWSH
FAILURE MEANS ONE SECOND OF FREEZING.
FAILURE...
...MEANS ONE SECOND.

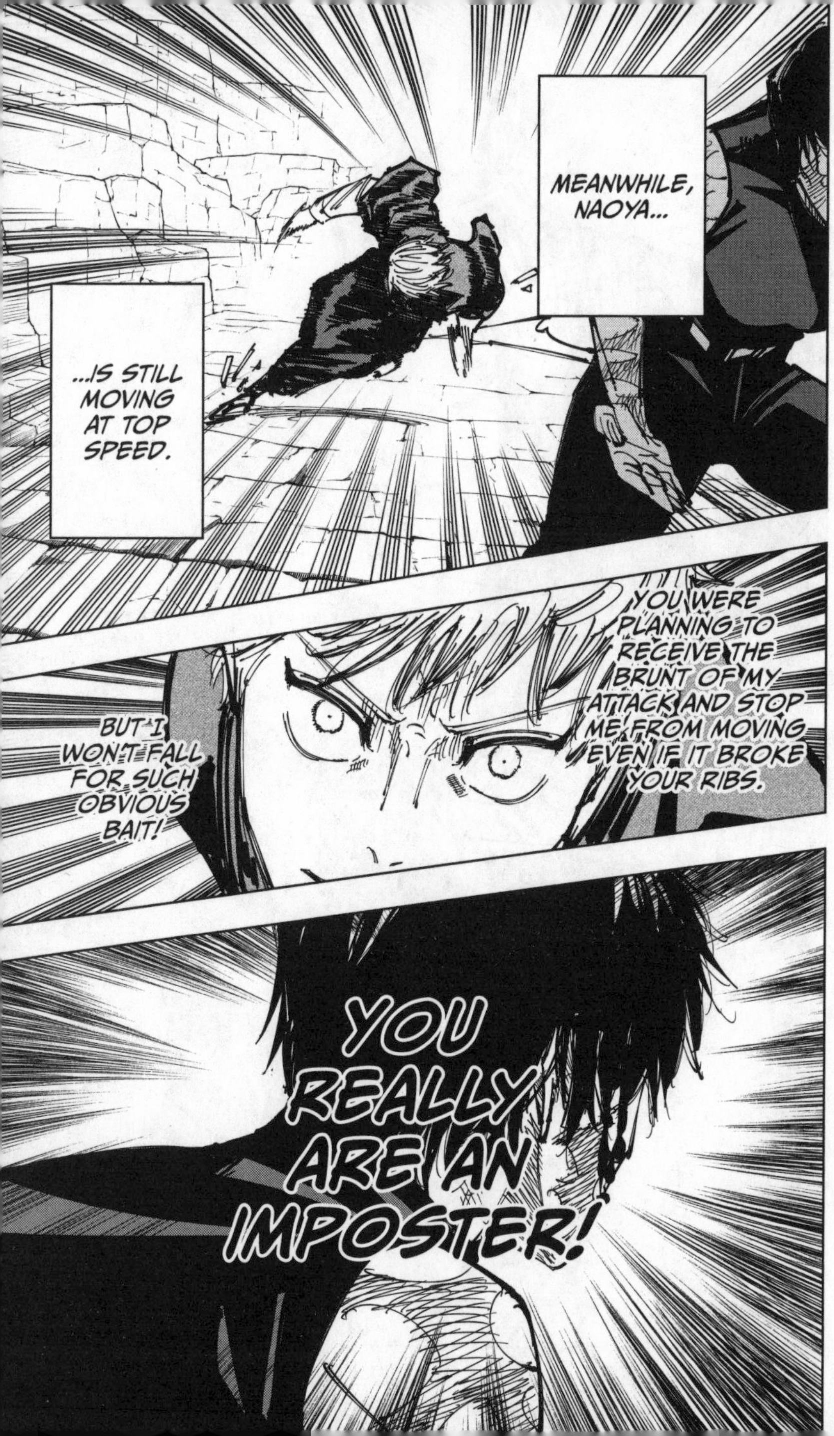
MEANWHILE, NAOYA...
...IS STILL MOVING AT TOP SPEED.
YOU WERE PLANNING TO RECEIVE THE BRUNT OF MY ATTACK AND STOP ME FROM MOVING EVEN IF IT BROKE YOUR RIBS.
BUT I WON'T FALL FOR SUCH OBVIOUS BAIT!
YOU REALLY ARE AN IMPOSTER!

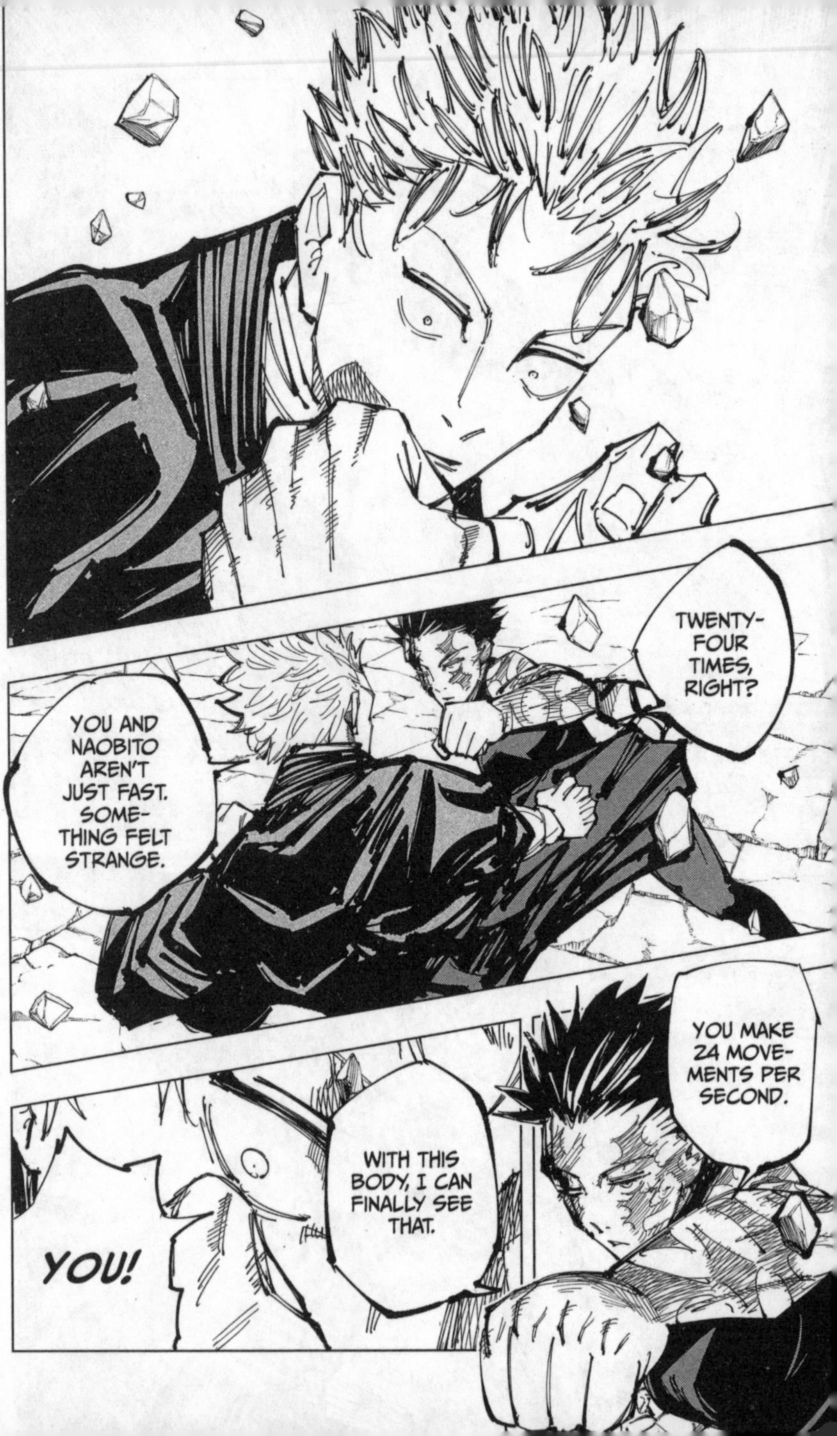
TWENTY-FOUR TIMES, RIGHT?
YOU AND NAOBITO AREN'T JUST FAST. SOME-THING FELT STRANGE.
YOU MAKE 24 MOVE-MENTS PER SECOND.
WITH THIS BODY, I CAN FINALLY SEE THAT.
YOU!

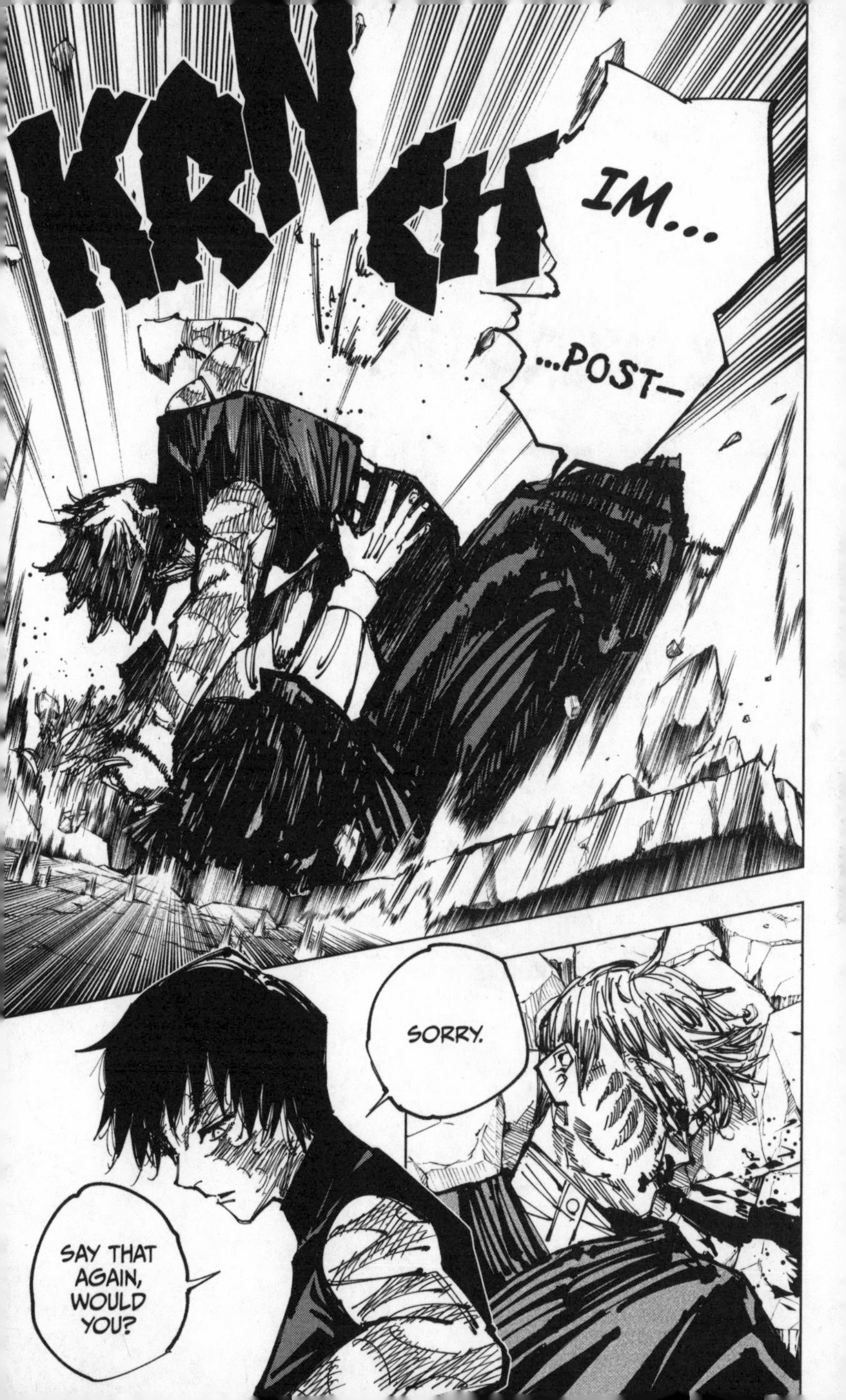
IM...
...POST—
KRNCH
SORRY.
SAY THAT AGAIN, WOULD YOU?

KUKURU UNIT HEI REVIEW!! ④

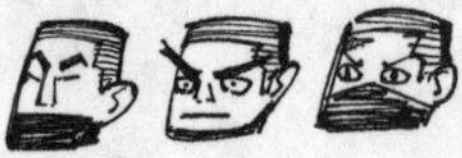

• **NAOYA ZEN'IN**

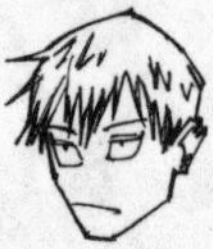

0.0 ☆☆☆☆☆

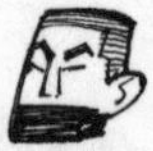

SCUM.

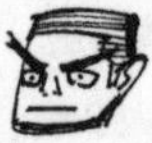

POOP.

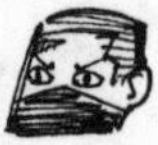

POOP SCUM.

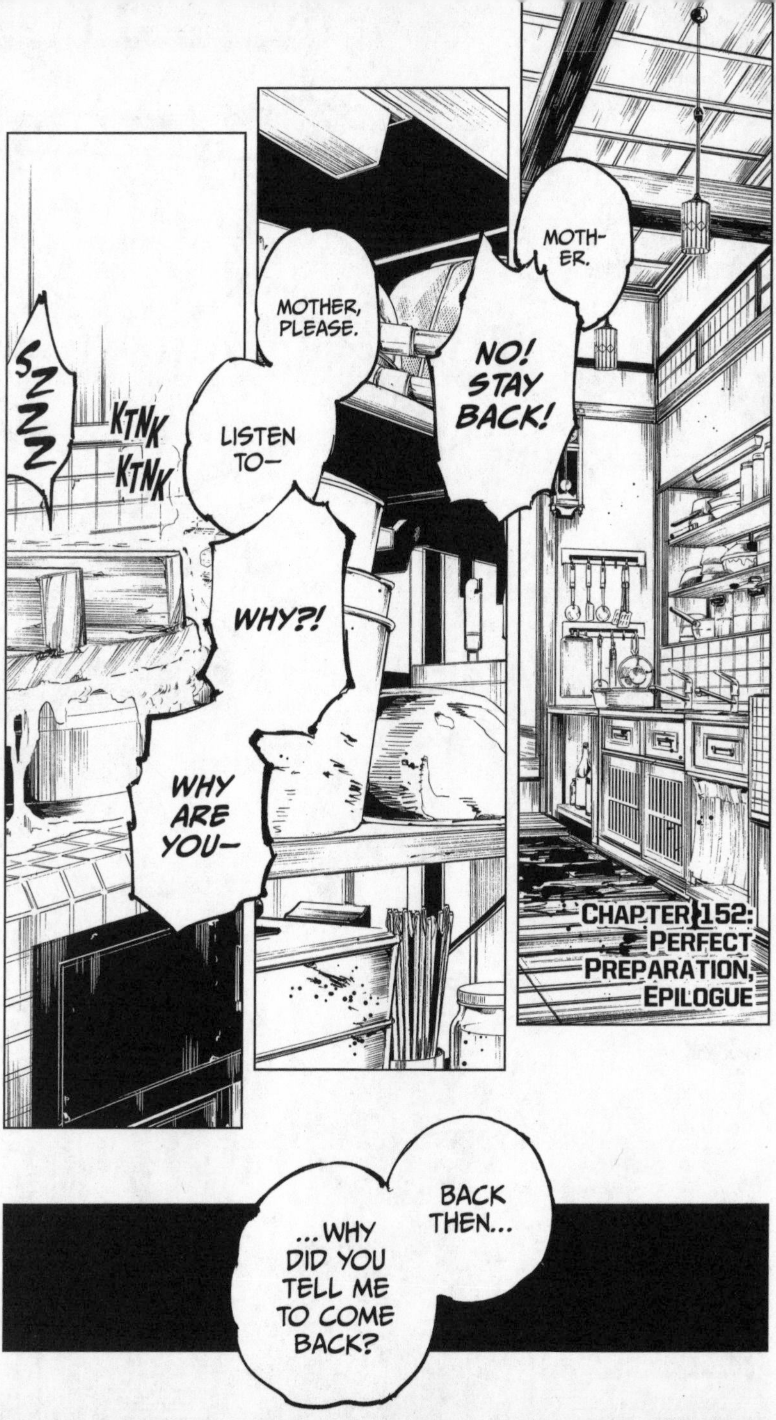
MOTH-ER.
NO! STAY BACK!
CHAPTER 152: PERFECT PREPARATION, EPILOGUE
MOTHER, PLEASE.
LISTEN TO–
WHY?!
WHY ARE YOU–
SZZZ
KTNK KTNK
BACK THEN...
...WHY DID YOU TELL ME TO COME BACK?

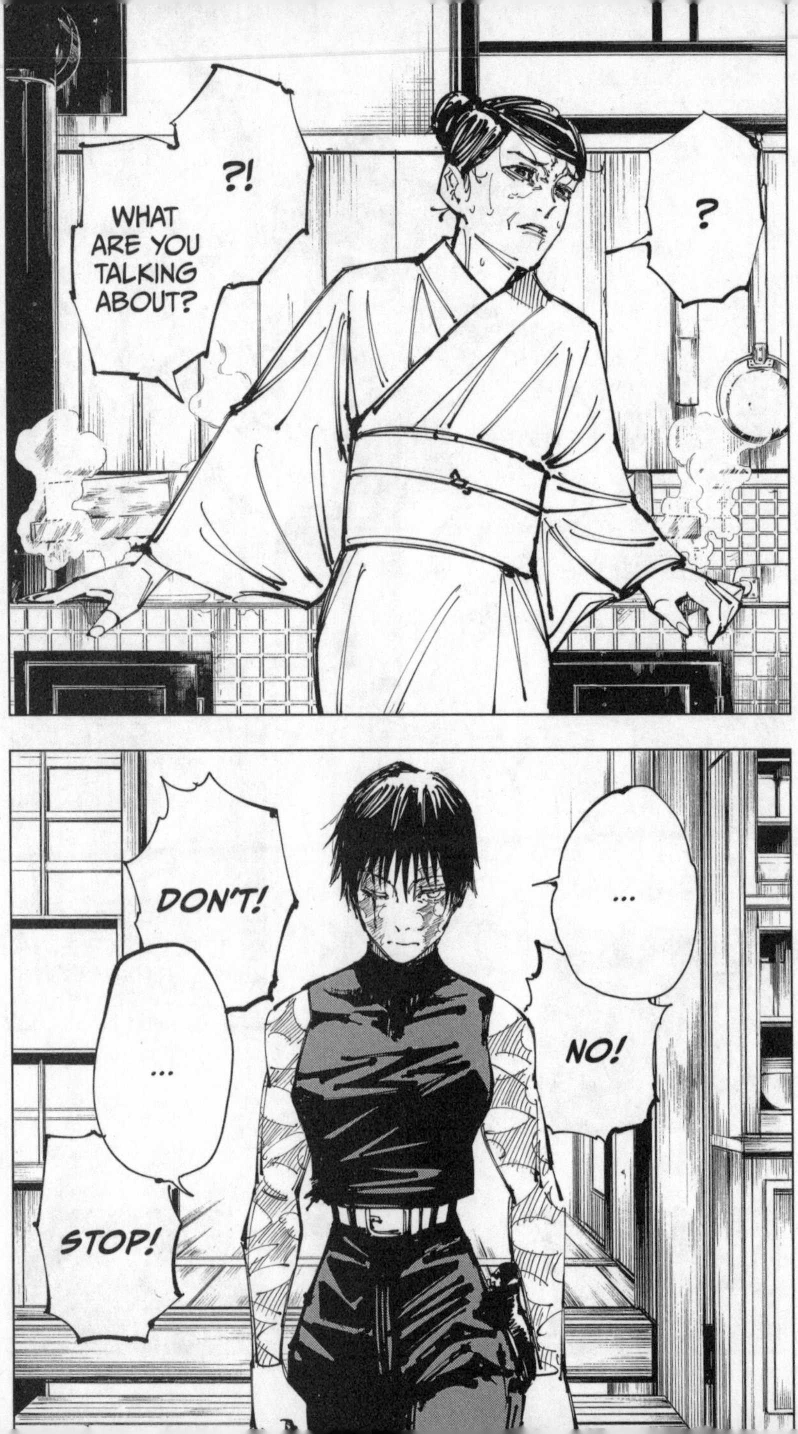
?
?!
WHAT ARE YOU TALKING ABOUT?
...
NO!
DON'T!
...
STOP!

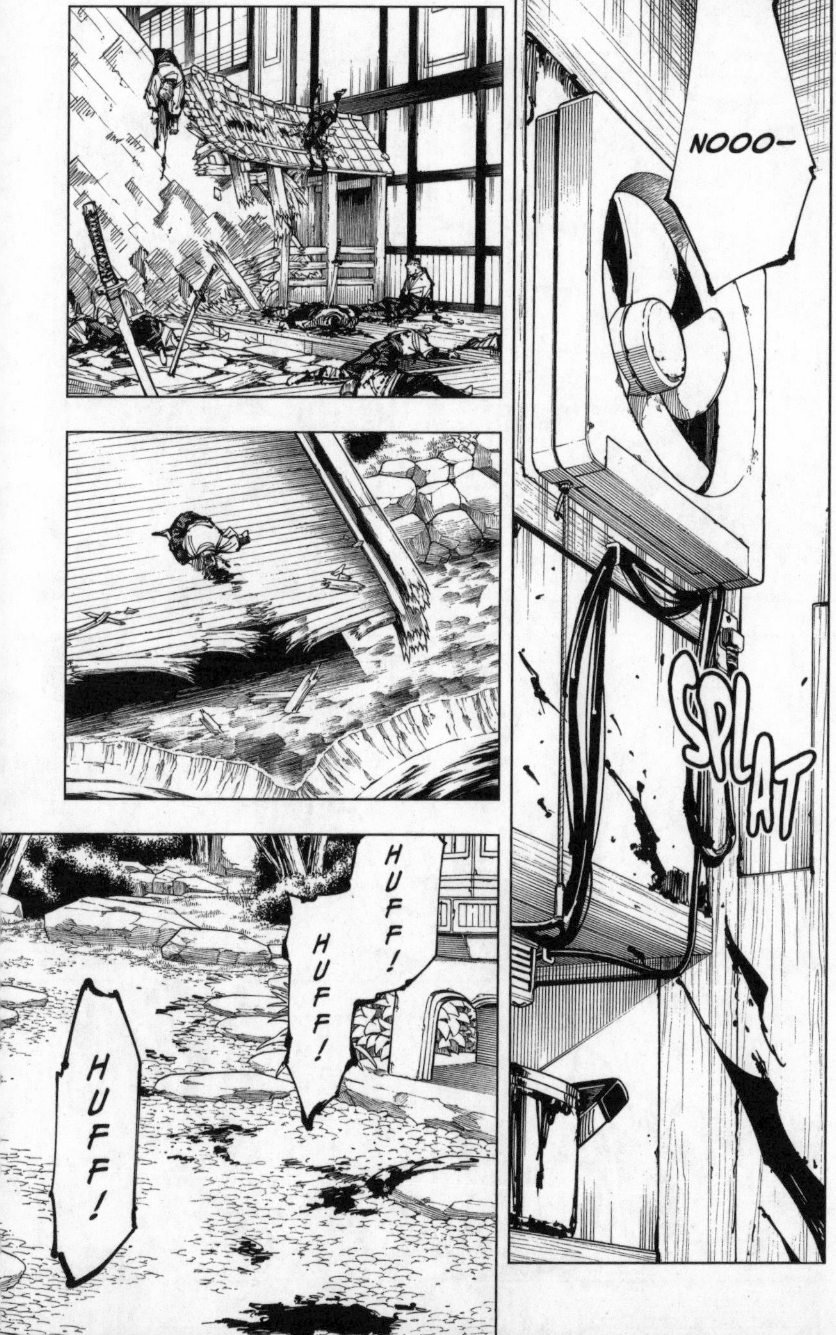
NOOO-
SPLAT
HUFF! HUFF!
HUFF!

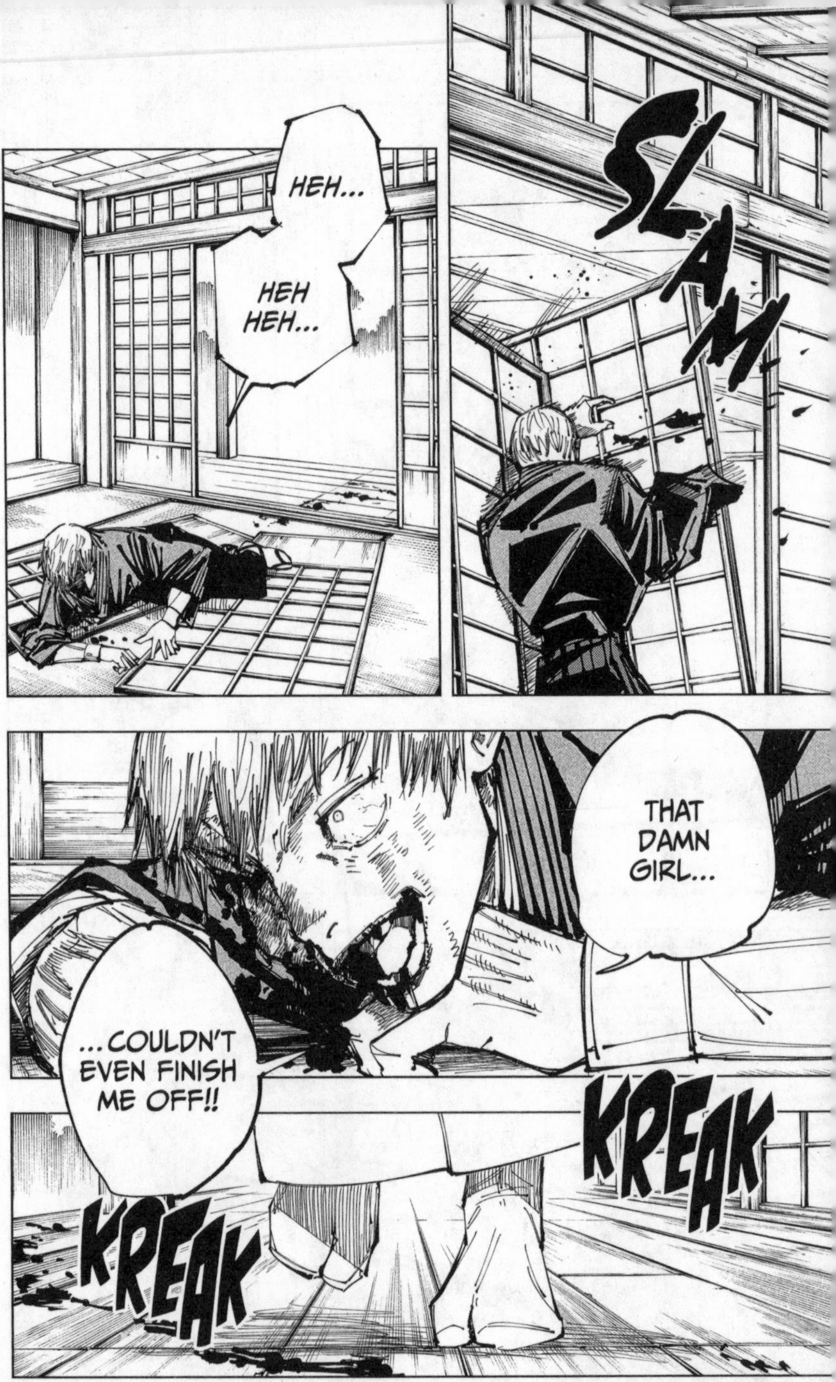
SLAM
HEH...
HEH HEH...
THAT DAMN GIRL...
...COULDN'T EVEN FINISH ME OFF!!
KREAK
KREAK

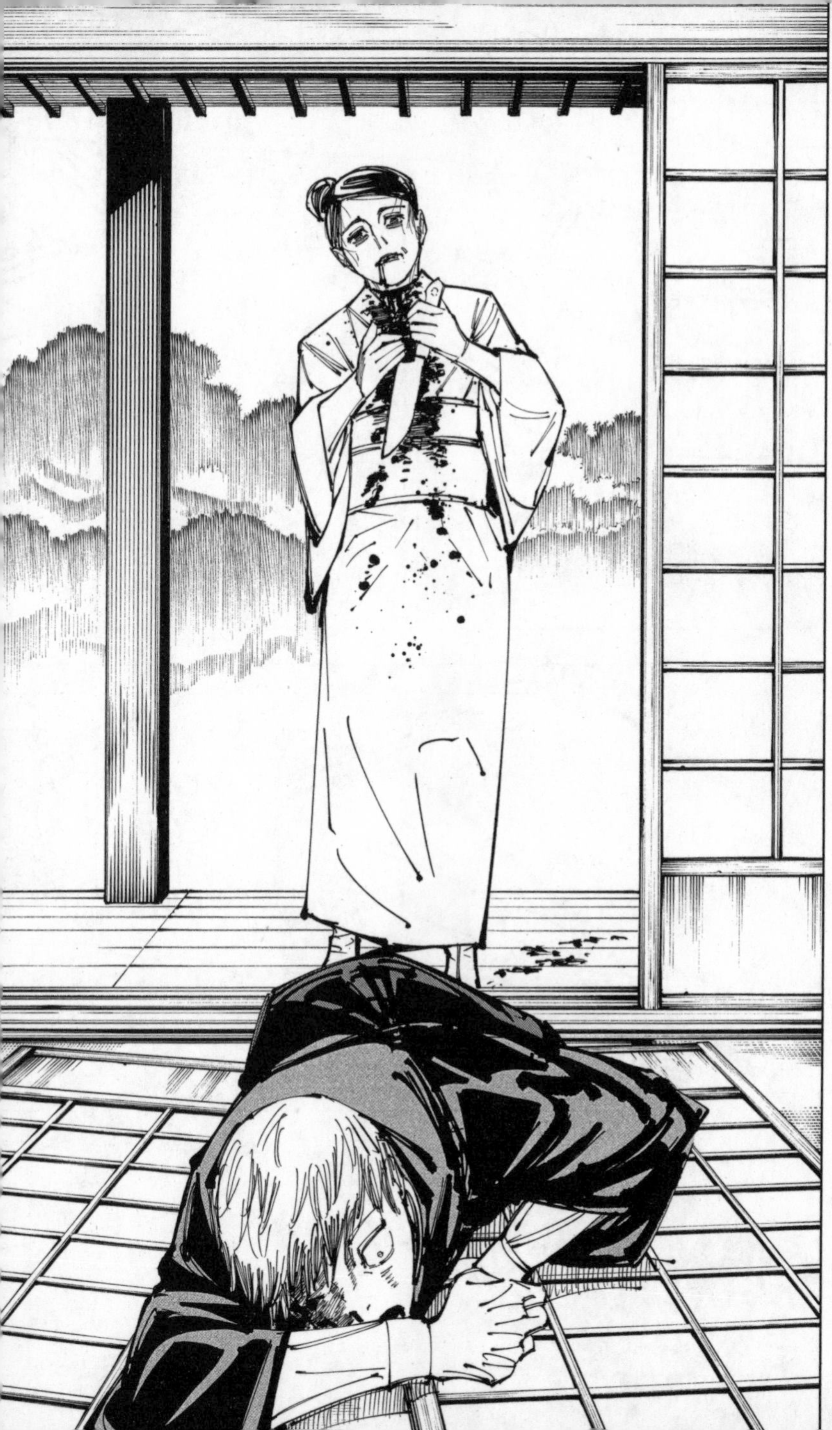

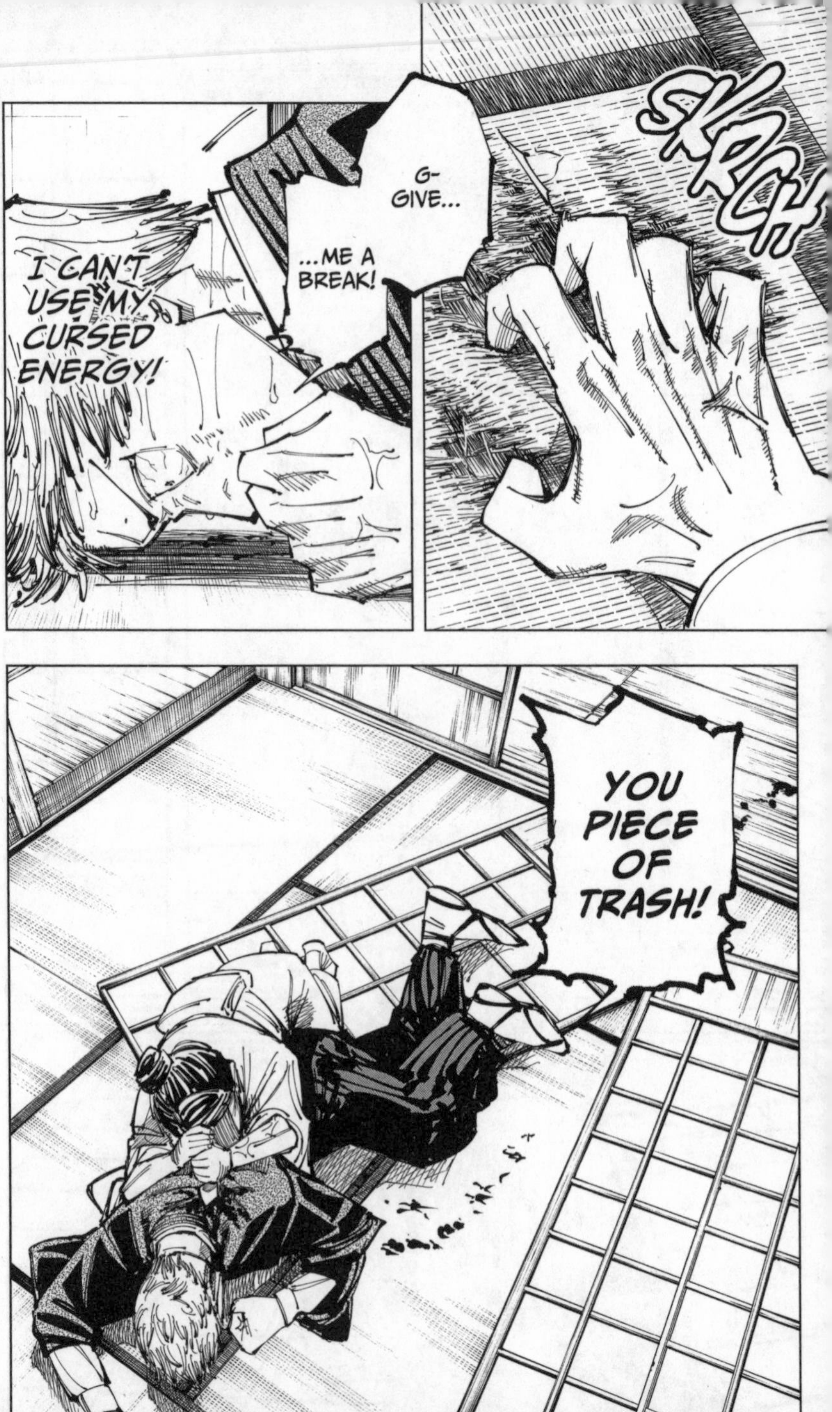
SKRCH
G-GIVE...
...ME A BREAK!
I CAN'T USE MY CURSED ENERGY!
YOU PIECE OF TRASH!

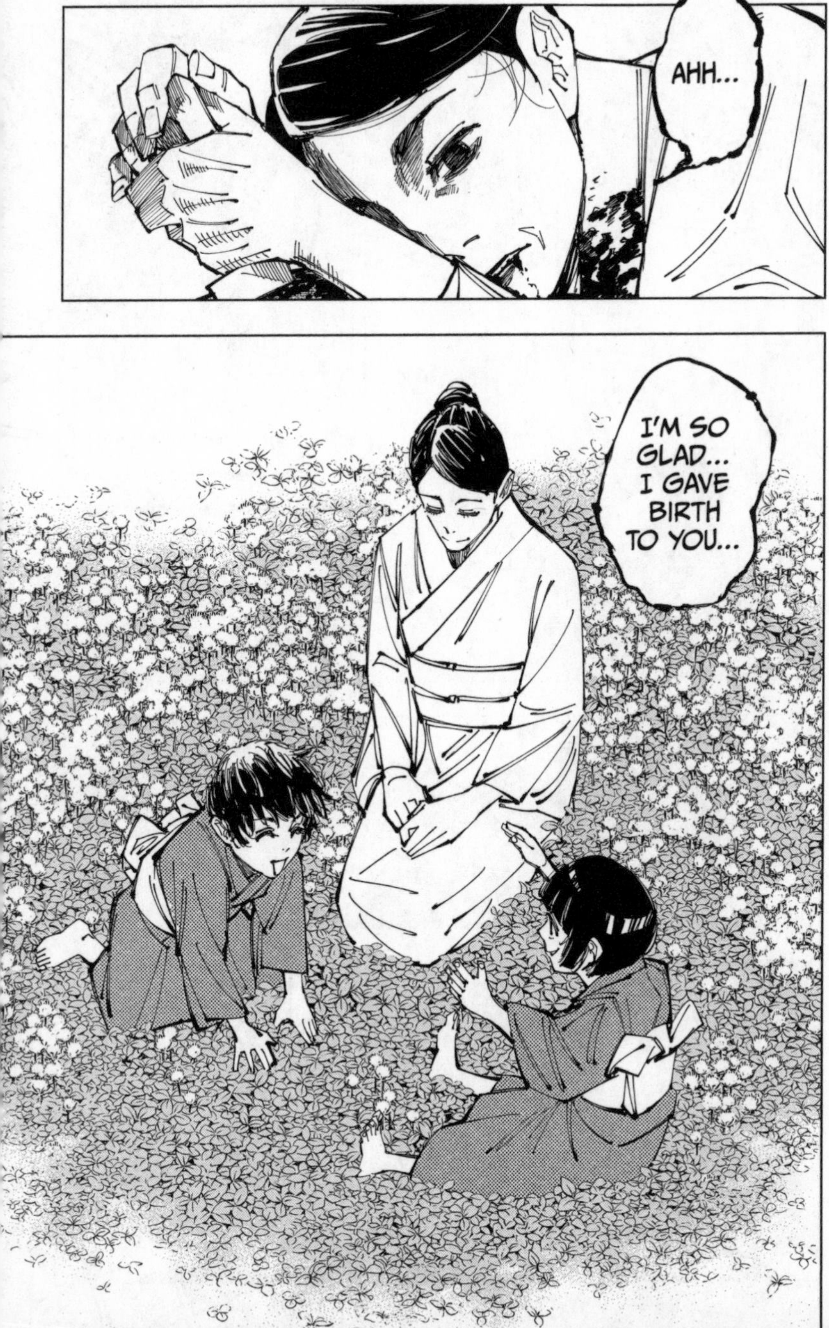
AHH...
I'M SO GLAD... I GAVE BIRTH TO YOU...

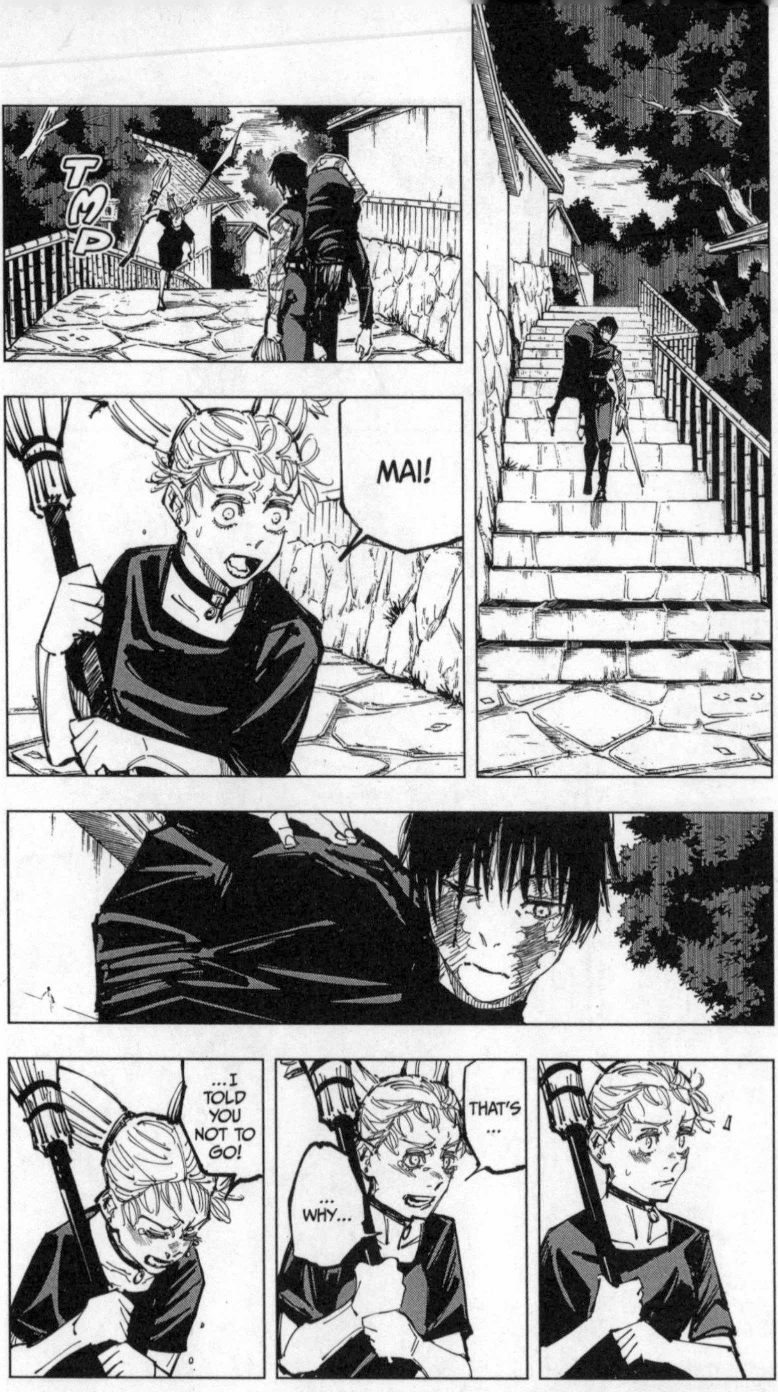

TMP
MAI!
THAT'S ...
... WHY...
...I TOLD YOU NOT TO GO!

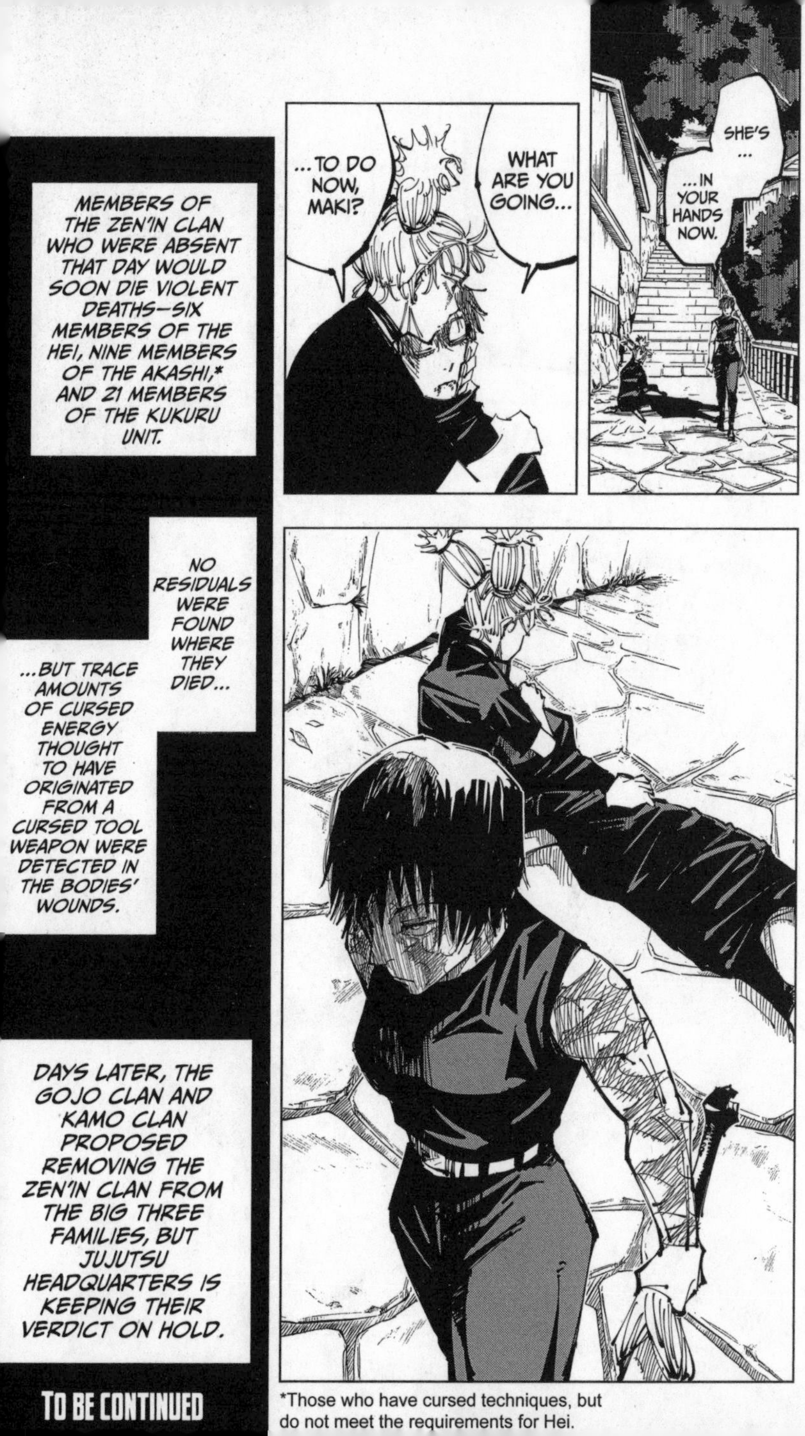
SHE'S ...
...IN YOUR HANDS NOW.
WHAT ARE YOU GOING...
...TO DO NOW, MAKI?
MEMBERS OF THE ZEN'IN CLAN WHO WERE ABSENT THAT DAY WOULD SOON DIE VIOLENT DEATHS—SIX MEMBERS OF THE HEI, NINE MEMBERS OF THE AKASHI,* AND 21 MEMBERS OF THE KUKURU UNIT.
NO RESIDUALS WERE FOUND WHERE THEY DIED...
...BUT TRACE AMOUNTS OF CURSED ENERGY THOUGHT TO HAVE ORIGINATED FROM A CURSED TOOL WEAPON WERE DETECTED IN THE BODIES' WOUNDS.
DAYS LATER, THE GOJO CLAN AND KAMO CLAN PROPOSED REMOVING THE ZEN'IN CLAN FROM THE BIG THREE FAMILIES, BUT JUJUTSU HEADQUARTERS IS KEEPING THEIR VERDICT ON HOLD.
TO BE CONTINUED

*Those who have cursed techniques, but do not meet the requirements for Hei.

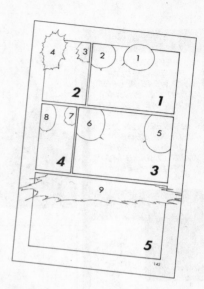

JUJUTSU KAISEN

reads from right to left, starting in the upper-right corner. Japanese is read from right to left, meaning that action, sound effects, and word-balloon order are completely reversed from English order.